Volvo 240 Series Owners Workshop Manual

by J H Haynes

Member of the Guild of Motoring Writers

and Bruce Gilmour

Models covered
UK: Volvo 244 and 245; DL, DLE, E, GL, GLE and Thor
USA: Volvo 242, 242 GT, 244 and 245, DL, GL and GT

Does not cover 244 GLT with 2.3 litre engine

ISBN 0 85696 591 X

Printed in England   *(270 - 9F3)*

HAYNES PUBLISHING GROUP
SPARKFORD YEOVIL SOMERSET ENGLAND
distributed in the USA by
HAYNES PUBLICATIONS INC
861 LAWRENCE DRIVE
NEWBURY PARK
CALIFORNIA 91320
USA

Acknowledgements

Special thanks are due to A B Volvo for the supply of technical information and some of the illustrations used in this manual. Castrol Limited provided lubrication data, and the Champion Sparking Plug Company supplied the illustrations showing the various spark plug conditions. The bodywork repair photographs used in this manual were provided by Lloyds Industries Limited who supply 'Turtle Wax', 'Dupli-color Holts', and other Holts range products. We are particularly grateful to John Tallis Motors Limited,

Bathwick Hill, Bath, who supplied the Volvo 244 used as our project car.

Lastly thanks are due to all of those people at Sparkford who helped on the production of this manual. Particularly, Brian Horsfall and Les Brazier who carried out the mechanical work and took the photographs respectively; Stanley Randolph who planned the layout of each page and Rod Grainger the editor. The supplementary Chapter dealing with later models was written by Peter Strasman.

About this manual

Its aim

The aim of this manual is to help you get the best value from your car. It can do so in several ways. It can help you decide what work must be done (even should you choose to get it done by a garage), provide information on routine maintenance and servicing, and give a logical course of action and diagnosis when random faults occur. However, it is hoped that you will use the manual by tackling the work yourself. On simpler jobs it may even be quicker than booking the car into a garage and going there twice to leave and collect it. Perhaps most important, a lot of money can be saved by avoiding the costs the garage must charge to cover its labour and overheads.

The manual has drawings and descriptions to show the function of the various components so that their layout can be understood. Then the tasks are described and photographed in a step-by-step sequence so that even a novice can do the work.

Its arrangement

The manual is divided into thirteen Chapters, each covering a logical sub-division of the vehicle. The Chapters are each divided into Sections, numbered with single figures, eg 5; and the Sections into paragraphs (or sub-sections), with decimal numbers following on from the Section they are in, eg 5.1, 5.2, 5.3 etc.

It is freely illustrated, especially in those parts where there is a detailed sequence of operations to be carried out. There are two forms of illustration: figures and photographs. The figures are numbered in sequence with decimal numbers, according to their position in the Chapter — eg Fig. 6.4 is the fourth drawing/illustration in Chapter 6. Photographs carry the same number (either individually or in related groups) as the Section or sub-section to which they relate.

There is an alphabetical index at the back of the manual as well as a contents list at the front. Each Chapter is also preceded by its own individual contents list.

References to the 'left' or 'right' of the vehicle are in the sense of a person in the driver's seat facing forwards.

Unless otherwise stated, nuts and bolts are removed by turning anti-clockwise, and tightened by turning clockwise.

Vehicle manufacturers continually make changes to specifications and recommendations, and these when notified are incorporated into our manuals at the earliest opportunity.

Whilst every care is taken to ensure that the information in this manual is correct, no liability can be accepted by the authors or publishers for loss, damage or injury caused by any errors in, or omissions from, the information given.

Introduction to the Volvo 240

With the introduction of the Volvo 240 series another quality vehicle of conventional design is added to the Volvo stable. It is available with carburettor or fuel injection engines.

There is a choice of many additional features: Manual gearbox, with overdrive, automatic transmission, power steering, limited slip differential and air conditioning.

Overhaul and repair operations to the car are not complicated and all major components are fairly accessible.

Contents

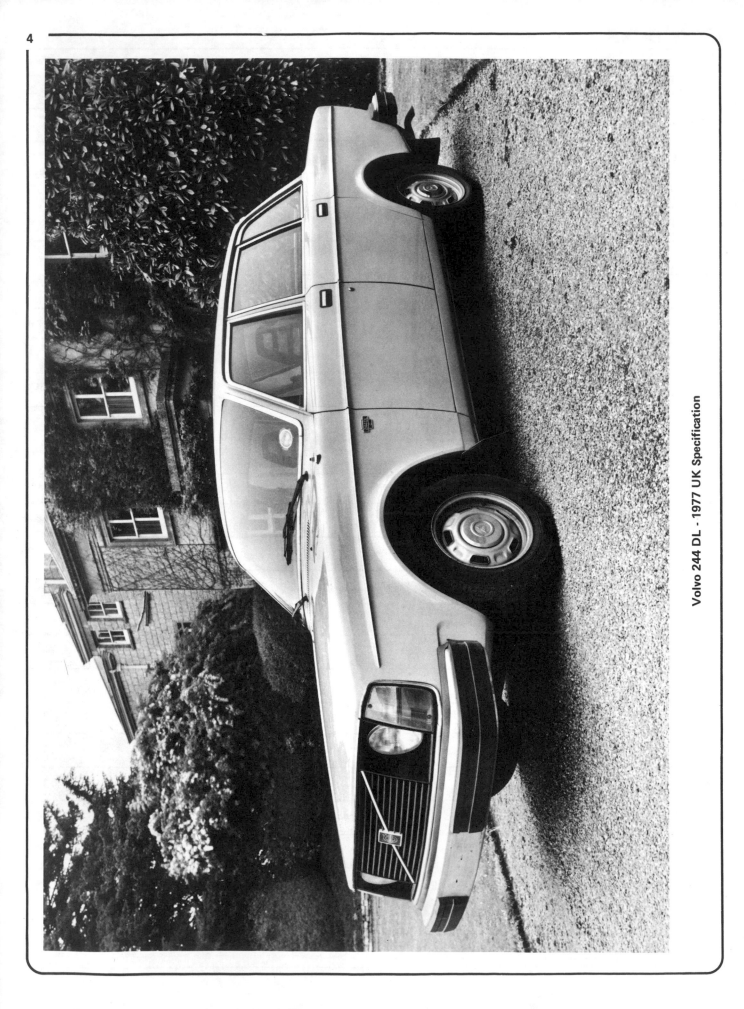

Volvo 244 DL - 1977 UK Specification

General dimensions, weights and capacities

Dimensions

Overall length:		
Early models	192.8 in (4898 mm)
Later models	192.4 in (4888 mm)
Overall width	67.2 in (1707 mm)
Overall height:	
Saloon	56.2 in (1427 mm)
Estate	57.5 in (1460 mm)
Wheelbase:	
Manual steering	103.9 in (2640 mm)
Power steering	104.3 in (2650 mm)
Front track:	
Early models	55.9 in (1420 mm)
Later models	56.3 in (1430 mm)
Rear track:	
Early models	53.15 in (1350 mm)
Later models	53.5 in (1360 mm)
Turning circle (between kerbs)	32 ft 6 in (9.8 m)

Weights

Kerb weights (approx):	
242, 244 and 245 (UK)	2830 lb (1285 kg)
GT and DL (240 and 242) (US)	2891 to 2999 lb (1312 to 1362 kg)
GL (244) (US)	2933 to 3065 lb (1332 to 1392 kg)
Estate (245) (US)	3129 to 3162 lb (1421 to 1436 kg)
Maximum trailer weight	2000 lb (908 kg)

Capacities

Engine:	
B20 (ohv)	6.6 Imp pints (4.0 US qt, 3.75 litres)
B17A, B19 and B21	6.8 Imp pints (4.1 US qt, 3.85 litres)
Manual transmission:	
M40, M45	1.3 Imp pints (0.8 US qt, 0.75 litre)
M41	2.8 Imp pints (1.7 US qt, 1.6 litres)
M46	4.0 Imp pints (2.4 US qt, 2.3 litres)
Automatic transmission:	
BW 35	11.3 Imp pints (6.8 US qt, 6.4 litres)
AW 55 and early BW 55	11.4 Imp pints (6.85 US qt, 6.5 litres)
BW 55 (later models)	12.1 Imp pints (7.3 US qt, 6.9 litres)
Rear axle	2.3 Imp pints (1.4 US qt, 1.3 litres)
Cooling system	16.7 Imp pints (10.0 US qt, 9.5 litres)
Fuel tank	13.2 Imp gal (15.8 US gal, 60 litres)

Use of English

As this book has been written in England, it uses the appropriate English component names, phrases, and spelling. Some of these differ from those used in America. Normally, these cause no difficulty, but to make sure, a glossary is printed below. In ordering spare parts remember the parts list will probably use these words:

English	American	English	American
Aerial	Antenna	Layshaft (of gearbox)	Countershaft
Accelerator	Gas pedal	Leading shoe (of brake)	Primary shoe
Alternator	Generator (AC)	Locks	Latches
Anti-roll bar	Stabiliser or sway bar	Motorway	Freeway, turnpike etc
Battery	Energizer	Number plate	License plate
Bodywork	Sheet metal	Paraffin	Kerosene
Bonnet (engine cover)	Hood	Petrol	Gasoline
Boot lid	Trunk lid	Petrol tank	Gas tank
Boot (luggage compartment)	Trunk	'Pinking'	'Pinging'
Bottom gear	1st gear	Propeller shaft	Driveshaft
Bulkhead	Firewall	Quarter light	Quarter window
Cam follower or tappet	Valve lifter or tappet	Retread	Recap
Carburettor	Carburetor	Reverse	Back-up
Catch	Latch	Rocker cover	Valve cover
Choke/venturi	Barrel	Roof rack	Car-top carrier
Circlip	Snap-ring	Saloon	Sedan
Clearance	Lash	Seized	Frozen
Crownwheel	Ring gear (of differential)	Side indicator lights	Side marker lights
Disc (brake)	Rotor/disk	Side light	Parking light
Drop arm	Pitman arm	Silencer	Muffler
Drop head coupe	Convertible	Spanner	Wrench
Dynamo	Generator (DC)	Sill panel (beneath doors)	Rocker panel
Earth (electrical)	Ground	Split cotter (for valve spring cap)	Lock (for valve spring retainer)
Engineer's blue	Prussian blue	Split pin	Cotter pin
Estate car	Station wagon	Steering arm	Spindle arm
Exhaust manifold	Header	Sump	Oil pan
Fast back (Coupe)	Hard top	Tab washer	Tang; lock
Fault finding/diagnosis	Trouble shooting	Tailgate	Liftgate
Float chamber	Float bowl	Tappet	Valve lifter
Free-play	Lash	Thrust bearing	Throw-out bearing
Freewheel	Coast	Top gear	High
Gudgeon pin	Piston pin or wrist pin	Trackrod (of steering)	Tie-rod (or connecting rod)
Gearchange	Shift	Trailing shoe (of brake)	Secondary shoe
Gearbox	Transmission	Transmission	Whole drive line
Halfshaft	Axleshaft	Tyre	Tire
Handbrake	Parking brake	Van	Panel wagon/van
Hood	Soft top	Vice	Vise
Hot spot	Heat riser	Wheel nut	Lug nut
Indicator	Turn signal	Windscreen	Windshield
Interior light	Dome lamp	Wing/mudguard	Fender

Miscellaneous points

An 'oil seal' is fitted to components lubricated by grease!

A 'damper' is a 'shock absorber', it damps out bouncing, and absorbs shocks of bump impact. Both names are correct, and both are used haphazardly.

Note that British drum brakes are different from the Bendix type that is common in America, so different descriptive names result. The shoe end furthest from the hydraulic wheel cylinder is on a pivot; interconnection between the shoes as on Bendix brakes is most uncommon. Therefore the phrase 'Primary' or 'Secondary' shoe does not apply. A shoe is said to be 'Leading' or 'Trailing'. A 'Leading' shoe is one on which a point on the drum, as it rotates forward, reaches the shoe at the end worked by the hydraulic cylinder before the anchor end. The opposite is a 'Trailing' shoe, and this one has no self servo from the wrapping effect of the rotating drum.

Buying spare parts and vehicle identification numbers

Buying spare parts

Spare parts are available from many sources, for example: Volvo garages, other garages and accessory shops, and motor factors. Our advice regarding spare part sources is as follows:

Officially appointed Volvo garages - This is the best source of parts which are peculiar to your car and are otherwise not generally available (eg. complete cylinder heads, internal gearbox components, badges, interior trim etc). It is also the only place at which you should buy parts if your car is still under warranty - non-Volvo components may invalidate the warranty. To be sure of obtaining the correct parts it will always be necessary to give the storeman your car's engine and chassis number, and if possible, to take the 'old' part along for positive identification. Remember that many parts are available on a factory exchange scheme - any parts returned should always be clean! It obviously makes good sense to go straight to the specialists on your car for this type of part for they are best equipped to supply you.

Other garages and accessory shops - These are often very good places to buy materials and components needed for the maintenance of your car (eg. oil filters, spark plugs, bulbs, fanbelts, oils and greases, touch-up paint, filler paste etc). They also sell general accessories, usually have convenient opening hours, charge lower prices and can often be found not far from home.

Motor factors - Good factors will stock all of the more important components which wear out relatively quickly (eg. clutch, oil filters, pistons, valves, exhaust systems, brake cylinders/pipes/hoses/seals/shoes and pads etc). Motor factors will often provide new reconditioned components on a part exchange basis - this can save a considerable amount of money.

Vehicle identification numbers

1   Although many individual parts, and in some cases sub-assemblies fit a number of different models it is dangerous to assume that just because they look the same, they are the same. Differences are not always easy to detect except by serial numbers. Make sure therefore, that the appropriate identity number for the model or sub-assembly is known and quoted when a spare part is ordered.

2   The final drive assembly has a number of its own which is carried on a plate fastened to the left-hand side of the casing. This plate gives the drive ratio, part number and serial number of the unit. The gearbox carries a similar plate on its underside giving the type designation, part number and serial number. On automatic transmission the plate is on the left-hand side of the casing.

3   The engine serial number appears on the left-hand side of the engine at the lip of the cylinder block just below the cylinder head.

4   The type designation and chassis number of the vehicle is stamped on the right-hand front door pillar and on a plate mounted on the luggage compartment rear wall (242/244) or on the side section under the right-hand rear side window (245).

5   The type designation, chassis number and code numbers for colour and upholstery appear on a plate located on the right-hand side wheel housing.

The engine serial number is stamped on the left-hand side of the engine block

This plate gives the type designation, chassis number and code numbers for colour and upholstery

Tools and working facilities

Introduction

A selection of good tools is a fundamental requirement for anyone contemplating the maintenance and repair of a motor vehicle. For the owner who does not possess any, their purchase will prove a considerable expense, offsetting some of the savings made by doing-it-yourself. However, provided that the tools purchased are of good quality, they will last for many years and prove an extemely worthwhile investment.

To help the average owner to decide which tools are needed to carry out the various tasks detailed in this manual, we have compiled three lists of tools under the following headings: Maintenance and minor repair, Repair and overhaul, and Special. The newcomer to practical mechanics should start off with the 'Maintenance and minor repair' tool kit and confine himself to the simpler jobs around the vehicle. Then, as his confidence and experience grows, he can undertake more difficult tasks, buying extra tools as, and when, they are needed. In this way, a 'Maintenance and minor repair' tool kit can be built-up into a 'Repair and overhaul' tool kit over a considerable period of time without any major cash outlays. The experienced do-it-yourselfer will have a tool kit good enough for most repair and overhaul procedures and will add tools from the 'Special' catagory when he feels the expense is justified by the amount of use these tools will be put to.

It is obviously not possible to cover the subject of tools fully here. For those who wish to learn more about tools and their use there is a book entitled 'How to Choose and Use Car Tools' available from the publishers of this manual.

Maintenance and minor repair tool kit

The tools given in this list should be considered as a minimum requirement if routine maintenance, servicing and minor repair operations are to be undertaken. We recommend the purchase of combination spanners (ring one end, open-ended the other); although more expensive than open-ended ones, they do give the advantages of both types of spanner.

> *Combination spanners - 10, 11, 13, 14, 17 mm*
> *Adjustable spanner - 9 inch*
> *Engine sump/gearbox/rear axle drain plug key (where applicable)*
> *Spark plug spanner (with rubber insert)*
> *Spark plug gap adjustment tool*
> *Set of feeler gauges*
> *Brake adjuster spanner (where applicable)*
> *Brake bleed nipple spanner*
> *Screwdriver - 4 in long x ¼ in dia (plain)*
> *Screwdriver - 4 in long x ¼ in dia (crosshead)*
> *Combination pliers - 6 inch*
> *Hacksaw, junior*
> *Tyre pump*
> *Tyre pressure gauge*
> *Grease gun (where applicable)*
> *Oil can*
> *Fine emery cloth (1 sheet)*
> *Wire brush (small)*
> *Funnel (medium size)*

Repair and overhaul tool kit

These tools are virtually essential for anyone undertaking any major repairs to a motor vehicle, and are additional to those given in the basic list. Included in this list is a comprehensive set of sockets. Although these are expensive they will be found invaluable as they are so versatile - particularly if various drives are included in the set. We recommended the ½ in square-drive type, as this can be used with most proprietary torque wrenches. If you cannot afford a socket set, even bought piecemeal, then inexpensive tubular box spanners are a useful alternative.

The tools in this list will occasionally need to be supplemented by tools from the Special list.

> *Sockets (or box spanners) to cover range 6 to 27 mm*
> *Reversible ratchet drive (for use with sockets)*
> *Extension piece, 10 inch (for use with sockets)*
> *Universal joint (for use with sockets)*
> *Torque wrench (for use with sockets)*
> *'Mole' wrench - 8 inch*
> *Ball pein hammer*
> *Soft-faced hammer, plastic or rubber*
> *Screwdriver - 6 in long x 5/16 in dia (plain)*
> *Screwdriver - 2 in long x 5/16 in square (plain)*
> *Screwdriver - 1 ½ in long x ¼ in dia (crosshead)*
> *Screwdriver - 3 in long x 1/8 in dia (electricians)*
> *Pliers - electricians side cutters*
> *Pliers - needle nosed*
> *Pliers - circlip (internal and external)*
> *Cold chisel - ½ inch*
> *Scriber (this can be made by grinding the end of a broken hacksaw blade)*
> *Scraper (this can be made by flattening and sharpening one end of a piece of copper pipe)*
> *Centre punch*
> *Pin punch*
> *Hacksaw*
> *Valve grinding tool*
> *Steel rule/straight edge*
> *Allen keys*
> *Selection of files*
> *Wire brush (large)*
> *Axle stands*
> *Jack (strong scissor or hydraulic type)*

Special tools

The tools in this list are those which are not used regularly, are expensive to buy, or which need to be used in accordance with their manufacturers instructions. Unless relatively difficult mechanical jobs are undertaken frequently, it will not be economic to buy many of these tools. Where this is the case, you could consider clubbing together with friends (or a motorists club) to make a joint purchase, or borrowing the tools against a deposit from a local garage or tool hire specialist.

The following list contains only those tools and instruments freely available to the public, and not those special tools produced by the vehicle manufacturer specifically for its dealer network. You will find occasional references to these manufacturers special tools in the text of this manual. Generally, an alternative method of doing the job without the vehicle manufacturers special tool is given. However, sometimes, there is no alternative to using them. Where this is the case and the relevant tool cannot be bought or borrowed you will have to entrust the work to a franchised garage.

> *Valve spring compressor*
> *Piston ring compressor*
> *Ball joint separator*
> *Universal hub/bearing puller*
> *Impact screwdriver*
> *Micrometer and/or vernier gauge*
> *Carburettor flow balancing device (where applicable)*
> *Dial gauge*
> *Stroboscopic timing light*
> *Dwell angle meter/tachometer*
> *Universal electrical multi-meter*
> *Cylinder compression gauge*
> *Lifting tackle (photo)*
> *Trolley jack*
> *Light with extension lead*

Buying tools

For practically all tools, a tool factor is the best source since he will have a very comprehensive range compared with the average garage or accessory shop. Having said that, accessory shops often offer excellent quality tools at discount prices, so it pays to shop around.

Remember, you don't have to buy the most expensive items on the shelf, but it is always advisable to steer clear of the very cheap tools. There are plenty of good tools around, at reasonable prices, so ask the proprietor or manager of the shop for advice before making a purchase.

Care and maintenance of tools

Having purchased a reasonable tool kit, it is necessary to keep the tools in a clean and serviceable condition. After use, always wipe off any dirt, grease and metal particles using a clean, dry cloth, before putting the tools away. Never leave them lying around after they have been used. A simple tool rack on the garage or workshop wall, for items such as screwdrivers and pliers is a good idea. Store all normal spanners and sockets in a metal box. Any measuring instruments, gauges, meters, etc., must be carefully stored where they cannot be damaged or become rusty.

Take a little care when the tools are used. Hammer heads inevitably become marked and screwdrivers lose the keen edge on their blades from time-to-time. A little timely attention with emery cloth or a file will soon restore items like this to a good serviceable finish.

Working facilities

Not to be forgotten when discussing tools, is the workshop itself. If anything more than routine maintenance is to be carried out, some form of suitable working area becomes essential.

It is appreciated that many an owner mechanic is forced by circumstance to remove an engine or similar item, without the benefit of a garage or workshop. Having done this, any repairs should always be done under the cover of a roof.

Wherever possible, any dismantling should be done on a clean flat workbench or table at a suitable working height.

Any workbench needs a vice: one with a jaw opening of 4 in (100 mm) is suitable for most jobs. As mentioned previously, some clean dry storage space is also required for tools, as well as the lubricants, cleaning fluids, touch-up paints and so on which soon become necessary.

Another item which may be required, and which has a much more general usage, is an electric drill with a chuck capacity of at least 5/16 in (8 mm). This, together with a good range of twist drills, is virtually essential for fitting accessories such as wing mirrors and reversing lights.

Last, but not least, always keep a supply of old newspapers and clean lint-free rags available, and try to keep any working area as clean as possible.

Spanner jaw gap comparison table

Jaw gap (in.)	Spanner size
0.250	¼ in AF
0.276	7 mm
0.313	5/16 in AF
0.315	8 mm
0.344	11/32 in AF; 1/8 in Whitworth
0.354	9 mm
0.375	3/8 in AF
0.394	10 mm
0.433	11 mm
0.438	7/16 in AF
0.445	3/16 in Whitworth; ¼ in BSF
0.472	12 mm
0.500	½ in AF
0.512	13 mm
0.525	¼ in Whitworth; 5/16 in BSF
0.551	14 mm
0.562	9/16 in AF
0.591	15 mm
0.600	5/16 in Whitworth; 3/8 in BSF
0.625	5/8 in AF
0.630	16 mm
0.669	17 mm
0.686	11/16 in AF
0.709	18 mm
0.710	3/8 in Whitworth; 7/16 in BSF
0.748	19 mm
0.750	¾ in AF
0.813	13/16 in AF
0.820	7/16 in Whitworth; ½ in BSF
0.866	22 mm
0.875	7/8 in AF
0.920	½ in Whitworth; 9/16 in BSF
0.937	15/16 in AF
0.945	24 mm
1.000	1 in AF
1.010	9/16 in Whitworth; 5/8 in BSF
1.024	26 mm
1.063	1.1/16 in AF; 27 mm
1.100	5/8 in Whitworth; 11/16 in BSF
1.125	1.1/8 in AF
1.181	30 mm
1.200	11/16 in Whitworth; ¾ in BSF
1.250	1¼ in AF
1.260	32 mm
1.300	¾ in Whitworth; 7/8 in BSF
1.313	1.5/16 in AF
1.390	13/16 in Whitworth; 15/16 in BSF
1.417	36 mm
1.438	1.7/16 in AF
1.480	7/8 in Whitworth; 1 in BSF
1.500	1½ in AF
1.575	40 mm; 15/16 in Whitworth
1.614	41 mm
1.625	1.5/8 in AF
1.670	1 in Whitworth; 1.1/8 in BSF
1.688	1.11/16 in AF
1.811	46 mm
1.813	13/16 in AF
1.860	1.1/8 in Whitworth; 1¼ in BSF
1.875	1.7/8 in AF
1.969	50 mm
2.000	2 in AF
2.050	1¼ in Whitworth; 1.3/8 in BSF
2.165	55 mm
2.362	60 mm

A Haltrac hoist and gantry in use during a typical engine removal sequence

Recommended lubricants and fluids

Component or system	Lubricant type or specification	Castrol product
1 Engine	Multigrade engine oil	GTX
2A Manual gearbox (with or without overdrive)		
M40 and M41	Hypoid gear oil SAE 80 or 90	Hypoy Light or Hypoy
M45 and M46	Automatic transmission fluid type F	TQF
2B Automatic transmission	Automatic transmission fluid type F	TQF
3 Rear axle*	Hypoid gear oil SAE 90...	Hypoy B
4 Front wheel bearings	Lithium-based grease	LM Grease
Hydraulic system	Hydraulic fluid to SAE J1703	Universal Brake and Clutch Fluid

If the vehicle is fitted with a limited slip differential a special lubricant is required. Consult your Volvo dealer.

Note: *The above are general recommendations only. Lubrication requirements vary from territory to territory. If in doubt, consult your nearest dealer or the operator's handbook supplied with the vehicle.*

Routine maintenance

For modifications, and information applicable to later models, see Supplement at end of manual

Introduction

Routine maintenance is a chore - however enthusiastic an owner or ardent a car lover you may be. A better name for it is preventive maintenance. This does not make it any less of a chore, but it is one of those chores which pays off.

It does this in three ways:

a) *It reduces wear and lengthens car life by ensuring that all parts that need it are properly lubricated.*

b) *It ensures that all small adjustments which make so much difference to the performance of the car - and in some cases neglect of these may mean disaster - are always correct.*

c) *Most important of all, by carrying out maintenance you give your car a thorough inspection.*

The maintenance tasks described below are in the main those recommended by Volvo, but we have added a few more to the list which practical experience has convinced us are well worth doing.

The recommended time intervals are applicable in temperate climates where the roads are reasonably dust-free and for yearly distances of 12,000 - 24,000 miles (20,000 - 40,000 kms). They may need to be modified where environmental conditions are extreme or distances driven are very much greater.

2 Weekly, before a long journey, or every 250 miles (400 kms)

1 Check the engine oil level which should be up to the 'Max' mark on the dipstick. Top-up the oil in the sump if necessary. On no account allow the oil to fall below the 'Min' mark on the dipstick.

2 Check the battery electrolyte level and top-up as necessary with distilled water. Make sure that the top of the battery is always kept clean and free of moisture.

3 Check the coolant level in the radiator or expansion tank. Top-up if necessary with the same mixture as is already in there - do not top-up antifreeze solution with water. Persistent need to top-up indicates leakage somewhere and should be investigated without delay.

4 Check the tyre pressures - and that includes the spare. The correct tyre pressures depend on the type of tyre that is being used and the vehicle load carried. The local Volvo garage, or indeed, any garage which deals in the make of tyre that is fitted, will be able to give this information. Keep the spare tyre at the highest pressures used as it can always be let down a little when it is fitted.

5 Refill the windscreen washer container with perfectly clean water. If it is necessary to add an antifreeze always use the sort specially made for windscreen washers. Check that the jets are operating correctly.

6 Check the windscreen wipers for correct operation and the blades for signs of deterioration. Renew the blades if their condition is suspect.

7 Check all the lights - notably the brake lights. When the car brakes suddenly, the car behind it needs all the warning it can get.

8 Check the level of the brake and clutch (when the hydraulic system is used as opposed to cable operation) hydraulic fluid reservoir/s. Top-up to the 'Max' mark if necessary.

3 Every 6,000 miles (10,000 km) or 6 months

1 Carry out the service operations in the weekly check.

2 Run the engine until it is hot and drain the engine oil. Refill with fresh oil.

3 Renew the engine oil filter.

4 Wipe the top of the carburettor suction chamber and top-up the carburettor until the fluid is 0.25 in (6 mm) from the top. For further

information see Chapter 3.

5 Check the carburettor adjustments, as described in Chapter 3. When fuel injection is fitted, further information will also be found in Chapter 3, but it may be as well to leave this to the local Volvo garage.

6 Check the cooling and heater systems for signs of leakage. Be sure that all hose clips are tight and that none of the hoses shows signs of cracking.

7 *Carburettor engine only.* Clean the filter in the fuel pump. For further information, refer to Chapter 3.

8 Check the fanbelt for signs of wear. If necessary set the tension, as described in Chapter 2.

9 Lubricate all throttle and engine control linkages with a little engine oil.

10 Check the adjustment of the handbrake and footbrake. If it was necessary to make an appreciable adjustment to the handbrake inspect the linkage for wear. Full information will be found in Chapter 9.

11 Carefully examine all the brake hydraulic pipes, hoses and unions for signs of leakage. The flexible hoses must not rub against any part of the car when the steering is turned through both locks.

12 Lubricate all moving parts of the handbrake system.

13 Clean and adjust the spark plugs, as described in Chapter 4.

14 Check the state of charge of the battery with an hydrometer. If it is not fully charged, and there is no immediate explanation of this (as, for example a slack fanbelt), have the battery checked by a local garage or preferably a specialist. If it is not in very good shape, it may be wise to consider replacement, especially in the winter.

15 Clean the battery terminals and smear them with petroleum jelly (vaseline) to prevent corrosion.

16 Check the alignment of the headlights and adjust, if necessary, as described in Chapter 10.

17 Check the steering box for leaks. Check oil level in reservoir (power steering).

18 Check the tyre wear pattern as, if irregular, it can indicate that the front suspension is out of alignment. If this does appear to be the case, the remedy is obvious and expert advice should be sought as soon as possible.

19 Wipe around the filler plug of the final drive unit (differential) and remove the plug. Check the oil level which should come up to the filler hole. If necessary, top-up with the correct lubricant. Refit the plug.

20 Check the propeller shaft for wear, as described in Chapter 7. Generally speaking, if wear is evident it would already have made its presence felt by causing vibration in the transmission system.

21 For cars with manual gearboxes, whether or not they are fitted with overdrive, wipe round the filler plug and check the oil level which should be up to the filler hole. If necessary, top-up with the correct lubricant.

22 *Automatic transmission.* The dipstick and filler tube is located in front of the bulkhead on the right-hand side of the engine. To check the oil level drive the car for a few miles to bring the fluid up to its normal operating temperature. With the car on a level surface move the selector to the 'P' position and allow the engine to idle for two minutes. With the engine still running, remove the dipstick, wipe clean with a non-fluffy rag, quickly insert fully and withdraw. If necessary, add fluid of the correct type to bring the level up to the 'Max' mark but take care not to overfill.

23 Check the exhaust system for leaks. If small blow holes are found, these can be rectified with a proprietary repair kit. However, this is a sign that corrosion is well advanced and the pipe or system will require renewal shortly. Check all exhaust mountings for tightness.

24 Check and, if necessary, adjust the clutch free-play. Where a cable system is used check the condition of the cable and lubricate with a little engine oil.

25 Check and adjust the distributor contact breaker points. Full information will be found in Chapter 4.

Fig. 1. B21A carburettor engine

1 Data plate
2 Oil dipstick, automatic transmission
3 Oil dipstick, engine
4 Brake fluid reservoir
5 Ignition coil
6 Battery
7 Ignition distributor
8 Oil filler cap, engine
9 Expansion tank, cooling system
10 Windscreen washer reservoir

Oil sump drain plug

Topping up with engine oil

Fig. 2. Checking the carburettor damper oil level

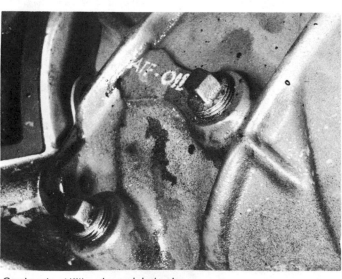

Gearbox level/filler plug and drain plug

26 Check ignition timing and reset if necessary, as described in Chapter 4.
27 Ideally the front wheel alignment should be checked and reset if necessary. This is best left to the local Volvo garage. See Chapter 11 for further information.
28 Generally, check the suspension and steering attachments for security and wear.
29 Check the valve clearances (B 20 engine) and reset if necessary. Full information will be found in Chapter 1.

---

4   Every 12,000 miles (20,000 km) or 12 months

---

1   Carry out the service items for the 6,000 mile (10,000 km) service.
2   Renew the spark plugs. Refer to Chapter 4.
3   Generally lubricate all locks, catches and hinges.
4   Thoroughly examine all electrical connections and fuel lines for signs of deterioration and damage.
5   Check the pad thickness of the front wheel brakes with the help of a mirror and 0.12 in (3 mm) wire gauge. If less than 0.12 in remains (the wire gauge will not fit), the pads should be considered worn out. If the wire gauge fits but the clearance is small it should be noted that the pads will not last another 12,000 miles (20,000 km).
6   Check the pad thickness of the rear wheel brakes. When 0.04 in (1 mm) remains between the base plate of the lining and the tensioning spring, the pads are worn out.
7   Check the valve clearances and reset if necessary. Full information will be found in Chapter 1.

Fig. 3. Lubrication points - body

No.	Lubricating point
1	Engine bonnet lock
2	Bonnet hinges
3	Sliding roof wind deflector
4	Door check assy.
5	Striker plates
6	Boot lid hinges
7	Door hinges
8	Door hinges Door stops
9	Front seat slide rails and latch devices
10	Window winders Lock device (on the inside of the doors)
11	Keyholes
12	Boot lid lock Keyhole

8   Clean the recirculation valve, pipes and connection nipple in the exhaust manifold.

5   Every 24,000 miles (40,000 km) or 18 months

1   Carry out the service items for the 6,000 and 12,000 mile service.
2   Drive the car until the oil in the transmission and final drive is thoroughly warm, drain and refill the systems.
3   Renew the air cleaner element, as described in Chapter 3.
4   *Fuel injection engine* - Change the fuel filter.
5   Check condition of crankcase ventilation hoses and for possible blockage. Remove and clean the nipple in the inlet manifold. Replace the flame guard.

6   Every two years

1   Drain and refill the cooling system with fresh coolant as described in Chapter 2.

7   Every 36,000 miles (60,000 km)

Change the timing gears drivebelt on B21 engines. Full information is given in Chapter 1.

8   Every three years

Drain the brake hydraulic system, renew all rubber seals and refill with fresh fluid. Bleed the system.

Jacking and towing

Jacking
The jack supplied with the car tool kit should be used only for changing a roadwheel. Whenever repair or overhaul operations are being carried out jack the car in the following positions and always supplement the jack with axle stands placed under the body side frame.
Raising the front end. Place the jack under the front axle member.
Raising the rear end: Place the jack under the tubular section of the axle casing as close to the trailing arm as possible.

Towing
Towing eyes are fitted to the front and rear of the car and any towing hooks or ropes should always be attached to these points only. Always remember to unlock the steering wheel in order to steer the car.
Bear in mind that the servo assistance does not function when the engine is not running, so the brake pedal will have to be depressed with greater force.
For cars with automatic transmission the gear selector must be in position 'N' and the car must not be towed for a distance exceeding 20 miles (32 km) or at a speed in excess of 20 mph (32 kph).
If it is necessary to tow a car with automatic transmission for more than 20 miles (32 km), remove the propeller shaft.

Chapter 1 Part A : Overhead camshaft engines

For modifications, and information applicable to later models, see Supplement at end of manual

Contents

Specifications

Engine (B 21) - general

	B 21A	B 21E
Type	B 21A	B 21E
Max output:*		
HP at rev/min DIN	100/5250	123/5500
KW at rev/min DIN	74/5280	90/5520
Max torque:*		
lbf ft at rev/min DIN	125/3000	125/3500
kgf m at rev/min DIN	17.3/3000	17.3/3500
Compression pressure at 250 - 300 rpm (warm engine turned over with starter)	128 - 156 psi (9 - 11 kg/sq cm)	128 - 156 psi (9 -11 kg/sq cm)
Compression ratio	8.5 : 1	9.3 : 1
Number of cylinders	4	4
Bore	3.622 in (92 mm)	3.622 in (92 mm)
Stroke	3.150 in (80 mm)	3.150 in (80 mm)
Capacity	130 cu in (2127 cc)	130 cu in (2127 cc)
Weight (approx.)	340 lb (155 kg)	365 lb (165 kg)

Typical figures which vary with emission control system and compression ratio

Pistons

Material	Light alloy
Permissible weight difference between pistons in same engine	0.35 oz (10 g)
Length	2.79 in (71 mm)
Clearance in bore	0.0004 - 0.0012 in (0.01 - 0.03 mm)
Compression rings:	
Number on each piston	2
Width	0.078 in (1.98 mm)
Gap	0.0138 - 0.0217 in (0.35 - 0.55 mm)
Side clearance in groove	0.0016 - 0.0028 in (0.040 - 0.072 mm)
Oil scraper ring:	
Number on each piston	1
Width	0.1566 - 0.1571 in (3.978 - 3.990 mm)
Gap	0.010 - 0.016 in (0.25 - 0.40 mm)
Side clearance in groove	0.0012 - 0.0024 in (0.030 - 0.062 mm)
Gudgeon pins (general):	
Arrangement	Fully floating with circlips at both ends
Fit in con-rod	Sliding fit
Fit in piston	Push fit
Gudgeon pin diameter:	
Standard	0.945 in (24.00 mm)
Oversize	0.947 in (24.05 mm)

Cylinder head

Material	Light alloy
Height between cylinder head joint face and face for bolt head	3.74 in (95.1 mm)

Valves

Inlet valves:	
Seat angle in cylinder head	45°
Valve seat angle	45.5°
Seat width in cylinder head	0.08 in (2 mm)
Valve head diameter	1.732 in (44 mm)
Stem diameter	0.3132 - 0.3138 in (7.955 - 7.970 mm)
Exhaust valves:	
Seat angle in cylinder head	45°
Valve seat angle	45.5°
Seat width in cylinder head	0.080 in (2 mm)
Valve head diameter	3.378 in (35 mm)
Stem diameter	0.3120 - 0.3126 in (7.925 - 7.940 mm)
Valve clearance - inlet and exhaust	
Adjusting cold	0.014 - 0.016 in (0.35 - 0.40 mm)
Adjusting warm	0.016 - 0.018 in (0.40 - 0.45 mm)

Valve guides

Length	2.047 (52 mm)
Inner diameter	0.3150 - 0.3159 in (8.000 - 8.022 mm)
Height above cylinder head face:	
Inlet	0.606 - 0.614 in (15.4 - 15.6 mm)
Exhaust	0.705 - 0.713 in (17.9 - 18.1 mm)

Valve springs

Free-length	1.77 in (45 mm)
With load of 62 - 70 lb (28 - 32 kg)	1.50 in (38 mm)
With load of 156 - 174 lb (72 - 80 kg)	1.06 in (27 mm)

Valve tappets

Diameter	1.4557 - 1.4565 in (36.975 - 36.995 mm)
Adjuster washer:	
Thickness	0.13 - 0.18 in (3.3 - 4.5 mm) in steps of 0.002 in (0.05 mm)

Crankshaft

Endfloat	0.0015 - 0.0058 in (0.037 - 0.147 mm)
Big-end bearing clearance	0.0009 - 0.0028 in (0.024 - 0.070 mm)
Main bearings clearance	0.0011 - 0.0033 in (0.028 - 0.083 mm)
Main bearing journals:	
Diameter:	
Standard	2.4981 - 2.4986 in (62.451 - 63.464 mm)
Undersize 1	2.4882 - 2.4886 in (63.197 - 63.210 mm)
Undersize 2	2.4781 - 2.4786 in (62.943 - 62.956 mm)
Width on crankshaft for flange bearing shell:	
Standard	1.5338 - 1.5351 in (38.960 - 39.000 mm)
Oversize 1	1.5438 - 1.5451 in (39.061 - 39.101 mm)
Oversize 2	1.5538 - 1.5551 in (39.163 - 39.203 mm)

Big-end bearing journals:

Bearing seat width	1.179 - 1.183 in (29.95 - 30.05 mm)
Diameter:	
Standard	2.1255 - 2.1260 in (53.987 - 54.000 mm)
Undersize 1	2.1155 - 2.1160 in (53.733 - 53.746 mm)
Undersize 2	2.1055 - 2.1060 in (53.479 - 53.492 mm)

Connecting rods

Endfloat on crankshaft	0.006 - 0.014 in (0.15 - 0.35 mm)
Length between centres	5.71 ± 0.0039 in (145 ± 1 mm)
Permissible weight difference between con-rods on same engine ...	35 oz (10 gramme)

Camshaft

Marking/MAX lift height:	
B21A 1975	A/0.39 in (9.8 mm)
B21A 1976 on	A/0.41 in (10.5 mm)
B21E	D/0.44 in (11.2 mm)
Number of bearings	5
Journal diameter	1.1437 - 1.1445 in (29.050 - 29.070 mm)
Radial clearance	0.0012 - 0.0028 in (0.030 - 0.071 mm)
Endfloat	0.004 - 0.016 in (0.1 - 0.4 mm)
Valve clearance for camshaft setting (cold engine)	0.028 in (0.7 mm)
Inlet valve should then open at:	
B21A 1975	5° btdc
B21A 1976 on	13° btdc
B21E	15° btdc
Diameter of camshaft bearings	1.1811 - 1.819 in (30.000 - 30.021 mm)

Timing gears

Number of teeth:	
Crankshaft gear	19
Intermediate gear	38
Camshaft gear	38
Drivebelt	123

Intermediate shaft

Number of bearings	3
Diameter bearing journal:	
Front	1.8494 - 1.8504 in (46.975 - 47.000 mm)
Intermediate	1.6939 - 1.6949 in (43.025 - 43.050 mm)
Radial clearance	0.0008 - 0.0030 in (0.020 - 0.75 mm)
Endfloat	0.008 - 0.018 in (0.20 - 0.46 mm)
Diameter of bearing in block:	
Front	1.8512 - 1.8524 in (47.020 - 47.050 mm)
Intermediate	1.6957 - 1.6968 in (43.070 - 43.100 mm)
Rear	1.6917 - 1.6929 in (42.970 - 43.000 mm)

Flywheel

Permissible axial throw (max)	0.002 in (0.05 mm) at diameter of 5.9 in (150 mm)

Lubrication system

Oil capacity:	
With oil filter	6.8 Imp pints (8.1 US pints : 3.85 litre)
Without oil filter	5.9 Imp pints (7.1 US pints : 3.35 litre)
Oil pressure at 2000 rpm (engine warm)	37 - 85 psi (2.5 - 6.0 kg/cm^2)
Oil filter - type	Full flow
Oil pump:	
Type	Gear type pump
Number of teeth on each gear	9
Endfloat	0.0008 - 0.0047 in (0.02 - 0.12 mm)
Radial clearance	0.0008 - 0.0035 in (0.02 - 0.09 mm)
Backlash	0.0059 - 0.0138 in (0.15 - 0.35 mm)
Relief valve spring length:	
Free-length	1.54 in (39.2 mm)
With load of 11 ± 0.8 lb (5 ± 0.4 kg)	1.03 in (26.25 mm)
With load of 15 ± 1.8 lb (7 ± 0.8 kg)	0.83 in (21 mm)

Torque wrench settings

	lbf ft	kgf m
Cylinder head (cold):		
Stage 1	44	6
Stage 2	81	11
Main bearings	92	12.5
Big-end bearings	46	6.3
Flywheel	52	7
Spark plugs	18	2.5
Camshaft bearings	15	2
Camshaft gear bolt	37	5

Intermediate shaft gear bolt	...	...	...	...	...	...	...	37	5
Oil sump bolts	...	...	...	...	...	...	...	8	1.1
Crankshaft gear bolt	...	...	...	...	...	...	...	122	16.5
Tensioner retaining nut	...	...	...	...	...	...	...	37	5

1 General description

The B21 engine is an in-line, four cylinder, fluid cooled, overhead camshaft engine. The B21 has two versions - B21A and B21E. The primary difference between them is in the different fuel systems they use. The B21A is a carburettor engine and the B21E has a fuel injection system of the Bosch CI type.

The B21E has a higher output, not only due to the fuel injection but also because of the higher compression ratio and a different type of camshaft with greater lifting height. The greater compression ratio on the B21E is achieved through flat piston crowns, while the pistons on the B21A have concave tops. Otherwise, the basic engine is the same for both versions.

The cylinder block is made of cast iron, in one piece, with the cylinder bores drilled directly in the block. An intermediate shaft for driving the ignition distributor, the lubricating oil pump and the fuel pump (B21A engines) is carried in three bearings on the left-hand side.

The cylinder head is made of aluminium alloy and the camshaft is carried in five bearings machined in the head and bearing caps. The cams of the camshaft operate directly on the valve tappets. The camshaft is driven by a toothed rubber belt, which also drives the intermediate shaft, from a pinion on the crankshaft.

The crankshaft has five main bearings which run in replaceable bearing shells. The connecting rods are made of drop forged steel and have pressed-in bronze bushings which act as bearings for the gudgeon pins at the small end. The big-end bearings are replaceable shell bearings.

The pistons are made of light alloy and have two compression rings and one oil scraper ring. The upper compression ring is chromed in order to reduce cylinder wear.

The cylinder head is bolted to the block (ie there are no studs in the block). The combustion chambers are cast and have separate inlet and exhaust ports, one for each valve. The valves are made of special steel and run in replaceable valve guides. Rubber seals are fitted on the top side of the inlet valve guides to prevent excessive oil from penetrating down between the guides and the valve stems. The seals are fitted only on the inlet valve guides where risk of oil being sucked in is greatest.

The engine lubrication system is of the conventional type with pressure lubrication of the main and big-end bearings, the intermediate shaft bearings and the camshaft bearings, and splash lubrication of the gudgeon pins and pistons. The camshaft works in a bath of oil which is fed from the camshaft bearings. The lubrication channel to the camshaft bearings comes from the main oil line. The three bearings on the intermediate shaft are supplied with oil through oilways from the main bearing housings. The engine timing gears are mounted on the outside of the engine and do not require any lubrication.

The gear type oil pump is driven by a gear on the intermediate shaft and has a spring-loaded ball-type relief valve fitted in the pump. On the discharge side of the pump there is a bleeder valve. In the event of the oil pump taking in air (eg. when taking a sharp bend with a low oil level), the bleeder valve ensures that the pump resumes its delivery in spite of the air mixture.

All oil supplied by the oil pump passes through a filter, located

Fig. 1.1. Cut-away view of B21A engine

Fig. 1.2. The intermediate shaft

1 *Front bearing*
2 *Gear for driving the ignition distributor*
3 *Cam for fuel pump*
4 *Intermediate bearing*
5 *Gear for driving oil pump*
6 *Support (used in manufacture)*
7 *Rear bearing*

on the right-hand side of the engine, before going to the various
lubricating points. The filter contains a bypass valve which allows oil
to bypass the filter should resistance to flow become excessive (blocked
filter) and a non-return valve which prevents the filter from being
emptied when the engine is switched off.

2 Engine removal - when is it necessary?

1   Because engine removal is a bothersome job for the ordinary owner
whose lifting tackle may well consist of nothing more than a barely
adequate pulley block, he will naturally want to do all he can with the
engine still in place. The Volvo owner is fortunate in that he can remove
the complete front section of the car and this gives very good access
to the front of the engine. This means that such jobs as replacing the
camshaft or timing gears present no problems with the engine in the
vehicle. Removing the sump is a little awkward and has a Section to itself later on (Section 38). Once it is removed, you can deal with the
big-end bearings, and with these removed and the head off you can
push the connecting rods up the cylinders and remove the
pistons.
2   This means that you can get at the engine sufficiently well to
give it a thorough examination in order to decide whether, for example,
it needs a re-bore or the crankshaft needs grinding, to say nothing
of carrying out quite a range of repairs, without having to take the
engine out of the car. Nevertheless, if you are faced with replacing
the crankshaft or main bearings or if you have got to do anything
on the flywheel more difficult than straightforward replacement of
the clutch assembly, you will have to take the engine out.

3 Engine - removal (general)

1   The engine can be removed and replaced quite easily with the
gearbox attached. However, we recommend that the automatic
transmission (where fitted) be removed before the engine
because of the high weight factor.
2   It is not necessary to remove the front section of the body when
removing the engine but to provide better access we removed the
front grille, cover plate and stay.
3   Although Volvo instructions for removing the engine make no
mention of dropping the front axle member slightly, we found this
to be necessary when removing the engine from the car shown in the
photographs. For this a mobile hoist, axle stands and a jack
are required.

4 Engine (carburettor models) - removal

1   Disconnect the leads from the battery.
2   Disconnect the windscreen washer hose and the engine compartment
light and cable from the bonnet. With the help of an assistant, take
the weight of the bonnet and remove the bolts securing the bonnet to
the bonnet hinges. Carefully lift the bonnet over the front of the car.
Store in a safe place, away from the immediate work area, where it
will not get scratched or damaged (photo).
3   Jack-up the front of the car and place axle stands or other secure
supports at the jacking points behind the front wheels. Chock the
rear wheels.
4   Remove the drain plug and drain off the oil into a container (photo).
5   Carefully drain the cooling system and remove the fan shroud
and the radiator, as described in Chapter 2.

4.2 Bonnet securing bolts

4.4 Sump drain plug

4.6a Remove the cover plate

4.6b Removing the cover plate stay

4.7 Removing the air cleaner

Fig. 1.3. Removing the servo pump (Sec. 4)

6 Remove the front grille, cover plate and stay (photo).

7 Remove the air cleaner, as described in Chapter 3 (photo).

8 *Cars with power steering:* remove the servo pump and bracket by removing the tensioning bolt and tilting up the pump. Lift off the belt and remove the bolts securing the bracket to the engine block.

9 *Cars with power steering and air-conditioning:* remove the servo pump by removing the bolts on the tensioning bar, lifting off the belt and placing the servo pump securely on the inside of the casing. Remove the pulley on the crankshaft, lift off the compressor belt and replace the pulley temporarily with two bolts. Remove the compressor and its bracket and place the compressor securely on the inside of the wheel arch (valance). *On no account disconnect the hoses from the compressor,* otherwise the air-conditioning system will have to be evacuated and this requires special equipment and may cause danger to health.

10 Disconnect the earth strap from the engine block, and the valve cover (photo).

11 Disconnect the low tension lead, and the high tension lead from the coil. Remove the distributor cap complete with plug leads (photo).

12 Disconnect the leads from the starter motor. Disconnect the lead from the charging regulator and remove the clamp (photo).

13 Disconnect the fuel inlet pipe from the fuel pump and blank-off the pipe.

14 Disconnect the servo brake hose from the engine and the heater hoses from the bulkhead at the rear of the engine block.

15 Disconnect the throttle and choke controls (photo).

16 Disconnect the leads from the water temperature and oil pressure switches.

17 Remove the pre-heating plate from the exhaust manifold.

18 Remove the nuts securing the exhaust pipe flanges (photo).

19 Remove the front engine mounting bolts (photo).

20 Remove the bracket for the front exhaust pipe clamp (photo).

21 Disconnect the clutch cable from the operating fork and its support on the clutch housing (cable actuation) or disconnect the hydraulic pipe from the slave cylinder (hydraulic actuation) (photo).

22 Release the rubber gaiter from the gearlever. Remove the retaining pin and the gearlever. Disconnect the lead for the reversing lights (photos).

Fig. 1.4. Removing the air-conditioning compressor (Sec. 4)

23 Disconnect the speedometer cable from the gearbox (photo).

24 Remove the bolts from the front propeller shaft, and lower it to the ground.

25 Disconnect the link arm from the gearlever end, (5 mm Allen key) and from the gearbox. On cars with overdrive disconnect the cable to the gearlever (photos).

26 Position a jack under the gearbox and remove the gearbox support member (photos).

27 Using a hoist and a suitable sling, support the weight of the engine/gearbox. Check that all controls, cables and pipes have been disconnected and tucked out of the way.

28 Commence lifting the engine, lifting the rear downwards to clear the bulkhead until the sump clears the front axle member. At this stage we found it necessary to slacken off the front axle member retaining bolts and drop the front axle member slightly to allow the sump to clear the axle, when being pulled forward (photos).

29 Continue lifting the unit and pull it forward clear of the engine compartment. Lower the engine to the ground and support it so that it can't fall over.

4.10 Earth strap from valve cover to bulkhead

4.11a Ignition coil with HT lead removed

4.11b Removing the distributor cap and plug leads

4.12 Disconnecting the leads from the starter motor

4.15 Disconnecting the throttle cable

4.18 Exhaust pipe disconnected

4.19 Removing the front engine mounting bolts

4.20 Removing the bracket for the front exhaust pipe clamp

4.21 Disconnecting the clutch slave cylinder

4.22a Removing the gear lever retaining pin

4.22b Lifting out the gear lever

4.22c Disconnecting the lead for the reversing light switch

4.23 Disconnecting the speedometer cable from the gearbox

4.25a Disconnecting the link arm at the gear lever

4.25b Removing the link arm from the gearbox

4.25c Gearbox with propeller shaft, speedometer cable and link arm disconnected

4.26a Gearbox support member retaining bolts

4.26b Gearbox flexible mounting

4.26c Gearbox mounting retaining nut

4.28a Lifting out the engine

4.28b The front axle member retaining bolts

5 Engine (fuel injection models) - removal

1 The removal sequence is basically the same as that described in Section 4, but there are several points that should be noted, relative to the disconnecting of the fuel injection equipment.
2 Disconnect the crankcase ventilation hose.
3 Disconnect the four vacuum hoses from the engine.
4 Disconnect the clutch cable from the clamp on the starter motor.
5 Disconnect the cable to the air-conditioning from the solenoid valve on the shutter housing (where fitted) and pull the cable forward.
6 Remove the tank cap (to eliminate any over pressure in the system). Disconnect the hose from the filter and the return hose from the return pipe. Remove the guard plate for the pre-engaging resistor (Fig. 1.5). On later models the pre-engaging resistor is mounted behind the radiator grille.
7 Disconnect the plug contacts from the pre-engaging resistor, four on the cable harness and bands, two from the relay and one from the pre-engaging resistor switch.

6 Engine (automatic transmission models) - removal

When automatic transmission is fitted it is recommended that because of the weight involved, the automatic transmission unit should be removed first, as described in Chapter 6, and then the engine removed in the normal way.

7 Engine - dismantling (general)

1 The essential preliminary to dismantling an engine is cleaning. The ideal way to do this is to brush the engine all over with paraffin or, better, 'Gunk' or a similar commercial solvent. Allow it to stand for a while and then hose it down. Where the dirt is thick and deeply embedded, work the solvent into it with a wire brush. If the engine is very dirty a second application may be necessary here and there.

Fig. 1.5. Disconnecting the fuel hoses (Sec. 5)

1 Hose from filter   3 Guard plate retaining screws
2 Return pipe hose

Finally, wipe down the outside of the engine with a rag. If it is not possible to use a pressure hose to remove the dirt and solvent, cleaning will be much more laborious, but however laborious it is, it will pay in the long run. After all, the engine has got to be cleaned at the end of the dismantling process, so it might just as well be as clean as possible at the start.

2 Clean each part as the engine is stripped. Try to ensure that everything taken off - down to the smallest washer - goes back exactly where it came from and exactly the same way round. This means laying the various bits and pieces out in a tidy manner. Nuts, bolts and washers may often be replaced finger tight from where they were removed.

3 Most parts can easily be cleaned by washing them in paraffin and wiping down with a cloth, but do not immerse parts with oilways in paraffin. They are best wiped down with a petrol or paraffin dampened cloth, and the oilways cleaned out with nylon pipe cleaners.

4 Re-use of old gaskets is false economy. Oil and water leaks will always result even if nothing worse. Always use genuine Volvo gaskets obtainable from Volvo garages. Volvo say that jointing compound should not be used with any of their gaskets.

5 Do not throw the old gaskets away as the engine is stripped down. These may be used for checking the pattern of new ones or as templates for making gaskets for which replacements are difficult to obtain. Hang up the old gaskets as they are removed.

6 In this Chapter we have described the order in which we stripped down the engine shown in most of the photographs. Where it seems necessary we have explained why we removed or did not remove certain parts at certain times. Generally speaking when stripping an engine it is best to work from the top down, at least once you have removed the gearbox. Support it with wood blocks so that it stands firmly on its sump or the base of the crankcase to start with. When the stage of removing the crankshaft and connecting rods is reached, turn it on its side and carry out all subsequent work with it in this position.

8 Engine - dismantling procedure

1 Remove the bolts securing the gearbox to the engine and separate the gearbox and engine (photo).

2 Remove the exhaust manifold (photo).

3 Disconnect the ignition setting sender (17 mm open ring spanner).

4 *Carburettor engines:* disconnect the fuel pump to carburettor pipe, the coolant hose to the inlet manifold, the vacuum hose and the crankcase ventilation hose. Remove the inlet manifold and fuel pump (photo).

5 *On fuel injection engines:* disconnect the crankcase ventilation hose, the lead and fuel line from the cold-start valve, the lead and hoses from the auxiliary air valve. Remove the cold-start valve (5 mm Allen key) and the auxiliary air valve. Remove the stay between the block and

8.1 Separating the gearbox and engine

8.2 Removing the exhaust manifold

8.3 Disconnecting the ignition setting sender

Fig. 1.6. Disconnecting the vacuum hose (Sec. 8)

Fig. 1.7. Disconnecting the crankcase ventilation hose (Sec. 8)

8.4 Removing the fuel pump

inlet manifold and the vacuum hose, slacken the upper hose clamp at the rubber bellows and remove the inlet manifold. Disconnect the pipes to the injectors, the electrical connections and remove the fuel distributor and control pressure regulator.

6   Remove the starter motor, the temperature sensor and, on E type engines, the thermal timer sensor.

7   Remove the engine mountings. Remove the bolt securing the dip-stick tube.

8   Disconnect the leads from the alternator, remove the bolts from the tensioning bar and lift off the belts. Remove the alternator and

bracket. Remove the fan (photos).

9   Remove the pulley from the water pump.

10 Disconnect the lead and remove the oil pressure sensor (photo).

11 Remove the oil filter (photo).

12 Remove the distributor (photo).

13 Remove the cover protecting the timing gears.

14 Remove the coolant pipe to the heater element and remove the water pump. Remove the thermostat housing, the thermostat and the lifting eye (photos).

15 Slacken the belt tensioner nut and slacken the belt by pushing the roller back against the spring. Lock the spring by inserting a 3 mm pin (eg. drill) in the hole on the thrust pin. Remove the toothed drive-belt.

16 Remove the retaining nut and washer and pull off the belt tensioner roller.

17 Restrain the camshaft from turning (a bar in one of the holes) and remove the camshaft gear retaining nut. The gear wheel and guide plates can be pulled off by hand.

18 Remove the six bolts securing the crankshaft pulley and lift off the pulley. Remove the centre bolt from the front of the crankshaft and remove the front hub (photo).

19 Remove the crankshaft gear and guide plate. Use a puller, if necessary.

20 Remove the retaining bolt and gearwheel from the intermediate shaft.

21 Remove the cable harness and the rear part of the belt guard. Remove the front sealing flange and press out the seals (photo).

22 Remove the oil pump pinion cover and lift out the oil pump pinion. Pull out the intermediate shaft taking care that the shaft gear does not damage the bearing bushing in the engine block (photo).

23 Remove the valve cover and gasket. Remove the cylinder head bolts,

Fig. 1.8. Removing the inlet manifold (Sec. 8)

Fig. 1.9. Removing the fuel distributor and control pressure regulator (Sec. 8)

1   Electrical connections   3   Retaining bolts
2   Injectors

Fig. 1.10. Removing the temperature sensor (Sec. 8)

1   Temperature sensor   2   Thermal timer sensor (E engines)

8.8a Alternator earth cable

8.8b Removing the alternator

8.10 Removing the oil pressure sensor

8.11 The oil filter

8.12 Removing the distributor

Fig. 1.11. Removing the drivebelt guard casing (Sec. 8)

8.14a Disconnecting the pipe from the water pump to the heater element

8.14b Removing the thermostat housing and the lifting eye

Fig. 1.12. Releasing the tension on the drivebelt and removing the tensioner roller and drivebelt (Sec. 8)

8.18 Removing the crankshaft gear and guide plate

8.21 Removing the bolts securing the rear part of the belt guard

8.22 Taking off the oil pump pinion cover and lifting out the oil pump pinion

Fig. 1.13. Withdrawing the intermediate shaft (Sec. 8)

8.24a Removing the clutch assembly

8.24b Pilot bearing retaining circlip

10 mm(3/8 in) Allen key, and lift off the head.

24 Unscrew the bolts holding the clutch assembly to the flywheel a little at a time, keeping them in step to avoid the risk of distorting the clutch cover. Mark the clutch assembly and flywheel to identify position for replacement and remove the clutch assembly. Remove the circlip retaining the pilot bearing and remove the washer and bearing (photos).

25 Restrain the flywheel from turning and remove the eight retaining bolts. Remove the flywheel taking care not to push in the ignition setting sender. On cars with automatic transmission a carrier plate with ring gear, a support plate and flange are fitted in place of a flywheel (photo).

26 Remove the reinforcing bracket. Remove the rear sealing flange and press out the seal.

27 Remove the sump. Remove the oil pump and the 'O' ring seals from the block and also from the pipe, if fitted (photo).

28 Check the marking on the connecting rods and caps, and mark

the pistons accordingly, so that they can be identified regarding their respective cylinders when being refitted. The five main bearing caps are marked 1 to 5 with No. 1 at the front. When removing bearing shells, mark them too, so that they can be refitted in the same location if they are not being renewed.

29 Remove the pistons and connecting rods by removing the bearing caps and shells and pushing the connecting rods through the cylinders and steadying the pistons as they emerge. Take care not to scratch or damage the pistons as they are removed (photo).

30 Remove the main bearing caps and lift out the crankshaft. Remove the spacer sleeve on the front end of the crankshaft. Remove the bearing shells from the engine block and caps (photos).

9 Cylinder head, valves and camshaft - overhaul

1 Remove the spark plugs and injectors (if fitted).

8.25 Removing the flywheel retaining bolts

Fig. 1.14. Reinforcing bracket retaining bolts (Sec. 8)

8.27 Removing the oil pump

Fig. 1.15. Identification marking on connecting rods and caps (Sec. 8)

8.29 Removing the connecting rod caps

8.30a Lifting out the crankshaft

8.30b Remove the main bearing shells from the engine block

2   Check the marking on the camshaft bearing caps, they are numbered 1 - 5 from the front (Fig. 1.16). Slacken off the cap retaining nuts, evenly and in rotation till the tension is off the camshaft, then remove the bearing caps and the camshaft. Remove the front seal and the half-moon shaped rubber seal at the rear of the cylinder head.

3   Lift out the valve tappets and remove the rubber rings. Identify the tappets to their location so that they can be fitted in the same position on reassembly (photo).

4   Clean the oil and grease off the cylinder head and remove the carbon from the combustion chambers and valve heads with a scraper or a rotary wire brush.

5   Using a suitable valve spring compressing tool, compress the spring until the collets are free from their recess, remove the collets, release the pressure on the spring, lift off the upper spring retainer, the spring and the lower spring retainer. Push the valve through the valve guide and remove it. If the valve seems a tight fit in the guide, this may be because the upper part of the stem has carbon on it. Give it a clean in this case. Remove the valve stem seals from the inlet valve guides (photos).

6   Keep the valves lined up in the order you remove them, and place them with their springs and retainers together with their tappets.

7   With the valves removed, clean out any carbon from the ports. Examine the valve seats, if they are only slightly pitted it is possible to make them smooth again by grinding the valves against the seats, as described in Section 11. Where pitting is very deep they will have to be recut: a job for the specialist with the necessary equipment.

8   Check the valve guides with the valve stems to ensure that they are a good fit: the stems should move easily in the guides without side play. Worn guides can be extracted and new ones installed but this should be left to your Volvo agent.

9   Examine the valves, checking them for straightness and the condition of the face. Slight pitting can be removed by grinding-in, but if the pitting is deep the valve will have to be machine ground by a specialist.

Fig. 1.16. Checking the marking on the camshaft bearing caps and cylinder head (Secs. 9 and 27)

10 The camshaft and its bearings in the cylinder head are part of the Volvo engine which seems virtually everlasting. If there should be noticeable play between the camshaft and its bearings, or if the bearings are damaged then the cylinder head will have to be renewed as the bearings are machined in the head. If very light scratches are present on the camshaft these can be removed by gently rubbing down with a very fine grade emery cloth or oil stone. The greatest care must be taken to keep the cam profiles smooth.

10 Tappets and adjuster washers - inspection

1   Examine the tappets for scoring or damage. Place them in the cylinder head and check that they move easily but have no noticeable side play.

2   Check the condition of the adjuster washers; if they show signs of wear they must be renewed.

11 Valves and valve seats - grinding-in

1   Grinding-in is essential when fitting valves whether these, or their seats, be new or old. As well as removing every trace of scoring, it ensures that the valve face and the seat have exactly the same slope and hence a reasonably wide area of contact. Where new valves are being fitted to correctly re-cut seats, grinding is still essential, because - as you can see from the specifications at the start of the Chapter - a valve face is cut to an angle which is very slightly less than that of the face in the cylinder head and consequently the contact area is very small. The correct area of contact is obtained by grinding.

2   Valve grinding is a simple matter, needing only fine and coarse carborundum paste, an inexpensive tool and a great deal of patience. Fig. 1.17 illustrates the procedure. Place the cylinder head upside down on a bench with a block of wood at each end to give clearance for the valve stems.

3   Smear a trace of coarse paste on the seat face, apply a suction tool to the valve head and insert the valve into the cylinder head. Press lightly on the tool using the palms of the hands and rotate the tool with a to-and-fro motion, then lift the valve from the seat and give it a quarter or half a turn before repeating the process. When a dull, matt, even surface finish is produced on both the valve seat and the valve, wipe off the coarse paste and carry on with the fine paste, lifting and turning the valve as before. When a smooth unbroken ring of light grey matt finish is produced on both valves and valve seat faces, the grinding operation is complete.

Aim to get a seat width in accordance with the Specifications at the start of the Chapter. If the seat is too wide, you can reduce the width by carefully rounding off the corners with an oil stone.

4   When the grinding is complete, clean away every trace of grinding compound with paraffin or petrol. Take great care that none is left in the ports or the valve guides.

12 Pistons and piston rings - examination and renovation

1   If the old pistons are to be refitted, carefully remove the piston

9.3 Lift out the tappets

9.5a Compressing the valve spring and removing the collets

9.5b Lifting out the valve spring

Fig. 1.17. Valve grinding, using hand suction tool. Lift off seat occasionally to spread grinding paste evenly over seat and valve face (Sec. 11)

Fig. 1.18. Measuring the piston ring gap with feeler gauge (Sec. 12)

Fig. 1.19. Measuring piston ring clearance in groove with feeler gauge (Sec. 12)

rings and then thoroughly clean them. Take particular care to clean out the piston ring grooves. Do not scratch the comparatively soft material of the pistons in any way. Piston rings can be easily removed by raising one end and slipping a thin metal strip (such as an old feeler gauge of around 0.020 in (0.05 mm) underneath it. Slide the strip round the piston easing the ring out of the grooves as you go.
2   If new rings are to be fitted to the old pistons, then the top ring should be stepped so as to clear the ridge left above the previous top ring. If a normal but oversize new ring is fitted it will hit the ridge and break, because the new ring will not have worn in the same way as the old.
3   Before fitting the rings on the pistons, put them in the cylinder bore at a point below the bottom limit of their travel and check their gap (Fig. 1.18). This should be between 0.016 - 0.022 in (0.40 - 0.55 mm). If the ring gap is too small rub down the ends of the ring with a very fine file until it is correct. To keep the rings square in the bore for measurement, line them up with a piston in the bore.
4   Check the fit of the piston rings in the grooves by rolling them

13.1 Slot on piston top (must face forward when piston is fitted in cylinder)

round the groove and inserting the feeler gauges (Fig. 1.19). For correct clearances, see Specifications at the beginning of this Chapter. Note that of the two compression rings, the chromium plated one goes at the top. The scraper ring, which is grooved fits in the bottom groove.
5   In engine manufacture the cylinders are all machined simultaneously and because of this have very slight differences in diameter. This is allowed for by selecting pistons to fit each bore; this is why it is so important when refitting old pistons that they should be replaced in the cylinders that they came from.

13 Gudgeon pins - general

1   The gudgeon pins are retained in the pistons by circlips and can easily be pushed out of the pistons when these are removed. When you separate the connecting rod from the piston, mark the connecting rod so that you can refit it the same way round. There is no need to mark the piston as this has a small slot (which must always face forwards when the piston is in the engine) on the top (photo).
2   The fit of the gudgeon pin in the connecting rod should be such that it can be pushed out with light thumb pressure but should have no noticeable looseness. It should fit in the piston so that you can push it through by hand, against light resistance. If the gudgeon pin hole in the piston is worn, an over-sized gudgeon pin must be fitted. In this case the holes must be reamed out in line to the correct measurement (see paragraph 4).
3   If the bush in the connecting rod is worn, it can be pressed out and a new bush pressed in. The new bush must be reamed to the correct fit.
4   Reaming is best carried out by someone who has suitable machinery and experience. If you do not come within this category, have it done through your Volvo agent.

14 Intermediate shaft - inspection

1   Examine the pinions for the distributor and oil pump for chipping or damage. Check the fuel pump operating cam for wear.
2   Check the shaft in its bearings in the engine block. If there is noticeable play between the intermediate shaft and its bearings, they will have to be renewed, but this is a highly specialised job, involving the reaming of three bearings in line - definitely a task for the specialist.

15 Crankshaft and bearings - examination and renovation

1   Inspect the bearing shells for signs of general wear, scoring, pitting and scratches. The shells should be a matt grey in colour. If any trace of copper colour is noticed, it is an indication that the bearings are

badly worn, because the white metal is plated onto a copper coloured underlay.

2   The bearing shells will have figures stamped on them to indicate their size, and naturally ensure that the shells purchased are of the same size as the ones taken out.

3   Examine the bearing surfaces on the crankshaft for signs of scoring or scratches and check their ovality with a micrometer. Take measurements at a number of positions on each surface, paying particular attention to the surfaces of which the bearing shells show signs of wear. If there are differences in diameter of more than 0.002 in (0.05 mm) on the main bearing surfaces or 0.003 in (0.07 mm) on the big-end surfaces the crankshaft must be reground. It is probably worthwhile regrinding the crankshaft if it is found that the bearings are worn and the crankshaft ovality is appreciably more than half these figures.

4   Regrinding the crankshaft and subsequent fitting of under-sized bearing shells is a job for the specialist. If the reground crankshaft is returned with the bearing shells fitting to the surface, be sure not to change them round when refitting.

5   **Never** make any attempt to cure a noisy big-end by filing the bearing cap and/or working on the bearing shell.

16 Flywheel starter ring gear - renewal

1   The ring gear is a shrink fit on the flywheel. Replacing it needs care but is not really very difficult. Remove the old ring by drilling through it at the root of the gear teeth at two diametrically opposite points, being careful not to drill the actual flywheel. Drill as big a hole as possible and then break the ring gear with a hammer and cold chisel.

2   Heat up the new ring in the oven, setting the thermostat to 220°C (430°F). If possible, put the flywheel in the refrigerator or deep

freeze for an hour or so at the same time.

3   Before the ring has time to cool, fit it over the flywheel and clamp it in position so that as it cools down it will be accurately positioned.

4   After refitting a ring, the flywheel (ideally the flywheel assembled to the crankshaft), should be balanced. Any out of balance is rectified by drilling on the flywheel close to, but not on, the joint between the wheel and the ring gear.

5   Do not be tempted to heat the ring gear with a flame. It is case-hardened and if the temperature is raised much above 220°C (430°F) locally the casing will be softened.

17 Oil pump - overhaul

1   Dismantling the pump is straightforward: pull the delivery pipe out of its socket, remove the wire clip and take off the strainer. Remove the four bolts and remove the cover, the spring and ball. Remove the gears.

2   Clean the parts in petrol and wipe them dry with a non-fluffy cloth.

3   Examine the gears and housing for damage. Check the cover for wear. Fit the gears and check the backlash, this should be between 0.006 and 0.014 in (0.15 and 0.35 mm). Check the endfloat as shown in Fig. 1.22, this should be 0.0008 - 0.0047 in (0.02 - 0.12 mm). Check for wear by fitting the drive gear; the gear should rotate freely without side play. If wear is apparent the pump will have to be renewed.

4   Check the relief valve spring against the Specifications at the beginning of this Chapter, if it does not meet the specifications it must be renewed.

5   The sealing rings at each end of the delivery pipe are made of special rubber and are manufactured to very close tolerances. Use only Volvo parts when renewing them. When assembling the pump coat them with soapy water to ease fitment.

Fig. 1.20. Dismantling the oil pump (Sec. 17)

Fig. 1.21. Checking the backlash (Sec. 17)

Fig. 1.22. Checking the endfloat (Sec. 17)

Fig. 1.23. Replacing the relief valve ball and spring (Sec. 17)

18 Engine - reassembly (general)

1 To ensure maximum life with minimum trouble from a re-built engine, not only must every part be correctly assembled but everything must be spotlessly clean, all the oilways must be clear, locking washers and spring washers must always be fitted where needed and all bearings and other working surfaces must be thoroughly lubricated during assembly. Before assembly begins, renew any bolts or studs whose threads are in any way damaged and wherever possible use new spring washers.

2 All bearing caps should be assembled with new bolts.

3 Be sure that where the instructions call for pressing on bearings, pressing in bushes, pressing on gears and so forth, suitable tools are used for doing the job. In most cases these can be made up with suitable bolts, lengths of tubing washers, bridging pieces etc. The point is that taking things off is, generally speaking, easier than putting them on, and in any case when removing a bearing which has already been condemned it doesn't matter whether it is damaged further or not. When replacing things however, one does not want the replacement to be damaged in any way. In the case of replacement bearings or replacement gears, there is no reason why one cannot have a rehearsal with the old ones.

4 Be sure all the gaskets needed are to hand.

5 Finally, when reassembling this engine regard a torque wrench as a necessity, not a luxury. The bolts and nuts for the big-ends and main bearing caps do not carry washers or split pins; they rely on accurate torque setting to stretch them just enough to ensure a really shakeproof assembly.

19 Crankshaft - refitting

1 Make sure that the crankcase is thoroughly clean and that all the oilways are clear. Inject oil into the oilways at several points with a forcefeed oil can or plastic bottle: this will have the two-fold benefit of checking that the oilways are clear and getting oil into them before you start assembly. Do the same with the crankshaft - it is particularly important to get as much oil as possible into the crankshaft oilways.

2 Remove every trace of protective grease from new bearing shells.

3 Wipe the seats of the main bearing shells in the crankcase clean and fit the appropriate shells in them. The rear shell incorporates thrust flanges. Note that the bearing shells have tabs on them which fit into grooves in the casing, so they can only be fitted the one way. If the old bearings are being refitted be sure to place them in their original positions (photo).

4 Oil the shells generously and place the crankshaft on top of them - be sure that it is the right way round (photo).

5 Wipe the bearing cap housings and fit their shells into them, keeping an eye on the order if necessary.

6 Oil the bearing surfaces of the crankshaft generously and fit the bearing caps over them, ensuring that they locate properly. The mating surfaces must be spotlessly clean or the caps will not seat correctly.

7 As each cap is fitted, put a new pair of fixing bolts through the holes and screw them up finger tight. Be sure the caps are fitted in their right order and the right way round.

8 When all the caps are fitted and the nuts finger-tight, check that the crankshaft rotates freely without any suggestion of high spots. If it does not, there is something wrong: do not go any further in the assembly until the cause has been found. The most likely cause is dirt on one of the bearing shells.

9 Tighten the bolts to a torque of 92 lb f ft (12.5 kg f m). Recheck the crankshaft for freedom of rotation (photo).

10 Check that the crankshaft endfloat lies within the Specifications at the beginning of this Chapter.

20 Pistons and connecting rods - reassembly

1 We have already considered the overhaul of the pistons, connecting rods and gudgeon pins and it only remains to assemble the connecting rods, gudgeon pins and pistons before fitting them into the cylinder block. Check that the connecting rods are the right way round and make sure that when the mark on the connecting rod lines up with the

19.3 Fitting the rear main bearing shell

19.4 Placing the crankshaft in the engine block

19.9 Tightening the main bearing cap bolts

20.1a Connecting rod big-end bearing assembly

20.1b Marking on connecting rod and cap

corresponding mark on the bearing cap, the cap itself is right way round, the piston is placed as in Fig. 1.24 with the slot in the head facing forwards (photos).

2   Assemble the connecting rods and gudgeon pins to the pistons, and fit the retaining circlips (photos).

3   Check that the piston ring grooves and oilways are thoroughly clean and that the clearance between piston rings and the edges of the grooves is correct (see Section 12 and Fig. 1.25).

4   Fit the piston rings to the pistons, remembering that the top compression ring is chromium plated and the oil control ring with its ridges and slots goes at the bottom. Piston rings should always be fitted over the top of the piston and not from the bottom. A simple method is to place three narrow strips of thin metal - old feeler gauges of about 0.020 in (0.051 mm) are ideal - at equal distances round the

Fig. 1.24. Slot on piston head must point forward and numbers on connecting rod must face right-hand side of engine block (oil filter side (Sec. 20)

piston and slide the piston rings over these. Stagger the gaps in the piston rings equally round the piston. Be very careful not to scratch the piston or damage the grooves when fitting piston rings. Mind too that you do not let the connecting rod bang against the piston as this may damage or distort it. Remember that the pistons are made of alloy and are comparatively soft.

5   Insert the pistons into the cylinders from the top, using a device like the one shown in the photograph to clamp the rings. If you haven't got the correct tool it is a very simple matter to make a substitute. We have used a large jubilee clip with success. Whatever you use, make sure that you do not scratch the piston. Gently tap the piston through the piston ring compressor into the cylinder. Ensure that each piston is the correct one for the bore and that the front of the piston (with the slot) faces forwards. Lubricate the piston well with clean engine oil.

6   As each piston is fitted, wipe the big-end bearing seat on the connecting rod perfectly clean and fit the shell bearing in position with its locating tab engaged with the corresponding groove in the connecting rod. The procedure and precautions are exactly the same as those needed for fitting big-end bearings as described in Section 19.

7   Generously lubricate the corresponding surfaces on the crankshaft with engine oil and draw the connecting rod on to it.

8   Fit the bearing shell to the connecting rod cap in the same way as with the connecting rod itself.

9   Generously lubricate the shell bearing and offer up the connecting rod bearing cap to the connecting rod. Join the cap to the rod with new fixing bolt and nuts (photo).

10 Tighten the retaining bolts evenly - in other words tighten each bolt a little at a time alternately - to a torque of 46 lb f ft (6.3 kg f m) (photo).

21 Oil pump - refitting

Fit new sealing rings on both ends of the delivery pipe. Make sure the pipe is located properly in the crankcase and the pump. Fit the pump retaining bolts.

20.2a Assembling the connecting rod, gudgeon pin and piston

20.2b Fitting the gudgeon pin retaining circlip

Fig. 1.25. Correct fitting of piston rings (Sec. 20)

20.5 Use a piston ring clamp when inserting the pistons in the cylinders

20.9 Fitting the connecting rod bearing cap

20.10 Tightening the connecting rod big-end bearing bolts

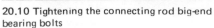

22 Rear sealing flange - refitting

1 Press a new seal into the sealing flange.
2 Clean the surface of the block and using a smear of grease stick the new gasket in place on the block.
3 Grease the rubber lip on the sealing ring and opposite surface on the crankshaft with mineral grease.
4 Fit the sealing flange taking great care that the rubber lip is not damaged by the edge of the crankshaft or twisted so that the spring jumps out of its position (photo).
5 Trim off the projecting parts of the gasket with a knife (photo).

23 Intermediate shaft and front sealing flange - refitting

1 Oil the intermediate shaft journals. Fit the shaft in the block taking care that the gears do not damage the bearing bushings in the block. Fit the spacer sleeve on the crankshaft (photos).
2 Clean the joint faces of the block and sealing flange, and fit a new gasket and the front sealing flange (photo).
3 Cut off the projecting parts of the gasket and fit the rear part of the belt guard and the cable harness (photo).

24 Sump - refitting

1 Ensure that the sump is really clean and that all traces of the old gasket have been removed from the flanges of the sump and the crankcase. Fit the new gasket to the crankcase.
2 Lightly grease the flange on the sump. Place the sump in position and fit the spring washers and bolts. Tighten the bolts to a torque of 6 - 8 lb f ft (0.8 - 1.1 kg f m) (photo).

25 Water pump - refitting

1 The water pump is simply screwed to the cylinder block, a gasket being required even though there is no water outlet from the pump into the side of the block. A sealing ring is placed in the groove at the top of the pump and will be compressed by the cylinder head when it is fitted (photos).
2 Fitting the water pump when the head is removed as we are doing here is somewhat simpler than fitting it with the head in position, because you have to push the pump up against the head, ensuring that the ring is properly located, as you put in the bolts. This will have to be done of course, if the pump has been removed for some reason when the head has not been taken off.

26 Flywheel and clutch - refitting

1 Turn the crankshaft so that No. 1 cylinder is at tdc (top-dead-centre).
2 Position flywheel (or flange plate in the case of automatic transmissions) on the crankshaft so that pin (A) is approximately 15° from the horizontal position and pointing away from the starter motor mounting as shown in Fig. 1.26. Note that there are two pins (A) and (B).
3 Fit the retaining bolts and tighten them to a torque of 53 lb f ft (7 kg f m) (photo).
4 Fit the input shaft bearing (packed with grease), the retaining washer and circlip. Fit the reinforcing bracket (photo).
5 Refit the clutch disc and pressure plate assembly and lightly secure it in position with its securing bolts (photo).
6 Carefully line-up the disc with the input bearing. This is ideally done by using the input shaft from the gearbox, if it is available, otherwise use a mandrel with a diameter same as the disc hub and having a spigot on the end which fits in the pilot bearing (photo).
7 When the clutch disc is correctly aligned tighten the clutch assembly securing bolts in stages in a diagonal and progressive manner.

22.4 Fitting the rear sealing flange (oil seal retainer)

22.5 Cutting off the projecting parts of the rear sealing flange gasket

23.1a Fitting the intermediate shaft in the engine block

23.1b When fitting the spacer sleeve, fit it the opposite way round to what it was at removal

23.2 Fitting the front sealing flange (oil seal retainer)

23.3 Rear part of the drive belt guard fitted in position

24.2 Fitting the sump

25.1a Fitting the water pump

25.1b Water pump in position and sealing ring fitted

Fig. 1.26. Locating the flywheel in correct position on the crankshaft. Do not confuse pin A with pin B (Sec. 26)

26.3 Tightening the flywheel bolts

26.4 Fitting the reinforcing bracket

26.5 The clutch disc is marked to identify the side fitted towards the flywheel

26.6 Using the gearbox input shaft to align the clutch disc

27.1 Fit new valve stem seals on inlet valve guides

27 Cylinder head and camshaft - reassembly

1 Fit new valve stem seals on the inlet valve guides (photo).
2 Unless parts have been renewed, refit the valves, springs and tappets in the positions from which they were removed. Oil the valve stems before inserting them in the valve guides (photo).
3 Over each valve fit the lower spring retainer, the valve spring and the upper spring retainer. Using a valve spring compressing tool, compress the spring and fit the collets in the recess in the valve stem and release the compression tool. Fit the rubber ring, refer to Fig. 1.27. (photos).

Fig. 1.27. Valve and valve spring assembly (Sec. 27)

1 Rubber ring
2 Upper spring retainer
3 Collets
4 Valve spring
5 Valve stem seal (inlet only)
6 Lower spring retainer

4 Oil the bearing seats for the camshaft, the bearing caps, the camshaft and the tappets. Fit the tappets and the adjuster washers. Place the camshaft in the cylinder head (photo).
5 Coat the face of the front cap that mates with the cylinder head with a sealing compound. Fit the caps, with the markings aligned as shown in Fig. 1.16, and the retaining nuts. Screw down the nuts in an even and progressive manner to compress the valves springs without putting uneven stress on the camshaft. Torque tighten the nuts to 15 lb f ft (2 kg f m).
6 Before fitting the camshaft seal apply mineral grease to the rubber lip of the seal and the corresponding surface on the camshaft. Take care not to damage the seal against the edge of the camshaft. Fit the seal so that a new wear surface is obtained against the camshaft.
7 Fit the rear guide plate, the gearwheel with the slot on the gear located on the pin on the camshaft end, then the front guide plate, washer and retaining bolt. Restrain the gear wheel from turning and torque tighten the bolt to 37 lb f ft (5 kg f m).
8 Fit the torque tighten the spark plugs to 18 - 22 lb f ft (2.5 - 3 kg f m) on carburettor engines or fit the retainers for the injectors and the injectors (fuel injection engines). Use new 'O' ring seals.

28 Cylinder head - refitting

1 Check that both cylinder block and cylinder head mating faces are perfectly clean.
2 Lubricate each cylinder with engine oil.
3 Always use a new cylinder head gasket. The old gasket will be compressed and incapable of giving a good seal. Do not smear grease or gasket cement on either side of the gasket.
4 Place the gasket on the cylinder block the right way up and carefully aligned with the bolt holes in the block.
5 Place the cylinder head in position, being careful to align the bolt holes accurately, and fit the cylinder head bolts (photo).
6 Tighten the cylinder head bolts, in two stages, in the numerical sequence shown in Fig. 1.28; tighten the bolts to the specified torque.

27.2 Fitting valve on cylinder head

27.3a Compressing the valve spring

27.3b Retaining collets fitted in position

27.3c Don't forget the rubber ring

27.4 Fit the tappets and adjuster washers

28.5 Fitting the cylinder head

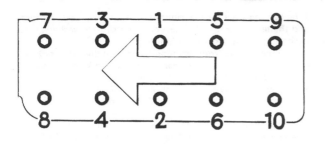

Fig. 1.28. Numerical tightening sequence for cylinder head bolts
(Secs. 28, 67 and 69)

Fig. 1.29. Aligning the crankshaft timing mark (Sec. 30)

29.3 Fitting the gear wheel on the intermediate shaft

Fig. 1.30. Aligning the intermediate shaft timing mark (Sec. 30)

29 Crankshaft and intermediate shaft seals and gears - refitting

1   Fit a new sealing ring on the crankshaft. Before fitting, grease the
seal rubber lip with mineral grease and take care not to damage the seal
against the edge of the spacer sleeve. If the spacer sleeve has not been
renewed, locate the seal so that a new contact surface is obtained.
2   Fit the intermediate shaft seal observing the same procedure.
3   Fit the gear wheel on the intermediate shaft, and restraining the
shaft from turning, fit the retaining bolt and tighten to a torque of
37 lb f ft (5 kg f m) (photo).
4   Fit the guide plate on the crankshaft, the gear, the front hub and
the centre bolt. Tighten the centre bolt to a torque of 122 lb f ft
(16.5 kg f m) while restraining the crankshaft from turning by blocking
the flywheel.

30 Toothed drivebelt - refitting

1   Fit the belt tensioner and retaining nut. Tighten the nut and remove
the pin (fitted at disassembly) compressing the spring.
2   Rotate the crankshaft to where the timing marks coincide, Fig. 1.29.
3   Rotate the intermediate shaft to where the marks coincide, Fig. 1.30.
4   Place the valve cover in position and rotate the camshaft to where the
marks coincide, Fig. 1.31.
5   Fit the toothed belt on the crankshaft gear. Ensure that the belt is
in good condition and clean, with no trace of oil or grease. New belts
have a colour marking. Set the double lines on the belt against the
crankshaft mark, the next line should then be opposite the intermediate
shaft mark and the other mark opposite the camshaft mark (photo).
6   Stretch the belt and fit it on the camshaft gear and belt tensioner.
Do not use any tools for this as they might damage the belt.
7   Slacken the tensioner retaining nut, so that the spring tensions
the belt and then re-tighten the nut (photo).
8   Rotate the engine clockwise and then check that the belt marks are
correctly aligned. Retension the belt and tighten the nut to a torque of

Fig. 1.31. Aligning the camshaft timing mark (Sec. 30)

37 lb f ft (5 kg f m).
9   Fit the pulley on the front hub (if the car has air-conditioning, fit
the pulley temporarily with two bolts).
10 Fit the belt guard casing.

31 Valve clearance - adjustment

1   Lift off the valve cover and turn the engine to the firing position for
No. 1 cylinder (both cams on No. 1 cylinder pointing obliquely upwards
at equal angles, and the ignition mark on crankshaft pulley at 0°). Always
turn the crankshaft with the centre bolt.
2   Measure the valve clearance with a feeler gauge (photo).

30.5 Toothed drive belt marking

30.7 Tensioning the belt

31.2 Measuring the valve clearance with a feeler gauge

Clearance when checking:

Cold engine: 0.012 - 0.018 in (0.30 - 0.45 mm)
Warm engine: 0.014 - 0.020 in (0.35 - 0.50 mm)

Clearance when adjusting:

Cold engine: 0.014 - 0.016 in (0.35 - 0.40 mm)
Warm engine: 0.016 - 0.018 in (0.40 - 0.45 mm)

The clearance is the same for inlet and exhaust valves.

3   To adjust the clearance turn the tappets so that the slots are at right angles to the camshaft. Position the Volvo tool 5022 as shown in Fig. 1. 32, and depress the tappets so that the adjuster washers can be removed.

4   Remove the adjuster washer and fit a washer of the correct thickness to obtain the specified clearance. Adjuster washers are available in different thicknesses between 0.130 and 0.180 in (3.30 and 4.50 mm) in steps of 0.002 in (0.05 mm). The thickness of the washer is marked on one side; always fit the washer with the marked face downwards. Oil the washer before fitting it. Remove the tappet depressing tool.

5   Rotate the engine to No. 3 cylinder firing position and proceed as for No. 1 cylinder, then to No. 4 cylinder and No. 2 cylinder.

6   If the Volvo tappet depressing tool is not available the tappet can be depressed by turning the engine till the cam depresses the tappet, then fitting a wedge to hold the tappet down while you turn the camshaft to the checking position and lift out the washer, as shown in photograph.

7   Fit the halfmoon-shaped rubber seal at the rear of the cylinder head. Place the gasket in position. Oil the camshaft and fit the valve cover. Attach the ignition setting indicator to the valve cover with one of the nuts (photos).

Fig. 1.32. Depressing the valve tappet. Note the position of the slots in the tappets. The tool bears upon the rim of the tappet (Sec. 31)

Fig. 1.33. Adjuster washer. Fit marked face downward (Sec. 31)

31.6 Keeping the tappet depressed with a suitable wedge and removing the adjuster washer

31.7a Fitting the valve cover gasket

31.7b Attaching the ignition setting sender to valve cover

32 Distributor - refitting

1   Rotate the crankshaft to the firing position for No. 1 cylinder. This is checked by looking through the valve cover filler hole to see the position of the camshaft cams, Fig. 1.34, and checking that the ignition mark on the crankshaft finally is at 0° on the graduated scale on the belt guard casing (photo).
2   Refer to Fig. 1.35. Turn the rotor so that the line marked on it is approximately 60° from the mark on the distributor housing.
3   Fit the distributor in position in the engine block and check that the mark on the rotor and the mark on the distributor housing are opposite each other. Fit the distributor retaining screw.
4   Remove the rotor, fit the seal and replace the rotor. Do not fit the distributor cap at this time as it may get damaged when refitting the engine in the car.

33 Fuel pump - refitting

1   Ensure that the mating faces of the cylinder block, spacer and fuel pump are clean with no traces of old gaskets.
2   Fit the bolts in the pump flange and place a gasket, the spacer and another gasket on the bolts.
3   Fit the assembly to the cylinder block and tighten the bolts.

34 Oil filter - refitting

1   When fitting the oil filter smear the filter rubber ring with oil. Screw on the filter, by hand, until it just touches the block. Then screw a further half turn by hand. Do not overtighten (photo).

35 Other fitments - refitting

1   When replacing the other fitments the procedure is the reverse of dismantling.
2   Don't forget the lifting brackets when fitting the thermostat housing, the inlet manifold the exhaust manifold (photos).
3   When fitting the exhaust always use new gaskets and position them with the marking 'UT' facing outwards. Centre the manifold round No. 1 cylinder lower stud and fit washers so that the marking UT/OUT faces outwards. Fit the lifting bracket at No. 3 cylinder. Tighten the nuts to a torque of 15 lb f ft (2 kg f m) (photo).
4   When fitting the alternator, tension the belt, as described in Chapter 2.
5   When fitting the cold start valve (fuel injection engines) don't forget to connect the earth lead at one of the retaining screws.
6   When fitting the water pump to heater pipe always fit new rubber seals.
7   Fit the gearbox to the engine, this should be straightforward providing the clutch disc has been correctly aligned.

36 Engine - refitting

1   Refitting of the engine and gearbox is the reverse of the removal sequence. Make sure that all loose leads, hoses or pipes are tucked out of the way where they won't get caught up as the engine is lowered into position. If the front axle bolts have been slackened off don't forget to retighten them.
2   When the engine has been refitted check that all the items removed or disconnected at removal have been refitted and all connections made.
3   Check that the drain tap is closed, and drain plugs tightened. Fill the cooling system with coolant and the engine with the specified oil. Don't forget to check the gearbox oil level and fill as necessary. Make sure that all tools, rags, etc have been removed from the engine compartment (photo).

37 Engine - initial start-up after overhaul or major repair

1   Just have a quick look at the last item in the previous Section.
2   Make sure that your battery is fully charged - it may have to work hard before the engine starts.
3   If the fuel system has been dismantled, it will require quite a lot of

Fig. 1.34. Firing position for No. 1 cylinder (Sec. 32)

32.1 Graduated scale on belt guard casing

Fig. 1.35. Fitting the distributor (Sec. 32)

engine revolutions to get the petrol up to the carburettors. With the fuel injection engine, of course, this problem will not arise. If there is doubt about the state of charge of the battery, take the plugs out and the petrol will be pumped up with far less effort.
4   As soon as the engine fires and runs, keep it going at a fast tickover only (no faster) and bring it up to normal working temperature.
5   As the engine warms up, there will be odd smells and some smoke from parts getting hot and burning off oil deposits. Look for water or oil leaks which will be obvious if serious, particularly as the engine is so

34.1 Oil filter fitted in position

35.2a Fitting the thermostat

35.2b Fitting the inlet manifold

35.3 Don't forget the lifting eye when fitting the exhaust manifold

36.3 Don't forget to fill up with engine oil

nice and clean.

6   When the engine running temperature has been reached, adjust the idling speed as described in Chapter 3.

7   Let the engine run at normal temperature for ten minutes. Then switch it off, allow it to cool for at least 30 minutes and check the torque of the cylinder head bolts. Slacken each bolt in sequence, a quarter turn before tightening it. Only release and retighten one bolt at a time.

8   Then check to see if there are any lubricant or coolant drips. or coolant drips.

9   By now the reader will hardly be able to wait to get the car on the road and check that the ignition timing is correct and gives the necessary smoothness and power. Don't forget that although the old pistons and crankshaft may still have been used, new bearing shells will have been fitted. Treat it as a new engine and run-in at reduced revolutions for 500 miles (800 kms).

38 Oil sump - removal and refitting (engine in car)

1   Fit a lifting attachment to the lifting bracket at the thermostat housing and take the weight of the engine without lifting it. Remove the left-hand engine mounting bolts. If the car has air-conditioning first remove the compressor as described in Section 4, paragraph 9.

2   Drain the engine oil. Refit the plug after draining and tighten to a torque of 45 lb f ft (6 kg f m).

3   Remove the guard plate under the engine. Hoist the engine slightly and remove the left-hand engine mounting.

Fig. 1.36. Removing the sump with engine fitted in the car (Sec. 38)

4   Remove the reinforcing bracket and the sump bolts.

5   Release the sump, turn it as shown in Fig. 1.36 and take it out. Remove the gasket.

6   Refitting is the reverse of the removal sequence. Make sure the joint faces are clean. Always use a new gasket. Don't forget to refill with the specified engine oil.

See next page for 'Fault diagnosis - engine'.

39 Fault diagnosis - engine

When investigating starting and uneven running faults do not be tempted into snap diagnosis. Start from the beginning of the check procedure and follow it through. It will take less time in the long run. Poor performance from an engine in terms of power and economy is not normally diagnosed quickly. In any event the ignition and fuel systems must be checked first before assuming any further investigation needs to be made.

Symptom	Reason/s	Remedy
Engine will not turn over when starting switch is operated	Flat battery Bad battery connections Bad connections at solenoid switch and/or starter motor Defective solenoid Starter motor defective	Check that battery is fully charged and that all connections are clean and tight. Remove starter and check solenoid. Remove starter and overhaul.
Engine turns over normally but fails to fire and run	No spark at plugs No fuel reaching engine Too much fuel reaching the engine (flooding)	Check ignition system according to procedures given in Chapter 4. Check fuel system according to procedures given in Chapter 3. For carburettor engines: Slowly depress the accelerator pedal to floor and keep it there while operating starter motor until engine fires. Check fuel system if necessary as described in Chapter 3. For fuel injection engines: Flooding signifies malfunction of cold starting system - check cold start valve and thermal timer and their electrical connections.
Engine starts but runs unevenly and misfires	Ignition and/or fuel system faults Incorrect valve clearances Burnt out valves	Check the ignition and fuel systems as though the engine had failed to start. Check and reset clearances. Remove cylinder heads and examine and overhaul as necessary.
Lack of power	Ignition and/or fuel system faults Incorrect valve clearances Burnt out valves Worn out piston or cylinder bores	Check the ignition and fuel systems for correct ignition timing and carburettor settings. Check and reset the clearances. Remove cylinder heads and examine and overhaul as necessary. Remove cylinder heads and examine pistons and cylinder bores. Overhaul as necessary.
Excessive oil consumption	Oil leaks from crankshaft oil seal, valve cover gasket, oil sump gasket, or sump plug washer Worn piston rings or cylinder bores resulting in oil being burnt by engine. Smoky exhaust is an indication Worn valve guides and/or defective valve stem seals	Identify source of leak and repair as appropriate. Fit new rings - or rebore cylinders and fit new pistons, depending on degree of wear. Remove cylinder heads and recondition valve stem bores and valves and seals as necessary.
Excessive mechanical noise from engine	Wrong valve clearances Worn crankshaft bearings Worn cylinders (piston slap)	Adjust valve clearances. Inspect and overhaul where necessary. Inspect and overhaul where necessary.
Unusual vibration	Misfiring on one or more cylinders Loose mounting bolts	Check ignition system. Check tightness of bolts and condition of flexible mountings.

Chapter 1 Part B : Overhead valve engines

Contents

Specifications

Engine (B20) - general

	B20A	B20E
Type	B20A	B20E
Max. output:		
HP at rev/min DIN	82/4700	120/6000
KW at rev/min DIN	60/4680	73/6000
Max. torque:		
lb f ft at rev/min DIN	115/2300	110/3500
kg m at rev/min DIN	16/2300	15.2/3500
Compression pressure at 250-300 rpm (warm engine turned over with starter motor)	156 - 185 psi (11 - 13 kg/sq cm)	170 - 200 psi (12 - 14 kg/sq cm)
Number of cylinders	4	4
Compression ratio	8.7 : 1	10.5 : 1
Bore	3.5 in (88.9 mm)	3.5008 in (88.92 mm)
Stroke	3.150 in (80 mm)	3.150 in (80 mm)
Capacity	1986 cc	1986 cc
Weight (approx.)	341 lb (155 kg)	341 lb (155 kg)

Pistons

Material	Light alloy
Permissible weight difference between pistons on same engine ...	0.35 oz (10 g)
Length	2.79 in (71 mm)
Clearance in bore:	
B20A	0.0004 - 0.0012 in (0.01 - 0.03 mm)
B20E	0.0016 - 0.0024 in (0.04 - 0.06 mm)
Compression rings:	
Number on each piston	2
Width	0.078 in (1.98 mm)
Side clearance in groove	0.0016 - 0.0028 in (0.040 - 0.072 mm)
Oil scraper rings:	
Number on piston	1
Width	0.186 in (4.74 mm)
Side clearance in groove	0.0016 - 0.0028 in (0.040 - 0.072 mm)
Piston ring gap	0.016 - 0.022 in (0.40 - 0.55 mm)
Gudgeon pins (general):	
Arrangement	Fully floating with circlips at both ends
Fit in con-rod	Sliding fit
Fit in piston	Push fit

Gudgeon pin diameter:
    Standard ... ...   0.945 in (87.0 mm)
    Oversize ... ...   0.947 in (95.1 mm)

Cylinder head

Material ... ...   Light alloy
Height between cylinder head joint face and face for bolt heads:
    B20A ... ...   3.42 in (87 mm)
    B20E ... ...   3.34 in (84.9 mm)

Valves

Inlet valves:
    Seat angle in cylinder head ... ...   45°
    Valve seat angle ... ...   45.5°
    Seat width in cylinder head ... ...   0.08 in (2 mm)
    Valve head diameter ... ...   1.732 in (44 mm)
    Stem diameter ... ...   0.3132 - 0.3138 in (7.955 - 7.970 mm)
    Valve clearance (cold and warm) ... ...   0.016 - 0.018 in (0.40 - 0.45 mm)
Exhaust valves:
    Seat angle in cylinder head ... ...   45°
    Valve seat angle ... ...   44.5°
    Seat width in cylinder head ... ...   0.080 in (2 mm)
    Valve head diameter ... ...   1.378 in (35 mm)
    Stem diameter ... ...   0.3120 - 0.3126 in (7.925 - 7.940 mm)
    Valve clearance (cold and warm) ... ...   0.016 - 0.018 in (0.40 - 0.45 mm)

Valve guides

Length:
    Inlet ... ...   2.047 in (52 mm)
    Exhaust ... ...   2.323 in (59 mm)
Inner diameter ... ...   0.320 - 0.321 in (8.000 - 8.022 mm)
Height above cylinder head face:
    B20A ... ...   0.689 (17.5 mm)
    B20E ... ...   0.705 in (17.9 mm)
Valve stem clearance:
    Inlet ... ...   0.0012 - 0.0026 in (0.030 - 0.067 mm)
    Exhaust ... ...   0.0024 - 0.0038 in (0.060 - 0.097 mm)

Valve springs

Free-length ... ...   1.81 in (46 mm)
With load of 60 ± 5 lb (29.5 ± 2.3 kg) ... ...   1.57 in (40 mm)
With load of 181 ± 10 lb (87 ± 4.5 kg) ... ...   1.18 in (30 mm)

Lubrication system

Oil capacity:
    With oil filter ... ...   6.6 Imp pints (8 US pints/3.75 litres)
    Without oil filter ... ...   5.75 Imp. pints (7 US pints/3.25 litres)
Oil pressure at 2000 rpm (engine warm) ... ...   36 - 85 psi (2.5 - 6.0 kg/cm^2)
Oil filter:
    Type ... ...   Full flow
    Make ... ...   Wix or Mann
Oil pump:
    Type ... ...   Gear type pump
    Gear endfloat ... ...   0.0008 - 0.004 in (0.02 - 0.10 mm)
    Radial play ... ...   0.0032 - 0.0055 in (0.08 - 0.14 mm)
    Backlash ... ...   0.006 - 0.014 in (0.15 - 0.35 mm)
    Number of gearteeth   9
    Relief valve spring:
        Free-length ... ...   1.54 in (32.5 mm)
        With load of 11 ± 0.88 lb (5 ± 0.4 kg) ... ...   1.03 in (26.25 mm)
        With load of 15.4 ± 1.7 lb (7 ± 0.7 kg) ... ...   0.83 in (21 mm)

Crankshaft

Endfloat ... ...   0.0018 - 0.0054 in (0.047 - 0.137 mm)
Main bearing clearance ... ...   0.0011 - 0.0033 in (0.028 - 0.083 mm)
Big-end bearing clearance ... ...   0.0012 - 0.0028 in (0.029 - 0.071 mm)

Main bearings

Main bearing journals:
    Diameter:
        Standard ... ...   2.4981 - 1.4986 in (63.451 - 63.464 mm)
        Undersize ... ...   2.4881 - 2.4886 in (63.197 - 63.210 mm)
        Undersize ... ...   2.4781 - 2.4786 in (62.943 - 62.956 mm)

Big-end bearings
Big-end bearing journals:
   Diameter:

Standard	...	...	...	...	...	...	...	...	2.1255 - 2.1260 in (53.987 - 54.000 mm)
Undersize	...	...	...	...	...	...	...	...	2.1155 - 2.1160 in (53.733 - 53.746 mm)
Undersize	...	...	...	...	...	...	...	...	2.1055 - 2.1060 in (53.479 - 53.492 mm)

Connecting rods

Endfloat on journal		0.006 - 0.014 in (0.15 - 0.35 mm)
Permissible weight difference between con-rods of one engine		0.35 oz (10g)

Camshaft

Number of bearings	3
Running clearance	0.0008 - 0.0030 in (0.020 - 0.075 mm)
Endfloat	0.0008 - 0.0024 in (0.020 - 0.60 mm)

Camshaft marking:

B20A	A
B20E	D

Bearing journal diameter:

Front	1.8494 - 1.8504 in (46.975 - 47.000 mm)
Centre	1.6919 - 1.6929 in (42.975 - 43.000 mm)
Rear	1.4557 - 1.4567 in (36.975 - 37.000 mm)

Valve clearance for valve timing setting (cold engine):

B20A	0.043 in (1.10 mm)
B20E	0.055 in (1.40 mm)

Inlet valve should then open at:

B20A	10° ATDC
B20E	5.5° BTDC
Timing gear backlash	0.0016 - 0.0032 in (0.04 - 0.08 mm)

Flywheel

Permissible axial throw (max.)	0.002 in (0.05 mm) at a diameter of 5.9 in (150 mm)

Torque wrench settings

Cylinder head (see text):	lbf ft	kgf m
Stage 1	30	4.1
Stage 2	58	8
Stage 3	65	9
Main bearings	87 - 94	12 - 13
Big-end bearings	51 - 57	7 - 8
Flywheel	47 - 51	6.5 - 7
Spark plugs	25 - 29	3.5 - 4
Camshaft nut	94 - 108	13 - 15
Crankshaft pulley bolt	50 - 60	7 - 8
Oil sump bolts	6 - 8	0.8 - 1.1
Oil filter nipple	32 - 40	4.5 - 5.5

40 General description

The engine is a four cylinder, water-cooled, overhead valve unit, the valves being pushrod operated by a three bearing camshaft. It employs alloy pistons and a five bearing crankshaft. The big-end bearings are replaceable shells.

The three bearing camshaft is made of special grade cast iron and has case hardened cams. It operates the valves through the normal mechanism of tappets, pushrods and rockers. There are no inspection covers for the valve tappets since these are accessible after the cylinder head has been removed.

The connecting rods are made of drop forged steel and have precision machined bushes at the little end which act as bearings for the gudgeon pins.

The pistons are made of light alloy and have two compression rings and one oil scraper ring. The upper compression ring is chromed in order to reduce cylinder wear.

The cylinder head is bolted to the block (ie. there are no studs in the block). All the combustion chambers are machined throughout and have separate inlet and exhaust ports, one for each valve. The valves themselves have chromed stems and run in replaceable valve guides to which they are sealed with rubber seals.

The cylinder block is made of special cast iron and is cast as a single unit. The cylinder bores are machined directly in the block. The oilways in the block are arranged so that the oil filter, which is the full flow type, is directly attached to the right-hand side of the block.

The engine has a 'force' feed lubrication system. Pressure is provided by a gear pump driven from the camshaft and fitted under the crankshaft in the sump. The pump forces the oil past the relief valve (itself fitted inside the pump), through the oil filter and then through oilways out to the various lubrication points. All the oil supplied to the lubricating points first passes through the oil filter.

41 Engine - removal

The removal procedure is basically the same as for overhead camshaft engines, refer to Sections 3, 4 and 5 of Chapter 1/Part A.

42 Engine - dismantling procedure

1   Assuming that the engine is out of the car and on the work bench, first of all remove the inlet and exhaust manifolds for a carburettor engine or the inlet ducting and exhaust manifold in the case of a fuel injection engine and pull out the pipe that goes from the water pump along the side of the block to the heater. Once this is done there ceases to be any difference between fuel injection engines and carburettor engines, and the instructions which follow are equally applicable to both.

2   It is a good idea to start with the more cumbersome items as the remainder of the engine then gets progressively easier to handle. If the gearbox has not yet been removed, do so now by removing the bolts round the edge of the flywheel housing. Two of these anchor the starter motor which will now be freed.

3   Remove the rocker arm casing which is held down by small screws round its edges. Remove the four screws holding down the rocker arm

Fig. 1.37. Cut-away view of B20 engine

1 Cold air hose	22 Rocker arm shaft	44 Reinforcing bracket
2 Hot air hose	23 Spring	45 Bush
3 Flap, constant air temperature device	24 Pushrod	46 Seal
4 Fuel line	25 Bearing bracket	47 Oil pump
5 Thermostat	26 Rocker arm casing	48 Main bearing cap
6 Valve tappet	27 Rubber seal	49 Delivery pipe
7 Valve spring	28 Rubber terminal	50 Main bearing shell
8 Washer	29 Rubber seal	51 Crankshaft
9 Valve collet	30 Cylinder head	52 Sump
10 Exhaust valve	31 Vacuum hose	53 Piston rings
11 Connection for crankcase hose	32 Vacuum governor	54 Connecting rod cap
12 Valve tappet seal	33 Distributor	55 Connecting rod
13 Intake valve	34 Condenser	56 Camshaft
14 Oil filler cap	35 Valve tappet	57 Piston
15 Carburettor	36 Retainer	58 Bush
16 Damping device	37 Flywheel casing	59 Big-end bearing shell
17 Air cleaner	38 Engine block	60 Gudgeon pin
18 Hose for crankcase gases	39 Gear wheel	61 Washer
19 Vacuum hose for distributor	40 Pilot bearing	62 Spacing ring
20 Choke wire	41 Flywheel	63 Camshaft gear
21 Rocker arm	42 Flange bearing shell	64 Nut
	43 Sealing flange	65 Crankshaft gear

66 Hub	
67 Washer	
68 Bolt	
69 Pulley	
70 Key	
71 Seal	
72 Fan	
73 Oil nozzle	
74 Key	
75 Timing gear cover	
76 Coolant inlet	
77 Gasket	
78 Water pump	
79 Gasket	
80 Pulley	
81 Alternator	
82 Sealing ring	
83 Cylinder head gasket	
84 Tensioner	
85 Water distributing pipe	
86 Thermostat	
87 Coolant outlet	

42.3a Removing the rocker arm assembly

42.3b Lifting out the push rods

42.3c Removing the thermostat

42.3d Lifting out the tappets

42.4a The water pump has a gasket between it and the cylinder head

42.4b These rubber rings seal the water pump outlets to the cylinder head

42.5 Removing the crankcase breather

42.7 Timing marks on the crankshaft pulley

42.8 Remove the central bolt and the pulley will come off without difficulties

assembly and lift it off. Take out the pushrods and put them in a safe place. There is no advantage in keeping them in order though this is a good idea for valves. Remove the thermostat. Unscrew the bolts holding down the cylinder head and place it on one side. Lift out the tappets with pliers (photos).

4   It is now easy to remove the water pump. Notice how it is sealed to the cylinder head by two rings. It can of course be removed and fitted with the cylinder head in position (photos).

5   The fuel pump (on a carburettor engine) and the crankcase breather are easy to deal with. The crankcase breather is fastened to the case by a single screw (photo). The oil filter simply unscrews. The neat way in which the alternator is fixed makes its removal a simple matter.

6   As the distributor is timed, its removal is better left until the timing case has been taken off. This enables the position of the rotor arm shaft for a given timing setting to be noted and so ensure that the timing is the same when the distributor is replaced.

7   Before removing the crankshaft pulley, note the index mark on the timing cover and the figures on the edge of the pulley which indicate degrees before or after top dead centre for No. 1 (front) and No. 4

(back) pistons (see photo). This is not sufficient for checking the setting of the rotor arm in the distributor because it is not possible to determine which of these cylinders is firing without a further check.

8   Take out the central bolt and draw off the crankshaft pulley (photo).

9   Remove the timing case cover (photo) and take out the spring clip, retaining washer and felt ring. These have to be removed to permit the correct aligning procedure to be carried out when refitting, and in any event the felt ring should be renewed.

10 With the timing cover removed, the timing can be set for checking the position of the distributor rotor arm. Rotate the crankshaft until the timing dot on the crankshaft gear comes opposite the mark on the camshaft gear as shown in the photograph.

11 Mark the position of the distributor shaft which carries the rotor arm and also mark the position that the distributor assembly occuples relative to its clamp - just in case it is necessary to loosen the clamp later on. Now undo the fastening bolts and lift out the clamp and assembly as a unit. Follow this by lifting out the driving gear which is operated by the camshaft (photos).

12 Remove the nut from the camshaft and pull off its timing gear as

42.9 Removing the timing gears cover

42.10 The timing marks aligned

42.11a Withdrawing the distributor assembly

42.11b Lifting out the distributor drive gear

42.12a Pulling off the timing gear (be careful - it is a fibre gear)

42.12b Removing the camshaft thrust flange and spacing ring

42.12c Withdrawing the camshaft

41.12d The sleeve or 'hub' that takes the crankshaft pulley. Note the key that also keys timing gear. Just under tip of thumb you can see the nipple which directs oil onto gears

42.14 Restraining the flywheel from turning

42.15 The wired bolts securing the sealing flange (oil seal retainer)

42.18a The rear main bearing cap and shell. This is the only one which has flanges

42.18b With the crankshaft out of the engine it is easy to pull off the timing gear

shown in the photograph. Be careful not to push the camshaft backwards - certainly do not hammer it - because the hole in which it runs at the back of the cylinder block is supposed to be sealed off for life and it certainly won't be if the camshaft is hammered against it. The seal (or most of it) can be seen in the top left-hand corner of photograph 42.15. Now remove the thrust flange and the spacer ring behind it, and then withdraw the camshaft (photos). Now pull off the sleeve (called by Volvo a 'hub'). Start it on its way by getting a bit of purchase under the two holes on the timing gear. These holes are threaded, and bolts screwed into them can form the basis of a simple device for pulling the timing gear off. If however the crankshaft is being removed one can easily take it off later, which is what we did.

13 Unscrew the bolts holding the clutch housing to the flywheel a little at a time, keeping them all in step to avoid the risk of distorting the clutch housing. Mark the clutch housing and flywheel to identify position for replacement, and remove the clutch assembly from the flywheel.

14 Stop the flywheel from turning by wedging it with a screwdriver as shown in the photograph, undo the six bolts holding it to the crankshaft and lift it away, marking flywheel and shaft to identify position.

15 Undo the wired bolts holding on the sealing flange and remove it.

16 Remove the reinforcing plate and the sump. Undo the bolts fastening the oil pipe to the crankcase and remove the oil pump. Its delivery pipe simply pushes into a hole in the crankcase and it is sealed by a rubber ring.

17 Before proceeding any further have a look at the bearing caps. They are marked, either with dots as are shown in several of our photographs or with stamped figures to indicate their positions. When the bearing caps are refitted they must be put back in the same places and the same way round as they were before. The big-ends are marked 1, 2, 3 and 4, the front one (in accordance with time-honoured convention) being No. 1. The five main bearings are marked 1 — 5, No. 1 being at the front. It is easy to see which way round the caps are meant to be

because of the shape of the pads which carry the dots. Often these pads are circular, in which case it may be more difficult to remember how the caps have to go. If in doubt, put marks on. There should also be a mark on one side of the connecting-rod and a corresponding mark on the same side of the bearing cap which ensures that the piston as well as the bearing cap, goes back the same way round as it came out. If such marks are not visible then make some. When removing the shells, mark them too, so that if a later inspection reveals faults, its location can be found.

18 Now for each of the connecting-rods in turn, remove the bearing cap and shell, and push the connecting-rod up the cylinder, steadying the piston with the other hand as it emerges. Take great care when doing this that things do not get banged about or scratched, and in particular that the skirt of the piston does not knock against the connecting-rod. Remove the main bearing caps with their shells, and the crankshaft can be lifted out of the crankcase. Pull off the timing gear, now a very simple matter (photos).

19 Removal of a retaining clip and protecting ring at the back end of the crankshaft reveals the pilot bearing for the clutch (photo). There is no need to remove this in order to inspect it thoroughly, and we suggest that it is only removed for renewal purposes. It then does not matter if the removal process damages the bearing. If a puller which will do the job is not available, a suggested method is to fill the cavity behind the bearing with thick grease, push a circular drift which is a pretty good fit into the bearing, and give the drift a good blow with a hammer. The pressure exerted by the grease will then drive the bearing out.

43 Cylinder head, valves and cylinder block - overhaul

1 Clean the oil and grease off the cylinder head and remove the carbon from the combustion chamber and valve heads with a scraper or rotary wire brush.

2 Remove the valves by compressing the valve springs until the collets are free of the recesses in the spring retainers, remove the collets, release the pressure on the spring, lift off the spring and its retainer. Push the valve through the valve guide and remove it. If the valve seems a tight fit in the guide, this may be because the upper part of the stem has dirt or carbon on it. Give it a clean in this case. Remove the rubber seal from the end of the valve guide (photos). Keep the valves in the order in which you removed them. A good idea is to stick them through holes in a piece of thick paper. We like to stand them up when we have done this, and slip the spring and retainer belonging to each valve over the stem. Then if we find anything amiss with a valve seat we know at once which valve and spring to look at.

3 With the valve removed, clean out any remaining carbon from the ports. This done, examine the valve seats. If they are only slightly pitted you will be able to make them smooth again by grinding the valves against the seats. Where bad pitting has occurred they will have to be re-cut - a job for the specialist. Grinding the valves is described in Section 11.

4 Check the valve guides with the valve stems to ensure that they are a good fit; the valve stems should move easily in the guides without slop or side play. Worn guides can be extracted and new ones installed. The guides should project above the adjacent surface of the cylinder head by the amount shown in Fig. 1.38. After fitting new guides, check that they are free from burrs and that the valves move easily in them.

42.19 The pilot bearing for the gearbox input shaft

43.2a Compressing the valve springs ...

43.2b ... and removing the collets

43.2c Removing the rubber seals

Fig. 1.38. Replacing valve guides (Sec. 43)

B20A engine: A = 0.689 in (17.5 mm)
B20E engine: A = 0.705 in (19.9 mm)

Be sure to have the step end of the guides at the top.
5   Examine the valves, checking them for straightness and noting the condition of their faces. Slight pitting can be removed by grinding in, but if it is serious the valves will have to be refaced by a specialist.
6   Remove the carbon at the tops of the cylinder bores and polish them. Now examine them for scoring, scratching and wear. Start by carefully examining the top of the bores. If they are worn you will detect a very slight ridge at the top of the cylinder at the highest point the piston reaches. Using an internal micrometer, measure the maximum diameter of the cylinder just below this ridge and compare it with the diameter at the bottom where no wear has taken place. If the difference between these diameters exceeds 0.010 in (0.025 mm) you need a rebore. If a micrometer is not available remove the rings from a piston and insert it in its cylinder about ¾ in (19 mm) below the top of the bore. If a 0.010 in (0.025 mm) feeler gauge can be slid between the top of the piston and the cylinder on the right-hand side just below the ridge, a rebore is required. If the wear is less, the diameter difference or feeler gauge thickness will be correspondingly reduced. If it is around 0.004 in (0.010 mm) it is possible to purchase and fit special rings designed to cope with small amounts of cylinder wear and stop the engine burning oil.
7   Reboring followed by the fitting of over-sized pistons is a job for specialists and the local Volvo agent will be able to arrange for this to be done.

44 Piston and piston rings - examination and renovation

Refer to Section 12 of Chapter 1, Part A.

45 Gudgeon pins - general

Refer to Section 13 of Chapter 1, Part A.

46 Rockers and rocker shaft - overhaul

1   Remove the circlips from the ends of the shaft and take off the springs and rockers. Remove the plugs from the ends of the shaft and give it a good clean paying special attention to the oil holes through which the rockers are lubricated. Check the shaft for straightness by rolling it on a flat surface, and for wear which will show as ridges where the rocker arms were running. If any wear is present or the shaft is

appreciably distorted, replace it. Wear is likely to have occurred only if the rocker shaft oil holes have become blocked.
2   Check the rocker arms for wear on the rocker arm bushes. There should be no appreciable play between the rocker arm and the shaft. If there is, the bushes in the rocker arms can be pressed out and replaced but after replacement they must be reamed to fit the shaft correctly. If the equipment is not available have this done by the local Volvo garage.
3   Check the tip of the rocker arm where it bears on the valve for cracking or serious wear. If none is present the rocker arm may be refitted. Otherwise replace it - grinding the face is only a short term remedy because the arm is case-hardened.
4   Check the pushrods for straightness. If bent they must be renewed.

47 Tappets (cam followers) - inspection

Clean these thoroughly and look them over for any indentation on the end that bears on the camshaft. Check that they are a reasonable fit in the cylinder block. It is very unusual to find anything wrong with the tappets.

48 Camshaft - inspection

1   The camshaft and its bearing bushes in the cylinder block are another part of the Volvo engine which seems virtually everlasting. If there is noticeable play between the camshaft and its bearings, they will have to be replaced, but this is a highly specialised job, involving as it does the reaming of three bushes in line - definitely a task for the specialist.
2   The camshaft itself should show no sign of wear. If very light scoring marks are present they can be removed by gently rubbing down with a very fine emery cloth or an oil stone. The greatest care must be taken to keep the cam profiles smooth.

49 Timing gear - overhaul

The Volvo timing system is simplicity itself; only two gears, nothing to adjust. If the fibre gear on the camshaft is worn, replace it. The only thing to notice is the oil spray nipple which can be seen just under the thumb in photo 42.12d. Take this out and give it a good clean.

50 Crankshaft and bearings - examination and renovation

Refer to Section 15 of Chapter 1, Part A.

51 Starter ring gear - renewal

Refer to Section 16 of Chapter 1, Part A.

52 Oil pump - overhaul

Refer to Section 17 of Chapter 1, Part A.

53 Engine - reassembly (general)

Refer to Section 18 of Chapter 1, Part A.

54 Crankshaft - refitting

Refer to Section 19 of Chapter 1, Part A.

55 Pistons and connecting rods - reassembly

Refer to Section 20 of Chapter 1, Part A.

56 Camshaft and timing gear - reassembly

1 Oil the camshaft well and insert it into the block, being careful to keep it straight so that the edges of the cams (which are very sharp) do not hit the bearing bushes and damage them. This is an operation that should be taken gently.
2 When the camshaft is in place, fit the spacing ring over the end and follow this by the retaining flange. Bolt the retaining flange to the block and bend the tab washers over the bolt.
3 Fit the camshaft gear to the shaft, not forgetting the Woodruff key. Press it on gently, using a tool which depends on a bolt screwing into the centre of the crankshaft, see Fig. 1.39. Don't hammer it on - see Section 42, paragraph 12 for the reason. Take care with this gear - it is a fibre one and can easily be damaged. Put the nut on the camshaft (there is no washer) and tighten it to 94 - 108 lb f ft (13 - 15 kg fm). Do not try to prevent the gear from turning by putting a screwdriver between the teeth. Some sort of device carrying two bolts which can be pushed into two of the holes in the gear will do the trick with perfect safety.
4 Turn the camshaft and the crankshaft so that when you fit the crankshaft gear with the key in its correct position the timing marks will line up as shown in photo 42.10. Press the gear onto the crankshaft, noting that the key will stick out in front of the gear and engage with the sleeve which you fit next (see photo 42.12d).

57 Distributor - refitting

1 With the timing marks aligned, fit the drive pinion for the distributor in the position required for the distributor rotor to take up the position that was marked for it when the engine was taken apart (see Section 42, paragraph 10). Oil the pinion and its shaft well before fitting them. Fit the distributor flange, using a new gasket. This fitting is the reverse of the dismantling process.
2 Just to check the position of the rotor we mention here that when the timing marks are coincident cylinder No. 4 is at the top end of its compression stroke. Hence the rotor should be selecting the plug on No. 4 cylinder and the points should just have opened.

58 Oil pump - refitting

This is a very simple matter - the driving dog on the oil pump must engage with the dog on the shaft of the distributor drive spindle, and the delivery pipe must be pushed home into its socket in the crankcase. Oil the pump well before assembly and ensure that the flange on the pump is bedding against its mating surface in the crankcase before it is fastened down.

59 Rear sealing flange - refitting

1 Wipe the surface of the cylinder block clean, smear the new gasket very lightly with grease so that once placed on the surface it will not move about and carefully position the gasket on the cylinder block.
2 Refit the sealing flange, but do not at this stage have the felt ring fitted into the flange. Fit the bolts with their spring washers but do not tighten them for the moment.
3 Carefully centre the sealing flange, using feeler gauges to ensure that the distance between the sealing flange and the end of the crankshaft is the same all the way round. Be very careful when moving the flange not to damage the gasket.
4 When it is right, first of all do up the bolts finger-tight and then tighten them up with a spanner as with a cylinder head - each one a little at a time, in crosswise order. Finally, wire them up (see photo 42.15).
5 Oil the felt ring well and fit it into the flange, following it with the washer and circlip. Make sure that the circlip is properly embedded in its groove.

60 Sump - refitting

Refer to Section 24 of Chapter 1, Part A.

Fig. 1.39. Fitting the camshaft gear (Sec. 56)

61 Fuel pump - refitting

Refer to Section 33 of Chapter 1, Part A.

62 Flywheel and clutch - refitting

1 Clean the mating faces of the crankshaft, flywheel and (in the case of automatic transmission), the spacing and support plates. Refit the flywheel (and support plates if present) to the crankshaft, taking note of any position marks you made when dismantling. Tighten the bolts to a torque of 36 - 40 lb f ft (5 - 5.5 kg fm) (see photo 42.14).
2 Refit the clutch disc and clutch assembly. Refer to Chapter 1, Part A, Section 26 paragraphs 5 to 7.

63 Oil filter - refitting

Refer to Section 34 of Chapter 1, Part A.

64 Valves and springs - refitting to cylinder head

1 Unless there has been some renewal, each valve and spring should be put back in the guide from which it was removed.
2 Fit each valve and valve spring in turn, wiping down and lubricating the valve stem as it is inserted into the guide.
3 As each valve is inserted, slip a new rubber sealing ring over the stem and onto the top of the valve guide.
4 Slip the spring over the stem of the valve and fit the retaining cap into the top of the spring. Position the compressor so that the bottom part of it bears on the head of the valve. Depending on what sort of compressor is being used it may be necessary to rig up some arrangement of wooden wedges or the like to achieve this. Whatever method is being used, be careful not to scratch the valve head, the combustion chamber or the mating surface of the cylinder head.
5 Compress the valve spring until the cotters can be slipped into place in the cotter grooves. It will be helpful to grease the cotters which sometimes had the annoying habit of falling out of the grooves at the critical moment and disappearing under the bench.

65 Water pump - refitting

Refer to Section 25 of Chapter 1, Part A.

66 Tappets (cam followers) - refitting

1 Lubricate the tappets generously, inside and out and insert them in the bores before fitting the cylinder head.

67 Cylinder head - refitting

1   Refit the cylinder head as described in Chapter 1, Part A, Section 28, paragraphs 1 to 5.
2   Tighten the cylinder head bolts in the order shown in Fig. 1.28 to the Stage 1 specified torque bringing them up to this in two stages. This is not the final tightening value: there will be further tightening, first after the rocker arm assembly has been fitted and finally after running the engine. These will be dealt with in due course (see Sections 69 and 73).

68 Rocker arms and rocker shaft - assembly and refitting

1   Assembling the rocker arms on the rocker shaft is simply a reversal of the dismantling process and calls for no particular comment. Squirt oil into the rocker shaft and oil all the bits and pieces generously.
2   Fit the pushrods, making sure that they are sitting on top of the tappets. Turn the crankshaft to such a position that the pushrods are all lower than the block (ie. that the valve would be closed if the rocker assembly were fitted).
3   Fit the rocker arm and shaft assembly to the cylinder head.
4   Volvo do not lay down a torque wrench setting for the rocker shaft fixing bolts. We feel that it is a good idea if they are evenly tightened with a torque wrench and suggest a setting of 25 lb f ft (3.4 kg fm).

69 Valve clearance adjustment and cylinder head tightening

1   When the rocker arm assembly has been refitted as just described in Section 68, tighten the cylinder head nuts in the proper order (Fig. 1.28) to the Stage 2 specified torque. Adjust the valve clearances between limits 0.002 in (0.05 mm) greater than those laid down in the Specifications. The correct setting will be made when the final cylinder head tightening is carried out after the engine has been run. The simplest method of setting the valve clearances is to use two feeler gauges, one for the lower limit and one for the upper limit. Adjust the clearances so that the thicker feeler gauge will not go between the rocker arm and the valve and the thinner one will fit in quite easily.
2   It is important that the clearance of a valve is set when the tappet operating it is well away from the peak of its cam. This can be done by carrying out the adjustments in the following order, which also avoids turning the crankshaft more than necessary.

Valve fully open	Check and adjust
Valve No. 8	*Valve No. 1*
Valve No. 6	*Valve No. 3*
Valve No. 4	*Valve No. 5*
Valve No. 7	*Valve No. 2*
Valve No. 1	*Valve No. 8*
Valve No. 3	*Valve No. 6*
Valve No. 5	*Valve No. 4*
Valve No. 2	*Valve No. 7*

3   Just in case one of our readers doesn't know how to set the valve clearances, we show a photograph of it being done. The locknut on the rocker arm is slackened off and the screw turned to raise or lower the rocker on the pushrod. If two feeler gauges are used as we have suggested, the reader will soon learn what the fit of the thin one feels like when the clearance has been set so that the thicker one won't go in.

70 Timing gear cover and crankshaft pulley - refitting

1   Though we have fitted the timing gears we have not so far dealt with the timing case cover. The photo shows the preliminary to fitting it - a new gasket fitted to a clean surface very lightly smeared with grease. Fit the cover to the cylinder block, making sure that its mating surface is perfectly clean and very lightly greased, and do up the bolts finger-tight.
2   Align the cover so that the crankshaft extension is perfectly central in it. It should be possible to insert a 0.004 in (0.02 mm) feeler gauge comfortably all round it. Recheck this after fully tightening the fixing bolts.

69.3 Adjusting the valve clearance

70.1 Preparing to fit the timing case cover

71.3 Checking the fan belt tension

3 Fit a new felt ring (well oiled). Follow this with the retaining washer and circlip. Check that the circlip is properly embedded in its groove.

71 Other fitments - refitting

1 The remaining fitments call for no special instructions. Provided mating surfaces are absolutely clean, with no more than a thin smear of grease used to keep the thinner gaskets in position, you cannot go wrong. The fitting procedures are simply the reverse of dismantling.
2 When you fit the thermostat, remember to fit the clips that carry the clutch cable and the fuel pipe.
3 Fitting the alternator and water pump pulley brings us to the problem of tensioning the fanbelt. Settle for 0.5 in (13 mm) of lateral movement at the mid-point position between the alternator pulley and the crankshaft pulley. Don't have the belt too tight - if you do the alternator and water pump bearings wear rapidly. On the other hand, if the belt slips because it is too loose, it will get hot and very soon pack up. Proper maintenance will prevent this; the only point we are making here is that when tightening a fanbelt you should remember that fanbelts are cheaper and easier to replace than alternators and water pumps (photo). We have not yet mentioned the crankcase breather, which should be given a new seal ring and bolted down with its single bolt. The crankcase ventilation system is covered in Chapter 3.
4 Fit as much of the carburation or fuel injection system as was on the engine when you took it out of the car. We suggest that you don't fit the distributor cap and plug leads at this stage; distributor caps are all too easily damaged.
5 We suggested that in the beginning the engine should be put back in the car with the gearbox attached. If you now fit the gearbox and bellhousing you are at least ready to re-unite the car and engine which by now you are probably beginning to think had been parted for far too long.

72 Engine - refitting

Refer to Section 36 of Chapter 1, Part A.

73 Engine - initial start-up after overhaul or major repair

The procedure is the same as described in Section 37 with the exception of the torque loading of the cylinder head bolts, which is given in the Specifications (Stage 3 torque).

74 Sump - removal and refitting (engine in car)

Refer to Section 38 of Chapter 1, Part A.

75 Fault diagnosis - engine

Refer to Section 39 of Chapter 1, Part A.

Chapter 2 Cooling and heating systems

For modifications, and information applicable to later models, see Supplement at end of manual

Contents

Specifications

Type
... ... Sealed system with expansion tank

Pressure valve opens at
B20 engine	10 psi (0.7 kg/sq cm)
B21 engine	9.2 to 12 psi (0.65 to 0.85 kg/sq cm)

Capacity
... ... 16.0 to 16.5 Imp pints (9.6 to 9.9 US qts, 9.1 to 9.4 litres)

Thermostat (B20A)

	Type 1	Type 2
Type	Wax	Wax
Marking	170°	82°
Starts to open at	75 - 78°C (168 - 172°F)	81 - 83°C (177 - 181°F)
Fully open at	89°C (192°F)	90°C (195°F)

Thermostats (B21A & B21E)

	B21A	B21E
Type	Wax	Wax
Marking	92°C	82°C
Starts to open at	91 - 93°C (196 - 199°F)	81 - 83°C (177 - 181°F)
Fully open at	102°C (216°F)	92°C (198°F)

Fanbelts
B20A	HC-38 x 888
B21A (35A alternator)	HC-38 x 925
B21A (55A alternator)	2 x HC-38 x 925
B21E	2 x HC-38 x 925

1 General description - cooling system

1 A sealed type cooling system is used on engines fitted to the Volvo 240 series. A diagram of the cooling system is given in Fig. 2.1.

2 The engine coolant is circulated by a thermo-syphon, water pump assisted system, and the coolant is pressurised. This is primarily to prevent premature boiling in adverse conditions and to allow the engine to operate at its most efficient running temperature, this being just under the boiling point of water.

3 With this type of cooling system the overflow pipe from the radiator is connected to an expansion tank, which makes topping-up virtually unnecessary. The coolant expands when hot, and instead of being forced down an overflow pipe and lost, as with the earlier systems, it flows into the expansion tank. As the engine cools the coolant contracts and because of the pressure differential, flows back into the radiator.

4 The cap on the expansion tank is set at a pressure which will increase the boiling point of the coolant to just above that at normal atmospheric pressure.

5 The cooling system comprises the radiator, top and bottom hoses, the expansion tank, the water pump, the fan and the thermostat. A drain tap is provided on the right-hand side of the cylinder block. The radiator does not have a cap as the system is filled through the expansion tank. The radiator is of the horizontal type having the tanks standing along the sides of the matrix.

6 The system functions as follows: Cold coolant from the radiator circulates up through the lower radiator hose to the water pump, where it is pushed round the water passages in the cylinder block helping to keep the cylinder bores and pistons cool. The coolant then travels up into the cylinder head and circulates around the combustion spaces and valve seats. Then, when the engine is at its normal operating temperature the water flows out of the cylinder head, past the now open thermostat, through the top hose and into the radiator. The coolant flowing down through the radiator matrix is cooled by the time it reaches the bottom hose when the cycle is repeated.

7 When the engine is cold, the thermostat (a valve which opens and closes according to coolant temperature), maintains the circulation of the same coolant in the engine and only when the correct minimum temperature is reached, as given in the Specifications, does the thermostat begin to open, allowing coolant to return to the radiator.

Fig. 2.1. The cooling system (Sec. 1)

2 Cooling system - draining and filling

Volvo recommend the use of a 50% Volvo antifreeze/water mixture all the year round as the antifreeze prevents rusting. The coolant should be changed every two years at the beginning of the winter. If water only is being used in the system, a rustproofing medium should be added.

1 With the cooling system cold remove the expansion tank cap. Do not remove the tank cap while the engine is hot, as the sudden drop in pressure will cause the coolant to boil.

2 Remove the expansion tank cap. If the system is being drained for reasons other than the renewal of the coolant, place containers to collect the coolant for re-use. Disconnect the bottom radiator hose and open the drain tap on the right-hand side of the engine.

3 Before filling flush the system with clean water. Close the drain tap and connect the bottom radiator hose. Set the heater control to maximum heat.

4 Fill the system with coolant until the level in the expansion tank is at the 'Max' mark or slightly higher. Run the engine for several minutes at different speeds. If necessary, top-up with more coolant and then refit the expansion tank cap. After driving for a short time, check the coolant level again and top-up with more coolant - it takes some time before the system is completely free of air.

Fig. 2.2. The expansion tank (Sec. 2)

3 Radiator - removal and refitting

1 Drain the cooling system, as described in Section 2.

2 Remove the two screws securing the fan shroud and move the shroud rearwards. Disconnect the top radiator hose at the radiator and the expansion tank hoses from the radiator (photo).

3 On cars with automatic transmission, disconnect the oil pipes from the radiator and blank-off the pipes.

4 Remove the two radiator retainers and lift out the radiator (photos).

5 Replacement of the radiator is the reverse of the removal sequence. Fill the cooling system, as described in Section 2. Run the engine at its normal operating temperature and check for leaks at the hose joints.

4 Radiator - inspection and cleaning

1 With the radiator out of the car, any leaks can be repaired by soldering or repaired with a fibre glass paste. Clean out the inside of the radiator by flushing with clean water, turn it upside-down and reverse flush the matrix. Clean the exterior of the radiator by hosing down with a strong jet of water to clean away road dirt and dead flies, etc., which may be lodged in the matrix.

2 Inspect the radiator hoses for cracks, internal or external perishing and damage caused by over-tightening of the hose clips. Renew defective

3.2 Removing the shroud securing screws and disconnecting the top radiator hose

3.4a Removing the radiator retainers

3.4b Lifting out the radiator

Fig. 2.3. Coolant path - (left) thermostat closed - (right) thermostat open (Sec. 5)

1	To radiator	3	Cylinder head	5	Distributor pipe	7	From radiator
2	Thermostat	4	By-pass	6	Water pump		

hoses. Examine the hose clips and renew them if they are rusted or distorted.

5 Thermostat - removal, testing and refitting

1   The action of the thermostat is shown in Fig. 2.3. Note the definite change-over action when the coolant is allowed to flow through the main hose which is connected from the top of the thermostat casing to the radiator: the circulation path to the water pump is closed up by the tongue on the bottom of the thermostat. For proper operation of the system, therefore, you should be careful not to bend or twist this tongue when removing or fitting the thermostat.

2   To replace a faulty thermostat, lower the level of the coolant in the engine by partially draining the system through the tap on the cylinder block. Collect the coolant in a clean container for using again.

3   Remove the nuts securing the thermostat housing and lifting eye. Lift off the housing and remove the thermostat.

4   Clean off the contact faces of the head and the housing, fit a new thermostat, in the identical position, and a new gasket. Refit the housing and the lifting eye. Refill the system through the expansion tank.

5   To check the performance of a suspect thermostat, suspend it in a container of water which can be heated. As the water warms up, note the temperature at which the thermostat begins to open and also that at which the fully open position is reached. Compare these with the figures in the Specifications at the beginning of this Chapter.

6   Generally speaking, when the thermostat fails it remains shut. This

leads to overheating, and if for any reason you are unable to replace the thermostat you should remove it and run the car without it. This is alright as a temporary measure, but in this situation the engine takes longer to warm up on starting and also there is no regulation of the coolant system to keep the engine at its optimum operating temperature. Therefore, always renew the thermostat at the first opportunity.

6 Water pump - removal and refitting

If the water pump starts to leak, shows signs of excessive movement of the shaft, or is noisy during operation, it should be renewed.
1   Drain the cooling system, as described in Section 2. Remove the two screws securing the fan shroud and push the shroud back over the fan.
2   Remove the fan centre bolt. Remove the fan and the shroud. Slacken the tensioner bolt and remove the belts from the alternator. Remove the fan hub retaining bolts, the fan spacer and pulley.
3   On B21A and B21E engines remove the timing gear cover. Disconnect the radiator hose and the return water pipe. Remove the bolts securing the pump and remove the pump.
4   Remove residue of old gasket on the cylinder block mating surface and also clean the rubber ring contact surface on the cylinder head. Fit a new rubber sealing ring on the new pump, ensure you fit the correct ring. Varying heights of rings are available to allow for different thickness of cylinder head gaskets.
5   Fit a new gasket against the cylinder block, use a smear of grease to hold it in position. Press the pump upwards against the cylinder head and fit the retaining bolts. Fit a new rubber ring on the water return pipe, fit the pipe and the retaining bolts. Connect the lower radiator hose.
6   Fit the timing gear casing (B21A and B21E engines). Fit the fan pulley. Fit and tension the belts, as described in Section 7. Position the fan shroud and fit the fan. Fit the fan shroud retaining screws. Fill the system as described in Section 2.

7 Fanbelts - general

1   According to the type of engine, either one or two fanbelts are fitted. Proper tensioning of the fanbelt will ensure that it has a long and useful life. Where twin belts are fitted always renew both at the same time, even if only one is defective.
2   Adjust the tension by slackening the tensioner bolt of the alternator. With a properly tensioned belt it should be possible to depress it 5/16 in (5 - 10 mm), midway between the fan and the alternator (see Fig. 2.5) with normal force (approx. 18 lb [8 kg]). Always check, and if necessary, adjust the tension on newly fitted belts after 300 miles (500 km) driving.
3   Check regularly to make sure that belts are in good condition and are clean. Worn or dirty belts can cause poor cooling and poor alternator output.

8 Cooling fan - general

1   The B20 and B21 engines have a fixed plastic cooling fan and a slipping viscous drive coupling.
2   At low speeds, the blades revolve at the same speed as the water pump shaft to which it is attached, but as the water pump speed increases the fan speed levels off and for shaft speeds of over 4000 rpm it actually drops as shown in Fig. 2.6.
3   Fig. 2.7. gives a diagram of the fan coupling. The central hub is bolted to a flange which is in turn bolted to the front of the water pump pulley. The fan itself is bolted to the back of the coupling unit with four bolts.
4   The disc attached to the central hub is covered with friction material which causes it to drag against the viscous liquid with which the coupling is filled. Because of the energy dissipated the liquid gets quite hot - hence the cooling fins.
5   It is highly unlikely that this unit will give trouble unless due to wear or mechanical damage the oil leaks out. It is unlikely that this leakage would pass undetected. You can check that all is well with the fan by turning the blades by hand and noting the slight resistance produced in the coupling. If you want to be really fussy you can mark

Fig. 2.4. The water pump

1 Housing	5 Lock spring
2 Impellor	6 Shaft with ball bearings
3 Seal ring	(integral unit)
4 Flange	7 Wear ring

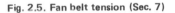

Fig. 2.5. Fan belt tension (Sec. 7)

Fan speed

Input speed, rpm (water pump)

Fig. 2.6. Speed graph for viscous fan coupling (Sec. 8)

the fan pulley and the fan itself with chalk, and check their speeds with a stroboscope for comparison with Fig. 2.6.
6   If anything goes wrong with the fan coupling it is very unlikely that you will be able to repair it. The only remedy is renewal.

9 Pressurising of cooling system - general

1   The expansion tank filler cap is provided with a valve which opens at a pressure of 10 psi (0.7 kg/sq cm) above atmospheric on B20 engines or 9.2 to 12 psi (0.65 to 0.85 kg/sq cm) on B21 engines.

Fig. 2.7. Viscous slip coupling (Sec. 8)

1 Fan blade	7 Centre bolt
2 Bolt	8 Hub
3 Oil	9 Friction material
4 Seals	10 Rubber ring
5 Washer	11 Housing
6 Flange, water pump	

2 If for any reason the water in the system approaches boiling point, air and possibly steam will be driven out through the cap. When the system cools down again another valve in the cap opens to relieve the partial vacuum that would otherwise occur.
3 If the coolant is very close to boiling point, it will certainly start to boil when the expansion chamber cap is removed and coolant may well be forced out and make a mess in the engine compartment which needs to be wiped up as the glycol has a corrosive action. For this reason you should be very careful about opening the cap when the temperature gauge needle is reading high. Put a rag over it, turn it slightly and allow the pressure to dissipate before you remove the cap entirely.

10 Temperature gauge sensor unit - general

1 The sensor for the coolant temperature gauge is a semi-conductor device whose electrical resistance varies with temperature. It is supplied with a constant voltage via the temperature indicator on the instrument panel (see Chapter 10). The variations of resistance cause a varying current to pass through the sensor, and this current is registered on the indicator as a variation in temperature.
2 The sensor is located on the left-hand side of the cylinder head beside the rear inlet port.
3 To remove it, partially drain the cooling system through the tap in the cylinder block (removing the filler cap in the expansion tank) until the level has fallen to just below the cylinder head. To check this, unscrew the sensor slightly and see if there is any tendency for coolant to leak out. When enough coolant has been drained from the system the sensor can be unscrewed and removed for checking.
4 To check the sensor attach temporary extension leads to the device (one from the tag on the top to the lead in the cable harness, the other from the metal part to the frame of the car) and suspend it in a container of water which is then heated up to boiling point (an electric immerser is suitable for this). You can check that the needle on the indicator rises smoothly as the water temperature rises, finishing well up in the red when the water starts to boil. Do not forget that the boiling point of water in free air is somewhat lower than the boiling point reached in the sealed system (see Section 9).

11 Fault diagnosis - cooling system

Symptom: excessive rise in coolant temperature.
1 *Broken or loose fanbelts.*
2 *Low coolant level in system.*
3 *Faulty thermostat.*
4 *Ignition too far retarded.*
5 *Incorrect fuel mixture.*
6 *Blocked radiator tubes.*
7 *Brakes binding.*
Symptom: loss of coolant.
1 *Leaking hoses or joints.*
2 *Leaking radiator or drain tap.*
3 *Expansion tank cap defective.*
4 *Defective cylinder head gasket.*
Note: Unlike an open cooling system, the sealed system loses little or no coolant unless there is a definite leak somewhere or overheating is so pronounced that it would be detected quite apart from its effect on the coolant level.

12 Heating system - general description

1 The heating system is a combined warm air/fresh air system. Incoming air is blown by a fan through the miniature radiator in the heater unit and out into the car. The fresh air can be heated and directed to the required areas of the car by various controls.
2 The ducting system varies with the model and year, but all employ the same heating unit. A typical combined heater and fresh air unit is shown in Fig. 2.8. A heat control valve keeps the heated air at a predetermined and constant temperature. This is achieved by the thermostat which is incorporated in the control valve. If the coolant temperature increases, the thermostat capillary expands and acts on the valve in the control system to reduce the flow of coolant.
3 The heater has two separately controlled outputs - floor ducts and defrosters. These are regulated by flaps which are connected by cables to the control unit fixed to the dashboard. A similar cable arrangement from this unit operates the heat control valve. The heater unit is shown in Fig. 2.9.

13 Heater unit - removal and refitting

1 Disconnect the battery for safety reasons.
2 Remove the combined instrument panel (see Chapter 10).
3 Disconnect the hoses to the control valve, the defroster hoses and the control wires. Remove the switch for the fan and disconnect the cables to the fan motor.
4 Unbolt the fuse box from the heater, and then the control valve and the upper hose to the heater unit. Take great care with the control valve and the copper pipe attaching it to the heater as these are easily damaged.
5 Plug the outlets on the heater so that the remaining coolant does not run into the car - antifreeze is not good for paintwork. Disconnect the earthing cable from the right-hand bracket, remove the four screws which hold the heater unit to the brackets and free the drain hose. The heater unit and control valve can now be removed.
6 Refitting is a straightforward reversal of this procedure. Handle the control valve and its connecting pipe with care.

14 Heater unit - overhaul

1 Remove the four rubber bushes on the sides of the heater unit. Mark the fan casing so that you don't have to worry which way round it goes when reassembling. Remove the spring clips (Fig. 2.10) which hold the heater together and separate the two halves. This exposes the radiator system with its thermostatic control and the fan motor.
2 Inspect the radiator for signs of leakage and check that all is well with the flap system. Give it a drop of oil here and there. The only other overhaul procedure is replacement of the motor should its bearing be worn. The mounting plate for the motor is attached to the fan casing by bent over tabs. Straighten these carefully, and remove the mounting plate from the casing. The motor can then be unscrewed from the mounting plate.

Fig. 2.8. Combined warm air/fresh air unit
(Sec. 12)

1 Turbine
2 Capillary tube for heater control valve
3 Heater control valve
4 Shutter, air vent left floor
5 Vacuum motor
6 Shutter, left defroster nozzle
7 Vacuum motor
8 Return spring for vacuum motor
9 Evaporator (only on vehicles with air
   conditioning)
10 Air intake cover
11 Heater matrix
12 Vacuum motor for air intake cover
13 Fan motor
14 Central unit
15 Blow-in valve
16 Air conditioning switch
17 Fan motor switch
18 Vacuum motor
19 Shutter, right air duct, rear floor
20 Air duct to rear floor
21 Knob, air intake cover
22 Knob, defroster shutter
23 Knob, floor shutter
24 Temperature controls

Fig. 2.9. Heater unit (Sec. 12 and 13)

1	Heat control valve	4	Fan casing
2	Heater casing	5	Fan
3	Matrix		

3 On reassembly, scrape off the old sealing compound at the various
joints in the heater and replace this with a suitable soft sealing agent.
On reassembly use new spring clips and replace the rubber bushings.

15 Heater control unit - general

1 The complete unit is fixed to the dashboard with three nuts. To
remove it, first take out the panel below the dashboard and then free
the cables from the heater unit and control valve.
2 Pull the illuminating lamp and holders out of the unit, leaving them

Fig. 2.10. Removing the spring clips on the heater (Sec. 14) (open
pliers to expand the clips)

Fig. 2.11. Heater matrix system (Sec. 14)

1	Water hose, output	5	Control cable
2	Water hose, input	6	Capillary tube for heater
3	Matrix		control valve
4	TEMP control	7	Heater control valve

Fig. 2.13. Air conditioner installed - B21 engine (Sec. 16)

1 Compressor		*4 Drier*
2 Air pump or idler	*3 Condenser*	
pulley	*4 Drier*	
	5 Evaporator	

1 Compressor		*4 Drier*
2 Servo pump		*5 Evaporator*
3 Condenser		

suspended in the wiring, undo the nuts and lift out the unit.

3   Check that the wheels and cables are operating freely. Oil where necessary. Replace any damaged or worn parts.

16 Air-conditioning system - general

1   The air-conditioner is of the compressor type, which means that the refrigerant is circulated by a compressor.

2   Fig. 2.12 and 2.13 show the layout of the air-conditioning units. The system is divided into the main components as follows: condenser, receiver-drier, thermostatic expansion valve and the evaporator. The evaporator and expansion valve are placed in front of the heater matrix assembly inside the car and the other components in the engine compartment.

3   There is little that can be done to it by way of maintenance, apart from keeping one's eye on the compressor drivebelt and the pipeline connections. *Never disconnect any part of the refrigeration circuit*, but have the system discharged by your dealer. The escape of refrigerant gas can injure your health.

Chapter 3 Part A: Fuel system - carburettor models

For modifications, and information applicable to later models, see Supplement at end of manual

Contents

Specifications

Fuel pump

Type	Diaphragm pump
Make, designation	Pierburg APG
Fuel pressure, measured at same level as pump (1000 rpm)	1.5 - 3.5 psi (0.11 - 0.25 kg/sq cm)

Carburettors

	B20A	**B21A**
Make, designation	SU	Zenith-Stromberg
Designation	HIF-6	175 CD 2SE
Number	1	1
Size (air intake diameter)	1.75 in (44.5 mm)	1.75 in (44.5 mm)
Metering needle, designation	BCJ	B1 ED
Idling speed	700 rpm	850 rpm
Oil for damping cylinder	Automatic transmission fluid	

Max. exhaust CO content:*	**Adjusting value**	**Checking value**
B20A (1975)	2.5%	1.5 - 4%
B20A (1976)	1.5%	0.5 - 4%
B21A	2.5%	1.5 - 4%

Fuel type

USA models	RON 91, leaded or unleaded
All other models	RON 93, leaded or unleaded

Also refer to vehicle decal or handbook

1 General description

The basic fuel system comprises a single fuel tank, mounted at the rear of the car, from which petrol is pumped by a mechanical pump to the horizontally mounted carburettor. The air filter is of the replaceable paper type.

In order to meet air pollution regulations in North America, and elsewhere, modifications and improvements to the basic fuel system have been introduced over the years. Positive crankcase ventilation and improved fuel utilisation during initial warm-up deal with pollution due to products of combustion, while a recycling system prevents petrol vapour from reaching the atmosphere.

2 Fuel pump - general description

1 The fuel pump used in the 240 series is a Pierburg APG, diaphragm type pump.

2 The basic components of the fuel pump are:
A petrol chamber incorporating a filter
An outlet valve
An inlet valve
A diaphragm
A spring which pushes on the diaphragm
A lever which pulls the diaphragm
A small spring against which the lever operates
The inner end of the lever is linked to a rod attached to the diaphragm.

3 If there is no petrol in the pump the diaphragm is pushed up by the spring so that the space inside the fuel chamber is a minimum. In this case, the outer end of the lever is in its lowest position.

4 The lever is operated by a cam on the engine camshaft. The cam pushes the lever upwards, the diaphragm is drawn downwards, the space inside the fuel chamber increases and petrol is sucked in to fill the resulting vacuum. When the cam leaves the lever, the diaphragm

returns to its original position, but the inlet valve stops the petrol from returning to the tank.

5   As this operation is repeated, the fuel chamber soon fills with petrol which passes through the outlet valve and outlet pipe to the carburettor float chamber. When the float chamber is full, the carburettor needle valve closes and no more petrol can pass along the pipe.

6   When this happens, the diaphragm cannot return to its original position. Soon the pump becomes full of petrol and the diaphragm is extended downwards, holding the lever away from the cam on the camshaft which operates it.

7   When the level in the carburettor float chamber drops, the needle valve opens and petrol can once more pass along the outlet pipe. The diaphragm moves upwards as it pushes the petrol out, the lever moves closer to the cam and the diaphragm is operated until the pump is again filled up.

3   Fuel pump - importance of efficient operation

1   Pumping takes place only when the pump is not full of petrol. The more effectively the pump is working, the less often the lever and diaphragm will have to move. If there is any fuel starvation, you can be sure that the pump is working much harder than it ought, and consequently wearing much faster. If the inefficiency is due to wear, that wear will progress at an ever increasing rate.

2   Any air leakage on the inlet side will cause the pump to take in air and so reduce its efficiency. Very often mechanical pumps are fitted below the level of the petrol tank so that the inlet pipe does not empty back into the tank if there is air leakage. This means that there is no direct indication that leakage is occurring and causing the pump to work harder than it ought, so it is a good idea to check that all is well on the inlet side of the fuel pump from time to time.

4   Fuel pump - removal and refitting

1   Remove the fuel inlet and outlet connections from the fuel pump and plug the ends of the pipes to stop loss of fuel and the entrance of dirt.

2   Unscrew the bolts holding the pump body to the crankcase and lift it away.

3   Remove the fuel from the pump - by operating the lever a few times - before dismantling it.

4   Refitting is the reverse process to removal. Inspect the gaskets on either side of the insulating block and if they are damaged replace them with new ones.

5   Fuel pump - dismantling

1   Thoroughly clean the outside of the pump with paraffin or a proprietary solvent and then dry. To ensure correct reassembly mark the upper and lower body flanges.

2   Take off the cover and remove the gasket and fuel strainer.

3   Undo the six screws joining the upper and lower pump housing and separate these, freeing the diaphragm which is sandwiched between them. Be very careful not to damage the diaphragm in the process.

4   Remove the circlip from the lever shaft, push out the shaft, remove the lever and its return spring.

5   Remove the diaphragm with the spring, spring guide and rubber seal. The spring can be removed after the rubber seal has been levered over the nylon washer.

6   Remove the screw on the underside of the upper body section, take out the stop arm and the leaf spring inlet valve (see Fig. 3.1).

6   Fuel pump - inspection and reassembly

1   Thoroughly clean all parts in paraffin. Dry off and examine each part for signs of wear. As we have already pointed out, very little mechanical wear can be accepted. Look for it on the rocker arm pin or bearing holes, the face of the cam lever and the linkage between the cam lever and the diaphragm pull rod. Renew any part about which you are doubtful.

2   The diaphragm and pull rod (a single assembly) must be renewed if there are any signs of wear or cracking in the diaphragm.

Fig. 3.1. Pierburg fuel pump (Sec. 5)

1	Lower pump housing	9	Inlet pipe
2	Rubber seal	10	Strainer
3	Guides	11	Cover with gasket
4	Diaphragm spring	12	Return spring
5	Diaphragm	13	Spring holder
6	Stop arm	14	Lever
7	Spring	15	Circlip
8	Upper pump housing	16	Lever shaft

Fig. 3.2. Underside view of upper body, Pierburg fuel pump (Sec. 6)

A   Inlet valve   B   Stop arm

3   Check that the seating surface for the inlet valve spring is clean and smooth and that the port edges are free from burrs. There is no provision for removing the outlet valve, but it never seems to give any trouble. Ensure that it is clean before you reassemble the pump.

4   To reassemble, first install the cam lever and its pivot pin in the lower body. Replace the lever return spring.

5   Assemble the diaphragm spring, seal and washer in the order in which they were dismantled and centre the diaphragm in the return spring. Engage the diaphragm pull rod with the lever and position the diaphragm so that the holes round its edge are exactly in line with those on the body flange. When all is correctly positioned, check that the pull rod is properly seated in the lever fork and that everything operates smoothly.

6   To fit the upper half of the body, hold the diaphragm against the flange by pushing on the lever while placing the upper body in position, with the alignment marks made on the two flanges coinciding. Insert the six screws and tighten them until the heads just engage with the

spring washers. Check that the diaphragm is correctly centred and that it does not overlap the edge at any point. Then tighten the screws alternately until all are fully home.

7 Replace the filter gauze and refit the top cover using a new gasket. Do not overtighten the screw on the top cover or you may distort the cover and be troubled with leakage at the joint.

7 Fuel pump - testing

1 Hold the pump steady in the protected jaws of a vice. Fit two short lengths of plastic tube to the inlet and outlet pipes and take the inlet tube to a container of paraffin (much safer than petrol) set a short distance away, with the paraffin level slightly above that of the pump. Insert the end of the outlet pump into a measuring jar set a little below the pump. Pump with the lever arm until paraffin is coming through without bubbles. Once pumping is established the pump should deliver not less than 1.75 fl oz (50 cc) in 10 strokes. If the delivery is below this, it indicates a faulty valve or weak diaphragm return spring. If bubbles appear continuously in the output, an air leak somewhere in the chamber is the cause.

2 Empty the pump of paraffin and remove the plastic tubes. Push up the cam lever, cover the end of the inlet pipe with one finger and then release the cam lever - a distinct suction should be felt, the lever should return very slowly, and on removing the finger there should be an inrush of air as the lever springs back.

8 Fuel tank - cleaning filter

1 At the intervals specified in Routine Maintenance the fuel level sender unit must be removed from the fuel tank and the filter which is attached to it must be cleaned.

2 To remove the sender unit disconnect the battery earth terminal and lift the mat in the boot.

3 Remove the cover plate and disconnect the earth wire and the lead from the sender unit terminal.

4 Make up a tool similar to the one shown in Fig. 3.3 to engage in the sender unit cover plate cut-outs and turn it in an anticlockwise direction.

5 Refitting is the reversal of removal. Always fit a new gasket.

9 Carburettor (SU) - general description

1 The variable choke SU carburettor is a relatively simple instrument. It differs from most other carburettors in that instead of having a number of various fixed jets for different conditions, only one variable jet is fitted to deal with all possible conditions.

2 Air passing rapidly through the carburettor draws petrol from the jet so forming the petrol/air mixture. The amount of petrol drawn from the jet depends on the position of the tapered carburettor needle, which moves up and down the jet orifice according to the engine load and throttle opening, thus effectively altering the size of jet so that exactly the right amount of fuel is metered for the prevailing road conditions.

3 The position of the tapered needle in the jet is determined by engine vacuum. The shank of the needle is held at its top end in a piston which slides up and down the dashpot in response to the degree of manifold vacuum.

4 With the throttle fully open, the full effect of inlet manifold vacuum is felt by the piston which has an air bleed into the choke tube on the outside of the throttle. This causes the piston to rise fully, bringing the needle with it. With the accelerator partially closed, only slight inlet manifold vacuum is felt by the piston (although, of course, on the engine side of the throttle the vacuum is greater), and the piston only rises a little, blocking most of the jet orifice with the metering needle.

5 To prevent the piston fluttering and giving a richer mixture when the accelerator is suddenly depressed, an oil damper and light spring are fitted inside the dashpot.

6 The only portion of the piston assembly to come into contact with the piston chamber or dashpot is the actual central piston rod. All the other parts of the piston assembly, including the lower choke portion, have sufficient clearance to prevent any direct metal to metal contact which is essential if the carburettor is to function correctly.

Fig. 3.3. Fuel level sender unit

1 Filter	2 Tool for releasing sender unit flange

7 The correct level of the petrol in the carburettor is determined by the level of the float chamber. When the level is correct the float rises and, by means of a lever resting on top of it, closes the needle valve in the cover of the float chamber. This closes off the supply of fuel from the pump. When the level in the float chamber drops as fuel is used in the carburettor, the float drops. As it does, the float needle is unseated so allowing more fuel to enter the float chamber and restore the correct level.

10 Carburettor (SU-HIF6) - removal and refitting

1 Remove the air cleaner.

2 Detach the fuel pipe from the carburettor float chamber union.

3 Disconnect the distributor vacuum pipe from the carburettor.

4 Note the throttle and choke control connections and then disconnect them.

5 Remove the carburettor retaining nuts and withdraw the carburettor from the inlet manifold.

6 Cover the inlet manifold aperture with masking tape or blank off with a rag to prevent dirt ingress.

7 Refitting the carburettor is the reverse of the removal sequence. Always use new gaskets. Top-up the carburettor damper.

11 Carburettor (SU-HIF6) - dismantling, inspection and overhaul

1 Assuming that the carburettor is on the workbench, start by cleaning the exterior thoroughly with paraffin or a proprietary solvent, using a stiff brush where necessary.

2 Undo the cap at the top of the carburettor and withdraw it complete with the small damper piston. Empty the oil from the dashpot.

3 Mark the position of the float chamber cover relative to the body and remove it by unscrewing the four screws holding it down. Empty out any fuel still in the fuel chamber.

4 The float is held to the body by a spindle having a screw head on it (shown in Fig. 3.5). Unscrew and remove the spindle with its sealing washer, remove the float, unscrew the needle valve socket and remove it and the needle.

5 Dismantle the various control linkages, being sure that it is understood how the linkages work before they are taken off. It is an easy matter to sort this out before taking them apart, but much more difficult when they are in bits.

6 Unscrew the nut holding the fast idle cam - having first straightened its tab washer, take off the cam and its spring which is contained in a small housing behind it. Undo the two screws holding down this housing and pull on the spindle which held the fast idle cam and the whole cold start assembly will come out of the body. It is shown in Fig. 3.4.

7 Undo the screws holding the throttle disc into its shaft, being careful not to put too much pressure on the shaft in the process (support it with the other hand). Remove the disc and withdraw the throttle shaft.

8 Mark the flanges and remove the top part of the body (suction chamber) and the piston. Be careful of the needle on the end of the piston - a good idea is to stand the piston on a narrow-necked jar with the needle hanging inside it.

Fig. 3.4. SU HIF 6 carburettor - exploded view

2 Housing
3 Plug
4 Bushing
5 Key
6 Screw
6a Nipple
7 Bearing
8 Gasket
9 Screw
10 Jet
11 Bi-metal assembly
12 Spring
13 Screw
14 O-ring
15 Adjuster screw
16 Needle valve with seat
17 Float
18 Gasket
19 Spindle
20 Cover
21 Rubber ring
22 Spring washer
23 Screw
24 Spindle
25 Throttle disc
26 Screw
27 Seal ring
28 Throttle return lever
29 Adjuster screw
30 Adjuster screw
31 Spring
32 Distance sleeve
33 Spring
34 Throttle actuating lever
35 Throttle pick-up lever
36 Bushing
37 Lockwasher
38 Nut
39 Cold start device spindle
40 Valve sleeve
41 O-ring
42 Gasket
43 Seal ring
44 Guide
45 Retainer
46 Screw
47 Return spring
48 Fast idle cam
49 Screw
50 Lockwasher
51 Nut
52 Vacuum chamber
53 Piston
54 Screw
55 Spring
56 Jet needle
57 Spring
58 Guide
59 Damper
60 Gasket
61 Screw

Fig. 3.5. Jet and float assembly (Sec. 11)

1 Fixing screw for bi-metal   3 Bi-metal assembly
  assembly   4 Float valve retainer
2 Spring   5 Drilling to cold start valve

Fig. 3.6. Testing fit of piston in suction chamber (Sec. 11)

    A Rubber or cork plugs

Fig. 3.7. Removal of bi-metal strip from jet (Sec. 11)

9 Unscrew the jet adjusting screw and remove the bi-metal assembly holding the jet.

10 The carburettor is now sufficiently dismantled for inspection to be carried out. One or two adjusting screws and the like have been left in the body, but it is recommended that these are only removed when actually ensuring that the various channels are clear. Generally speaking, the SU carburettor is very reliable but even so it may develop faults, which are not readily apparent unless a careful inspection is carried out, yet may nevertheless effect engine performance. So it is well worthwhile giving the carburettor a good look over when it has been dismantled.

11 Inspect the carburettor needle for ridging. If this is apparent it will probably be found that there is corresponding wear on the inside of the jet. If the needle is ridged, it must be replaced. Do not attempt to rub it down with abrasive paper as carburettor needles are made to very fine tolerances.

12 When replacing the needle locate it in the piston as shown in Fig. 3.6. The supporting stubs should be flush with the piston and the engraved line should point directly away from the channel in the piston face. Note that this makes the needle incline in the direction of the carburettor air cleaner flange when the piston is fitted.

13 Inspect the jet for wear. Wear inside the jet will accompany wear on the needle. If any wear is apparent on the jet, replace it. It may be unhooked from the bi-metal spring and this may be used again (see Fig. 3.7).

14 Inspect the piston and the carburettor body (suction chamber) carefully for signs that these have not been in contact. When the carburettor is operating the main piston should not come into contact with the carburettor body. The whole assembly is supported by the rod of the piston which slides in the centre guide tube, this rod being attached to the cap in the top of the carburettor body. It is possible for wear in the centre guide to allow the piston to touch the wall of the body. Check for this by assembling the small piston in the carburettor body and sliding the large one down, rotating it about the centre guide tube at the same time. If contact occurs and the cause is worn parts, replace them. In no circumstances try to correct piston sticking by altering the tension of the return spring, though very slight contact with the body may be cured - as a temporary measure - by polishing the offending portion of the body wall with metal polish or extremely fine emery cloth.

15 The fit of the piston in the suction chamber can be checked by plugging the air hole in the body and assembling the piston in the chamber without its return spring, fitting the damper piston without filling the dashpot with oil. If the assembly is now turned upside down as shown in Fig. 3.6 the piston would sink to the bottom in 5 - 7 seconds. If the time is appreciably less than this, the piston and suction chamber should both be replaced since they are matched to each other.

16 Check for wear on the throttle shaft and bushes through which it passes. Apart from the nuisance of a sticking throttle, excessive wear here can cause air leaks in the induction system adversely affecting engine performance. Worn bushes can be extracted and new bushes fitted if necessary. For inspection and overhaul of the cold start device see Section 12.

17 Reassembly is a straightforward reversal of the dismantling process. During reassembly the float level can be checked and adjusted if necessary as described in Section 13. When assembling the jet, screw up the adjusting screw so that the upper edge of the jet comes level with the bridge, then turn it 2½ turns clockwise. This gives the initial position for jet adjustment. Fig. 4.5 shows the jet assembled on the bi-metallic strip in the main body and also indicates the correct positioning of the float valve retainer on the tab on the float arm.

18 When the carburettor is assembled, the dashpot should be filled with automatic transmission fluid to within 0.25 in (6 mm) of the top of the cylinder before re-inserting the damper piston. Check that the piston is operating properly by lifting it with the lifting pin and letting it fall. It should hit the bridge of the carburettor with an audible metallic click. If it does not, perhaps the needle is fouling the jet (it is supposed to touch it lightly). This should not occur with careful assembly; there is no provision for centering the jet but if it is properly assembled this is not necessary.

12 Carburettor (SU-HIF6) - cold start device

1 The cold start device is shown assembled in Fig. 3.8 and a diagram is given in Fig. 3.9 from which it will be seen that as the spindle

(which also carries the fast idle cam) revolves, a 'V' shaped slot in the spindle progressively opens a channel between the float chamber and throttle chamber. At the same time a small air channel is opened so that a little air is mixed with the incoming vapour.

2   The fast idle cam operates the throttle by acting on a stop screw on a lever on the throttle shaft.

3   The whole device can be removed from the carburettor body (see

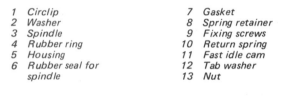

Fig. 3.8. SU HIF 6 carburettor - cold start device (Sec. 12)

1	Circlip	7	Gasket
2	Washer	8	Spring retainer
3	Spindle	9	Fixing screws
4	Rubber ring	10	Return spring
5	Housing	11	Fast idle cam
6	Rubber seal for	12	Tab washer
	spindle	13	Nut

Fig. 3.9. SU HIF 6 - cold start device (Sec. 12)

A	Disengaged	10	Spring retainer
B	Engaged	11	Screw
1	Carburettor housing	12	Packing
2	Channel from float chamber	13	V-slot
3	Stop tab for lever	14	Valve housing
4	Channel for additional air	15	Rubber ring
5	Tab washer	16	Spindle
6	Cam for fast idle	17	Washer
7	Nut	18	Circlip
8	Sealing	19	Channel to carburettor
9	Return spring		throttle chamber

Section 11, paragraph 6) and dismantled for cleaning and inspection. If kept oiled it should give no trouble. Should the spindle or the housing show signs of wear they should both be replaced.

13 Carburettor (SU-HIF6) - checking the float level

1   This is best checked with the carburettor body upside-down. The float will then be resting on the needle valve. The lowest part of the float should then be just a little higher than the face of the carburettor body, as illustrated by Fig. 3.10.

2   The distance between the float and the flange (measurement 'A' in Fig. 3.10) should be between 0.02 - 0.06 in (0.5 - 1.5 mm).

3   The level can be adjusted by carefully bending the metal tab on the float arm. Do not attempt to bend the arm itself. If there is a plastic tab instead of metal one, no adjustment is possible but it is unlikely to be needed.

4   There is no reason why this measurement should not be checked with the carburettor in-situ, holding the float against the flange whilst it is being done. It is awkward but possible.

14 Carburettor (SU-HIF6) - tuning

1   Before tuning the carburettor check that the valve clearances, spark plug gaps, contact breaker settings and ignition timing are all correct, that there is no air leak on the intake system and that the vacuum ignition advance tube is in place. Make the final adjustments with the engine at its normal running temperature and finish off by setting the throttle stop to give the proper idling speed when the air cleaner and crankcase ventilation pipes (which are removed when tuning so that you can check piston position etc.) have been refitted.

2   Unscrew the throttle adjusting screw until it is just clear of the throttle lever with the throttle closed. Check that the cold start lever is fully closed (cold start device out of action) and that the fast idle adjusting screw is well clear of the cam. Failure to observe this may result in the throttle being held open when, by external examination, it appears closed. Turn the throttle adjusting screw one and a half turns clockwise to open the throttle for a datum position.

3   Lift the piston with the piston lifting pin, checking that it falls freely when the pin is released.

4   Lift the piston high enough to reveal the bridge and jet. Turn the jet adjusting screw to bring the top of the jet flush with the bridge, or as near the top as possible. Turn the jet adjusting screw two turns clockwise to set the jet height to a datum position.

5   Start and run the engine until it reaches normal working temperature, and continue to run for approximately five minutes at the correct temperature until an even temperature is established.

6   Increase the engine speed to 2500 rpm for approximately 30 seconds. This will clear the plugs and any condensed fuel from the inlet manifold walls.

7   Adjust the throttle adjusting screw to obtain the correct idling speed as given in Specifications at the beginning of this Chapter.

8   Set the correct mixture strength by adjustment of the jet adjusting screw (turn clockwise to enrich and anticlockwise to weaken) until the fastest engine speed (with given throttle adjusting screw position) is obtained. The fastest engine speed must be obtained when adjusting from a weak setting and approaching a rich setting, so having found the correct setting, turn the screw anticlockwise until a small but perceptible

Fig. 3.10. SU HIF 6 - float level (Sec. 13)

A = 0.02 - 0.06 in (0.5 - 1.5 mm)

Fig. 3.11. SU HIF 6 carburettor - tuning and adjustment (Sec. 14)

1 Piston/suction chamber	5 Fast-idle adjusting screw	9 Auto ignition connection
2 Jet adjusting screw	6 Piston lifting pin	10 Cold start enrichment lever (cam lever)
3 Float chamber	7 Fuel inlet	11 Crankcase ventilation tube
4 Throttle adjusting screw	8 Vent tube (alternative positions)	

fall in speed is noticed, then turn the screw clockwise very slowly until the maximum speed is regained. If the correct position is 'overshot', open the throttle to clear the engine, return to the weak setting and repeat the tuning procedure.

9 Following the mixture strength setting, the idling speed may need re-adjusting by adjustment of the throttle adjustment screw to restore the specified speed.

10 It is at this stage that the exhaust gas analysing test should be applied, if the tuning were being performed by an operator with this facility. The mixture strength obtained by very careful application of the procedures given above, gives only an approximation to correct carburation: final adjustment being made in conjunction with the exhaust analysis equipment to bring the carbon monoxide (CO) percentage within the specified limits. Therefore, in countries where stringent exhaust emission control laws exist, the foregoing tuning procedures must be regarded as for information or emergency use only.

11 To set the fast idle pull out the choke control on the instrument panel until the arrow marked on the cam is directly under the fast idle adjusting screw. Turn the screw to obtain a fast idle speed of 1100 to 1600 rpm. In very cold conditions it may be desirable to set the idling speed slightly faster.

12 Lock both adjusting screws, taking care not to disturb the settings. Refit the air cleaner.

15 Carburettor (Stromberg) - general description

1 The Stromberg type 175 CD-2SE carburettor is used on some models in the Volvo 240 series.

2 The carburettor has been specially designed to reduce exhaust emission to a minimum and to be compatible with other devices in the exhaust emission control system.

3 The carburettor is fitted with a temperature compensator which acts as an air valve during periods of high under-bonnet or fuel temperature levels.

4 A hot-start valve is fitted to offset the effects of accumulations of fuel vapour which occur in the carburettor intake during periods of high under-bonnet temperatures. This vapour originates from the

carburettor float chamber and makes it difficult to start the engine in hot conditions. The valve discharges the fumes to atmosphere under throttle closed conditions and then deflects them into the air cleaner where they are drawn into the engine as soon as the engine starts running.

16 Carburettor (Stromberg) - removal and refitting

The sequence for the removal of the Stromberg carburettor is basically the same as that for the SU carburettor. Refer to Section 10 for removal procedure.

17 Carburettor (Stromberg) - dismantling, inspection and overhaul

1 With the carburettor removed from the car, clean away all external dirt.

2 Set the carburettor on the bench and arrange to have two or three small containers ready for screws and small components that can easily get lost.

3 Mark the position of the float chamber lid relative to the body and remove it by unscrewing the six screws holding it down. It is sealed to a blind plug which holds the jet in position. Ease it off carefully, turning it to-and-fro. Empty out any fuel still in the float chamber.

4 Carefully push out the pin on which the float is pivoted to the main body, take out the float and unscrew the needle valve assembly.

5 Dismantle the various linkages on the body and remove the temperature compensating device, the bypass valve and the cold start device (Figs. 3.14 - 3.17).

6 Undo the cap at the top of the body and remove it complete with the damper piston. Empty the oil from the dashpot. Remove the upper part of the carburettor body, marking the flanges so that you will not have to think twice about its position when replacing it. Remove and dismantle the piston, needle and diaphragm assembly. Treat this assembly carefully - a good idea is to stand the piston in the top of a jar with the needle hanging down inside.

7 Remove the blind plug from the main body, being careful not to

Fig. 3.12. Major components of Stromberg carburettor (Sec. 17)

Fig. 3.13. Stromberg carburettor - cross-section through drive (Sec. 17)

damage the surface where it seals to the float chamber cover. Underneath it you will see a tube which is pressed into the main body and communicates with the jet. The jet itself is pressed into the body from the other end. Its removal and replacement is a matter for the specialist.

8   Undo the screws holding the throttle disc into its shaft, being careful not to put too much pressure on the shaft in the process (support it with the other hand). Remove the disc and withdraw the throttle shaft.

9   The carburettor is now sufficiently dismantled for inspection to take place. One or two adjusting screws still remain in the body, but these are best removed as you clean out the various airways and

replaced immediately. Generally speaking the Stromberg carburettor is very reliable but even so it may develop faults which are not readily apparent unless a careful inspection is carried out, yet may nevertheless affect engine performance. So giving the carburettor a good looking over when dismantled, is well worthwhile.

10 Start by cleaning the various parts, making sure that the air channels in the main body are completely clear. This is best achieved by blowing through them.

11 Inspect the carburettor needle for ridging. If the needle is ridged, it must be renewed - do not attempt to rub it down with abrasive paper as carburettor needles are made to very fine tolerances.

Fig. 3.14. Stromberg carburettor - temperature compensator (Sec. 17)

1 Rubber seal	7 Screw for cover
2 Rubber seal	8 Cross-slotted screw
3 Valve	9 Adjustment nut
4 Bi-metal spring	10 Housing
5 Cover	11 Identity label
6 Screw for temperature compensator	

Fig. 3.15. Stromberg carburettor - cold start device (Sec. 17)

A Cold start device 'off'	B Cold start device fully 'on'
1 Passage from float chamber	3 Pierced disc
2 Passage to throttle chamber	4 Channel disc
	5 Housing

12 Where the jet is removable, inspect it for wear. Wear inside the jet may well accompany wear on the needle. If the jet is worn, replace it. Where the jet is pressed into the main body, it can be examined from above. Replacement, if worn, is a matter for the specialist.

13 Examine the diaphragm and replace it if it shows any sign of weakness or cracking. Examine the piston, in particular the dashpot cylinder on the top of it but unless there has been any maltreatment (such as dropping) it is unusual to find anything wrong. Check that the damper piston has a to-and-fro movement along its shaft of between 0.04 - 0.07 in (1.1 - 1.9 mm) and that it moves perfectly freely. This movement is essential for proper damping action. If there is any fault in the assembly, replace it complete.

14 Check for wear on the throttle shaft and the bushes through which it passes. Apart from the nuisance of a sticking throttle, excessive wear here can cause air leaks in the induction system (though this is less likely when the bushes are sealed) affecting the performance. Worn bushes can be extracted and new bushes fitted if necessary.

15 Reassembly is largely a reversal of the dismantling procedure, but the following internal adjustments and checks must be carried out during the process.

Fig. 3.16. Stromberg carburettor - bypass valve - diagram (Secs. 17 and 18)

1 Adjusting screw
2 Rubber ring
3 Cover
4 Nut
5 Spring
6 Drilling to underside of diaphragm
7 Diaphragm
8 Outlet channel for fuel/air fixing
9 Valve
10 Inlet channel for fuel/air mixing
11 Flap
Shading A = Vacuum   B = Fuel/air mixture

Fig. 3.17. Stromberg carburettor - bypass valve dismantled (Secs. 17 and 18)

1 Gasket	7 Cover screw
2 Housing	8 Cover
3 Gasket	9 Rubber ring
4 Diaphragm	10 Adjusting screw
5 Gasket	11 Spring
6 Fixing screws	

16 Thoroughly clean the channels of the bypass valve.

17 When refitting the cold start device to the carburettor, make sure that the mating surfaces are completely clean and smooth: there is no gasket. The outer end of the spindle carries a combined choke control lever and fast idling cam. The cam bears an engraved mark which should be set opposite the fast idle screw when the fast idling is adjusted.

18 Check that the temperature compensator valve moves easily in its housing. If necessary, it can be centred by slackening its crosshead screw which secures the bi-metallic strip and adjusting its position.

19 Float adjustment is illustrated in Fig. 3.18. It is achieved by bending the lug on the float arm which bears on the needle valve. With the carburettor body inverted, check the dimensions 'A' and 'B' and bend as necessary. It is possible to carry out this adjustment with the carburettor in-situ by pressing the float lightly against the needle valve, but a great deal more awkward. Do not try to bend the arm between the float and the needle valve.

Fig. 3.18. Stromberg carburettor - float level (Sec. 17)

A = 0.35 - 0.51 in (9 - 13 mm)
B = 0.59 - 0.67 in (15 - 17 mm)

Fig. 3.19. Stromberg carburettor - tuning and adjustment (Sec. 19)

20 When refitting the flexible diaphragm, make sure that the lugs engage correctly in both the carburettor body and the piston.
21 Finally fill the dashpot with automatic transmission fluid to within 0.25 in (6 mm) of the top of the carburettor before inserting the damper piston.

18 Carburettor (Stromberg) - bypass valve

1 The purpose of this valve is to ensure that when the throttle is shut off with the engine running at high speed a certain amount of air still enters the engine, ensuring proper burning of the mixture and reducing noxious emissions from the exhaust. It is entirely self-contained, functioning automatically as the result of the high vacuum that occurs when the throttle is shut off under these conditions. In effect it slows up the rate at which the engine reduces speed when the throttle is closed. Once normal idling speed is reached, the valve ceases to operate.
2 It consists of a diaphragm clamped to a machined face on the wall of the unit by a cover. At the centre of the diaphragm is a combined metal valve plate and spring register, into which fits a compression

spring located at the other end over a spigot in the cover. The spring loads the valve plate to the closed position. The cover also forms a diaphragm control chamber, being connected to the engine intake manifold by a small bore pipe.
3 Depression, sensed in the diaphragm chamber, will lift the valve at a predetermined value, dictated by the compression spring preload, and admit air from the mixing chamber into the intake manifold, thus bypassing the throttle plate and limiting the depression. The maximum bleed flow is controlled by an orifice fitted in the bypass passage.
4 The bypass valve is preset and no attempt may be made to adjust it in service.

19 Carburettor (Stromberg) - tuning

1 Before adjusting the carburettor, check that the valve clearances, spark plug gaps, contact breaker settings and ignition timing are all correct, that there is no leakage in the intake manifold and that the vacuum ignition advance tube is in place. Make the final adjustments with the engine at its normal running temperature, and finish off by setting the throttle stop to give the specified idling speed when you have refitted the air cleaner and crankcase ventilation pipes.
2 Screw up the idling trimmer screw (see Fig. 3.12) as far as it will go and then undo it two full turns. Now run the engine until it reaches operational temperature, adjust the engine speed, to that given in Specifications at the beginning of this Chapter, by means of the throttle stop screw and then adjust the idling trimmer to give smoothest engine running on idling and good pick-up on acceleration. Should the idling speed increase when adjusting this screw, correct on the throttle stop screw.
3 Pull out the choke control on the instrument panel 0.9 - 1 in (23 - 25 mm) and adjust the cable so that the mark on the fast idle cam comes opposite the centre-line of the fast idle screw.
4 Jet adjustment should ideally (and in some parts of the world, by legal requirement) be set for minimum CO emission using the appropriate test gear and then sealed. In countries or states where stringent exhaust emission control laws exist the foregoing tuning procedure must be regarded as general information or for emergency use only.
5 When using a CO meter to set the carburettor, warm the engine up from cold and carry out the adjustment within eight minutes of the cooling thermostat opening. This can be ascertained by feeling the radiator top hose and when it suddenly turns warm, the thermostat will have opened.
6 The CO content should be as given in Specifications at the beginning of this Chapter and adjustment is carried out with the idling trimmer screw. If the CO content cannot be reduced to the specified level, suspect a fault in the temperature compensator on the front face of the carburettor.

20 Closed crankcase ventilation system - general

1 For efficient engine operation it is necessary that pressure should not build up in the crankcase. In times past this has been taken care of by providing a simple breathing device (sometimes, but not always, fitted with an oil trap) which vented the crankcase fumes to atmosphere. Such a device is found on early Volvo engines, but now all Volvo engines are fitted with a closed crankcase ventilation system in which the build-up of crankcase pressure is prevented without allowing it to breathe directly into the atmosphere.
2 Fig. 3.20 illustrates the system employed by Volvo on the B20 series. Clean air from a subsidiary filter in the air cleaner assembly is drawn into the crankcase via a small flame trap in the crankcase breather. The oil filler cap is connected to the inlet manifold through a nipple which restricts the amount of air drawn into the manifold while at the same time causing pressure in the crankcase to be lower than atmospheric, thus ensuring that air is drawn in from the air intake. When the throttle is fairly wide open, the vacuum in the inlet manifold is less than that in the air cleaner, and vapour flows out of the crankcase along both routes. Much of this enters the air cleaner via the subsidiary insert, where it is remixed with fuel vapour and again enters the engine.
3 The only attention the system requires is periodical cleaning of the nipple and flame guard. To ensure that pollution of the atmosphere is kept to a minimum, ensure that the flexible pipes and their clips are in good condition and airtight.

Fig. 3.20. Closed crankcase ventilation (Sec. 20)

1 Cleaner insert
2 Pipe for fresh air supply to crankcase
3 Nipple
4 Pipe for crankcase gases
5 Flame guard

Fig. 3.21. Constant air temperature device (Sec. 21)

1 Thermostat   5 Flaps
2 Lock nut   6 Warm air intake
3 Air feeler connection 7 Cold air intake
4 Flap control

Fig. 3.22. Constant air temperature device (Sec. 21)

1 Hot - open for warm air   4 Shutter
2 Cold - open for cold air   5 Warm air intake
3 Tab   6 Cold air intake

21 Constant temperature air device - general

1 In order to ensure that the air entering the carburettor is rapidly raised to a temperature which thereafter remains constant, air at atmospheric temperature from an intake in the front of the car is mixed with air which has passed over a hot spot on the exhaust system, in a box which incorporates a flap controlled by a thermostat. A view of this box with the hose connections removed is given in Fig. 3.21.

2 Inside the box is a flap which in one extreme position completely blanks off the warm air intake and in the other blanks off the cool air intake. Fig. 3.22 shows the small tab found on either side of the box indicating the position of the flap. When it points to 'hot' the cold air intake is completely shut off and the warmest possible air is fed to the carburettor(s), the reverse happening when it points to 'cold'.

3 To check the operation of the thermostat, remove the unit from the car and test it in warm water. The flap should shut off the hot air intake (tab pointing to 'cold') at a temperature of 95 - 105°F (35 - 41°C) and shut off the cold air intake at 70 - 77°F (27 - 31°C).

4 The device is very unlikely to go out of adjustment, but the thermostat may possibly cease to function properly. If so, the complete device should be replaced.

5 When fitting, note that the thermostat should be in the middle of the air flow and that any hose clamp screws should be on top of the housing.

22 Evaporative fuel vapour control system - general description

1 In hot countries the problem of atmospheric pollution by evaporation of petrol, from motor cars, is a serious one. In California, it has been estimated that a car left out all day can lose as much as a gallon of

Fig. 3.23. Evaporative system (Sec. 22)

A Engine idling (top)   B Engine running (bottom)

1 Fuel tank   7 Control rod (connected
2 Expansion tank   to throttle)
3 Venting filter   8 Air cleaner
4 Air valve   9 Carburettor
5 Diaphragm   10 Float chamber
6 Hot start valve   11 Intake manifold

fuel by evaporation. Even if the average figure is less than a hundredth of this, when one considers all the cars there are in California the fact that legislation has been introduced enforcing evaporation control is not surprising.

2   The sources of evaporation are:
   a) *The carburettor float chambers*
   b) *The fuel tank*

In the control system used by Volvo, when the engine is switched off or idling the vapour from these two sources is channeled into an absorptive element made up of active carbon granules which soak up the fumes like a sponge. When the engine is running, air is drawn through the active carbon element into the carburettor air intake, purging the element and drawing in vapour from the fuel tank as it is generated. At the same time the channel from the float chamber is diverted from the filter direct to the carburettor intake.

3   Fig. 3.23 shows how the system operates. When the engine is idling or switched off, the hot start valve has its plunger in the up position and any petrol vapour coming from the float chamber is fed into the filter. At the same time the main fuel tank can evaporate into an expansion tank where a certain amount of condensation can occur, the remaining vapour being passed to the filter also. The air valve on top of the filter, which is operated by engine vacuum, is closed when the engine is idling and the filter is cut off from the air intake. This is the position shown in Fig. 3.23.

4   When the engine is running normally the vacuum falls sufficiently to let the air valve open and at the same time the plunger of the hot start valve is lowered by its control lever. Vapour from the float chamber is now taken via the hot start valve into the air cleaner, while vapour from the circulation tank and the filter is sucked into the carburettor throttle chamber where it mixes with what is already being provided by the carburettor. The air drawn through the filter removes fuel fumes stored in the active carbon element.

23 Air cleaner - general description

1   There are two types of air cleaners fitted to carburettor engines. One type has a disposable element while the other is of sealed, throw-away type. Removal, dismantling, reassembly and refitting are obvious and straightforward. Attention to the air cleaner element is of paramount importance if engine efficiency is to be maintained. If operating conditions are particularly dusty, this component should be given frequent attention.

2   The complete filter or its element should be replaced every 24000 miles (40000 km).

24 Exhaust system (all models) - removal and refitting

See Section 58 of Chapter 3, Part B.

25 Fault diagnosis - fuel system and carburation

We give in the following table a few of the symptoms of carburettor or fuel system trouble, possible causes and remedies. Always bear in mind that it is very difficult to distinguish between ignition faults and carburettor faults in many cases. The golden rule should be - before starting on the carburettor, make 100% certain of the ignition. Ignition faults are easy to check, ignition adjustments, when required, are easy to make, and furthermore when adjustment is required as a result of normal wear and tear this adjustment is much more likely to be in the ignition than in the carburettor. The following table, therefore assumes that all is in order in the ignition system.

Symptom	Reason/s	Remedy
Smell of petrol when engine is stopped	Leaking pipes or unions	Tighten or renew as necessary.
	Leaking fuel tank	Fill fuel tank to capacity and examine carefully at seams, unions and filler pipe connections. Renew tank.
Smell of petrol when engine is idling	Leaking fuel lines or unions between pump and carburettor	Check lines and unions and tighten or repair.
	Overflow of fuel from float chamber due to wrong level setting, ineffective needle valve or punctured float	Check fuel level setting and condition of float and needle valve and renew if necessary.
Excessive fuel consumption for reasons not covered by leaks or float chamber faults	Worn needle and/or jet	Replace.
	Sticking needle or piston	Check correct movement of needle and piston assembly, as detailed in this Chapter.
Difficult starting, uneven running, lack of power, cutting out	Blockages in carburettor	Clean out float chamber and body.
	Float chamber fuel level too low or needle valve sticking	Dismantle and check fuel level and needle valve.
	Fuel pump not delivering sufficient fuel	Check pump delivery and clean or repair as required. Check for blockage in fuel pipes.
	Intake manifold gaskets leaking or manifold fractured	Check tightness of mounting nuts and inspect manifold.
Difficulty in starting not associated with faults already given	Over-rich mixture entering cylinders as a result of too much use of choke control or depressing the accelerator pedal when starting	Keep your foot off the accelerator pedal until the engine fires. If 'over-choking' has already occurred, push the pedal right down to the floor and operate the starter. Usually this will clear the fault. It will clear itself in time anyway.
Engine does not respond properly to throttle pedal	Sticking piston or needle	Check correct movement of piston.
	Damper piston not working properly	Check free play or damper piston on its rod.
	Oil level in dashpot low	Top-up.
Engine idling speed drops markedly after a long period of idling (in warm weather especially)	Defective temperature compensator (Stromberg)	Adjust or replace as necessary.
	Hot start valves sticking in run position	Determine cause, adjust or replace as necessary.
Engine does not take up proper idling speed when throttle released	Sticking controls	Clean and oil as required.
	Defective bypass valve (Stromberg) or relief valve in throttle flap (SU)	Correct defect or replace as necessary.

Chapter 3 Part B: Fuel system - fuel injection models

For modifications, and information applicable to later models, see Supplement at end of manual

Contents

Specifications

Pressure

System pressure	65 - 75 psi (4.6 - 5.3 kg/sq cm)
Closing pressure	24 psi (1.7 kg/sq cm)
Control pressure	53 ± 2.8 psi (3.7 ± 0.2 kg/sq cm)

Fuel pump

Type	Electric rotor pump
Capacity	1.32 to 1.52 Imp pint (1.58 to 1.82 US pints, 0.75 to 0.86 litres) per 30 sec at 71 psi (5 kg/sq cm)
Current consumption	8.5 amps (max)

Fuel filter

Type	Paper filter
Change interval	24,000 miles (40,000 km)

Auxiliary air valve

Fully open at	−30ºC (−22ºF)
Fully closed at	+70ºC (158ºF) (after 5 minutes driving with ambient temperature +20ºC (68ºF)

Air filter

Type	Paper filter
Change interval	24,000 miles (40,000 km)

Idling speed ... ... 900 rpm (manual), 800 rpm (automatic)

Maximum exhaust CO content* ... ... 1.7 to 2.3%

Refer also to individual vehicle decal or handbook

Fuel type

USA	91 RON unleaded
Germany	97 RON
Others	93 RON leaded or unleaded

26 Fuel injection system - description of operation

1   The best way to an understanding of the working of the fuel injection engine is to consider the basic operation of the normal carburettor system.

Obviously, the more fuel an engine burns the more power it will give out. Notice that we say burns - fuel taken in and not burnt will add to your petrol consumption without doing anything to help you along.

To ensure that the fuel is properly burnt, it must be mixed with air in the right proportions. If the mixture is too rich, there will not be enough oxygen to support combustion, as every motorist who has ever used his choke too enthusiastically will realise. If it is too weak, the burning process is slow and irregular - sometimes it is still going on when the inlet valve opens and flames shoot through the carburettor/s as a result.

The basic function of the fuel system, then, is simply to provide the amount of fuel the engine needs at any given time, mixed with the amount of air required to ensure that it is properly burnt.

2   The modern carburettor solves this problem by reversing it. For a given throttle setting, the engine will suck in a certain amount of air per stroke. A measure of the amount of air going in is the amount of suck which occurs on the carburettor side of the throttle, ie. the degree of vacuum set up there. This pressure drop causes the carburettor to release an amount of petrol vapour suitable to the amount of air going in.

This is not an easy problem to solve, as is obvious when one looks at the complexity of a modern carburettor. Quite apart from the initial case when the engine is cold and the vapour starts to condense before it ever enters the cylinders, we find devices for modifying apparent size of jet (the vacuum controlled piston and needle arrangement used by the carburettors described in this manual) or various arrangements of subsidiary jets, tubes in which the petrol level rises and so on.

On top of this, we are faced with difficulties caused by temperature variations. The proportion of air to petrol varies with the temperature of the air being mixed in, basically because when air is warm the same weight of air occupies more space and it is weight of air to weight of fuel that we have to worry about, not volume to volume. Also, quite

apart from this, the required mixture depends on the temperature inside the cylinder and generally speaking the carburettor has no way of knowing what this is. In an ordinary carburettor system, these problems are to some extent side-stepped because the engine temperature and the air temperature stabilise themselves after the engine has been running for a while.

Elaborate arrangements are made for stabilising the temperature of the input air on carburettor engines; as we shall see, the problem is tackled in a different way in the fuel injection engine and the thermostatically operated flap and branch pipe to a hot spot on the exhaust system are conspicuous by their absence.

Cold starting is a problem on its own. The mixture is arbitrarily enriched so that in spite of condensation which may occur on the way there is a reasonable chance that some at least of the cylinders will receive mixture of a strength which will ignite when a spark appears. Where these devices are automatically controlled, they come off when the engine temperature has reached a certain level.

3   Over the years, the carburettor manufacturers have solved their various problems in different ways, all to some extent compromises, as is shown by the variety of carburettor designs. In the last few years, insistence on the reduction of atmospheric pollution has made the carburettor designers task more difficult. The electronic fuel injection system tackles these problems in an entirely different way from the traditional carburettor approach.

27 CI fuel system - control principle

1   The models in the Volvo 240 series having fuel injection engines are equipped with a CI system. CI stands for continuous injection, which means the injection valves of the system are always open, that is, are always injecting fuel when the engine is running. The amount of fuel is not controlled by variation of the injection time but through variation of the fuel flow through the injectors.

2   The CI system principle is to measure continuously the airflow into the engine and let this airflow control the amount of fuel fed to the engine. The measuring of the induced air and the control of the fuel flow is provided by an air-fuel control unit which is the 'heart' of the CI system. The air-fuel control unit consists of an airflow

Fig. 3.24. Fuel injection system - general lay-out (Sec. 27)

1 Injector	5 Intake manifold	8 Air cleaner	11 Fuel filter
2 Auxiliary air valve	6 Air flow sensor	9 Thermal time switch	12 Safety relay
3 Idle adjustment screw	7 Fuel distributor	10 Control pressure regulator	13 Pump relay
4 Cold start injector			

air flow sensor   fuel distributor

Fig. 3.25. Air-fuel control unit (Sec. 27)

Fig. 3.26. The air flow sensor - operation (Sec. 27)

1　Lever
2　Control plunger
3　Balance weight
4　Metering slot
5　Control plunger

Fig. 3.27. Air-fuel control unit - schematic (Sec. 27)

1　Air flow sensor plate
2　Lever
3　From fuel pump
4　Pressure regulating valve
5 . To injector
6　Control plunger head
7　To control pressure regulator
8　Plunger
9　Line pressure regulator
10　To fuel tank
11　Balance weight

sensor and a fuel distributor.

3　The airflow sensor consists of a plate in a venturi. The air flows upwards through the venturi and lifts the plate to let air pass through. A large airflow lifts the plate to a high position, a small airflow to a low position.

4　The movement of the airflow sensor plate is transferred by a lever to a control plunger in the fuel distributor. The lever is provided with a balance weight which equalizes the weight of the plate and the lever.

5　The control plunger is located in a cylinder which is provided with four metering slots, one for each engine cylinder. When lifted, the edge of the control plunger head uncovers the metering slots. A high airflow sensor plate position corresponds to a large uncovered metering slot area; a low position to a small area.

6　The difference between the fuel pressure ahead of the slot and after the slot must be constant in order to ensure that the quantity of fuel passing through the metering slots is proportional to the uncovered metering area. This is ensured by four pressure regulating valves, one for each metering slot, which maintain a constant pressure drop of 1.4 psi (0.1 kg/sq cm) over the slot.

7　Refer to Fig. 3.27. The dark shaded area shows the fuel flow to and from the slots, and the lightly shaded area shows a control pressure which prevents the control plunger from reacting too strongly to rapid increases of induced air.

28 Fuel injection system - general description

Air system

1　Besides the airflow control unit, the CI system consists of several other components. Figure 3.28 shows a diagram of the system.

2　The air cleaner has a replaceable paper type cartridge which should be replaced every 24,000 miles (40,000 km).

3　The airflow sensor controls the flow of air to provide a correct fuel-air mixture at all loads. The throttle is located in the intake manifold and is controlled by the throttle pedal. An idle adjustment screw is located in a channel bypassing the throttle. It increases or decreases the area of the bypass channel and thus controls the idling speed.

4　The auxiliary air valve is located on the intake manifold and like the idling adjustment screw, bypasses the throttle. A bi-metallic spring (Fig. 3.31) presses on the valve when the engine is cold and thereby the bypass air channel is kept open. Current flows through the coil when the starter motor is operated and when the engine is running. The coil heats the bi-metallic spring which decreases the pressure on the valve which is gradually closed by the coil spring.

Fuel system

5　The fuel system consists of the fuel pump, fuel accumulator, fuel filter, fuel distributor and injectors as well as the control pressure regulator and line pressure regulator. The components are described in the order the fuel travels through the system.

6　The fuel pump is a roller-type pump combined with an electric motor and is located in front of the fuel tank. If the fuel pressure should become excessive (pinched fuel line, etc.) a built-in relief valve allows the fuel to circulate inside the pump. In the rest position pressure is maintained in the system by a check valve in the fuel pump outlet (Fig. 3.32).

7　The fuel accumulator is located close to the fuel pump and helps accumulate and maintain pressure in the fuel system when the fuel pump check valve has closed (Fig. 3.33).

8　The fuel filter is located in the system between the fuel accumulator and the fuel distributor. The direction of flow is marked by arrows on the housing.

9　The fuel distributor controls the amount of fuel to the injectors in relation to the airflow. It consists of a line pressure regulator which controls the pressure to the fuel distributor; a control plunger, which controls and distributes the fuel to the injectors, and four pressure regulator valves which maintain a constant pressure difference between inlet and outlet of the control plunger (Fig. 3.34).

10　The line pressure regulator controls the fuel pressure to the fuel distributor. It closes the tank recirculation line if the fuel pressure is below 65.3 psi (4.6 kg/sq cm).

11　The fuel control unit plunger opens the metering slots according to the airflow sensor plate position, when the plate position is high more fuel is directed through the pressure regulating valves.

Air
Atmospheric
pressure

Air
Under
pressure

Fuel
Line pressure 4.5
kp/cm^2

Fuel
Pressure-
less

Fuel
Injection
pressure,
approx
3 kp/cm^2

Fuel
Control pressure, approx
3.7 kp/cm^2
(hot engine)

Fig. 3.28. The CI system - schematic diagram (Sec. 28)

1 Fuel tank
2 Fuel pump
3 Pressure accumulator
4 Fuel filter

5 Air cleaner
6 Air flow sensor
7 Fuel distributor
8 Throttle

9   Idle adjustment screw
10 Auxiliary air valve
11 Cold start injector
12 Intake manifold

13 Control pressure regulator
14 Injector

Fig. 3.29. Cut-away view of the air flow sensor (Sec. 28)

Fig. 3.30. Location of idling adjustment screw (Sec. 28)

1 Venturi
2 Sensor plate
3 Adjustment screw
4 Balance weight

5 Balance weight screw
6 Roller
7 Link
8 Lever

Fig. 3.31. Auxiliary air valve (Sec. 28)

1 Coil	3 Bi-metallic spring
2 Valve	4 Coil spring

Fig. 3.32. Fuel pump (Sec. 28)

1 Armature	4 Pump rotor
2 Relief valve	5 Outlet
3 Inlet	

Fig. 3.33. The fuel accumulator (Sec. 28)

1 Inlet	5 Stop
2 Outlet	6 Spring
3 Pressure chamber	7 Plunger
4 Diaphragm	

Fig. 3.34. The fuel distributor (Sec. 28)

1 Line pressure regulator	3 Pressure regulator valves
2 Control plunger	

15 The injectors have a spring-controlled valve which opens at a fuel pressure of 51 psi (3.6 kg/sq cm). The fuel pressure opens the valve and that makes the injection continuous, while the fuel flow varies according to the air inducted (Fig. 3.35).

16 The cold start injector supplies extra fuel for cold starting. The injection time is controlled by the thermal time switch and provides extra fuel for 12 seconds at −20ºC (5ºF). The cold start injector is injecting fuel only when the starter motor is operating. It stops injecting fuel if the engine starts, and the starter stops operating, before the time permitted by the thermal time switch is up (Fig. 3.36).

17 The thermal time switch determines the cold start injector operating time. It is a sealed unit, having contacts controlled by a bi-metallic spring. The bi-metallic spring has two coils one activated from the cold start injector and the other from the starter. The contacts are closed at below +35ºC (95ºF). When the starter operates current flows from the starter to the cold start injector and, via a coil and the contacts, to earth. At the same time current flows from the starter, via the second coil and the contacts, to earth. The cold start injector operates as long as the contacts are closed and the starter is operating. The current flowing from the starter to the coil heats the bi-metallic spring, the contacts open and the cold start injector stops operating. The heating time varies with the engine temperature: the warmer the engine the shorter the heating time for the bi-metallic spring and consequently also the injection time.

12 Some of the fuel from the fuel distributor inlet is diverted to the control plunger top side. From there it travels first to a control pressure regulator and then to the tank. The control pressure is controlled by the control pressure regulator and is normally 53 ± 2.8 psi (3.7 ± 0.2 kg/sq cm). The control pressure fuel acts on top of the control plunger and dampens the movement of the airflow sensor plate during fast acceleration.

13 The control pressure regulator controls, during the warm-up period, the control pressure in relation to the engine temperature so that the fuel mixture is enriched .

14 The pressure regulating valves provide a constant pressure drop across the metering slots, independent of the amount of fuel passing through the slots. This is necessary in order to achieve an injection rate proportional to the positions of the control plunger and the airflow sensor plate.

Fig. 3.35. Fuel injector (Sec. 28)

1   Retainer   3   Spring
2   Injector body   4   Valve

Fig. 3.36. Cold start injector (Sec. 28)

1   Solenoid coil   3   Actuator
2   Return spring   4   Gasket

Fig. 3.37. Thermal time switch (Sec. 28)

1   Contacts   3   Lead to starter motor
2   Bi-metallic spring   4   Lead to cold start injector

Fig. 3.38. Electrical system (Sec. 28)

1   Starter motor   7   Cold start injector
2   Ignition coil   8   Air-fuel control unit
3   Fuse box   9   Auxiliary air valve
4   Main relay   10 Control pressure regulator
5   Fuel pump relay   11 Fuel pump
6   Thermal time switch

Electrical system

18 Figure 3.38 shows the layout of the electrical system and the electrical system wiring diagram is shown in Fig. 3.39.

19 When the ignition is switched on, current flows from the ignition coil terminal '15' to the main relay terminal '86', through the relay coil to terminal '85' and finally to the air-fuel control unit and earth. The main relay is thus activated.

20 When the ignition key is turned to the starting position, current flows from the starter terminal '50' to the main relay terminal '87', through the closed contacts to terminal '30' and to the pump relay terminal '86'. From there through the relay coil to terminal '85' and earth. The pump relay is thus activated.

21 Current flows from fuse '7' to the pump relay terminal '30', through the closed contacts to terminal '87', to the fuel pump and earth. The fuel pump is thus activated and pumps fuel. The control pressure regulator and the auxiliary air valve are activated at the same time as the fuel pump.

22 When the starter motor is operating or after the engine has started, the contacts at the air-fuel control unit open, the earth circuit is opened, and the main relay is deactivated. Current now flows from terminal '86' to terminal '87a', through the contacts to terminal '30'. The fuel pump relay is still activated and the pump is operating.

There is no current flow to the main relay terminal '87' when the engine is running and the starter motor not operating.

23 If the engine stops (with the ignition still switched on), the contacts at the air-fuel control unit close. Main relay terminal '85' is earthed, the relay is activated, and terminal '30' is connected to terminal '87'. As there is no current flow to terminal '87', the pump relay is deactivated and the fuel pump stops working.

24 The cold start injector is activated only when the starter motor is operating and the engine temperature at the same time is so low that the thermal time switch cuts in.

25 The illustrations used are of a B20E engine which has the induction system on the right-hand side of the engine. On B21E engines the induction system is on the left-hand side of the engine, otherwise the two systems are basically the same.

29 Fuel tank filter - cleaning

1   The filter should be cleaned at intervals of 15,000 miles (25,000 km).
2   Remove the plug from the bottom of the tank (Fig. 3.40) and clean it.
3   When refitting, ensure that the suction pipe is centred in the flange

hole, otherwise the filter can get damaged and, at worst, this could shut off the fuel supply.

30 Fuel tank - description, removal and refitting

1   The fuel tank is mounted at the rear of the car and is of a fuel evaporative control type.
2   To remove the tank, withdraw the floor panel from the boot,

Fig. 3.39. CI fuel system wiring diagram (Sec. 28) (see caption to Fig. 3.38)

disconnect all hoses and electrical leads from the tank, unscrew and remove the mounting screws. Cut round the sealing mastic and lift the tank out.
3   On cars fitted with a fuel evaporative control system the fumes from the tank are stored in a canister charged with activated charcoal until the engine is started when the fumes and vapour are drawn from the canister into the inlet manifold or duct and burned during the normal combustion cycle.
4   No maintenance is necessary except to occasionally check the security of the connecting hoses.
5   Refitting of the tank is a reversal of removal but always renew the sealing mastic round the edge of the fuel tank mounting.

31 Fuel tank sender unit - removal and refitting

Removal of the fuel tank sender unit is described in Section 8 of Chapter 3, Part A.

32 Air-fuel control unit - removal and refitting

1   Clean round all the fuel connections before disconnecting them.
2   Remove the rubber bellows and the strap for the injector pipes.
3   Remove the injector pipes and the control pressure pipe from the distributor.
4   Disconnect the cold start injector and recirculation pipe lines. Pull at the electrical plug connection.
5   Disconnect the fuel line at the filter.
6   Remove the air-fuel control unit retaining screws and lift it out. Collect the gasket.
7   Refitting is the reverse of the removal sequence. Always fit a new gasket.

Fig. 3.40. Fuel tank (Secs. 29 and 30)

1   Fuel output
2   Level sender unit
3   Hose connecting tank and
    equalizing valve
4   Venting filter hose
5   Equalizing valve
6   Connection for return line
7   Hose
8   Breather pipe
9   Equalizing hose
10 Expansion tank
11 Baffle can
12 Fuel filter

Fig. 3.40a. Fuel tank filter (Sec. 29)

Fig. 3.41. Removing the air-fuel control unit (Sec. 32)

33 Air-fuel control unit - dismantling and inspection

1   Clamp the unit lightly in a vice, do not use force or you are likely to damage it.

2   Remove the three securing screws and carefully lift off the fuel distributor taking care that the control plunger does not fall out and get damaged. **Note:** The fuel distributor must not be dismantled.

3   Remove the two retaining screws and lift off the bridge piece.

4   Remove the balance weight.

5   Remove the lever with the adjustment arm by removing the circlip, washer, rubber seal, springs and balls as well as the shaft.

Fig. 3.42. Removing the bridge piece (Sec. 33)

Fig. 3.43. Undoing the screw to remove the balance weight (Sec. 33)

Fig. 3.44. Using circlip pliers when removing the adjustment arm shaft retaining circlip (Sec. 33)

6   Wash the control plunger in petrol and blow it off with compressed air. Check the plunger for damage. If the plunger is worn or damaged, the fuel distributor must be renewed; any attempt to clean the slots will do more harm than good. Renew any worn or damaged parts.

34 Air-fuel control unit - reassembly

1   Place the lever and adjustment arm in position. The adjustment arm should be positioned so that the roller for the control plunger is towards the fuel distributor. Fit the shaft, balls, spring, rubber seals, washers and circlips.

2   Fit the balance weight and centre the lever. Tighten the balance weight screw.

3   Fit the sensor plate stop so that the spring and contact are on the right side, Fig. 3.46.

4   Centre the airflow sensor plate. The sensor plate must not touch the venturi at any point. If adjustment is needed, loosen the plate screw and reposition the plate.

5   Check that with the airflow sensor plate at rest it is level with or no more than 0.039 in (1 mm) below the venturi edge. Adjust, if necessary, at 'A' in Fig. 3.47, with needle nosed pliers.

6   Check the sensor plate for freedom of movement from low to high positions.

7   Fit the fuel distributor, taking care to avoid damaging the central plunger and O-ring. Always fit a new gasket. Tighten the retaining screws to 2.3-2.7 lb f ft (0.31-0.37 kg f m).

Fig. 3.45. Fitting the lever and adjusting arm (Sec. 34)

1	Housing	7	Circlip
2	Spring	8	Screw
3	Shaft	9	Balance weight
4	Ball	10	Lever
5	Seal	11	Adjusting arm
6	Washer	12	Sensor plate

Fig. 3.46. Fitting the air flow sensor plate (Sec. 34)

Fig. 3.47. Air flow sensor plate adjustment (Sec. 34)

Fig. 3.48. Exploded view of line pressure regulator (Sec. 35)

A O-ring
B Plunger
C Spring
D Shim
E Copper washer
F Plug

Fig. 3.49. Pressure gauge connected between the fuel distributor and the control pressure regulator (Sec. 36)

35 Line pressure regulator - testing

1 Refer to Fig. 3.48. Remove the plug taking care not to lose the shims in the plug.
2 Pull out the plunger and the spring. Remove the 'O' ring from the plunger.
3 Clean the parts and check them for damage. Renew defective parts, except the plunger which cannot be changed as it is matched with the fuel distributor. If it is defective change the distributor.
4 Fit a new 'O' ring on the plunger and refit the assembly using the same shims as were removed.

36 Line and rest pressure - testing

Line pressure
1 Connect a pressure gauge, with a three-way control lever as shown in Fig. 3.49, between the fuel distributor and the control pressure regulator.
2 Switch on the ignition and disconnect the lead at the airflow sensor, to start the fuel pump.
3 Check the line pressure on the gauge. It should be 65-75 psi (4.6-5.3 kg/sq cm).

4 If the line pressure is low the reasons could be as follows:

  a) *Fuel line leakage. Check and rectify.*
  b) *Line pressure regulator incorrectly adjusted. Adjust, as described in Section 37.*
  c) *If there is no line pressure with the pump operating, check for blockage of the fuel lines, filters or fuel distributor.*
  d) *Fuel pump defective.*

5 Excessively high pressure could be caused by:

  a) *Blocked recirculation line.*
  b) *Line pressure regulator incorrectly adjusted, refer to Section 37.*

Rest pressure
6 Reconnect the electrical lead to the airflow sensor.
7 After a few seconds check the rest pressure reading on the gauge. It should be 24 psi (1.7 kg/sq cm) minimum and 53 psi (3.7 kg/sq cm) maximum (injector opening pressure). Check that there is no noticeable drop in pressure within one minute. If the pressure is incorrect refer to Section 37, and adjust the line pressure regulator.
8 If the rest pressure drops too quickly check as follows:

  a) *Turn the lever on the gauge towards the control pressure regulator. If the pressure still drops too fast the control pressure regulator or its fuel lines are leaking and should be replaced.*
  b) *Block the fuel recirculation line after the fuel distributor. If the pressure stops dropping, the line pressure regulator or its 'O' ring is faulty. Refer to line pressure regulator checking, Section 35.*
  c) *Turn the gauge lever at right-angles to the connection from the fuel distributor. Remove the airflow sensor lead for a few seconds to bring up the line pressure, then reconnect the lead. Pinch the fuel feed hose from the tank to the pump. If the fuel pressure stops falling the fuel pump check valve is defective.*
  d) *Check the fuel lines for leaks.*

37 Line pressure regulator - adjustment

1 To adjust the line and rest pressure remove or add shims, as necessary, in the line pressure regulator.
2 There are two thicknesses of shims:

  0.0039 in (0.1 mm) = 0.8 psi (0.06 kg/sq cm) pressure difference
  C.0196 in (0.5 mm) = 4.3 psi (0.3 kg/sq cm) pressure difference

Use mainly the thick shims for adjustment. The thin shims are used when the line pressure is 69 psi (4.9 kg/sq cm) or more and the rest pressure at the same time is more than 24 psi (1.7 kg/sq cm).
Note: Both the line pressure and rest pressure are affected at the same time.

38 Control pressure - testing

  The engine must be cold (at ambient temperature) when the control pressure is being checked.
1 Connect the pressure gauge between the fuel distributor and the control pressure regulator with the gauge lever at right-angles to the connection to the fuel distributor.
2 Switch on the ignition and start the fuel pump by disconnecting the lead at the airflow sensor.
3 Check the control pressure against the chart, Fig. 3.50. As you can see from the chart the control pressure at 20°C (68°F) should be 20.6-24.8 psi (1.45-1.75 kg/sq cm).
4 If the control pressure is too low, try a new control pressure regulator. If the pressure is too high, the recirculation line may be blocked. If it is open, try a new control pressure regulator.
5 Reconnect the lead at the airflow sensor and switch off the ignition.

Fig. 3.50. Control pressure chart (Sec. 38)

Fig. 3.51. Replacing the cold start injector (Sec. 41)

Fig. 3.52. Replacing the auxiliary air valve (Sec. 43)

39 Injector - removal and refitting

1   Clean round the fuel injector and fuel pipe. Disconnect the fuel pipe.
2   Remove the injector retainer and the injector.
3   When refitting the injector fit a new rubber seal.
4   Reconnect the fuel pipe. Start the engine and check for leaks.

40 Injectors - testing

1   Check the injectors at rest pressure.
2   Remove the injector with the fuel line connected.
3   Lift the airflow sensor plate so that the metering slots in the fuel distributor open.
4   Injectors must not leak more than one drop in 15 seconds. Renew

leaking injectors. **Note:** If all the injectors leak the reason may be an excessive rest pressure, see Section 36.

41 Cold start injector - removal and refitting

1   Disconnect the electrical plug. Clean round the fuel pipe connection and disconnect the pipe.
2   Remove the two retaining screws and the cold start injector and seal.
3   Refit the injector, use a new seal, and fit the retaining screws.
4   Reconnect the fuel pipe and electrical plug.

42 Cold start injector - testing

1   With the engine cold remove the cold start injector, leaving the fuel and electrical supply connected.
2   Hold the injector over a container (a glass jar is ideal), switch on the ignition and run the starter motor.
3   The cold start injector should spray for 12 seconds at an engine temperature of −20°C (−4°F), Higher temperatures decrease the injection time and it ceases completely above +35°C (95°F).
4   If no fuel appears, remove the plug and check that when the starter motor is turned, 12V appears across the socket pins. If it does the injector must be faulty and will have to be renewed. If there is no voltage the wiring or thermal time switch is faulty.

43 Auxiliary air valve - removal and refitting

1   Disconnect the plug and hoses.
2   Remove the retaining screws and the auxiliary air valve.
3   When replacing the valve do not forget to connect the earth wire to one of the retaining screws.
4   Reconnect the hoses and plug.

44 Auxiliary air valve - testing

1   Remove the hoses and electrical connection.
2   Check that the valve is open, it should be half open at +20°C (68°F). It is completely closed when the engine is hot. Use a mirror and a light to check.
3   Reconnect the electrical plug. The valve should close completely within 5 minutes.
4   If the valve has not closed, tap lightly on the valve, if it closes it is OK (engine vibrations normally contribute to closing).
5   If it stays open check for voltage at the plug; if the voltage is ok, replace the air auxiliary valve.

45 Control pressure regulator - removal and refitting

1   Clean round the fuel line connections.
2   Remove the straps from the fuel lines and disconnect the hose from the fuel distributor and the return hose. Remove the electrical plug connection.
3   Remove the two retaining screws and the control pressure regulator. Disconnect the fuel supply hose.
4   Refit the pressure regulator and connect the hoses and plug. Do not forget the earth wire which should be connected to one of the retaining screws.
5   Check the control pressure: refer to Section 38.

46 Fuel filter - removal and refitting

1   Clean round the hose connections.
2   Disconnect the hoses, remove the attaching screws and the filter.
3   Remove the unions and washers from the filter and fit them on the replacement filter.
4   Refit the filter and connect the pipe lines. An arrow on the filter casing shows the direction of flow, make sure it is the right way round.
5   Switch on the ignition. Disconnect the plug at the airflow sensor and check that the fuel filter connections are not leaking.

6   Reconnect the plug at the airflow sensor and switch off the ignition.

47 Thermal time switch - testing

1   Run the engine until the temperature is above +35°C (+95°F).

Fig. 3.53. Replacing the control pressure regulator

Fig. 3.54. Removing the fuel filter

Fig. 3.55. Fuel pump and accumulator assembly

1 Outlet hose	5 Guard plate
2 Accumulator	6 Inlet hose
3 Bracket	7 Fuel pump
4 Rubber mounting	8 Pump to accumulator hose

2   Remove the cold start injector and hold it over a glass jar. Operate the starter motor.
3   The cold start injector should not spray, as the engine is hot. If it does spray, the thermal timer switch is faulty and should be renewed.
4   Refit the cold start injector.

48 Thermal time switch - removal and refitting

1   Disconnect the electrical lead.
2   Partly drain the coolant or have a small plug ready to block the orifice, then unscrew the timer from the block.
3   Replace the timer and reconnect the electrical lead.
4   Top-up the coolant system.

49 Fuel pump and accumulator - removal and refitting

1   Clean round all the hose connections so that dirt will not get into the pump.
2   Disconnect the battery earth terminal.
3   Pinch the fuel inlet hose with a clamp.
4   Disconnect the fuel inlet and outlet hoses.
5   Remove the retaining nuts, the fuel pump and accumulator, and the guard plate.
6   Disconnect the electrical plug and the fuel accumulator hoses.
7   Separate the bracket, rubber mountings, accumulator and fuel pump.
8   Refitting is the reverse of removal. Always fit a new fuel hose between the fuel accumulator and the fuel pump at every removal.

50 Fuel pump check valve - renewal

1   Remove the fuel pump, as described in Section 44.
2   Clamp the pump in a vice by its bracket. Never hold the pump other than by the bracket.
3   Screw out the check valve and make sure that no dirt enters the pump.
4   Refit the check valve, always use a new gasket. Torque tighten to 12 - 16 lb f ft (1.6 - 2.2 kg f m). Do not overtighten as you will damage the threads in the fuel pump housing.
5   Refit the fuel pump: refer to Section 49.

51 Throttle plate - adjustment

1   Loosen the locknut and turn the stop screw out until it is clear of the throttle lever stop (Fig. 3.57).
2   Turn the screw in, until it touches the stop, then a further ½ turn. Tighten the locknut.
3   Check that the throttle shaft lever touches the full throttle stop when the throttle pedal is fully depressed.

52 Idling speed - adjustment

1   Run the engine until it is at normal running temperature.
2   Adjust the idling speed to 900 rpm, manual transmission, or 800

Fig. 3.56. Fuel pump check valve

1 Gasket	2 Check valve

rpm automatic transmission, with the throttle closed by turning the idling adjustment screw (see Fig. 3.30).

3   If the idling speed cannot be lowered to the specified speed, the throttle valve plate must be slightly open, check the setting, as described in Section 51.

53 Air filter - element renewal

1   Release the clamps securing the rubber bellows and remove the bellows.
2   Disconnect the electrical plug at the fuel distributor.
3   Undo the clips and remove the air cleaner upper part including the fuel distributor and move it to the side.
4   Remove the air cleaner element and fit a new replacement.
5   Refit the upper part of the cleaner and the rubber bellows. Reconnect the electrical plug at the fuel distributor.

Fig. 3.57. Throttle plate adjustment (Sec. 51)

Fig. 3.58. Replacing the air cleaner filter element (Sec. 53)

54 Emission control systems - general description

1   In order to reduce engine and exhaust pollution to a minimum, various control systems are used. Certain devices (EGR; Air Injection System; Catalytic Converter; Lambda-sond sensor) are not fitted to all cars, but only to those vehicles destined for territories where stringent control regulations are in force.
2   The crankcase breather system and the fuel evaporative control system (see Sections 20 and 22) are integral parts of the overall emission control system.
3   The EGR (Exhaust Gas Recirculation) system is a method of re-cycling the engine exhaust gases by returning them to the combustion chambers where they reduce the combustion temperature and restrict the volume of noxious gases produced.
4   The arrangement includes a vacuum-operated valve, an air shutter and connecting pipes.
5   The Air Injection System is a method of injecting clean air to the exhaust ports in order to promote the complete combustion of exhaust gases before they are emitted from the exhaust system. The air supply is taken from the 'clean' side of the air cleaner, compressed by an air pump, which is driven by a belt from the engine crankshaft pulley and injected through a nozzle.
6   Components of the system include a diverter valve, an anti-backfire valve and an air manifold.
7   A Catalytic Converter is a device fitted to the exhaust system ahead of the silencer. It is made up of ceramic cores coated with platinum palladium which act as catalysts to absorb combustible elements remaining in the exhaust gases without being destroyed themselves.
8   See Section 59 for details of the Lambda-sond sensor.

Fig. 3.59. EGR valve (Sec. 54)

Fig. 3.60. Air injection system (exhaust emission control) (Sec. 54)

1   Air pump   3   Backfire valve
2   Diverter valve   4   Air manifold

55 EGR valve - servicing/mileage recorder - resetting

1   Every 25,000 miles (40,000 km) the EGR valve should be cleaned and checked. A mileage recorder is fitted under the fascia panel which causes two contacts to close at the specified mileage and to light up a warning lamp on the instrument panel as a reminder to the driver that the valve is due for servicing.

2   To clean the valve, disconnect the connecting pipes and unscrew and remove it. Using a wire brush clean away all the deposits, also clean the intake manifold nipple.

3   To reset the mileage recorder after having serviced the valve, remove the rear cover on the odometer and then depress the reset button (Fig. 3.64).

Fig. 3.61. Diverter valve (Sec. 54)

Fig. 3.62. Anti-backfire valve (flame trap) (Sec. 54)

Fig. 3.63. Catalytic converter (Sec. 54)

1   Stainless steel cover   3   Steel wool
2   Ceramic material

4   The EGR valve should be renewed at intervals of 30,000 miles (48,000 km).

5   To check the operation of the EGR system after refitting the valve, connect the distributor vacuum hose to the EGR vacuum chamber, start the engine and let it idle. The engine should run unevenly or stall. If this does not occur check that the return pipe and the EGR line are not blocked. If the pipes are clear and the engine still runs smoothly renew the valve complete.

56 Throttle and micro-switch - adjustment

1   Switch on the ignition (do not start the engine).

2   Disconnect the lead at the micro-switch (this is the lead connected between the micro-switch and the solenoid valve) and connect a test lamp in series between the disconnected lead and the micro-switch terminal.

3   Release the locknut on the throttle plate stop screw and back off its screw so it does not interfere with setting the throttle adjustment. The test light should go out and stay out for now.

4   Turn the throttle plate stop screw until it touches the stop, and then a further ½ turn. Tighten the locknut. Check that the throttle plate is free and does not stick in the closed position.

5   Insert a 0.060 in (1.5 mm) feeler gauge under the throttle stop screw, Fig. 3.66. The test light should still be out.

6   Screw in the micro-switch screw until the light just comes on. You will also hear the switch click. Tighten the locknut and remove the feeler gauge. Reconnect the micro-switch lead.

Note: Whenever the throttle plate adjustment screw is adjusted the micro-switch must also be adjusted.

7   To check the adjustment, insert a 0.056 in (1.4 mm) feeler gauge under the throttle plate stop screw - the test light should stay on. Insert a 0.072 in (1.8 mm) feeler gauge under the stop screw and the light should go out.

Fig. 3.64. Mileage recorder fitted in conjunction with EGR valve - arrow indicates reset button (Sec. 55)

Fig. 3.65. Adjusting the throttle plate stop screw (Sec. 56)

Fig. 3.66. Adjusting the micro switch (Sec. 56)

1.5 mm
0.060"

Fig. 3.67. Rear exhaust silencer installation diagram - arrow points to front of car (Secs. 24 and 58)

15°

56

VOLVO

Fig. 3.68. Lambda-sond oxygen sensor (Sec. 59)

57 Air Injection System and Catalytic Converter - testing

1   Regular maintenance consists of maintaining the tension of the compressor drivebelt and the security of all hose connections. The compressor drivebelt should have a deflection of 0.5 in (12.7 mm) at the centre of its longest run. To adjust the belt, slacken the mounting and adjustment bolt. If the drivebelt breaks, the anti-backfire valve must be renewed.
2   The compressor is a lubricant-sealed type and when faulty must be exchanged for a new unit.
3   The diverter valve is located on the engine compartment rear bulkhead and the anti-backfire valve (flametrap) is mounted on the air manifold.
4   To check the anti-backfire valve disconnect the discharge hose at the diverter valve. Suck the hose and check for leakage. If leaking, renew the anti-backfire valve.
5   To check the diverter valve disconnect the discharge hose and block it with a plug (preventative measure). Check that air is blowing from the discharge hole when the engine is idling. (Do not attempt to block the outlet, especially at high speeds, as this could ruin the compressor if the diverter valve is defective). If the diverter valve is faulty it must be renewed.
6   A defective catalytic converter is indicated by excessive CO readings. It is renewed as a unit.

58 Exhaust system (all models) - removal and refitting

1   The exhaust system is suspended on rubber rings and shackles.
2   To remove the system, remove the pre-heater plate (carburettor engines) or the air cleaner, battery and EGR valve hose (fuel injection engines).
3   Disconnect the intermediate pipe from the front silencer. Plenty of freeing fluid will be required for this!
4   Remove the rubber suspension rings from the front silencer.
5   Remove the rubber suspension shackles from the rear silencer and lower the intermediate pipe, rear silencer and tailpipe, all joined together.
6   Disconnect the exhaust downpipe brackets from the transmission and unbolt the downpipe from the manifold.
7   The foregoing operations should be followed if only certain sections of the system are to be renewed. If the complete system must be renewed, then it will be much easier if the old pipes are sawn through with a hacksaw in short lengths for removal.
8   When installing the new system, de-burr the connecting sockets and smear them with grease. Fit new clamps and suspension components if necessary.
9   Refitting is a reversal of removal but make sure that the rear silencer is inclined forward as shown in the diagram before tightening the pipe clamps (Fig. 3.67).

59 Lambda-sond sensor - general

1   Some 1977 models are fitted with Lambda-sond oxygen sensing device.
2   This device senses the level of oxygen in the exhaust gases. Should the level of oxygen exceed the optimum level the Lambda-sond unit triggers the fuel injection system to alter the air/fuel mixture being fed into the engine. This allows the Catalytic Converter to operate in optimum conditions and therefore ensures a really 'clean' exhaust.
3   The Lambda-sond oxygen sensor has an appearance somewhat similar to a spark plug and will be found screwed into the exhaust manifold, just above the downpipe flange. It is connected by a plug and electrical lead to an electronic module, then connected to a frequency valve on the fuel distributor.
4   The unit requires renewal at 15,000 miles (24,000 km) and the owner will be reminded of this when the 'EXH' light glows.

Fig. 3.69. Lambda-sond electronic module (Sec. 59)

Fig. 3.70. Lambda-sond frequency valve (Sec. 59)

60 Fault diagnosis - fuel injection system

We give in this Section a table detailing a few of the symptoms of fuel system trouble, possible causes and remedies. Always bear in mind that it is very difficult to distinguish between ignition faults and fuel system faults in many cases. The golden rule should be - before starting on the fuel system - make 100% certain of the ignition. Ignition faults are easy to check, ignition adjustments, when required, are easy to make, and furthermore when adjustment is required as a result of normal wear and tear this adjustment is much more likely to be in the ignition than in the fuel system. The following table assumes that all is in order in the ignition department.

Symptom	Reason/s
Smell of petrol when engine is stopped	Leaking fuel pipes or unions. Leaking fuel tank.
Smell of petrol when engine is idling	Leaking fuel lines or unions in fuel distribution system.
Difficult starting with cold engine	Leak in the intake system. Airflow sensor plate maladjusted. Fuel distributor or airflow sensor sticking or binding. Line pressure too low. Control pressure too high. Auxiliary air valve not opening. Cold start injector faulty. Thermal time switch faulty. Blocked fuel lines or filters.
Difficult starting with warm engine	Leak in the intake system. Airflow sensor plate maladjusted. Fuel distributor or airflow sensor sticking or binding. Line pressure too low. Cold start injector leaking. Air-fuel control unit leaking. Control pressure incorrect. Rest pressure incorrect. Injectors leaking.
Uneven running	Control pressure incorrect. Cold start injector leaking. Air-fuel control unit leaking. Auxiliary air valve not closing. Injectors leaking. Defective injector 'O'-ring seal. Air leak in intake system.
Poor performance, lack of power	Cold start injector leaking. Control pressure too high. Fuel starvation, blocked fuel lines, filters, injectors or fuel distributor. Intake system leaking.
Excessive fuel consumption not accounted for by external leaks	Control pressure too low. Cold start injector leaking. Faulty injectors.

Chapter 4 Ignition system

For modifications, and information applicable to later models, see Supplement at end of manual

Contents

Specifications

Ignition type

B20A, B21A	With breaker
B20E, B21E	Breakerless
Voltage	12 volts
Firing order	1 - 3 - 4 - 2

Ignition setting (vacuum disconnected)

At rev/min	700 - 800	2500
B20A	10° BTDC	23 - 27 BTDC
B20E	5° BTDC	
B21A 1975	12° BTDC	24 - 28 BTDC
B21A 1976 to 1979	15° BTDC	32 - 36 BTDC
B21E	8° BTDC	29 - 33 BTDC

Spark plugs

B20A	Bosch W 175T35
B20E	Bosch 200T35
B21A	Bosch W 175T30
B21E	Bosch W 200T30
Spark plug gap	0.028 - 0.031 in (0.7 - 0.8 mm)

Distributor

	B20A	B21A	B20E	B21E
Type No.	JFU4	JFU4	–	JGFU4
Direction of rotation	Anticlockwise	Clockwise	Anticlockwise	Clockwise
Contact breaker gap, in (mm)	0.014 (0.35)	0.016 (0.40)	–	–
Dwell angle at 500 rev/min	62 ± 3°	62 ± 3°	–	–

Ignition coil ... ...

Bosch 12V

Torque wrench setting

Spark plug	18 - 22 lb f ft (2.5 - 3 kg f m)

1 General description

1 Two types of ignition system are used on the Volvo 240 series: a conventional battery, coil and mechanical contact breaker type on carburettor engine, and on fuel injection engines a breakerless distributor is used. In the breakerless type the contact points have been replaced by an impulse sender. An electronic module has been added and triggering contacts are incorporated in the base of the distributor.

2 In order that the engine can run correctly it is necessary for an electrical spark to ignite the fuel/air mixture in the combustion chamber at exactly the right moment in relation to engine speed and load. The ignition system is based on feeding low tension (LT) voltage from the battery to the coil where it is converted to high tension (HT) voltage. The high tension voltage is powerful enough to jump the spark plug gap in the cylinders many times a second under high compression pressures, providing that the system is in good condition

and that all adjustments are correct.

3 The ignition system is divided into two circuits: the low tension circuit and the high tension circuit.

4 In the contact breaker type system, the low tension (sometimes known as the primary) circuit consists of the battery lead to the ignition switch, lead from the ignition switch to the low tension or primary coil windings, and the lead from the low tension coil windings to the contact breaker points and condenser in the distributor.

5 The high tension circuit consists of the high tension or secondary coil windings, the heavy ignition lead from the centre of the coil to the centre of the distributor cap, the rotor arm, and the spark plug leads and spark plugs.

6 The system functions in the following manner: Low tension voltage is changed in the coil into high tension voltage by the opening and closing of the contact breaker points in the low tension circuit. High tension voltage is then fed via the carbon brush in the centre of the distributor cap to the rotor arm of the distributor cap, and each time it

Fig. 4.1. B20A engine ignition system (distributor with contact breaker) (Sec. 1). LT circuit indicated by thick line

comes in line with one of the metal segments in the cap, which are connected to the spark plug leads, the opening and closing of the contact breaker points causes the high tension voltage to build up, jump the gap from the rotor arm to the appropriate metal segment and so via the spark plug lead to the spark plug, where it finally jumps the spark plug gap before going to earth.

7   The ignition is advanced and retarded automatically, to ensure the spark occurs at just the right instant for the particular load at the prevailing engine speed.

8   The ignition advance is controlled both mechanically and by a vacuum operated system. The mechanical governor mechanism comprises two weights, which move out from the distributor shaft, and so advance the spark. The weights are held in position by two light springs and it is the tension of the springs which is largely responsible for correct spark advancement.

9   The vacuum control consists of a diaphragm, one side of which is connected via a small bore tube to the carburettor, and the other side to the contact breaker plate. Depression in the inlet manifold and carburettor, which varies with engine speed and throttle opening, causes the diaphragm to move, so moving the contact breaker plate, and advancing or retarding the spark. A fine degree of control is achieved by a spring in the vacuum advance.

10 The various components of the breakerless electronic system are shown in Fig. 4.2. The distributor now contains a magnetic coil and a rotor disc which functions as an impulse sender.

11 An impulse goes from the distributor to the control unit. This closes and breaks the current to the ignition coil with the help of impulses from the impulse sender. Moreover, the dwell angle is regulated electronically. From the ignition coil the high tension impulse goes as usual to the spark plugs via the distributor rotor arm.

12 The ignition advance is still controlled by means of centrifugal weights and a vacuum chamber.

2   Contact breaker points - adjustment

1   Remove the distributor cap, the rotor arm and the protective cover. Clean the cap inside and out with a dry cloth. It is unlikely that the segments will be badly burned or scored, but if they are, the cap will have to be replaced.

2   Inspect the carbon brush in the top of the distributor cap and press it into its recess to test the spring.

3   Check the condition of the rotor arm and renew it if the metal contact is burned or loose. Slight burning can be cleaned up with a fine file.

4   Prise the contact breaker points apart and examine the condition of their faces. If they are rough, pitted or dirty, it will be necessary to remove them for resurfacing or for replacement points to be fitted.

5   With the points in a satisfactory condition, turn the engine till the heel of the breaker arm is on the highest point of one of the cams.

6   Measure the gap with a feeler gauge, it should be 0.014 in (0.35 mm)

2.6 Measuring the contact breaker gap

for B20A engines and 0.016 in (0.40 mm) for B21A engines (photo).

7   If the gap varies from this amount slacken the contact plate securing screw.

8   Place a screwdriver blade between the two 'pips' on the contact set and open or close the movable arm until the gap is correct. Tighten the securing screw.

9   On modern engines, setting the contact breaker gap in this way must be regarded as an initial setting only. For optimum engine performance, the dwell angle must be checked. The dwell angle is the number of degrees through which the distributor cam turns during the period between the instants of closure and opening of the contact breaker points. This can only be checked with a dwell meter. The correct dwell angle is as shown in Specifications. If the dwell angle is too large, increase the points gap; if it is too small, reduce the points gap.

10 With the gap correctly set, apply a smear of petroleum jelly to the high points of the distributor cam and refit the rotor arm and distributor cap. On some distributors an external lubricator is fitted into which two or three drops of engine oil should be injected.

3   Contact breaker points - renewal

1   Prise the springs which secure the distributor cap and withdraw the

Fig. 4.2. Breakerless electronic ignition system (Sec. 1)

1 *Battery*	4 *Pre-engaging resistance*	7 *Distributor cap*
2 *Ignition switch*	5 *Starter motor*	8 *Impulse sender*
3 *Control unit*	6 *Ignition coil*	9 *Spark plugs*

cap and lay it to one side.

2 Pull off the rotor arm, and remove the protective cover (if fitted).

3 Disconnect the low tension (LT) lead from the terminal on the inside of the distributor body.

4 Unscrew and remove the contact breaker securing screw and lift the contact breaker assembly from the baseplate.

5 Inspect the faces of the contact points. If they are only lightly burned or pitted then they may be ground square on an oilstone or by rubbing a carborundum strip between them. Where the points are found to be severely burned or pitted, then they must be renewed and at the same time the cause of the erosion of the points established. This is most likely to be due to poor earth connections from the battery negative lead to body earth or the engine to earth strap. Remove the connecting bolts at these points, scrape the surfaces free from rust and corrosion and tighten the bolts using a star type lock washer. Other screws to check for security are: the baseplate to distributor body securing screws; the distributor body to lockplate bolt. Looseness in any of these could contribute to a poor earth connection. Check the condenser (Section 5).

6 Refitting the contact breaker assembly is a reversal of removal and when fitted, adjust the points gap as described in the preceding Section. Lubricate the high points of the cam and apply two or three drops of engine oil to the felt pad on top of the distributor shaft.

4 Distributor (breakerless type) - maintenance

1 No routine maintenance operations are required on this type of distributor except to check that all leads, connections and vacuum hoses are secure.

5 Condenser - removal and testing

1 The condenser ensures that with the contact breaker points open, the sparking between them is not excessive to cause severe pitting. The condenser is fitted in parallel and its failure will automatically cause failure of the ignition system as the points will be prevented from interrupting the low tension circuit.

2 Testing for an unserviceable condenser may be effected by switching on the ignition and separating the contact points by hand. If this action is accompanied by a blue flash then condenser failure is indicated. Difficult starting, missing of the engine after several miles running, or badly pitted points are other indications of a faulty condenser.

3 The surest test is by substitution of a new unit.

4 The condenser may be internally or externally mounted according to distributor type but is simply removed after withdrawing the single securing screw.

6 Distributor - removal and replacement

1 Remove the distributor cap (photo).

2 Disconnect the low tension lead and the vacuum hose from the distributor.

3 On cars equipped with fuel injection system, disconnect the leads from the triggering contact assembly.

4 Unscrew and remove the flange bolts and withdraw the distributor from the engine.

5 Replace the distributor as described in Chapter 1, Section 32 or 57.

6 Refit the distributor cap, reconnect the low tension lead and the

triggering contact lead, (if applicable). Refit the vacuum hose to the vacuum capsule.

7 Distributor (contact breaker type) - dismantling

1   Remove the rotor arm and the protective cover (if fitted).

2   Remove the circlip for the pull rod from the vacuum unit and take off the unit.

3   Mark the location of the spring clips for the distributor cap (to save trouble on assembly) and remove them. Remove the terminal from the low tension lead and the condenser. Your distributor may possibly be different from that shown in Fig. 4.4 but the principle is the same. The terminal is screwed through to the breaker plate and must be removed before this can be released (Fig. 4.5).

4   With the LT terminal removed, the breaker plate can be lifted out revealing the centrifugal advance mechansim.

5   Looking at this, you will see that the breaker cam is free to move relative to the distributor driveshaft. It has a plate integral with it with projections which engage with two small weights attached to the top of the distributor shaft. These weights and the top of the distributor shaft are clearly shown in Fig. 4.6. When the weights move outwards under centrifugal force as the distributor shaft rotates they move the distributor cam round and so advance the ignition. A pair of small, but important, springs provide opposition for the weights to push against; upon these springs the proper working of the mechanism depends and you should be careful not to distort them in any way when you remove them. In a number of cases they are not identical, so watch for this and note which spring goes where, marking the distributor if necessary to

6.1 Location of distributor (ohc engine)

Fig. 4.3. Removing the vacuum capsule (Sec. 7)

Fig. 4.4. Distributor components, B20A engine (Sec. 7)

1 Distributor cap	14 Rubber seal
2 Distributor arm	15 Lubricator
3 Contact breaker	16 Primary connection
4 Lubricating felt	17 Distributor housing
5 Circlip	18 Centrifugal governor spring
6 Washer	19 Centrifugal weight
7 Vacuum regulator	20 Breaker camshaft
8 Cap clasp	21 Breaker cam
9 Fibre washer	22 Breaker plate
10 Steel washer	23 Lock screw for breaker
11 Driving collar	contacts
12 Lock pin	24 Rod brush (carbon)
13 Resilient ring	

Fig. 4.7. Tapping the housing, releases the circlip holding the cam to the driveshaft (Sec. 7)

Fig. 4.5. Removing the LT terminal and condenser (Sec. 7)

Fig. 4.8. Removal of driving collar (Sec. 7)

Fig. 4.6. Distributor driveshaft and weights (the cam and governor springs have been removed) (Sec. 7)

ensure that they go back in the right place. If you have to replace them, be sure that you get the right ones for your particular distributor.

6   With these springs removed, mark the cam and distributor shaft so that on reassembly the cam goes back in the correct position. Now hold the cam in a vice with protected jaws as shown in Fig. 4.7 and tap the distributor housing with a hide mallet or similar to release the breaker cam which is held in position by a clip. Draw the cam off the shaft, bringing with it the lubricating wick, the clip and a washer.

7   Undo the screws and remove the contact device where this is fitted.

8   Remove the resilient ring and mark the shaft and driving collar to ensure that when you put the collar back it is the correct way round. Drive out the pin and take the collar off the shaft (Fig. 4.8). .

9   Take the shaft out of the housing, being careful not to lose any of the spacing washers on the shaft.

10 Remove the spring clips which hold the centrifugal weights to the shaft and take off the weights (Fig. 4.6). .

8   Distributor (breakerless) - dismantling

1   Remove the rotor arm and protective cover.

2   Remove the vacuum capsule.

3   Remove the distributor cap clip assemblies. Note that the clip securing screws are of different lengths and if incorrectly replaced can project and damage moving parts. Always keep them with their respective clip assembly.

4   Remove the screw securing the impulse sender contact and pull it straight out (Fig. 4.10).

5   Using a pair of circlip pliers remove the circlip from the top of the distributor shaft and remove any shims located under it.

6   Remove the three screws which secure the impulse sender plate.

7   Lift off the rotor plate and small lock pin (Fig. 4.12).

8   Remove the second circlip and withdraw the impulse sender plate. Separate the impulse sender from its plate by removing the three securing screws (Fig. 4.13).

9   The rest of the dismantling procedure follows that described in Section 7, paragraphs 5 to 10.

9   Distributor - inspection and repair

1   Thoroughly wash all mechanical parts in petrol or paraffin and wipe dry using a clean non-fluffy rag.

2   Check the contact breaker points (if applicable) as described in Section 3.

3   Check the distributor cap for signs of tracking, indicated by a thin black line between segments. Replace the cap if this is evident. Check that the carbon brush moves freely in the centre of the distributor cap and replace it if it is worn or in bad condition.

4   If the metal portion of the rotor arm is badly burned or loose, renew the arm. Slight burning can be cleaned up with a fine file.

5   Examine the fit of the contact breaker plate on the base plate and also check the breaker arm pivot for looseness or wear. If necessary replace the plate.

6   Examine the centrifugal weights and pivot pins for wear in particular, the holes in the centrifugal weights should not be oval or deformed in any other way. The importance of the springs has already been mentioned and these should be checked and replaced if necessary.

7   Check the fit of the breaker cam on the distributor shaft. Play between the distributor shaft and the breaker cam must not exceed 0.004 in (0.1 mm). If the breaker cam itself shows signs of wear or scoring, replace it.

8   The play between the distributor housing and the driveshaft should

Fig. 4.9. Exploded view of breakerless distributor (Sec. 8)

1 Distributor assembly
2 Impulse transmitter
3 Shim
4 Rotor plate
5 Clrclip
6 Lock pin
7 Impulse sender contact
8 Protective cover
9 Rotor arm
10 Distributor cap
11 Vacuum governor
12 Retainer
13 Screw
14 Screw

Fig. 4.10. Removing the impulse sender contact (Sec. 8)

Fig. 4.11. Removing circlip and shims (Sec. 8)

Fig. 4.12. Removing the rotor plate and lock pin (Sec. 8)

1 Securing screw   2 Contact

Fig. 4.13. Removal of the impulse sender and plate (Sec. 8)

1   Spacing washer
2   Fibre washer
3   Bush
4   Bush
5   Lubricating felt
6   Fibre washer
7   Spacing washer

Fig. 4.14. Spacing washers and bushes for the driveshaft (Sec. 9)

Fig. 4.15. Alignment of rotor plate and lock pin (breakerless type distributor) (Sec. 10)

not exceed 0.008 in (0.2 mm). If the play is excessive, replace the bushes and, if this is insufficient, also the shaft.
9   Fig. 4.14 shows the assembly of bushes and washers on the drive-shaft. Replacement of the old bushes is a matter of driving or pulling them out and pressing or gently tapping the new ones in, one from each end with the felt lubricator between them. The lubricator and the bushes should be soaked in oil for at least half an hour before fitting.

The fibre washers at each end of the shaft should be next to the housing. The end play in the shaft should lie between 0.004 - 0.010 in (0.1 - 0.25 mm). If necessary this can be adjusted by altering the number of spacing washers on the distributor shaft.

10 Distributor - reassembly

1   Assemble the driving shaft into the housing as described in the previous paragraph (Section 9, paragraph 9).
2   One of the most important aspects of reassembly is lubrication. The cam lobes and the cam followers should all be lightly coated with grease and so should the weights. A touch of grease should also be applied where the pull rod from the vacuum regulator is attached to the breaker plate. Do not be too free with grease in this area - otherwise it may end up on the breaker contacts (mechanical breaker distributor).
3   On breakerless distributors the only lubrication permitted is applying a few drops of oil on the felt wick in the centre of the rotor shaft.
4   Assembly generally is a straightforward reversal of the dismantling procedure. To assemble the breaker cam on the drive shaft, slide the washer and circlip down the inside of the cam (using a suitable sleeve or two thin metal strips) until the circlip clicks into position. If you have replaced some of the parts whose position you marked when you were taking the distributor apart, be particularly careful about getting the new ones in the right position - you can easily be sure of this by checking with the old parts which you marked.
5   When fitting the rotor plate on breakerless distributors the slot should be opposite the ridge on the distributor shaft. Fit the lock pin so that the slot faces the ridge on the shaft (Fig. 4.15), otherwise the lock pin may be sheared off.

11 Ignition timing (contact breaker distributor)

1   Turn the engine until No. 1 piston is at TDC on the compression stroke and the timing mark on the crankshaft pulley is opposite the appropriate mark (as given in Specifications at the beginning of this Chapter) on the timing scale.
2   Release the clamp bolt on the distributor mounting and with the distributor cap remove, turn the distributor housing until the contact breaker points are just opening. This can be checked by connecting a test lamp between the distributor low tension terminal and a good earth and switching on the ignition. When the points have just opened, the test lamp will light up.
3   Tighten the clamp bolt and remove the test lamp, switch off the ignition and refit the distributor cap.
4   It is recommended that the timing is now checked with a strobo-scope as described in the following Section.

12 Ignition timing with a stroboscope

1   It is necessary to use this method where a breakerless type distributor is fitted. The method is recommended for all types of ignition.
2   Clean the timing mark on the crankshaft pulley and the timing scale on the cover. Mark the appropriate setting with quick drying white paint (or chalk).
3   Run the engine to normal operating temperature.
4   Disconnect the vacuum pipe from the distributor and plug it.
5   Connect a stroboscope in accordance with the manufacturer's instructions, usually between No. 1 spark plug and No. 1 HT lead.
6   Make sure the engine idling speed is correctly set.
7   Start the engine and point the stroboscope at the white marks. They will appear stationary and if the ignition timing is correctly set they will be in alignment. If they are not directly opposite each other, release the clamp bolt on the distributor mounting and turn the distributor one way or the other until the marks line up. Tighten the clamp bolt.
8   If the engine is now revved up, the white mark will move away from the fixed points indicating that the centrifugal advance mechanism is operating correctly. If the vacuum pipe is reconnected, the movement of the timing mark in relation to the fixed point will be greater when the engine speed is increased. This indicates that the vacuum advance is operating.

Measuring plug gap. A feeler gauge of the correct size (see ignition system specifications) should have a slight 'drag' when slid between the electrodes. Adjust gap if necessary

Adjusting plug gap. The plug gap is adjusted by bending the earth electrode inwards, or outwards, as necessary until the correct clearance is obtained. Note the use of the correct tool

Normal. Grey-brown deposits, lightly coated core nose. Gap increasing by around 0.001 in (0.025 mm) per 1000 miles (1600 km). Plugs ideally suited to engine, and engine in good condition

Carbon fouling. Dry, black, sooty deposits. Will cause weak spark and eventually misfire. Fault: over-rich fuel mixture. Check: carburettor mixture settings, float level and jet sizes; choke operation and cleanliness of air filter. Plugs can be re-used after cleaning

Oil fouling. Wet, oily deposits. Will cause weak spark and eventually misfire. Fault: worn bores/piston rings or valve guides; sometimes occurs (temporarily) during running-in period. Plugs can be re-used after thorough cleaning

Overheating. Electrodes have glazed appearance, core nose very white – few deposits. Fault: plug overheating. Check: plug value, ignition timing, fuel octane rating (too low) and fuel mixture (too weak). Discard plugs and cure fault immediately

Electrode damage. Electrodes burned away; core nose has burned, glazed appearance. Fault: pre-ignition. Check: as for 'Overheating' but may be more severe. Discard plugs and remedy fault before piston or valve damage occurs

Split core nose (may appear initially as a crack). Damage is self-evident, but cracks will only show after cleaning. Fault: pre-ignition or wrong gap-setting technique. Check: ignition timing, cooling system, fuel octane rating (too low) and fuel mixture (too weak). Discard plugs, rectify fault immediately

13 Ignition timing sender

1   In 1976 a new system for checking the firing position was introduced for the 21 engine. Instead of a stroboscope, a special engine instrument is used and is connected to a sender on the engine via a connection, and to the spark plug cable for No. 1 cylinder. The firing position can then be read off the instrument, (Volvo mono-tester - 999 9921).
2   The above makes it easier to check the firing position and adjustment can be more precise. It also reduces the risk of possible injury from the fan and belts.
3   The system consists of an electro-magnetic sender mounted in the engine block and two pins on the flywheel, Fig. 4.17. The position of the pins in relation to the sender corresponds to 12⁰ BTDC and 20⁰ ATDC for No. 1 cylinder.
4   The sender consists of a coil (resistance 15 ohms), wound round an iron core, and a cable integrated with the sender. This coil is connected to a connection terminal mounted on the valve cover.
5   To check the timing connect the tester to the battery positive terminal, battery negative terminal, ignition coil terminal 1, the sender connection on the valve cover and to the spark plug cable for No. 1 cylinder. The dial on the tester has a blue and a red scale. Push in the button and read off the red scale. The tester indicates when a spark is obtained in No. 1 cylinder, when the pins on the flywheel pass the sender, the tester gives a reading which shows the actual firing position.
Note: Although the 'timing sender' method of checking the timing is more precise, the timing can effectively be checked using the stroboscope as described in Section 12.

14 Spark plugs and HT leads

1   The correct functioning of the spark plugs is vital for the proper running and efficient operation of the engine.
2   At intervals of 6000 miles (10000 km) the plugs should be removed, examined, cleaned and if worn excessively, renewed. The condition of the spark plug can tell much about the general condition of the engine (see illustration).
3   If the insulator nose of the spark plug is clean and white, with no deposits, this is indicative of a weak mixture, or too hot a plug (a hot plug transfers heat away from the electrodes slowly - a cold plug transfers heat away quickly).
4   If the insulator nose is covered with hard black looking deposits, then this is indicative that the mixture is too rich. Should the plug be black and oily then it is likely that the engine is fairly worn as well as the mixture being too rich.
5   If the insulator nose is covered with light tan to greyish brown deposits, then the mixture is correct, and it is likely that the engine is in good condition.
6   If there are any traces of long brown tapering stains on the outside of the white portion of the plug, then the plug will have to be renewed, as this shows that there is a faulty joint between the plug body and the insulator, and compression is being allowed to leak away.
7   Plugs should be cleaned by a sand blasting machine, which will free them from carbon more completely than cleaning by hand. The machine will also test the condition of the plugs under compression. Any plug that fails to spark at the recommended pressure should be renewed.
8   The spark plug gap is of considerable importance, as, if it is too large or too small the size of the spark and its efficiency will be seriously impaired. The spark plug gap should be set to 0.028 - 0.032 in (0.7 - 0.8 mm).
9   To set it, measure the gap with a feeler gauge, and then bend open or close, the outer plug electrode until the correct gap is achieved. The centre electrode should never be bent as this may crack the insulation and cause plug failure, if nothing worse.
10 When replacing the plugs, remember to use new washers and replace the leads from the distributor cap in the correct firing order which is 1, 3, 4, 2, No. 1 cylinder being the one nearest the fan.
11 The plug leads require no maintenance other than being kept clean and wiped over regularly. At intervals of 6000 miles (10000 km) however, pull each lead off the plug in turn and remove it from the distributor cap. Water can seep down these joints giving rise to a white corrosive deposit which must be carefully removed from the end of each cable. At the same time, check that the suppressor connections are in good condition. If cracked or damaged they should be renewed.

Fig. 4.16. Ignition timing sender is mounted in front of the flywheel (Sec. 13)

Fig. 4.17. Volvo Mono-tester connected to the engine (Sec. 13)

15 Fault diagnosis - ignition system (contact breaker type)

Failures of the ignition system will either be due to faults in the HT or LT circuits. Initial check should be made by observing the security of spark plug terminals, Lucar type terminals, coil and battery connections. More detailed investigation and the explanation and remedial action in respect of symptoms of ignition malfunction are described in the following sub-Sections.

Engine fails to start

1   If the engine fails to start and the car was running normally when it was last used, first check there is fuel in the fuel tank. If the engine turns over normally on the starter motor and the battery is evidently well charged, then the fault may be in either the high or low tension circuits. First check the HT circuit. Note: If the battery is known to be fully charged, the ignition light comes on, and the starter motor fails to turn the engine check the tightness of the leads on the battery terminals and also the security of the earth leads to its connection on the body. It is quite common for the leads to have worked loose, even if they look and feel secure. If one of the battery terminal posts gets very hot when trying to work the starter motor this is a sure indication of a faulty connection to that terminal.
2   One of the commonest reasons for bad starting is wet or damp spark plug leads and distributor. Remove the distributor cap. If condensation is visible internally, dry the cap with a rag and also wipe over the leads. Replace the cap.
3   If the engine still fails to start, check that current is reaching the plugs, by disconnecting each plug lead in turn at the spark plug end, and hold the end of the cable about 3/16th inch (5 mm) away from the cylinder block. Spin the engine on the starter motor.
4   Sparking between the end of the cable and the block should be fairly strong with a regular blue spark. (Hold the lead with rubber to avoid electric shocks). If current is reaching the plugs, then remove them and clean and regap them. The engine should now start.
5   If there is no spark at the plug leads take off the HT lead from the

centre of the distributor cap and hold it to the block as before. Spin the engine on the starter once more. A rapid succession of blue sparks between the end of the lead and the block indicate that the coil is in order and that the distributor cap is cracked, the rotor arm faulty, or the carbon brush in the top of the distributor cap is not making good contact with the spring on the rotor arm. Possibly the points are in bad condition. Clean and reset them as described in this Chapter.

6   If there are no sparks from the end of the lead from the coil, check the connections at the coil end of the lead. If it is in order start checking the low tension circuit.

7   Use a 12v voltmeter or a 12v bulb and two lengths of wire. With the ignition switch on and the points open test between the low tension wire to the coil (it is marked +) and earth. No reading indicates a break in the supply from the ignition switch. Check the connections at the switch to see if any are loose. Refit them and the engine should run. A reading shows a faulty coil or condenser, or broken lead between the coil and the distributor.

8   Take the condenser wire off the points assembly and with the points open, test between the moving point and earth. If there now is a reading, then the fault is in the condenser. Fit a new one and the fault is cleared.

9   With no reading from the moving point to earth, take a reading between earth and the (−) terminal of the coil. A reading here shows a broken wire which will need to be renewed between the coil and distributor. No reading confirms that the coil has failed and must be renewed, after which the engine will run once more. Remember to refit the condenser wire to the points assembly. For these tests it is sufficient to separate the points with a piece of dry paper while testing with the points open.

Engine misfires

10 If the engine misfires regularly, run it at a fast idling speed. Pull off each of the plug caps in turn and listen to the note of the engine. Hold the plug cap in a dry cloth or with a rubber glove as additional protection against a shock from the HT supply.

11 No difference in engine running will be noticed when the lead from the defective circuit is removed. Removing the lead from one of the good cylinders will accentuate the misfire.

12 Remove the plug lead from the end of the defective plug and hold it about 3/16 in (5.0 mm) away from the block. Restart the engine. If the sparking is fairly strong and regular the fault must lie in the spark plug.

13 The plug may be loose, the insulation may be cracked, or the points may have burnt away giving too wide a gap for the spark to jump. Worse still, one of the points may have broken off. Either renew the plug, or clean it, reset the gap, and then test it.

14 If there is no spark at the end of the plug lead, or if it is weak and intermittent, check the ignition lead from the distributor to the plug. If the insulation is cracked or perished, renew the lead. Check the connections at the distributor cap.

15 If there is still no spark, examine the distributor cap carefully for tracking. This can be recognised by a very thin black line running between two or more electrodes, or between an electrode and some other part of the distributor. These lines are paths which now conduct electricity across the cap thus letting it run to earth. The only answer is a new distributor cap.

16 Apart from the ignition timing being incorrect, other causes of misfiring have already been dealt with under the section dealing with the failure of the engine to start. To recap - these are that:

a) *The coil may be faulty giving an intermittent misfire.*
b) *There may be a damaged wire or loose connection in the low tension circuit.*
c) *The condenser may be short circuiting.*
d) *There may be a mechanical fault in the distributor (broken driving spindle or contact breaker spring).*

17 If the ignition timing is too far retarded, it should be noted that the engine will tend to overheat, and there will be a quite noticeable drop in power. If the engine is overheating and the power is down, and the ignition timing is correct, then the carburettor should be checked, as it is likely that this is where the fault lies.

16 Fault diagnosis - Ignition system (breakerless type)

Symptom	Reason/s
Engine fails to start	Discharged battery or loose connections
	Fault in system component
	Disconnected system leads
	Incorrect air gap
Engine starts and runs but misfires	Faulty spark plug
	Cracked distributor cap
	Worn advance mechanism
	Incorrect timing
	Poor earth connections
	Incorrect air gap or faulty pick-up unit
Engine overheats	Incorrect timing
	Advance weights seized (retarded)
	Perforated vacuum pipe
Engine 'pinks'	Timing too advanced
	Advance weights seized (advanced)
	Broken weight spring

Chapter 5 Clutch

For modifications, and information applicable to later models, see Supplement at end of manual

Contents

Note: *For details on the hydraulic clutch used on right-hand drive models from 1975 onwards, see supplementary Chapter 13.*

Specifications

Type	Single dry plate, diaphragm spring
Size	8.5 in (215.9 mm)
Total friction area	68.2 in^2 (440 cm^2)
Throw-out fork free travel	
LH drive — cable-operated	0.12 - 0.16 in (3 - 4 mm)
RH drive — hydraulically-operated	Non-adjustable
Clutch pedal travel	
LH drive	6.0 in (150 mm)
RH drive	6.4 in (160 mm)

1 General description

1 The models covered by this manual which are fitted with manual transmission are fitted with an 8.5 in (215.9 mm) diameter diaphragm spring clutch operated by a cable connected between the release fork and the clutch pedal. On right-hand drive models from 1975 onwards, the clutch is hydraulically actuated. (Details of the hydraulic system appear in the supplementary Chapter 13). Two types of clutch are fitted which are interchangeable as complete assemblies, but not individual parts or friction discs.

2 A steel cover dowelled and bolted to the rear face of the flywheel has attached to it a pressure plate which (when the clutch is engaged) clamps a disc covered with high friction lining material to the flywheel. This disc has a central hub which engages with splines on the gearbox input shaft (first motion shaft). Thus when the clutch is engaged, the flywheel drives the gearbox through the disc and the whole assembly rotates at engine speed.

3 The gearbox input shaft is kept in alignment with the crankshaft because the end of it is held in a small bearing which is set in the end of the crankshaft. This bearing is known as the pilot bearing.

4 The pressure holding this sandwich together is exerted by a diaphragm spring fitted to the clutch cover. A diagram of this spring is given in Fig. 5.2. and you can see the central part of it quite clearly in the photograph.

In order to disengage the clutch, pressure is applied to the central part of the spring by a thrust bearing actuated by a lever attached to the flywheel housing. A look at Fig. 5.2 shows how this pressure acts to draw back the outer edge of the spring, so withdrawing the pressure plate. When the pressure plate is drawn back, the friction disc is no longer sandwiched between the flywheel and the pressure plate and ceases to be driven by the flywheel.

5 The thrust bearing is concentric with the gearbox input shaft, but in no way connected to it; the front part of the bearing revolves when it is in contact with the spring but the back part is stationary being attached to the release arm which is also stationary. When the clutch

Fig. 5.1. Two types of clutch cover (Sec. 1)

Fig. 5.2. Diagrammatic section through clutch assembly. Dimension 'A' representing deviation from flat on driving face, must not exceed 0.0012 in (0.03 mm) (Sec. 1)

Fig. 5.3. Clutch and cable control (Sec. 1)

1 Flywheel casing
2 Clutch cover
3 Clutch plate
4 Flywheel
5 Crankshaft
6 Pilot bearing
7 Circlip
8 Adjusting nuts
9 Return spring
10 Release fork
11 Dust cover
12 Release bearing
13 Input shaft (gearbox)
14 Cover (gearbox)
15 Support rings
16 Thrust spring
17 Pressure plate
18 Retainer
19 Clutch cable
20 Washer
21 Rubber bush
22 Washer
23 Nut
24 Pedal stop pin
25 Rubber sleeve
26 Bracket
27 Screw for pedal shaft
28 Return spring
29 Clutch pedal

1.4 This view of the clutch in the car clearly shows the segmental diaphragm spring

5.3a Removing the clutch thrust bearing (cable actuation, M40 gearbox)

5.3b Clutch thrust bearing and fork (hydraulic actuation, M45 gearbox)

Fig. 5.4. Clutch fork free play adjustment - 0.12 - 0.16 in (3 - 4 mm) (Sec. 2)

Fig. 5.5. Clutch pedal mounting (Sec. 4)

1 Clutch cable	6 Shaft
2 Rubber sleeve	7 Bush
3 Pedal stop	8 Return spring
4 Clutch pedal	9 Bracket
5 Bolt	

is engaged, the front of the bearing is not in contact with the spring and so does not revolve.

6   The central hub of the clutch friction disc is sprung in order to absorb transmission shocks and to help ensure a smooth take-off.

2   Clutch - adjustment

1   Engagement and disengagement of the clutch depends on the movement of the clutch lever which is actuated by the clutch cable. When the lever is pulled back, the clutch is disengaged, and when the lever is allowed to go forwards the bearing on the other end of it will move backwards and the centre part of the spring will also move backwards until the disc is firmly sandwiched between the plate and the flywheel. Once this has happened, the spring will cease to follow further movement of the bearing which will continue to move backward until the clutch cable is taut. It is obviously desirable that there should be some clearance between the spring and the bearing when the clutch is engaged.

2   The friction disc will wear in use and become thinner. When this has happened, the pressure plate will move a little closer to the flywheel when the clutch is engaged. The centre part of the spring will correspondingly move a little further backwards and the clearance between the spring and the thrust bearing will be reduced.

3   Clutch adjustment is effected by means of nuts which should be adjusted to give a clutch lever free travel of 0.12 - 0.16 in (3 - 4 mm). This free travel will be felt as free play movement of the clutch pedal. It is most important that this free play is always maintained. If you get to the stage where you cannot obtain it, then this is an indication that the friction disc is worn and requires replacement.

3   Clutch cable - removal and replacement

1   Unhook the return spring for the release lever.

2   Slacken off the two adjusting nuts that hold the outer cable sleeve to the housing boss and detach the inner cable from the clutch lever (photo).

3   Unscrew the rear adjustment nut from the cable sleeve and withdraw the cable from the housing boss.

4   Remove the clutch pedal bearing bolt and detach the inner cable from the pedal.

5   The cable can now be removed from the car.

6   Refitting the new cable assembly is the reverse sequence to removal. It will be necessary to adjust the cable as described in Section 2.

4   Clutch pedal and mounting - overhaul

1   Remove the panel under the dashboard which covers the pedal mounting. Details of the clutch pedal mounting are shown in Fig. 5.5.

2   Unhook the return spring for the pedal, slacken the nut and remove the pedal pivot bolt. Disconnect the pedal from the wire and remove the pedal.

3   The pedal runs on bushes bearing on a hollow shaft through which the bearing bolt passes. Take this shaft out, give the whole assembly a good clean and inspect for signs of wear and excessive play between the pedal and the shaft.

4   If necessary, drive out the bushes and replace them.

5   Inspect the tubular shaft for signs of wear (it is not very likely that you will find any) and replace it if necessary.

6   Replace the return spring unless you are perfectly sure that it is all right. It is most annoying if you have to do the work all over again because a silly little spring breaks, only weeks after you have had an assembly like this to pieces.

7   Grease the shaft, bushes and spring generously and reassemble. Remember to hook the cable on to the pedal before you bolt it to the mounting.

5   Clutch release thrust bearing - removal, inspection and replacement

1   The classic symptom of wear in the clutch release bearing - and it is one which should not be disregarded - is clutch squeal, heard when

you depress the clutch pedal. Before getting to this stage you may hear a whirring noise when you have the clutch pedal down.

2   The thrust bearing only has to perform when your foot is on the clutch pedal. If you use the clutch pedal as a foot-rest the thrust bearing may well be revolving even though there is no clutch slip; this is a temptation which it is well worthwhile to resist.

3   To remove the thrust bearing, remove the gearbox as described in Chapter 6. The bearing can now be removed from the release fork. On M45 gearboxes the thrust bearing is retained by a spring clip (photos).

4   Check the bearing by placing it on the bench and rotating it under light pressure. The bearing should turn easily with no suspicion of binding and there should be no suspicion of play when it is under pressure. If there is any doubt about it, replace it. The whole assembly is replaced; there is no question of dismantling it and fitting a new bearing inside. Be sure when getting hold of a replacement to specify the clutch type as the thrust bearings are not the same for the different clutch types.

5   Replacement is the reverse of the removal sequence. Adjust the clutch lever free travel as described in Section 2.

6   Clutch - removal

1   Remove the gearbox complete with the bellhousing as described in Chapter 6. This will give you a view of the flywheel and clutch.

2   Undo the screws attaching the clutch housing to the flywheel cross-wise a couple of turns at a time to prevent possible warping of the clutch housing. Remove the clutch as shown in Fig. 5.6. The disc is not attached to anything at this stage, hence the thumb in the hole to keep hold of it.

7   Clutch - inspection and overhaul

1   The view of the friction disc in the photograph shows what this should look like when it is in good condition. Inspect the friction disc for wear and contamination by oil.

2   Wear on the linings is gauged by the depth of the rivet heads below the surface of the friction material. If this is less than 0.025 in (0.6 mm) the linings are worn enough to justify renewal.

3   When one considers how easy it is to slip on a polished floor, it is surprising that the highly polished surfaces of the clutch are able to generate so much friction. This is the case because there is - or should be - a complete absence of any form of lubricant between the mating surfaces. Under these conditions, the smoother the surface the better the contact and consequently the surface of the friction facings should have the appearance of smoothly finished wood - the grain of the material being clearly seen. It should be quite light in colour. If oil has penetrated to this surface, it will have been burnt off and it will darken the face. If however, the polish of the facing remains such that the grain of the material can still be distinguished clearly this will have little effect on clutch performance. Naturally, if you feel that oil is - or has been - present in the clutch you will take good care to find out how it got there and put a stop to it. If a more severe degree of oil contamination has occurred, the surface may be affected in two ways depending upon the nature of the oil:

Fig. 5.6. Removing the clutch (Sec. 6)

7.1 Clutch friction disc

9.2 Clutch friction disc marking

Fig. 5.7. Clutch disc assembly (Sec. 7)

1 Disc	4 Damper spring
2 Facings	5 Hub
3 Spring	

a) The oil may burn off and leave a carbon deposit on the surface of the facings which become highly glazed and have a definite tendency to slip. In this condition the surfaces have the appearance of varnished wood and in general the grain of the material is hidden.

b) Oil may partially burn and leave a resinous deposit on the facings. This has a tendency to produce a fierce clutch and may also cause clutch spin due to the tendency of the face linings to stick to the surface of the flywheel or pressure plate.

4 If there are signs of severe overheating - brought about as a result of clutch slip - it is well to replace the disc complete. It may be distorted or the temper of the shock absorbing springs may have been affected. If only the friction lining is affected, it is quite practicable to replace this oneself rather than buy a complete replacement disc assembly. Most people feel it is hardly worth doing and we would be

inclined to agree with this. Nevertheless the linings and rivets are available as Volvo spares if you wish to have a go.

5 To replace the facings, first drill out the old rivets with an 0.14 in (3.5 mm) drill. Then check the clutch plate. The indentations on the tongues should be even. The clutch plate must not be warped. The clutch springs and rivets in the hub should fit securely and not show any signs of looseness. Check to make sure that there are no cracks. If the plate does not pass all these tests with flying colours, replace it.

6 Rivet on the new facings (preferably in a rivet press). The rivets should be inserted from the side on which the facing lies and riveted up from the opposite direction against the disc. Use alternative holes in the facing - the holes not occupied by rivets fixing one facing will contain the rivets for the other. After riveting - the faces should be quite flat and spaced from each other by the indentations on to the clutch disc. This spacing is most important in order to achieve smooth engagement of the clutch. Be sure that during these operations the clutch facings are kept absolutely free from oil.

7 The pressure plate assembly should be replaced complete if faulty. Check the pressure plate for damage by heat, cracks, scoring or other damage on the friction surface. Check the curvature of the pressure plate with a 9½ in (240 mm) steel straight edge placed diagonally across the friction surface. It is permitted for the plate to be very slightly concave, ie. the centre of the plate lies below the straight edge. The distance between the plate and the straight edge must not exceed 0.0012 in (0.03 mm), check this with feeler gauges. If the plate is convex, ie. the centre is higher than the edges, replace the assembly. Check the pressure spring carefully; if cracked or damaged in any other way, the assembly should be replaced.

8 Pilot bearing

1 This bearing is not all that easy to remove without damaging it. For this reason we recommend that you wash it out and inspect it while it is still in the crankshaft. This way you only have to remove it if you have already decided to replace it and your problems are simpler. Its removal is considered in Chapter 1.

2 Do not forget that the flywheel surface is an important component of the clutch. If the surface of the flywheel in contact with the clutch friction disc is uneven or burnt it should be reground. This is a job for the specialist. We suggest that if this is necessary, you take the flywheel and clutch assembly to the firm who is to do the grinding and have them balanced as a unit after the grinding has been carried out.

9 Clutch - replacement

1 Before you start, ensure that the clutch assembly and friction disc are completely free from oil. If necessary, wash in petrol and dry off with a clean rag.

2   To refit the clutch, place the friction disc against the flywheel. Make sure it is the right way round as fitment the wrong way would result in non-operation of the clutch. The friction disc is marked as shown in the photograph.

3   Replace the clutch cover assembly loosely on the dowels, replace the six bolts and spring washers and tighten them finger-tight so that the clutch disc is gripped but can still be moved.

4   The clutch disc must now be centralised so that when the engine and gearbox are mated, the gearbox input shaft splines will pass through the splines in the centre of the hub.

5   Centralisation can be carried out quite easily by inserting a round bar or long screwdriver through the hole in the centre of the clutch, so that the end of the bar rests in the small hole in the end of the crankshaft containing the input shaft bearing bush. Moving the bar sideways or up and down will move the clutch disc in whichever direction is necessary to achieve centralisation.

6   Centralisation is easily judged by removing the bar and viewing the driven plate hub in relation to the hole in the centre of the clutch cover assembly. When the hub appears exactly in the centre of the release bearing hole all is correct. Alternatively if an old input shaft can be used, instant fitment will result.

7   Tighten the clutch bolts firmly in a diagonal sequence to ensure that the cover plate is pulled down evenly and without distortion of the flange.

Fig. 5.8. Centralising the friction disc (Sec. 9)

8   Refit the gearbox as described in Chapter 6. Take care when inserting the input shaft into the clutch not to put any strain on the clutch assembly or input shaft.

9   Finally adjust the clutch cable as described in Section 2.

10 Fault diagnosis

Symptom	Reason/s	Remedy
Judder when taking up drive	Loose engine/gearbox mountings or over flexible mountings	Check and tighten all mounting bolts and replace any 'soft' or broken mountings.
	Badly worn friction surfaces or friction plate contaminated with oil deposits	Remove engine and replace clutch parts as required. Rectify any oil leakage points which may have caused contamination.
	Worn splines in the friction plate hub or on the gearbox input shaft	Renew friction plate and/or input shaft.
	Badly worn pilot bearing	Renew pilot bearing.
Clutch spin (failure to disengage) so that gears cannot be meshed	Clutch actuating cable clearance too great	Adjust clearance.
	Clutch hydraulic slave cylinder leaking	Renew seals
	Clutch friction disc sticking because of rust on lining or splines (usually apparent after standing idle for some length of time)	As temporary remedy engage top gear, apply handbrake, depress clutch and start engine. (If very badly stuck engine will not turn). When running rev up engine and slip clutch until disengagement is normally possible. Renew friction plate at earliest opportunity.
	Damaged or misaligned pressure plate assembly	Replace pressure plate assembly.
Clutch slip - (increase in engine speed does not result in increase in vehicle speed - especially on hills)	Clutch pedal free-play too little or non-existent resulting in partially disengaged clutch at all times	Adjust clearances.
	Clutch friction surfaces worn out (beyond further adjustment of operating cable) or clutch surfaces oil soaked	Replace friction plate and remedy source of oil leakage.
Clutch squeal when clutch is disengaged	Worn clutch release thrust bearing	Replace thrust bearing.

Chapter 6 Gearbox, overdrive and automatic transmission

For modifications, and information applicable to later models, see Supplement at end of manual

Contents

Specifications

Manual gearbox

Type

Without overdrive	... ...	M40	M45
With overdrive	... ...	M41	M46

Reduction ratios

1st gear	3.41 : 1	3.71 : 1
2nd gear	1.99 : 1	2.16 : 1
3rd gear	1.36 : 1	1.37 : 1
4th gear	1 : 1	1 : 1
Reverse	3.25 : 1	3.68 : 1
Overdrive	0.797 : 1	0.797 : 1

Lubrication

M40, M41	Gear oil, SAE 80W/90 or 80/90
M45, M46	Automatic transmission fluid Type F

Oil capacity

M40 and M45	0.75 litre (1.3 Imp pints - 1.6 US pints)
M41 (includes overdrive)	1.6 litre (2.8 Imp pints - 3.3 US pints)
M46 (includes overdrive)	2.3 litre (4 Imp pints - 4.8 US pints)

Tightening torques

Flange nuts - M40 and M45	69 - 76 lb f ft (9.5 - 10 kg fm)
- M41 and M46	119 - 130 lb f ft (16.5 - 18.0 kg fm)

Overdrive

Type	J
Application	Manual gearbox, type M41, M46
Ratio	0.8 : 1
Oil pressure	384 to 427 psi (27 to 30 kgf/cm^2)
Lubrication	In common with gearbox

Torque wrench settings

	lbf ft	kgf m
Casing nuts and bolts	7	1.0
Solenoid valve	37	5.0
Oil sump bolts	7	1.0
Relief valve plug	17	2.3
Oil pump plug	17	2.3
Pressure take-off plug	15	2.0
Output flange nut	135	18.6
Oil filter plug	17	2.3
Lubricating valve plug	10	1.3

Automatic transmission

Make and type ... ... Borg-Warner, Type 35 and 55

Reduction ratios

	BW35	BW55
1st gear	2.39 : 1	2.45 : 1
2nd gear	1.45 : 1	1.45 : 1
3rd gear	1 : 1	1 : 1
Reverse	2.09 : 1	2.21 : 1
Final drive	3.73 : 1	3.73 : 1

Size of torque converter ... ... 9.5 in (240 mm)
Torque ratio in converter ... ... 2 : 1 - 1 : 1

Weights

Gearbox	82 lb (37.2 kg)	
Converter case	6.6 lb (3.0 kg)	
Converter	24 lb (10.9 kg)	
Total without fluid	112 lb (51 kg)	
Total with fluid	126 lb (57.1 kg)	

Fluid type ... ... Automatic transmission fluid, Type F

Fluid capacity (from dry)

BW35	11.3 Imp pints (6.8 US qts, 6.4 litres)
BW55 (early)	11.4 Imp pints (6.95 US qts, 6.5 litres)
BW55 (later)	12.1 Imp pints (7.25 US qts, 6.9 litres)

Normal operating temperature of fluid ... ... Approx. 230 - 240°F (110 - 115°C)

Approximate shift speeds

Engine	Throttle position	1st–2nd km/h	mile/h	2nd–3rd km/h	mile/h	3rd–2nd km/h	mile/h	3rd–1st km/h	mile/h
B20A	Full throttle	43	27	70	43				
	kick-down	60	37	95	59	86	53	49	30
B21A	kick-down	62	39	105	65	95	59	49	30
B21E	kick-down	60	37	108	67	98	61	49	30

Normal stall speeds

B20A	2200 rev/min
B21A	2200 rev/min
B21E	2550 rev/min

Torque wrench settings (BW35) - see Supplement for BW55 and AW55

	lb f ft	kg fm
Torque converter - drive plate	25 - 30	3.5 - 4.1
Transmission case - converter housing	8 - 13	1.1 - 1.8
Extension housing - transmission case	30 - 55	4.1 - 7.6
Oil pan - transmission case	8 - 13	1.1 - 1.8
Outer lever - manual valve shift	7 - 9	1 - 1.2
Pressure point	4 - 5	0.6 - 0.7
Oil pan drain plug	8 - 10	1.1 - 1.4

1 Gearbox - general description

1 The M40 type gearbox fitted to the Volvo 240 series is illustrated in Fig. 6.1. Later models in the series have an M45 type gearbox. When an overdrive is fitted to these gearboxes, the complete assemblies become the M41 and M46, the gearboxes being unchanged. Both gearboxes are very similar, the main difference being that the M45 casing is shaped differently, with external reinforcing ribbing and the reverse gear on the left side. Also the layshaft is journalled in taper roller bearings instead of needle bearings, and the rear cover is in one piece.

2 The gearbox has four forward speeds and reverse, with synchromesh on all forward gears. Its design is conventional and the problems associated with dismantling, inspection and assembly are in no way typical. Coping with these problems is well within the scope of the intelligent owner mechanic, even though he may never have tackled a gearbox before. If your experience is limited. (and after all, the average gearbox doesn't go wrong all that often), we suggest that you give a little thought to the working of your gearbox before starting to take it apart.

3 Start by taking a look at Fig. 6.2. Ignoring for the moment the arrow we see two clusters of gears, and looking more closely at these we see that four pairs of gears are actually in mesh. Another pair of

1	Gear lever, upper part
2	Rubber bushes
3	Gear lever, lower part
4	Circlip
5	Spring
6	Washer
7	Bush
8	Protective cover
9	Gearbox cover
10	Protective cover
11	Rear cover
12	Ball bearing
13	Flange
14	Bush
15	Gear selector
16	Switch, reversing light and 'fasten seat belt' light
17	Shift fork, 1st-2nd gears
18	Flange
19	Shift link
20	Sleeve (reverse inhibitor)
21	Spring
22	Sleeve
23	Spring
24	Flange
25	Engaging sleeve and reverse gear
26	Synchromesh cone (baulk ring)
27	Bush (needle bearings)
28	2nd gear
29	Thrust washer
30	Circlip
31	Thrust washer
32	3rd gear
33	Bush (needle bearings)
34	Mainshaft
35	Spring
36	Interlock ball
37	Synchromesh hub
38	Flange
39	Spring
40	Spring
41	Flange
42	Engaging sleeve
43	Synchromesh cone (baulk ring)
44	Synchromesh cone (baulk ring)
45	Ball bearing
46	Roller bearing
47	Sealing ring
48	Front cover (input shaft bearing retainer)
49	Input shaft
50	Spacer washer
51	Thrust washer
52	Housing
53	Needle bearings
54	Spacer washer
55	Layshaft
56	Laygear
57	Reverse shaft
58	Reverse gear
59	Bush
60	Shift lever
61	Bush (needle bearings)
62	1st gear
63	Thrust washer
64	Speedometer gear
65	Sealing ring
66	Flange

Fig. 6.1. Cut-away view of M40 gearbox (Sec. 1)

gears doesn't quite make it, and indeed they are not even exactly in line. We know better than to suppose that by now you haven't looked at Figs. 6.3, 6.4, 6.5 and 6.6 as well and you will have seen that the upper one of this particular pair of gears can move to-and-fro and gets linked up with its opposite number by a subsidiary gear to provide reverse.

4   If we now consider the arrow in Fig. 6.2 which shows the way the drive is transmitted in bottom gear we at once realise that the two shaft ends at the top of the figure must belong to different shafts, because they are rotating at different speeds. The shaft on the left which we will call the input shaft is quite short; it only carries one of the gears and fits into the other shaft about mid-way between the gear pair on the left and the gear pair next to it. The shaft on the right, which we will call the output shaft, or mainshaft, carries the three other gears of the upper set, any one of which can be locked to it as described later. The gear on the input shaft is integral with it.

5   The lower set of gears is all one piece. This assembly is known as the layshaft. In practice the assembly has a hole through the middle of it and revolves on needle bearings on a spindle as shown in Fig. 6.1.

The left-hand gear is driven by the gear on the input shaft, causing the whole layshaft to rotate with a speed that always bears the same ratio to the engine speed.

6   Although the various layshaft gears are all revolving at the same speed the gears they drive on the mainshaft all revolve at different speeds because each one is a different size and consequently has a

different ratio to its opposite number on the layshaft. Gearbox ratios are selected by locking one or other of these gears to the mainshaft.

7   Details of the locking mechanism are considered later. At this stage it is sufficient to say that the locking is achieved by sliding operating sleeves along the mainshaft. If we look at Fig. 6.1 we see that there are two of these sleeves on the mainshaft. The one on the right is pushed over as far as it will go to the right and when it is in this position it locks the right-hand gear to the mainshaft. This gear now drives the mainshaft and we get the power transmission path indicated by the arrow. This particular gear is bigger than the other two, which means that its opposite number on the layshaft has got to be smaller than those driving its companions. Hence, this pair of gears has a larger reduction ratio than the others and gives us 'bottom gear'. In Fig. 6.3 we see the right-hand operating sleeve slid along the shaft as far as it will go to the left, in which position it locks the centre one of the three driven gears which is intermediate in size between the other two and gives us a reduced reduction ratio corresponding to 'second gear'. In Fig. 6.4 the right-hand operating sleeve is positioned mid-way between the two gears associated with it and in that position locks neither of them. The left-hand sleeve, however, has been moved over until it is close to the gear on its right, which it locks to the shaft. This is smaller than the other two driven gears and consequently gives less reduction - ie. 'third gear'. Fig. 6.5 shows the state of things for top gear. The left-hand sleeve is slid as far over to the left as it will go, and in this position it locks the input shaft direct to the output shaft. They operate as one shaft, not being driven through any gear train, hence the silence of top gear operation however rough the gearbox may be. Fig. 6.6 shows the set-up for reverse gear. Two gears set opposite each other on the mainshaft and the layshaft which do not engage directly are coupled together by a small pinion which is pushed into position when 'reverse' is selected. There is no particular significance in the fact that a driven gear for reverse forms part of an operating sleeve; this is simply a matter of engineering convenience. The sleeve is of course keyed to the shaft though it can slide along it freely.

8   The operating sleeves are pushed along the shafts by selector forks which are attached to selector rods. These rods carry dogs which are engaged by the gear lever. A simple interlock (described in Section 4, paragraph 3) prevents more than one selector rod being moved at a time. One selector rod is associated with each of the engaging sleeves and a third rod operates the lever that engages the reverse pinion.

9   Associated with the operating sleeves is the synchromesh mechanism which ensures that when a driven gear is about to be locked to the mainshaft - gear and mainshaft are rotating at the same speed. This is described in the next Section.

2   Synchromesh mechanism

1   We have already seen that when a gear is engaged, the gear wheel concerned is locked to the mainshaft by the engaging sleeve. Splines inside the engaging sleeve mesh with teeth on the hub of the gear wheel and simultaneously with the 'synchronising hub' on the mainshaft. In Fig. 6.2 the left-hand engaging sleeve is not locked to either of the gears on each side of it, but the right-hand sleeve is engaged with the gear on its right. You can see the synchronising hub on which it slides quite clearly on the left of it.

2   The purpose of the synchromesh is to provide an obstacle to travel of the engaging sleeve when the mainshaft (and hence the sleeve

Fig. 6.2. Power path - 1st gear (Sec. 1)

Fig. 6.3. Power path - 2nd gear (Sec. 1)

Fig. 6.4. Power path - 3rd gear (Sec. 1)

Fig. 6.5. Power path - 4th gear (Sec. 1)

Fig. 6.6. Power path - reverse (Sec. 1)

Fig. 6.7. Synchroniser sliding key and spring assembly (Secs. 2 and 10)

itself) is revolving at a different rate from the gear which it is desired to engage. The speed of this gear is determined by the engine speed via the layshaft. This obstacle is provided by the synchronising cone, which has teeth round its edge which get in the way of the synchronising hub when this is rotating faster or slower than the desired gear.

Photograph 5.5a gives a better idea of the mechanism than any drawing can. On the left we see the first speed gear (this photograph is the other way round to Figs. 6.2 - 6.6 which show the first speed gear on the right). It is displaced along the shaft - it would normally be running on the larger diameter portion. The hub of this gear has a taper on it and also carries the engaging teeth which do not show up well in this photograph but may be seen quite clearly in photograph 5.5b where this gear appears in the foreground. Returning to photograph 5.5a, it is easy to see that if the gear and the engaging sleeve are pressed together with the synchromesh cone between them the engaging sleeve will not get past the synchromesh cone unless the teeth on the cone line up with the splines inside the sleeve. If we now glance at Fig. 6.7 we see that the engaging sleeve has assembled inside it three sliding keys which are held in position by two circular springs. Two of these keys are clearly visible in photograph 5.5a, the one nearer the camera showing up very well as it has caught the light. Opposite this detent we can see a notch in the synchronising cone in which the key engages. If the cone is so positioned that one or other of the ends of the slot are touching the key the teeth on the cone get in the way of the splines on the engaging sleeve and this sleeve cannot get past it. If the gear wheel revolves faster or slower than the engaging sleeve, friction between the tapered part of the gear hub and the cone will push it one way or the other until it comes to rest against the key. If the relationship reverses, the cone will start to move relative to the engaging sleeve in the other direction and the time will come when the sleeve can slip past it. As soon as this happens the splines on the engaging sleeve pick up the engaging teeth on the gear and the synchromesh cone just sits between them while they revolve as one unit.

3 Gearbox - removal and replacement

1 Disconnect the battery, the reverse light cable and the connection at the overdrive, if fitted.
2 Drain the oil from the gearbox into a clean container (photo).
3 Disconnect the shift selector rod from the gearlever by removing the lock bolt and pushing out the pivot pin.
4 Remove the four clips and release the rubber gaiter from the tunnel. Remove the reverse inhibitor bracket (4 mm Allen key). Remove the circlip and lift out the gearlever.
5 Disconnect the clutch cable or slave cylinder. Remove the bolts securing the exhaust bracket to the clutch housing and the nut at the exhaust pipe. Remove the bracket.
6 Place a jack under the engine sump and remove the gearbox support member (photo).
7 Remove the bolts securing the front propeller shaft to the gearbox flange and tie the propeller shaft up with a piece of wire to keep it out of the way.
8 Disconnect the speedometer cable (photo).

9 Lower the rear end of the engine slightly and remove all the bolts attaching the clutch housing to the engine except the right upper bolt. On the B20 engine, the starter motor can now be removed, on the B21 engine you must first remove the starter motor front support bracket.
10 Support the gearbox and remove the upper right attaching bolt. Withdraw the gearbox and turn it so that the casing goes free from the tunnel as it is pulled backwards. Take care not to place any strain on the input shaft as the gearbox is removed. An extra pair of hands makes this job a lot easier.
11 Replacement is a reversal of the removal procedure. Do not forget to fill the gearbox with oil and ensure the drain and filler/level plugs are tightened.

4 Gearbox - dismantling

1 Give the whole exterior a thorough clean with paraffin or a detergent such as Gunk. As well as making the job more pleasant it is the only way to be certain that you will not get dirt inside the gearbox at some stage in the proceedings.
2 As the gearbox has been dismantled complete with the bellhousing, the clutch thrust bearing and its withdrawal fork are easily removed for inspection as described in Chapter 5.
3 Remove the cover. On the underside of the cover you will see the interlock plate with square bosses, these lock all selectors except the selector that is being operated so that only that particular selector can move - this also ensures that the gearlever is properly positioned over the selector you want because if it is not you will not be able to move the selector. A look at the photograph of the selectors as seen from the top of the box will show you at once how the system fits together. The action of the spring on the interlock plate makes the gearlever return to the right-hand side of the box. When you select reverse, you have to give an extra push to make the interlock plate overcome the resistance of the plunger which is backed by a fairly strong spring (photo).
4 Remove the three springs (normally held in by the lid) which press on locating balls for the selector rods (see photo). The balls can be left in the holes for the time being if you keep an eye on them.
5 Engage two gears at once by pushing both the forward speed selector rods as far in one direction as they will go. This locks the gearbox and enables you to undo the nut holding the flange on the mainshaft with difficulty. Pull the flange off the shaft with a puller if it will not respond to very gentle taps with a hammer. Now is as good a time as any to remove the speedometer drive pinion by undoing the screw that retains it. Follow this by removing the screws which hold the mainshaft bearing housing - this gives the shaft freedom of movement at this stage and makes subsequent dismantling a little easier. Note the sealing washers on these screws which go right through into the gearbox (photos).
6 Remove the cap covering the ends of the selector rods, take out the locking screws holding the selector fork and the engaging dogs to the two outer rods (this will release the lever actuating the reverse pinion as well) and withdraw the rods. Be careful in your choice of screwdriver

3.2 Drain and filler plugs

Fig. 6.8. Removing the gaiter clips (Sec. 3)

Fig. 6.9. Removing the reverse inhibitor bracket (Sec. 3)

Fig. 6.10. Removing the gear lever retaining circlip (Sec. 3)

Fig. 6.11. Bolts and nuts securing the exhaust pipe bracket (Sec. 3)

3.6 Gearbox support member securing bolts

3.8 Disconnecting the speedometer cable

4.2a Disconnecting the selector rod (M45)

4.2b Removing the gear lever carrier bracket (M45)

4.3a Lifting off the cover (M45)

4.3b The locking plate, its return spring and the plunger that loads the reverse position

4.3c The selector rods showing the dogs that engage with the gear lever

4.4 Removing the springs that hold down the lock balls

4.5a Removing the flange ...

4.5b ... the speedometer drive pinion ...

4.5c ... and the fixing screws for the mainshaft bearing housing

4.6a The cap covering the ends of the selector rods

4.6b On M45 gearbox, a one piece rear cover is fitted in place of the bearing housing and cap

4.7a Drive out the lock pin ...

4.7b ... this is what it looks like ...

4.7c ... and pull out the selector rod

4.9a Layshaft, laygear and needle roller bearings

4.9b Layshaft taper roller bearing (M45)

4.10a Removing the input shaft housing ...

4.10b ... followed by the input shaft

4.10c The needle bearing in the input shaft which supports the front end of the mainshaft

4.10d The input shaft with its integral fourth gear pinion and engaging teeth, and their associated synchromesh baulk ring

for undoing these screws - choose one that is a good fit in the slot. These screws are screwed in tightly because a lot depends on them (photos).

Go easy when you take the rods out; keep the dogs and selectors parallel with the shaft as they may jam if they get slightly askew.
7   The dog on the centre shaft is held in by a lock pin because a screw would get in the way of the gearlever. Move the selector as close as you can to the side of the gearbox (ie. put it in the 'first speed' position). Drive the pin out a little way, but not so far as to foul the teeth of the first speed gear on the layshaft which is underneath it. Having started the pin on its way, take the selector back past the first speed gear when you have enough room to drive it out. Having done this, you can withdraw the rod. With the rods out of the way you can take out the dogs and selector forks (photos).
8   Remove the bellhousing, which until now will have been serving as a most useful stand, being careful to use a correctly fitting key for the Allen screws - which hold it to the gearbox. These screws should be done up tightly and trying to unscrew them with a key which is not quite right will almost certainly damage them.
9   The rear end of the layshaft is normally half concealed by the mainshaft housing. If you turn the housing slightly the layshaft can be driven out rearwards, but do not do it for a moment. If you just drive out the shaft, 42 needles will be scattered all over the place. The difficulty arises because you have to drive out the shaft and allow the laygear to fall to the bottom of the gearbox casing before you can remove the mainshaft.

The ideal solution to the problem is to have a shaft or tube 1-1¼ inches (2.5 - 3.1 cms) shorter than the layshaft, ie a bit shorter than the layshaft itself, and having a diameter equal or slightly less than that of the shaft. If this shaft were driven into the middle of the laygear, the layshaft being removed, the laygear would fall to the bottom of the gearbox with the substitute shaft inside it retaining the needle bearings in position. Volvo have produced such a rod (Tool no. SVO 2907) and if you can borrow it from a Volvo agent that is fine, but if you are faced with making something we suggest that you do not bother at this stage, but just push out the shaft and allow the whole lot to drop to the bottom of the

gearbox. It will be much easier to devise something to use during reassembly (where it is almost essential) when you have the layshaft and bearings available to try out your system and see if it works. This is what we did, and in Section 13 we describe how we went about it.

Whatever you do about retaining the bearings at this stage, you will have to push out the layshaft and let the laygear drop to the bottom of the gearbox before you can deal with the mainshaft. This problem does not arise with the M45 gearbox as the layshaft is mounted in taper roller bearings. Simply drive the shaft to the rear to release the outer bearing and then forward to remove the front outer bearing (photos).
10 Undo the three Allen screws which hold the input shaft bearing retainer (note their O-ring seals - these screws go right through to the inside of the gearbox) take off the housing and withdraw the input shaft with its bearing. The inner end of this shaft contains 14 rollers on which the mainshaft runs - watch out for them.

There is a synchromesh cone associated with this shaft - keep corresponding cones and gears together so that when you inspect the components you know which is associated with what (photos).
11 On M45 gearboxes there is no input shaft housing. Remove the input shaft seal and withdraw the input shaft with its bearing (photo).
12 Take out the mainshaft assembly complete with its bearing housing. With the mainshaft out, you can now lift out the layshaft. Check that you have got all those needle rollers from inside the casing (photos).
13 On the M45 gearbox the rear cover having been removed it is necessary to remove the mainshaft bearing. Two screwdrivers under the circlip will start it on its way. Lift the mainshaft and then the layshaft out through the top of the gearbox (photos).

---

5   Mainshaft - dismantling

1   The photograph shows a view of the mainshaft and its associated components. The right-hand end enters the input shaft and the engaging sleeve picks up the engaging teeth on this shaft in top gear. The left-hand end (sticking out of the housing) normally carries a flange which

4.11 Removing the input shaft (M45)

4.12a The mainshaft assembly being removed

4.12b Removing the laygear

4.13a Starting the bearing on its way (M45) ...

4.13b ... and removing the mainshaft bearing

4.13c Lifting out the mainshaft assembly (M45) ...

4.13d ... followed by the layshaft (M45)

5.1 Mainshaft assembly

Fig. 6.12. Mainshaft of gearbox with overdrive. The shaft is being pressed out of its bearing (Sec. 5)

5.2a Remove the circlip retaining the synchromesh hub ...

5.2b ... and slide off the hub and the engaging sleeve as a unit

Fig. 6.13. Pulling off the front synchroniser (Sec. 5)

5.2c Then take off the synchronising baulk ring ...

5.2d ... the third gear pinion and the spacer ring behind it ...

5.3a ... revealing the circlip holding the second spacer gear

5.3b Remove the circlip and the spacing ring behind it

engages with the propeller shaft. Where overdrive is fitted, the left-hand end of the mainshaft is a lot longer and carries an eccentric for operating the overdrive oil pump. The bearing housing is different because it does not have to carry the speedometer drive. The bearing housing and rear end of this mainshaft are shown in Fig. 6.12. The eccentric for operating the pump is keyed on to the shaft just behind the shoulder. Once this is removed, the remainder of the instructions in this and the next Section apply equally to both types of shaft.

2 Remove the circlip at the end of the shaft remote from the bearing housing and slide off the synchronising hub and engaging sleeve as a single unit, then the synchronising cone and third speed gear. If the hub is a tight fit on the shaft, use a puller with its ends tucked behind the third speed gear as shown in Fig. 6.13. You know this is the third speed gear because it is the smallest of the three forward gears and so gives the least reduction ratio apart from the direct drive for top gear (photos).

3 Slide off the synchronising cone, the second speed gear and the spacing ring behind it. This brings you to the circlip retaining the second speed gear, and slide off the gear (photos).

Remove this circlip and spacing ring that lies between it and the second speed gear, and slide off the gear.

4 Slide off the synchronising cone and the engaging sleeve which also serves as a member of the reverse gear train. In this case you cannot take the synchronising hub with it as with the fourth speed/third speed engaging sleeve (paragraph 3) because the hub is in one piece with the shaft. When you pull it off, watch for the detents and spring which will fall out.

5 Using the first speed gear as a support, drive or push out the mainshaft from the bearing housing. A hide mallet carefully applied will do the trick or you can use a suitable puller or a home-made substitute.

The spacing ring and first speed gear can now be slid off the shaft, followed by the first speed synchronising cone (photos).

6 Remove the circlip from the mainshaft bearing housing and lift out the bearing. This reveals the speedometer pinion unless you have the overdrive version in which the speedometer is naturally driven from the overdrive unit. Notice the way the friction drive spring for the pinion is fitted (photos).

7 Remove the oil seal from the other side of the bearing housing.

6 Input shaft - dismantling

1 The input shaft bearing is held on by a circlip and removal calls for no special comment. Note that this circlip comes in alternative thicknesses and is selected to be a snug fit in the groove. Bear this in mind if you have to renew the shaft or circlip.

7 Layshaft assembly (M45) - dismantling

1 Examine the taper roller bearings and renew if defective. Remove the defective bearings with a puller and press fit the replacement bearings (photo).

8 Gearbox components - examination

1 If the gearbox has been stripped because of some specific fault such as failure to stay in a selected gear, difficulty in engaging gear, or the sort of noise which can no longer be ignored, the cause of the fault will usually be pretty obvious (see also Fault Diagnosis, Section 18). A not so obvious cause of noise and trouble is bearing wear, which it is well worthwhile to rectify by replacing the bearings concerned before things get to such a state that you have to replace a shaft.

2 If you can detect slop in the bearings when they are still full of oil they are obvious candidates for the scrap heap, but otherwise you should give them a good wash in paraffin or cleaning fluid with a final rinse in White Spirit. You can then examine them for signs of wear, scoring, blueing or excessive play - ie. any play that you can actually feel. If you are in any doubt at all, replace them. In fact there is a lot to be said for replacing the bearings as a matter of course.

3 If the synchromesh cones show signs of wear or have a battered look around the slots that engage with the detents, they should be replaced. Once again, it is a good idea to replace them as a matter

5.3c Slide off the second gear pinion

5.5a The front gear and its baulk ring coming off the mainshaft. (Note the engaging sleeve is still in position)

5.5b Mainshaft components (engaging sleeves assembled on synchronising hubs)

5.6a Remove the circlip from the bearing housing ...

5.6b ... which is then easily pushed out

5.6c Removing the speedometer drive pinion ...

5.6d ... and its driving spring

7.1 Layshaft assembly (M45)

Fig. 6.14. Fitting the mainshaft bearing into its housing (M40) (Sec. 10)

of routine - they are not expensive.

4   Examine the teeth of all gears for signs of uneven/excessive wear and chipping. If a gear is in a bad state have a good look at the gear it engages with - you may have to replace this too, a nuisance if it happens to be on the layshaft which will then have to be replaced complete.

5   All the gears should be a good running fit on the shaft with no signs of rocking. The fourth/third speed synchronising hub should not be a sloppy fit on the shaft splines.

6   All parts of the selector mechanism should be examined for wear. This includes the selector forks - Volvo have thoughtfully fitted engaging pins on the first/second speed selector fork so that you do not have to replace the whole lot if these get worn.

7   We think it is false economy not to renew the oil seals, but if you intend to use the old ones again check that they are in good condition.

9   Gearbox - reassembly

1   Assembling the gearbox is a slightly tricky business, but there is nothing really to worry about. It is not the sort of job in which, if you make a mistake, you find out about it disastrously some months later. It is more like a jigsaw puzzle - once you have done it you know it is right. The chief precaution you need to take if you have not worked on a gearbox before is to allow yourself a lot more time than you think you can possibly need.

2   You may also like to give yourself a revision course on gearbox design before you start. Take a look first at Fig. 6.5. This shows the input shaft locked to the mainshaft by the synchronising sleeve on the left which is pushed over to the left as far as it will go. This is of course the forward end of the gearbox. Obviously as we change from fourth speed to third speed this is the synchronising sleeve that moves, so we know at once that the third speed gear is at the front end of the mainshaft, near where it joins the input shaft. The next two gears must be second and first, with the reverse gear forming part of the synchronising sleeve which slides between them. The gear stick comes backwards to engage second speed and forwards to engage first speed, so we know that the synchronising sleeve moves forwards to engage second speed and backwards to engage first speed, just as the other synchronising sleeve moves forwards to engage fourth speed and backwards to engage third speed. This means that the first speed gear (the biggest one, having the most reduction) must be at the back end of the mainshaft.

3   With the biggest gear at the back, naturally we have to have the smallest gear on the layshaft also at the back. So now we know which way round and in what order you have to put the various gears. Obviously the cone surfaces on each pair of gears have to face each other so we know which way round on the mainshaft the gears have to go. A look at the layshaft reveals that the reverse gear is close to the second speed gear; this tells you that the reverse gear teeth on the synchronising sleeve on the mainshaft must be near the second speed gear, ie. they must face the front. Once you have the logic of the thing in mind, you will not need to keep referring to Fig. 6.5 or any other figure to see which way round and where the various gears have to go.

4   Assembly of the M45 mainshaft is basically the same as described in Section 10 for the M40, except there is no bearing housing, the bearing being fitted on the shaft.

10   Mainshaft - reassembly

1   Where applicable, assemble the speedometer drive gear into the bearing housing (see photographs 5.6c and 5.6d).

2   Using a suitable drift, press the mainshaft bearing into the housing (see Fig. 6.14). You can easily make a substitute for the Volvo drift shown in the Figure and use your vice as a press. Smear the bearing and housing with oil and be sure that the bearing goes in perfectly straight.

3   Smear the oil seal with oil and fit it the correct way round, ie. the thin end towards the gearbox.

4   Before fitting the bearing housing to the shaft, assemble the first speed/second speed engaging sleeve with its detents and springs over the synchroniser hub on the shaft (photo and Fig. 6.7). The groove on the synchroniser faces the rear of the shaft, ie. the flange end or, if overdrive is fitted, the long splined end. Then slip the first gear and its synchronising cone on to the shaft (both gear and synchronising sleeve, of course, must have their tapered ends facing the synchronising hub), assemble the housing on to the shaft and fit the circlip. Assemble the second and third speed gears and the third/fourth speed synchroniser on to the shaft, using the dismantling photo sequence 5.2, 5.3 and 5.5 in reverse order as guidance. The parts should be well smeared with oil before assembly. There is nothing particular to watch unless you are fitting new circlips, when you should be sure that these are selected to be a snug fit in the grooves; they are supplied in different thicknesses (photos).

11   Input shaft - reassembly

1   Press the bearing on to the input shaft, having smeared both with oil using a suitable substitute for the tool shown in Fig. 6.15.

2   Grease the 14 mainshaft bearing rollers and assemble these in the input shaft (see photo 49d). From now on the input shaft must be handled with a steady hand in order that the rollers do not get jolted out of place.

12   Reverse pinion - reassembly (M40)

1   If you have removed it, reassemble the idler pinion for the reverse train with its shaft into the casing. Note that the shaft end must protrude 0.28 - 0.30 in (7.0 - 7.6 mm) outside the housing (see Fig. 6.16).

13   Layshaft (M40) - assembly

1   Whatever you did on dismantling, you will have to have some sort of retainer for the needle bearings inside the laygear which you can rely on to hold them in place while you fiddle about with it during reassembly of the gearbox. We used a tube of slightly smaller diameter than the layshaft; slotting its ends and opening them out until they were a good fit inside the needle bearing assembly (photo).

2   Using the layshaft as a steady, fit the spacing washers and bearing needles into the laygear, using plenty of grease to anchor

10.4a The sliding keys are inserted between the engaging sleeve and the synchronising hub ...

10.4b ... backed by a spring at each end (see Fig. 6.7)

10.4c Select circlips which fit snugly in their grooves they are supplied in different thicknesses

2412

Fig. 6.15. Fitting the ball bearing on the input shaft (Sec. 11)

7,3 ±0,3mm
0.29"±0.012"

1

2

Fig. 6.16. Fitting the reverse pinion shaft (M45) (Sec. 12)

1 Reverse shaft   2 Gearbox casing

13.1 A piece of copper tube with the ends flared out a little made a successful needle roller bearing retainer for the layshaft

13.2a To reassemble the layshaft needle bearings, first insert a spacing ring ...

13.2b ... then using plenty of grease ...

them. The grease will stick better if the laygear is really clean and dry. Then slide the retainer in, letting it push the layshaft out of the laygear (photos).

14 Assembling components into gearbox casing (M40)

1 Press the input shaft bearing into the gear case as far as it will go (ie. until its retaining clip touches the case). Now stick the thrust washers for the layshafts to the inside of the case with grease. If the case and washers are clean and dry they will stick all right.

2 Now comes the bit where a steady hand and deliberate movement is all important. Give things a jolt now, and they will come unstuck - literally. With the case standing upright on the bench, position the layshaft on the bottom of the case centrally and the right way round, ie. with the larger gears at the input shaft end.

3 Check that the rollers in the input shaft are properly in place and that the thrust washers are aligned with the holes for the layshaft. Slip the synchronising cone over the input shaft, and then pass the mainshaft through the hole in the end of the case (do not forget

13.2c ... and the layshaft as a steady, insert the needle roller bearings in the laygear ...

13.2d ... followed by the second spacer

13.2e Then insert the retainer, letting it push the shaft through the laygear

14.5 Fixing the mainshaft bearing housing

14.6 Don't cover up this hole when fitting the gasket for the input shaft housing

15.1 Be sure the selector forks are in place before you put the rods back

its gasket!) and gently engage it with the input shaft, pushing the housing into the hole in the casing as far as it will go.

4   Now comes the most ticklish bit. If it does not come off first time the penalty is not very severe - you will simply have to remove the mainshaft, reposition the thrust washers and if you are very unlucky take out the layshaft and reposition some of its rollers. To avoid this irritating frustration, proceed deliberately and gently. Get hold of the gear case, positioning your forefingers in the holes for the layshaft so that if necessary you can prevent the thrust washers from sliding right over the holes. Gently turn the case upside down so that the laygear comes to rest on the mainshaft with its ends more or less opposite the holes for the layshaft. If the thrust washers have moved slightly, align them with the holes and then insert the layshaft. Push the shaft through the laygear, letting it drive out the retaining tube. When the end of the shaft appears in the hole at the far end of the case, you have won.

5   Do not be tempted to pick up the gearbox from the bench until you have fixed the mainshaft bearing housing in its correct position - and for the overdrive gearbox this involves fitting the spacing flange for the overdrive unit with its gasket and the tab washers (new of course) for the bottom pair of fixing bolts. Do not forget the sealing washers for the fixing bolts (photo).

6   Slide the circular gasket over the input shaft, making sure that it is the proper way round - there is a hole in the gearbox casing which must be lined up with the hole in the gasket. This provides a path for oil to reach the input shaft bearing. Push the housing over the shaft and fasten to the gear case with its three fixing bolts, not forgetting their O-ring seals (photo).

7   Replace the speedometer drive pinion in the bearing housing where applicable.

15 Selectors (M40) - assembly

1   Place the two selector forks in their correct positions (the photo shows which way round they go) before you insert any of the selector rods.

2   Insert the centre rod and drive in the lock pin which anchors the

selector fork to it.

3   Insert the first/second speed rod, fitting the dog to it so that when positioned on the shaft by its grubscrew it slopes towards the dog on the centre shaft. Tighten the grubscrew for the fork and the dog (photo).

4   Fit the remaining selector rod whose dog operates the lever which moves the reverse idler gear.

5   Place the interlock balls and springs in position and fit on the gearbox cover. Check that all gears engage and disengage freely.

6   Fit the cover over the ends of the selector rods.

7   For a gearbox without overdrive, engage two gears at once, thus locking the output shaft and fit the flange. For a gearbox with overdrive, fit the eccentric which operates the oil pump on the mainshaft, using a circlip which fits snugly into the groove.

8   Assemble the clutch housing to the gearbox and fit the clutch release lever and thrust bearing.

16 Assembling components into gearbox casing (M45)

1   Fit the reverse gear selector rod and dog. Do not fit the dog lock pin yet.

2   Fit the reverse gear and shaft. Check and if necessary adjust reverse gear shaft position. The shaft must be flush with the housing $\pm$ 0.002 in (0.05 mm) (photo).

3   If necessary, adjust the clearance between reverse gear and selector. Adjust by driving in the shift selector bearing pin with a drift. Correct clearance 0.004 - 0.079 in (0.1 - 2.0 mm), see Fig. 6.17.

4   Place the layshaft in the bottom of the casing.

5   Place the mainshaft in the casing and fit the axial washer and bearing on the mainshaft. The spacer ring must be fitted on the bearing, Fig. 6.18.

6   Press the mainshaft bearing into position. Push the reverse gear towards the centre of the gearbox to prevent teeth from clashing and becoming damaged. The bearing spacer ring should be against the casing when bearing is in its correct position.

7   Grease and fit roller bearing in the input shaft. Place the 4th synchronising hub and fit the input shaft to the mainshaft. Press in the shaft

15.3 Use a suitable screwdriver for this important tightening operation

16.2 Fitting the reverse gear and shaft

Fig. 6.17. Adjusting the clearance between reverse gear and selector (Sec. 16)

Fig. 6.18. Fitting the mainshaft bearing (M45) (Sec. 16)

Fig. 6.19. Input shaft with roller bearing in position (Sec. 16)

Fig. 6.20. Input shaft with spacer ring fitted (Sec. 16)

16.10 Fitting the layshaft outer bearings

as far as possible.

8   Place the layshaft so that the bearings are located in their housings.

9   Pull out the input shaft far enough, so that the spacer ring can be fitted on the bearing, then push in the shaft so that the spacer ring is against the casing.

10 Fit the layshaft outer bearing (photo).

11 Determine the thickness of shims for the input shaft by measuring (use a depth micrometer) the distance between the outer edge of the input shaft bearing and the casing, and the distance between the clutch housing contact face and the bottom of the bearing seat. The permitted axial clearance is 0.0004 - 0.0059 in (0.01 - 0.15 mm). When calculating the thickness of shim required do not forget to allow for a gasket thickness of 0.0098 in (0.25 mm) (Fig. 6.21).

12 Grease the gasket and shims to keep them in position on the casing and fit the clutch housing, tighten the retaining bolts to a torque of 25 - 36 lb ft (3.5 - 5.0 kg m) (Fig. 6.22). Fit the clutch withdrawal fork and thrust bearing as described in Chapter 5.

Fig. 6.21. Measuring the distance between the clutch housing contact face and bottom of bearing seat

16.13a Fitting the selector rods and dogs

Fig. 6.22. Fitting the clutch housing (Sec. 16)

16.13b Fitting selector lock pin

Fig. 6.23. Lock pins fitted flush in selector forks and dogs (Sec. 16)

16.15 Speedometer pinion fitted on mainshaft

13 Place the selector forks in position (they are both the same) and fit the selector rods and dogs. Fit the lock pins and drive them in flush with the upper edge of the dogs and selector forks, Fig. 6.23. Take care not to drive them in too far as they will foul the gears (photos).

14 Determine the thickness of shims for the layshaft and mainshaft by the same method as for the input shaft, paragraph 11 above. Permissible axial clearance:

Layshaft - 0.0009 - 0.0039 in (0.025 - 0.10 mm)
Mainshaft - 0.0004 - 0.0060 in (0.01 - 0.15 mm)

Do not forget to include a gasket thickness of 0.0098 in (0.25 mm) in your calculations.

15 Fit the speedometer pinion with flange facing the bearing (photo).
16 Place the shims for layshaft on the bearing and the mainshaft shims in the rear cover, use grease to hold in position. Fit gasket and rear cover. Tighten rear cover bolts to a torque of 25-36 lb f ft (3.5-5 kg f m).

17 Engage two gears at the same time and fit the flange. Tighten to a torque of 67-88 lb f ft (9.3 - 12.2 kg f m) (photo).
18 Fit the speedometer drive and retainer.
19 Place the gasket, interlock balls and springs in position and fit the gearbox cover. Tighten the bolts to a torque of 11-18 lb f ft (1.5-2.5 kg f m). Check that all gears engage and disengage freely.
20 Fit the reverse light contact and the rear selector rod. Fit the gearlever carrier (photos).

---

17 Gearbox - refitting in vehicle

This calls for no special comment, being simply a reversal of the removal procedure which has already been described in Section 3. Do not forget the electrical connection to overdrive unit, if fitted, and the reversing light. Do not forget to fill up with oil and check the drain and filler/level plugs for tightness.

Fig. 6.24. Tightening the rear cover bolts (Sec. 16)

Fig. 6.25. The speedometer drive and retainer (Sec. 16)

16.17 Fitting the gearbox flange

16.20a Fitting the reverse light contact

16.20b Fitting the gearlever carrier

18 Fault diagnosis - manual gearbox

Symptom	Reason/s
Weak or ineffective synchromesh	Synchronising cones worn, split or damaged. Baulk ring synchromesh dogs worn or damaged.
Jumps out of gear	Incorrectly assembled synchro units. Gearbox coupling dogs badly worn. Selector fork rod groove badly worn. Incorrect assembly of selector components.
Excessive noise	Incorrect grade of oil in gearbox or oil level too low. Bearings worn or damaged. Gear teeth excessively worn or damaged. Shimming of layshaft and/or mainshaft incorrect (M45 gearbox). Layshaft thrust washers worn (M40).
Excessive difficulty in engaging gear	Clutch pedal adjustment incorrect.

19 Overdrive - general description

1   The overdrive is essentially an extra gearbox, automatically control-led, driven by the output shaft of the main gearbox and producing on its own output shaft a step-up ratio of 0.797 : 1. The 'gear change' is controlled hydraulically, the hydraulic control valve being operated by a solenoid. The electrical connections to the solenoid are taken through a switch on the cover of the main gearbox which ensures that overdrive can only be brought into operation when the car is in top gear.

2   A cut-away illustration of the overdrive and an exploded view are shown in Figs. 6.26 and 6.27.

3   The heart of the overdrive is the epicyclic gear system whose com-ponents are shown in Fig. 6.27. These parts are assembled on the elongated mainshaft which extends from the main gearbox. Two of these parts, the planet carrier and the unidirectional clutch, are splined to the mainshaft and always revolve, therefore, at mainshaft speed. The unidirectional clutch sits inside the output shaft and ensures that if nothing else is driving the output shaft it will be driven by the gear-box mainshaft. In this manner, of course, the 1 : 1 ratio is obtained.

When this occurs, the planet carrier and the annulus on the output shaft are revolving at the same speed so the planet gears within the planet carrier are not being driven forwards or backwards and remain stationary on their splines. This means that the sun wheel must also be revolving at the same speed as the planet carrier and the annulus. The sun wheel is splined to the sliding clutch member and this too is revolving at the mainshaft speed. In practice the sliding clutch member is held against the tapered extension of the mainshaft when the 1 : 1 ratio is required and the whole gear system is locked together (Fig. 6.28).

4   To obtain the step-up ratio, the sliding clutch member is drawn away from the output shaft annulus and comes up against the outer casing of the gearbox which holds it stationary. It is still splined to the sun wheel, so this, too, is prevented from turning. This is shown in Fig. 6.28. The planet carrier continues to revolve at mainshaft speed, but because the sun wheel is stationary the planet wheels turn around their spindles in the planet carrier. This means that the outer teeth of the planet wheel (which mesh with the annulus) are moving relative to the planet carrier, and this makes the annulus move faster than the planet carrier.

Fig. 6.26. Cut-away view of overdrive unit (Sec. 19)

1	Thrust bearing	13	Uni-directional clutch	25	Solenoid	37	Pump cylinder
2	Thrust bearing retainer	14	Oil trap	26	Piston seal	38	Magnet
3	Sunwheel	15	Ball bearing	27	Piston	39	Pre-filter
4	Clutch sliding member	16	Bush	28	Operating valve	40	Fine filter
5	Brake ring	17	Thrust washer	29	Orifice nozzle	41	Pump plunger
6	Clutch member linings	18	Speedometer driving gear	30	Cylinder top	42	Connecting rod
7	Planet gear	19	Spacer	31	Cylinder	43	Front casing
8	Needle bearing	20	Ball bearing	32	Spring	44	Input shaft (gear-box mainshaft)
9	Shaft	21	Output shaft	33	Large piston	45	Eccentric
10	Planet carrier	22	Oil seal	34	Small piston	46	Bridge piece
11	Oil thrower	23	Coupling flange	35	Base plate	47	Spring
12	Uni-directional clutch rollers	24	Rear casing	36	Check valve for oil pump		

Fig. 6.27. Exploded view of overdrive unit (Secs. 19, 23, 24 and 26)

1	Nut	28	Key	57	O-ring
2	Lockwasher	29	Resilient ring	58	Cylinder
3	Bridge piece	30	Circlip	59	O-ring
5	Breather	31	Eccentric	60	Plug
6	Front casing	32	Piston pin	61	Spring
7	Gasket	33	Gasket	62	Ball
8	Brake ring	36	Stud	63	Non-return body
9	O-ring	37	Orifice nozzle	64	O-ring
10	O-ring	38	Seal	65	Pump body
11	Seal	39	Plug	66	Pump plunger
12	Gasket	40	O-ring	67	Washer
13	Solenoid	41	End piece	68	Fine filter
14	Bolt	42	Piston	69	Seal
15	Thrust bearing retainer	43	Washer	70	Plug
16	Spring	44	Spring	71	Data plate
17	Thrust bearing	45	Retainer	72	Screw
18	Circlip	46	Spring	73	Planet gear and carrier
19	Circlip	47	Screw	74	Sunwheel
20	Circlip	48	Screw	75	Clutch sliding member
21	Stud	49	Holder	76	Pre-filter
22	Piston seal	50	Spring	77	Gasket
23	Piston	51	O-ring	78	Magnet
24	Connecting rod	52	Plug	79	Base plate
25	Non-return ball	53	Nut	80	Bolt
26	Non-return valve spring	54	Piston	81	Resilient washer
27	Plug				

84	Bush
85	Thrust washer
86	Oil thrower
87	Circlip
88	Uni-directional clutch
89	Stud
90	Resilient washer
91	Nut
95	Speedometer pinion
96	O-ring
97	Bush
99	Bolt
100	Retainer
101	Oil seal
102	Stud
106	Speedometer driving gear
110	Output shaft
111	Ball bearing
112	Spacer
113	Rear casing
114	Ball bearing
115	Oil seal
116	Flange
117	Washer
118	Nut

Fig. 6.28. Working principle of overdrive (Sec. 19)

1   Direct drive
2   Overdrive
A   Non-rotating parts
B   Parts rotating at the same speed as the input shaft
C   Parts rotating at a higher speed than the input shaft

Fig. 6.29. Cut-away view of relief valve (Secs. 20 and 23)

1 Dashpot piston	9 Relief valve spindle
2 Dashpot sleeve	10 Residual spring
3 Dashpot spring cup	11 Relief valve spring cup
4 Dashpot spring	12 Relief valve spring
5 Relief valve for lubricating oil pressure	13 Double dashpot spring
6 Drilling from oil pump	14 Restrictor plug
7 Drilling to mainshaft	15 Drilling from operating valve
8 Relief valve body	16 Dashpot plug

Note - lower dashpot and item 13 are omitted in later models

Fig. 6.30. Cut-away view of oil pump (Sec. 20)

1 Mainshaft	8 O-ring
2 Eccentric	9 Valve seat
3 Connecting rod	10 Spring
4 Gudgeon pin	11 Plug
5 Piston	12 O-ring
6 Cylinder	13 Pre-filter
7 Ball	

5   To 'change gear', therefore all that is necessary is to slide the clutch member along the mainshaft. This member is pushed forwards by four coil springs anchored by bridge pieces through a thrust bearing assembly. When the hydraulic system is actuated, two pistons push on the bridge pieces and draw the sliding member along the shaft until it comes up against the outer case. This changes the drive ratio as already described.

6   The sliding member is bolted to bridge pieces. Behind these bridge pieces are hydraulically operated pistons which are able to push the bridge pieces away from the case against the action of the clutch return springs when the hydraulic pressure is great enough. This means that changing gear is simply a matter of raising the oil pressure applied to the pistons. The oil pressure is generated in the first instance by a piston pump which is driven by an eccentric release valve which gives either a low pressure or a high pressure according to whether the solenoid is energised or not (details of how this is done is given in Section 20). The oil reaches the pistons through oilways in the casing.

20 Hydraulic pressure control

1   The solenoid operated control valve is a simple double-ended affair which is sprung against a seating and blocks off the oil inlet to the valves when the solenoid is not energised. When voltage is applied to the solenoid, the valve is pushed against its spring until it comes up

against a lower seating, allowing oil to flow through the control valve and into the relief valve via the orifice nozzle. To see how this affects the relief valve take a look at Fig. 6.29.

2   The key to this figure is the small piston which when pushed down by oil pressure building up in the inlet channel uncovers drillings in the body which allows oil to flow into channel and also to the relief valve, which sets a limit on the pressure that can build up. This cylinder acts against a complex arrangement of dashpots and springs which eventually all push against a large piston at the bottom of the valve. When oil is admitted into the lower input channel by the action of the control valve, this piston is pushed upwards compressing the springs and thus making it harder for the small piston to be pushed down. The oil pressure builds up until this piston eventually moves against the increased spring pressure and a new state of equilibrium is reached.

3   The oil pump (shown in Fig. 6.30) is simple in principle, oil being drawn in on the up stroke of the plunger and pushed past the ball valve into the outlet channel on the down stroke. It draws oil from the bottom of the case which acts as a sump and the system incorporates a filter, just like the oil system in a car engine.

4   As well as supplying the hydraulic system, the oil pump provides pressure lubrication via a drilling in the gearbox mainshaft which connects with the channel. The oil finds its way through the unidirectional clutch, and via the planet gear back to the bottom of the overdrive case.

21 Overdrive unit - removal and replacement

1   It is helpful, before removing the overdrive, to start the car and engage and disengage the overdrive with the clutch pedal depressed. This will avoid leaving any residual torque in the mainshaft, planet carrier and unidirectional clutch. If this has not been done, disconnect the propeller shaft and then, of course, achieve the same object without

moving the car.

2   Place a jack under the engine sump and remove the gearlever and gearbox support member as described in Section 3. Disconnect the propeller shaft, the exhaust pipe bracket and the electrical lead.

3   Lower the engine enough to let you get at the upper fixing nuts holding the overdrive unit to the spacing flange. Remove the nuts and withdraw the unit leaving the spacing flange on the gearbox.

4   Refitting to the gearbox is dealt with in Section 27.

22 Overdrive overhaul - preliminaries

1   Overhauling an overdrive presents special problems to the owner mechanic whose workshop facilities are limited. These arise from the fact that the unit incorporates a hydraulic mechanism which depends for its operation on the same oil that lubricates the gears. Absolute cleanliness is therefore essential. We recommend that for anything other than the simplest check the unit is removed from the vehicle, thoroughly cleaned, and then taken to a work place where scrupulous cleanliness can be maintained throughout the whole time that the unit is dismantled. Any lower standard than this is asking for trouble. Another set of problems is posed by the multiplicity of small parts in the hydraulic units. The best - almost the only - way to cope with these is to lay out the bits and pieces in order as they are disassembled, on a clean surface (a table covered with newspaper for example) where they can be covered over and left undisturbed. Putting them in small separate containers is very much a second best; if this is not done a lot of time will be wasted during reassembly making sure that everything is in the right place and the right way round.

2   Dismantling and reassembling the mechanical bits and pieces presents no special problem apart from the requirement for extreme cleanliness. Have the outside spotlessly clean before starting. This is more than just a good idea - it is essential. Smear all parts with oil as they are assembled.

3   Dismantling an overdrive unit is a job which needs better working conditions than the average owner has available and every bit of care and thoroughness that can be mustered.

4   If the overdrive is in working order prior to overhaul, it is worth-while to check the oil pressure. Volvo recommend that this is done while the car is being driven and their agents have a special pressure gauge with suitable adaptors to fit to the different models of over-drive unit. When driving on direct drive at about 25 mph (40 kph) the pressure should be about 21 lb/sq in (1.5 kg/sq cm). When the overdrive is engaged, the pressure should rise to 380-425 lb/sq in (27-30 kg/sq cm). When the overdrive is disengaged, the pressure should drop to about 21 lb/sq in (1.5 kg/sq cm) within three seconds.

23 Solenoid, oil pump, hydraulic valves - dismantling

1   Remove the baseplate and the pre-filter and drain the oil into a perfectly clean container if you are proposing to use it again. **Warning:** If the overdrive has been running just before you drain it, the oil may be hot enough to scald you.

2   Remove the solenoid, using a 1 in (25 mm) open-ended spanner on the hexagon. The solenoid and operating valve form an integral unit which cannot be dismantled further and must be replaced complete if faulty.

3   Removing the baseplate and pre-filter will have revealed three plugs which retain the fine filter, oil pump and relief valve (see Fig. 6.31). To make a suitable tool for removing these plugs, get hold of two small bolts whose heads fit into the holes in the plugs and screw these into a pair of holes in a length of metal strip. If the surface of your strip rests against the plugs and the bolt heads are a reasonable fit in the holes you will be able to remove the plugs quite easily without trouble or damage (see Fig. 6.32). It is well worthwhile taking the trouble to make some-thing like this rather than simply pushing bolts into the holes in the plugs - a method which will certainly lead to loss of time and loss of temper.

4   Remove the fine filter and its seal which are under the largest of the three plugs. Then turn your attention to the awe-inspiring assort-ment of bits and pieces which go to make up the relief valve. Check each part as it comes out against the exploded view in Fig. 6.27 and the cut-away view in Fig. 6.29, (the secondary dashpot is not present in later models). We strongly recommend that you lay the pieces out somewhere where they will not be disturbed or get dirty. Draw out

Fig. 6.31. Three plugs under the baseplate and pre-filter hold the fine filter (shown dismantled), the relief valve and the oil pump (Sec. 23)

1   Filter   2   Seal   3   Plug

Fig. 6.32. Tool for applying correct torque when refitting plugs: To obtain correct tightening torque - connect spring balance to 'Q', keep-ing it at right angles to tool (Sec. 23)

'Q' - Balance hole   P - Pegs for holes in plugs A = 12 in (30 cm)
Balance reading of 16 lbs (7.33 gm) = 16 lbs ft (2.2 kg m) of torque

Fig. 6.33. Removal of relief valve with wire hook (Sec. 23)

the body of the relief valve as shown in Fig. 6.33, which also illus-trates the seating at the top of the valve for the small piston and the positioning of the ball valve which limits the pressure that can build up in the relief valve. The pump plunger can now be detached from the actuator and withdrawn through the pump body, which can then be withdrawn itself using a wire hook if necessary.

24 Overdrive mechanical components - dismantling

1   The numbers in brackets in this Section refer to Fig. 6.27.

2   Mount the unit vertically in a vice with wooden or copper jaw inserts, front end upwards. It is assumed that at this stage the solenoid and intermediate flange have been removed.

3   Straighten the locking tabs and unscrew the nuts for the piston bridge pieces (1,2,3) and remove the bridge pieces.

4   Unscrew the nuts holding together the front and rear sections of the casing (6,113) which have the brake ring (8) sandwiched between them. These should be slackened off gradually all round in case there is a difference in tension in the clutch sliding member return springs (16). The front casing and brake ring can now be lifted off the studs in the back case as shown in Fig. 6.34.

5   If necessary, use a copper drift to help free the brake ring from the casing.

6   Remove the clutch sliding member return springs and lift this member out complete with thrust bearing and sun wheel.

7   Lift out the planet carrier complete.

Fig. 6.34. Dismantling the overdrive (Secs. 24 and 26)

Fig. 6.35. Uni-directional clutch assembly (Secs. 24 and 26)

1 Spring	2 Cage	3 Hub

8   Removal of the pistons (23) from the front casing is best done with a small sucker (you can cut down one that is too big), unless you have compressed air available, when you can blow it out.

9   From the front casing remove the pump connecting rod (24).

10   To dismantle the clutch sliding member assembly, first remove circlip (20) and pull out the sun wheel. Then remove the circlip (19) and separate the bearing (17) and its housing (15) from the clutch sliding member. Finally, remove circlip (18) and press the bearing out of its housing.

11   Turning now to the rear casing, remove the bolt (99) and pull out the speedometer pinion and its associated bits and pieces.

12   Remove the flange nut and pull the flange off the shaft. Be sure that the centre part of your puller does not damage the thread at the end of the shaft - particularly if you are using a home-made device.

13   To disassemble the output shaft assembly, first press the output shaft out of the casing, then extract the inner bearing, freeing the speedometer pinion and spacer, then press out the rear bearing. These operations may make a bigger demand on the owner's workshop facilities than he is able to meet. We suggest, therefore, that having removed the oil seal (115) you check the assembly for lateral play after having washed all the oil out with paraffin followed by white spirit and if you find all is well leave it assembled; if not, have the bearings renewed at a local garage or workshop equipped for the job.

14   Remove circlip (87), take off oil thrower (86) and remove the unidirectional clutch from the annulus. Be doubly careful with the unidirectional clutch - make quite sure which way round it goes and mark it in some way to ensure that it goes back correctly, and watch the rollers as the clutch comes out - they are not attached in any way and like all such objects they have a wonderful instinct for concealment. Having got them all safely, have a good look at the way the spring and the cage are assembled in the outer frame of the unidirectional clutch. Compare the actual device with Fig. 6.35 which by itself may not be very revealing but will certainly serve as a reminder when you have seen the real thing.

15   Examine the bush (84) in the middle of the annulus before deciding to remove it, check that it is free from scores. Fit the output shaft to the gearbox mainshaft and check that there is no undue slop. If the bush is worn fit a new one. Be careful when fitting that it goes in straight and is not distorted or it will have to be reamed true.

25 Overdrive - inspection

1   No one will dismantle an overdrive unless he is certain that there is something wrong with it - excessive noise, failure to engage or disengage properly, or something of that sort. The nature of its shortcomings will have given a clue as to what to look for on dismantling and it may well be that the fault will be revealed before dismantling is complete. If this does happen, it still makes good sense to dismantle completely and give the whole thing a thorough inspection.

2   First of all, wash out all the passages in the casings and make sure that they are clean and dry. Two common domestic objects go a long way towards substituting for the compressed air so freely mentioned in service manuals and so rarely found in owner's workshops; the

ordinary hair drier and an empty plastic washing-up liquid container. This latter with its small rounded nozzle is a most useful device so long as it is clean and dry.

3   Give all the hydraulic bits and pieces a good wash and a good look over. Examine the seatings of all valves for possible scoring.

4   Wash the various bearings and the unidirectional clutch pieces in white spirit, dry them thoroughly with lint-free rag and inspect for excessive play and signs of wear.

5   Examine the various gears for signs of wear and damage. Make sure that the bush on the sun wheel is not worn. If it needs replacement, get a new sun wheel complete with bush - the bush must be concentric with the gear wheel and to achieve this is a factory job.

6   Check the pistons which act on the bridge pieces for signs of wear. Replace them if they are not perfect.

7   Check the brake ring for abrasion, cracks or wear.

8   Check the linings on the clutch sliding member for burning or wear.

9   Check the solenoid with a 12 volt battery and an ammeter. Current consumption should be about 2 amps and there should of course be no hesitation about its operation when it is disconnected from the unit. This should be checked again when the solenoid-operated control valve or control valve mechanism has been reassembled.

26 Overdrive - reassembly

1   Use new gaskets, O-rings, tab washers and oil seals when reassembling. If you are in any doubt about the filters, renew these too. The cost of these items is a small price to pay for peace of mind.

2   Absolute cleanliness is, of course, even more important during reassembly than during dismantling. Give every part a quick cleanliness check and smear it with oil as you reassemble it.

3   To assemble the rear casing and output shaft, press the front bearing on to the output shaft, followed by the speedometer spacers. Press the rear bearing into the rear casing using a drift similar to that shown in Fig. 6.36. Support the output shaft on a wooden block and then press the rear casing onto the shaft by pushing on the rear bearing with the same drift. Fig. 6.36 shows this process almost completed. As mentioned in Section 24, paragraph 13, this pressing operation may prove difficult for the average owner and it may be a good idea to have it done by a specialist.

4   Press in the oil seal, lubricating it well first. Get it the right way round - see Fig. 6.27.

5   Fit the coupling flange, washer and nut. Tighten the nut to a torque of 80-100 lb f ft (11-14 kg f m).

6   Assemble the unidirectional clutch cage on the hub with the spring as shown in Fig. 6.35, so that when viewed as in Fig. 6.37 the cage is sprung anticlockwise. Rotate the cage clockwise as far as it will go and lock it in this position with a temporary wedge. Position the rollers in the cage and tie them in with string.

7   Insert the thrust washer and follow this by the clutch in the centre of the output shaft, easing the string off the rollers when they are held by the mainshaft and removing the temporary wedge. Fit the oil

Fig. 6.36. Pressing the output shaft and its bearing into the rear casing (Sec. 26)

Fig. 6.37. Assembling the uni-directional clutch (Sec. 26)

1   Wedge

Fig. 6.38. Fitting the uni-directional clutch into the output shaft (Sec. 26)

thrower and circlip.

8   Reassemble the speedometer pinion and bush in the casing.

9   Position the planet gear assembly in the output shaft annulus. Note that when the overdrive is fitted to the gearbox the splines in the planet carrier will have to line up with those in the unidirectional clutch - both these items being splined to the gearbox mainshaft. Volvo make a special splined tool for ensuring this and you may care to make something that will do the same thing - perhaps either a wooden dowel with one or more 'splines' made of metal strip - but it can be done without as there is no centering problem - it is simply a matter of getting the splines lined up. You could do this at the last minute with a thin screwdriver pushed up the middle of the assembly.

10   Turning now to the clutch unit, first press the ball bearing into its retainer and fit the circlip (Fig. 6.27, Nos. 15, 17, 18 - numbers in brackets in the following paragraphs also refer to this figure).

11   Put the bolts (14) through their holes on the retainer and press the bearing with retainer on to the clutch sliding member. Fit the circlip (19). Fit the sun wheel and its circlip (20).

12   Insert the sun wheel into the planet cluster and fit the four thrust springs (16) on to the bolts. The clutch/output shaft assembly is now complete.

13   Now is a good time to consider exactly how you are going to ensure that those splines are lined up. It is better to solve this problem on the bench than underneath the car.

14   Assembly of the hydraulic components in the front case calls for no particular comment, being simply a reversal of the dismantling process. Do not forget a light smear of oil on everything. Put the actuating pistons (23) back in the case before assembling the valves and pump to avoid possible trouble with air pressure behind them.

15   Install the brake ring on the front casing and reassemble the front and rear casings with the brake ring between them exactly as they were taken apart (see Fig. 6.34). Tighten the fixing nuts evenly, a little at a time all round to avoid any possibility of distortion from the tension in the clutch springs. Note that the two upper fixing nuts have copper washers. Do not forget the tag washers on the nuts for the bridge pieces.

16   Finally, fit the solenoid and check its operation.

27 Overdrive - refitting to gearbox

1   It is as important to preserve cleanliness during this operation (carried out underneath the car in all probability) as it is when assembling the overdrive unit on a specially cleaned work bench. When working underneath the car it is easy to accidentally dislodge dirt from the subframe; this dirt then rains down - and could enter the overdrive unit if precautions are not taken during refitment. To avoid this problem, it is suggested that newspaper is stuck above the gearbox area so that at least the fall-out does not descend all over the overdrive. If the car is well jacked-up there will be more room to work and that is a help.

2   Do not forget the gasket.

3   When the overdrive unit is offered up to the gearbox the splines on the mainshaft will enter the unidirectional clutch at much the same time as the eccentric enters the connecting rod for the pump. However, thanks to the generous chamfer provided on this component it will pull itself into line if it is not exactly right to start with. The secret of success is to arrange matters by lining up the mainshaft splines, their opposite numbers on the unidirectional clutch and the planet gear cage and the pump connecting rod so that the unit can be slid straight on to the intermediate flange (attached to the gearbox) and pick up the holes on the flange with the studs - all this without having to turn the overdrive unit. Careful alignment before starting and a small amount of rocking just as the studs enter the intermediate flange should do the trick. If it does not, the best thing to do is to withdraw the unit and do the lining up again.

4   The rest of the installation is a simple reversal of the removal procedure.

5   Finally, do not forget to fill the unit with oil until level with the bottom of the filler plug hole in the side of the case. Check the oil after the car has been driven 6-9 miles (10-15 kms).

28 Fault diagnosis - overdrive

Listed overleaf are the commonest troubles experienced with overdrive and some possible causes. Start at the top of the list when looking for a fault and work through it. The overdrive is a well tried and well proven mechanism and - as the list reveals - trouble is more often due to causes outside the overdrive unit itself than within it.

Overdrive will not engage

1 *Faulty solenoid*
2 *Fault in electric wiring*
3 *Faulty gearbox switch*
4 *Faulty overdrive selector switch*
5 *Faulty relay (if fitted)*
6 *Low oil level in overdrive unit*
7 *Faulty non-return valve in oil pump*
8 *Blocked oil filter*

Overdrive will not release

Note: This fault should be attended to immediately. Above all, do not reverse when overdrive is engaged as this will cause considerable damage.

1 *Fault in electrical wiring, (voltage permanently on solenoid)*
2 *Control valve sticking*
3 *Mechanical damage in overdrive (note that when found this may be the result of the trouble and not its original cause)*
4 *Sticking unidirectional clutch*

Clutch slip in overdrive

1 *Low oil level in overdrive unit*
2 *Control valve incorrectly adjusted or not operating properly*
3 *Worn linings on clutch sliding member*

Noise

As the overdrive ages, normal wear may give rise to a certain amount of noise when the unit is in overdrive. Regard any harsh noise with the utmost suspicion. The only way you can be reasonably certain that the noise in your unit is significant or not is to consult someone who has the experience necessary to judge it.

29 Automatic transmission - general description

The Borg-Warner Model 35 automatic transmission fitted to the Volvo 240 series comprises two main components, a three element hydrokinetic torque converter coupling capable of torque multiplication at an infinitely variable ratio between 2 : 1 and 1 : 1 and a hydraulically operated epicyclic gearbox providing three forward ratios and reverse.

The automatic transmission is connected to an oil cooler which is housed in the bottom of the radiator. On some earlier models the oil cooler may not be fitted.

The control lever (which is mounted on the floor) has six positions: Position 'P' locks the transmission for parking; 'R' is reverse; 'N' is neutral; 'D' is the normal driving position; '2' stops the gearbox from engaging its third gear; '1' keeps the gearbox in first gear.

The BW55, introduced in 1977 has a different internal gearing system and the brake band systems have been replaced by multi-disc brake systems which do not require any adjustment. In respect of the operations dealt with in this manual both units are practically the same.

30 Automatic transmission - repair and maintenance

Because of the complexity of this unit, it is not recommended that the owner should attempt to dismantle it himself. If performance is not up to standard or some failure occurs, your Volvo garage should be called in. They will have special equipment for accurate fault diagnosis and rectification. Bear in mind that many tests of the unit are best carried out when it is still in the car, so if there is trouble, do not remove the unit from the car before placing it in the hands of the repairer.

The following Sections, therefore, confine themselves to adjustments and servicing information. Instruction for removal is given because this is an essential preliminary to removing the engine.

31 Fluid level - checking

1 Put gear selector in 'P'. Start the engine and allow it to idle. Shift into the various positions. Dwell in each position 4-5 seconds.
2 Shift back to 'P' and wait two minutes before checking the oil level.
3 Top up as necessary. The difference between the 'MIN' and 'MAX' levels is 1 pint (0.6 litre).

32 Speed selector linkage - adjustment

1 Place the control lever in '2'.
2 Disconnect the selector rod from the lever on the side of the transmission housing and then set the lever in position '2'. This is the first detent towards the rear of the car from the fully forward position.
3 Release the lock nut on the rod and adjust the length of the rod so that when it is reconnected there will be a clearance of about 0.04 in (1 mm) as shown at B in Fig. 6.40. Now move the control lever to 'D' and check that there is a similar gap at A.
4 Check that this clearance remains when the hand control is moved to '1' and 'P'. Make any minor adjustments which may be necessary and then tighten the locknut on the link rod.

33 Downshift cable - adjustment

1 The downshift cable is fitted with a crimped stop when it is set during production of the car. Should this stop have been removed or if it is loose on the cable, adjustment can only be carried out in the manner described in Section 34.
2 Check that the engine idling speed is correct.
3 Adjust the outer cable threaded adjuster until there is a gap between the end of the crimped stop and the end of the threaded adjuster of 0.04 in (1 mm).
4 Check that with the accelerator pedal fully depressed, the throttle lever is open fully to its stop.

Fig. 6.39. Borg-Warner Automatic Transmission type 35 (Sec. 29)

Fig. 6.40. Selector controls adjustment (Sec. 32)

Fig. 6.41. Selector control linkage (Sec. 32)

1	Selector lever knob, upper section	11	Shaft
2	Selector lever knob, lower section	12	Lever
3	Washer	13	Gearshift rod adjuster
4	Spring	14	Lock nut
5	Push rod	15	Control rod
6	Selector lever	16	Lever
7	Shift positions cover	17	Bracket
8	Shift positions light	18	Cable, shift positions light
9	Inhibitor plate	19	Detent
10	Housing	20	Button

34 Downshift cable - renewal and setting (BW35)

1   Remove the oil pan drain plug and drain the transmission fluid into a clean container. Remove the oil pan.
2   Disconnect the downshift cable at the carburettor end and then unscrew the outer cable locknuts and separate the cable from the support bracket.
3   Rotate the cam of the downshift valve until the nipple on the end of the inner cable can be released from the cam.
4   Unscrew the outer cable union from the transmission casing and remove the cable assembly.
5   The new cable will be supplied with the stop on the inner cable loose (uncrimped). Do not lubricate the new cable before installation.
6   Screw the new cable into the transmission casing and engage the inner cable with the downshift valve cam.
7   Attach the upper end of the cable to the throttle lever and the support bracket but leave the locknuts loose.
8   With the accelerator pedal fully released, adjust the locknuts at the upper end of the outer cable so that the cam to valve plunger relationship is as shown at 'A' in Fig. 6.42. Now have an assistant fully depress the accelerator pedal and check that the cam to valve plunger relationship is as shown at 'B'.
9   When adjustment is correct, tighten the cable locknuts and then crimp the stop to the inner cable so that there is a gap between it and the end face of the threaded adjuster of the outer cable of 0.04 in (1 mm).
10 Refit the oil pan and refill the transmission with fluid.
11 See Chapter 13 for BW55 and AW55 transmissions.

35 Starter inhibitor switch - replacement

1   Disconnect the switch leads and remove the contact.
2   Fit a new gasket on the contact. Screw in the contact and tighten to 10 lb f ft (1.4 kg f m).
3   Connect the leads and check that the engine can only be started

Fig. 6.42. Downshift valve cam relationship to accelerator pedal (Sec. 34)

A   Fully released   B   Fully depressed

with the selector in 'P' and 'N' and that the reversing light is on with the selector in 'R'.

36 Rear brake band - adjustment (BW35)

1   This is not a routine operation and should only require attention if after reference to Fault Diagnosis, Section 41, its adjustment is called for.
2   Access to the rear brake band adjuster is obtained after removing the interior mats from the front compartment, withdrawing the air duct and transmission tunnel cover. Remove the rubber plug from the hole in the transmission tunnel.
3   Release the locknut of the brake band adjuster screw and tighten the screw to 10 lb f ft (1.4 kg f m). Now unscrew the adjuster screw one complete turn and tighten the locknut without disturbing the setting.
4   Refit the transmission tunnel components.

37 Automatic transmission unit - removal and replacement

1 Withdraw the fluid dipstick and drain the fluid. On BW35 remove the drain plug; on BW55 removal of the filler tube drains the transmission. Be careful if the car has just been driven as the fluid will be very hot and can easily scald. Remove the guard plate from underneath the engine.

2 Disconnect the downshift cable at the engine end and detach it from its support bracket.

3 Disconnect the exhaust downpipe from the manifold.

4 Unless the car is on ramps or over an inspection pit it must be raised, and supported very securely, to provide adequate clearance for the torque converter housing to pass beneath the car as the transmission is removed.

5 Unbolt and remove the semi-circular cover plate from the lower front face of the torque converter housing.

6 Disconnect the front of the propeller shaft from the output flange of the transmission.

7 Disconnect the speed selector link rod from the lever on the side of the transmission casing.

8 Unbolt and remove the reinforcing bracket from the rear of the engine sump. Disconnect the oil cooler pipes.

9 Remove the starter motor.

10 Unscrew and remove the bolts which secure the torque converter to the driveplate. These bolts are accessible through the starter motor aperture. Each bolt can be brought into view by turning the crankshaft with a spanner on the pulley bolt.

11 Place a jack and a block of wood as a spreader under the rear end of the engine sump and take the weight of the engine.

12 Disconnect the transmission rear mounting and remove the support member and exhaust bracket.

13 Disconnect the speedometer cable from the transmission.

14 Unscrew the oil filler pipe union (BW35), remove the pipe and plug the hole in the transmission casing.

15 Lower the jack under the engine sump until the transmission is lowered about two inches at its rear end.

16 Disconnect the leads from the starter inhibitor switch and the earth strap.

17 Remove the bolts which secure the torque converter housing to the engine.

18 Using either a trolley jack or the help of two assistants withdraw the transmission rearwards. As soon as the torque converter housing starts to separate from the engine, use a thin lever to keep the torque converter pressed fully to the rear and in engagement with the oil pump drive dogs.

19 If required, the drive plate can be unbolted from the crankshaft rear mounting flange. This may be necessary if the starter ring gear is worn.

20 Installation is the reversal of the removal procedure but before offering the transmission to the engine, make sure that the torque converter is pushed fully to the rear so that the oil pump drive dogs are fully engaged. Keep the torque converter in this position until the torque converter housing is fully engaged with the engine.

21 Refill the unit on completion with the correct grade and quantity of fluid.

38 Fault diagnosis and rectification

1 The test procedure with its accompanying diagnosis and rectification instructions given in Section 40 will enable the owner to decide for himself whether or not the automatic transmission unit is faulty and, if faults are present, whether he himself will be able to rectify them or whether the fault must be corrected by a Volvo agent.

2 Test No 3 in this procedure is described in a little more detail in the remainder of this Section.

3 Before carrying out a stall test, make sure that the engine is developing full power and is properly adjusted. An engine which is not developing full power will affect the stall test reading.

4 Allow the engine and transmission to reach correct working temperatures.

5 Connect a tachometer to the vehicle.

6 Chock the wheels and apply the handbrake and foot brake (an assistant will be needed for this).

7 Select position '1' and run the engine with the accelerator pedal fully depressed. Check the engine speed against the figures specified at the beginning of this Chapter. Repeat the procedure with the selector in position '2'. The implications of speed readings, outside the specification, and other possible symptoms are discussed in Section 40, Test 3.

8 Do not carry out a stall test for a period longer than 10 seconds, otherwise the transmission will overheat.

39 Converter fault diagnosis

1 Inability to start on steep gradients, combined with poor acceleration from rest and low speed, indicate that the converter stator unidirectional clutch is slipping. This permits the stator to rotate in an opposite direction to the impeller and turbine and torque multiplication cannot occur.

2 Poor acceleration in third gear above 30 mph (48 kmph) indicates that the stator unidirectional clutch has seized. The stator will not rotate with the turbine and impeller and the 'fluid flywheel' phase cannot occur. This condition will also be indicated by excessive overheating of the transmission although the stall speed may be correct.

40 Road test procedure

The following test procedure may well be carried out periodically by the owner who is concerned with ensuring that his automatic transmission remains in tip-top condition. It will indicate the necessity for adjustment and may well reveal faults at an early stage, before they make themselves obvious by producing catastrophic failure.

We recommend that, even if you think you have found the cause of any trouble, you carry the tests through completely once you have started. One fault may give rise to another and it is as well to be sure that you know the full extent of the trouble, if any.

The test procedure follows:

Road test	Fault diagnosis	Rectification (see chart overleaf)
1 Check that the starter will operate only with the selector lever in 'P' and 'N' and that the reverse light operates only in 'R'	Starter will not operate in 'P' or 'N' Starter operates in all selector positions	19 20
2 Apply the hand and foot brakes and with the engine idling select 'N—D', 'N—2', 'N—1' and 'N—R'. Gearbox engagement should be felt in each position	Excessive bump on engagement of 'D', '2', '1' or 'R'	4, 3

3   Check the stall speed in '1' and 'R'. Do not stall for more than 10 seconds or transmission will overheat (see Section 38)

High stall speed:	
a) With slip and squawk in '1'	1, 2, 3, 13a, c, f, 11
b) With slip and squawk in 'R'	1, 2, 3, 13a, c, f, e, 12
Low stall speed: more than 600 rev/min below that specified (see Specifications)	21
Low stall speed: less than 600 rev/min below that specified (see Specifications)	23

4   With transmission at normal running temperature, select 'D' release the brakes and accelerate with minimum throttle. Check for 1—2 and 2—3 shifts. Confirm that third gear has been obtained by selecting '2' when a 3—2 shift should be felt

Note: A feature of this transmission is that a slight increase in throttle depression between 15 and 30 mph (25 and 48 kmph) may produce a 3—2 down-shift (part throttle down-shift)

No drive in 'D', '2' or '1'	1, 2, 3, 13a, 11, 16
No drive in 'D', drive in '1'	1, 2, 3, 16
No drive in 'D', '2', '1' or 'R'	1, 2, 3, 13a, 11, 16, 17
Delayed or no 1—2 shift	3, 14, 13a, 5, 6
Slip on 1—2 shift	2, 3, 5, 6, 7, 13c, f
Delayed or no 2—3 shift (if normal drive in 'R', omit 12)	3, 14, 13g, h, c, d, 5, 6, 12
Slip or engine run-up on 2—3 shift	2, 3, 5, 13a, c, 12
Bumpy gear-shifts	3
Drag on 'D' and '2'	8
Drag on binding on 2—3 shift	5, 6

5   From a standing start; accelerate using 'kick-down'. Check for 1—2 and 2—3 shifts at speeds specified at start of Chapter

Slip and squawk or judder on full throttle take-off in 'D'.	1, 2, 3, 13a, c, 11
Loss of performance and overheating in third gear	21
Other possible faults are as given in test No. 4	Continue as in test 4

6a   At 40 mph (65 kmph) in top gear release the accelerator and select '2' or '1'. Check for 3—2 shift and engine braking. Check for 2—1 roll out
b   At 15 mph (25 kmph) in second gear release the accelerator and select '1'. Check for 2—1 shift

No. 3—2 down-shift or engine braking	1, 5, 6, 7, 12
No. 2—1 down-shift and engine braking	8, 9, 10

7a   At the speed specified for 3—2 shift, in 3rd gear, depress the accelerator to kick-down, when the gearbox should down-shift to second gear.
b   At the speed specified for 3—1 shift, in second gear, depress the accelerator to kick-down when the gearbox should down-shift to first gear

Transmission will not down-shift	3, 13f, g, 14
Transmission will not down-shift	3, 13f, g, 14

8a   Stop, engage '1' and accelerate to 20 mph (30 kmph), check for clutch slip or breakaway noise (squawk) and that no up-shift occurs
b   Stop, engage 'R' and reverse the vehicle using full throttle if possible. Check for clutch or breakaway noise (squawk)

Slip, squawk or judder on take-off in '1'	1, 2, 3, 13, 11
Transmission up-shifts	1
Slip, squawk or judder on take-off in 'R'	1, 2, 3, 13b, c, e, f, g, 12
As above, with engine braking available in '1'	1. 2. 3
Slip but no judder on take-off in 'R'. No engine braking available in '1'	1, 2, 3, 8, 9, 10
Drag in 'R'	5
No drive in 'R', no engine braking in '1'	1, 2, 3, 8, 13e, f, g, 9, 10, 12
As above, with engine braking in '1'	1, 2, 3, 13e, 12

9   Stop the vehicle facing downhill, apply the brakes and select 'P'. Release the brakes and check that the pawl holds. Re-apply the brakes before disengaging 'P'. Repeat facing uphill

Parking pawl inoperative	1, 15
Miscellaneous:	
Screech or whine increasing with engine speed	17
Grinding or grating noise from gearbox	18
Knocking noise from torque converter area	22
At high speeds in 'D', transmission down-shifts to second ratio and immediately up-shifts back to third ratio	12

RECTIFICATION CHART

X 1   Check manual linkage adjustment
X 2   Recheck fluid level
X 3   Check adjustment of down-shift valve cable
X 4   Reduce engine idle speed
  5   Check self-adjusting mechanism of front band (BW35)
  6   Check front servo seals and fit of tubes
  7   Check front band for wear (BW35)
  8   Check adjustment of rear band (BW35)
  9   Check rear servo seal and fit of tubes
 10   Check rear band for wear (BW35)
 11   Examine front clutch, check ball valve and seals, also
       forward sun gear shaft sealing rings. Verify that cup
       plug in driven shaft is not leaking or dislodged
 12   Examine rear clutch, check ball valve and seals
       Verify that rear clutch spring seat inner lip is not
       proud. Check fit of tubes

 13   Strip valve bodies and clean, checking:
       a. Primary regulator valve sticking
       b. Secondary regulator valve sticking
       c. Throttle valve sticking
       d. Modulator valve sticking
       e. Servo orifice control valve sticking
       f. 1 to 2 shift valve sticking
       g. 2 to 3 shift valve sticking
       h. 2 to 3 shift valve plunger sticking
 14   Strip governor valve and clean
 15   Examine parking pawl, gear, and internal linkage
 16   Examine one-way clutch
 17   Strip and examine pump and drive tangs
 18   Strip and examine gear train
X 19   Adjust starter inhibitor switch inwards
X 20   Adjust starter inhibitor switch outwards
X 21   Replace torque converter
X 22   Examine torque converter drive plate for cracks or fracture
X 23   Check engine performance

Items marked thus X can be carried out by the owner as they do not involve stripping down the unit.

Chapter 7 Propeller shaft

For modifications, and information applicable to later models, see Supplement at end of manual

Contents

Specifications

Type ... ...   Tubular, divided, three universal joints and one support bearing.

Universal joints
Make ... ...   Hardy-Spicer
Type ... ...   Needle bearings

1 General description

1 The propeller shaft couples two rotating parts which move independently of each other. The engine moves a comparatively small amount in its mounting, while the rear axle has a considerable degree of fore-and-aft displacement. Hence the universally accepted arrangement of universal joints and sliding splines. Because the propeller shaft rotates without being rigidly clamped anywhere, it has to be very carefully balanced or it will vibrate. This balance is lost if the shaft is distorted and runs out of true. Wear in the universal joints will allow it to rotate off centre and this too will produce vibration.

2 The Volvo propeller shaft is made in two parts. The front part is coupled by a universal joint to a flange on the gearbox or, if fitted, the overdrive unit, and is supported at its other end by a ball bearing in a flexible rubber housing. This arrangement takes care of engine movement

3 The rear half has two universal joints. At one end it terminates in a flange which is connected to the rear axle and at the other end the universal joint is connected to a splined shaft which slides into the front part. The spline allows for the fore-and-aft movement of the rear axle.

4 The universal joints are of grease-sealed type and require no regular lubrication.

2 Propeller shaft - removal

1 The easiest way is to remove the two parts separately. Start by removing the bolts between the universal joint and the rear axle flange, lowering the shaft and withdrawing it to the rear. The splined part will pull straight out of the centre bearing (photo).

2 Remove the nuts and bolts joining the gearbox or overdrive flange to the universal joint. Put a couple of bolts back in the holes to take the weight while you undo the two screws fixing the support bearing housing to the chassis (photos).

3 Remove the front half of the propeller shaft with the bearing housing attached.

3 Support bearing - removal

1 Bend back the tab washer and unscrew the nut on the end of the propeller shaft. The bearing and its housing can now be withdrawn from the shaft.

2 Dismantle the housing and take the bearing out. The bearing housing assembly is shown in Fig. 7.2.

Fig. 7.1. Propeller shaft assembly (Sec. 1)

1 *Flange on gearbox*	3 *Front section of shaft*	5 *Intermediate universal joint*	7 *Rear universal joint*
2 *Front universal joint*	4 *Support bearing*	6 *Rear section of shaft*	8 *Flange on rear axle*

2.1 Removing the bolts attaching the universal joint to the rear axle flange

2.2a Bolt fitted temporarily at gearbox flange while removing the support bearing housing screws

2.2b Propeller shaft support bearing

Fig. 7.2. Cut-away view of support bearing (Sec. 3)

1	Dust cover	6	Floor tunnel
2	Ball bearing	7	Splined shaft
3	Rubber housing	8	Rubber cover
4	Dust cover	9	Cap
5	Nut	10	Front section of shaft

Fig. 7.4. Driving bearings through yoke. The bearing on the left has already been driven through (Sec. 4)

Fig. 7.5. When both bearings have been driven through, the yoke will come away (Sec. 4)

Fig. 7.3. Removing circlip which retains bearing cup (Sec. 4)

4 Universal joints - dismantling

1   Remove the circlips which retain the bearings for the spiders.
2   Support one yoke of the joint in a vice. Take care when doing this not to distort the shaft which is hollow.
3   Drive the spider as far as it will go in one direction; this will make the bearing cap stick out of the yoke.
4   Repeat the process in the opposite direction. You will now find

that the spider can be taken out of the yoke.
5   Drift the bearing cups out of the yoke.

5 Propeller shaft - checking

1   The approved test is to mount the shaft between centres and check for run-out along the whole length. If it is more than 0.010 inches (0.25 mm) out of true it should be replaced. If, like most owners, you don't have measuring equipment of this sort of accuracy, get someone to do it for you if you have any suspicion of vibration. This small tolerance emphasises the importance of correct balancing.
2   It also shows that even minor damage can be a source of trouble. Inspect the shaft for this and renew if necessary.

6 Support bearing - inspection

Examine the support bearing by pressing the bearing races against each other by hand and turning them in opposite directions. The bearing should run easily without binding at any point. If it does not, renew it.

7 Universal joints - inspection and reassembly

1 Wash out the needle bearings thoroughly, finishing off with white spirit to remove all traces of cleaning fluid and grease. Check for signs of wear, rust or blueing. Check that their rubber seals are undamaged.

2 Check spiders for signs of wear.

3 If as in paragraph 1 and 2 any imperfection is revealed replace the spiders and the bearings.

4 If the yokes are damaged or the bearing cups are a loose fit in them, replace the shaft concerned. The yokes cannot be removed from the shaft.

5 To reassemble universal joints, fill the bearings half-full of grease and check that the needle rollers are located neatly round the inside of the cup. Push the spider over to the side of the yoke on which you are fitting a bearing so that you can be sure that the bearing cup slides on to the shaft when you fit it (Fig. 7.6). Drive the bearing home gently with a drift just less than a bearing cup diameter and put in the circlip. Do the same on the other end. Take care not to trap the needle rollers.

8 Propeller shaft - refitting

1 Refitting is the reverse of the removal sequence, as described in Section 2.

9 Fault diagnosis - propeller shaft

Fig. 7.6. Push the spider as far through the yoke as possible and slide the bearing over it when reassembling (Sec. 7)

2 Alternatively, if you have someone to assist you, there is something to be said for assembling both halves of the propeller shaft and the support bearing housing into a single unit before refitting it to the car. This will ensure that the splines and centre bearing do not collect dirt in the process. The splines should be lubricated with molybdenum disulphide grease before assembling.

3 When assembling, it is important that the yoke on the front section of the propeller shaft and the yoke on the splined shaft are correctly lined up, as shown in Fig. 7.1.

Any trouble occuring in the propeller shaft and the universal joints usually consists of noise caused by vibration and clunking or clicking sounds. Vibration can be recognised by a growling noise which becomes louder as the speed increases. The clunking noise occurs when drive from the engine is transmitted to the rear axle and then conversely changing to the over-run condition.

Symptom	Reason/s	Remedy
Vibration	Support bearing dry or worn	Renew the bearing.
	Support bearing loose in housing	Renew the bearing and housing.
	Propeller shaft bent	Renew the shaft.
Clunking noise	Needle bearings in universal joints worn	Renew the needle bearings.

Chapter 8 Rear axle
and suspension; wheels and tyres

For modifications, and information applicable to later models, see Supplement at end of manual

Contents

Specifications

Rear axle

Type	Hypoid, semi-floating
Track	53.15 in (1350 mm)
Reduction ratio	3.73 : 1, 3.9 : 1, 4.10 : 1, or 4.30 : 1
Backlash	0.005 - 0.007 in (0.13 - 0.18 mm)
Oil capacity	2.3 Imp. pints (1.3 litres/2.7 US pints)

Torque wrench settings

	lb f ft	kg f m
Flange nut	180 - 220	24 - 30
Differential bearing caps	50	7
Crownwheel bolts	60	8
Wheel nuts	70 - 100	10 - 14
Hub bearing retaining plate	36	5 ·

Suspension

Type	Trailing arms, torque rods, track rod, coil springs and shock absorbers	
Springs:	**242, 244**	**245**
Wire diameter	0.472 in (12 mm)	0.51 in (12.95 mm)
Coil diameter	5.04 in (128 mm)	5.11 in (129.9 mm)
Number of turns	8	8.35
Shock absorbers:		
Type	Double-acting hydraulic telescopic	

Roadwheels

Type	Disc
Size	5J x 14 or 5.5J x 14

Tyres

Type	Tubeless
Size	175 R 14, 185 R 14 or 185/70 R 14

1 Rear suspension - general description

1 A diagram of the rear suspension is given in Fig. 8.1. The rear axle assembly is supported on two arms pivoted to the chassis and sprung against it by coil springs. It is steadied by torque rods attached to the same brackets on the chassis as the support arms but taken to points nearer the middle of the rear axle assembly. All cars except the 245 model are equipped with a rear stabilizer fitted between the support arms.

2 Hydraulic shock absorbers are attached between the body and the support arms and a single tie or 'Panhard' rod extends from an anchorage on the axle casing to a bracket on the opposite side of the body.

2 Shock absorbers and springs - removal and refitting

1 Jack-up the axle and remove the wheel.

2 With the spring under compression (ie. with the axle jacked up after you have removed the wheel) you can remove the shock absorber. If you are only concerned with removing the spring, it is sufficient to let go one end of the shock absorber.

3 To remove the spring, undo the top and bottom attachments while it is still under compression and then take the compression off by jacking-up the body and if necessary letting down the axle, until you are able to take out the spring and its spacers.

4 Refitting is a reversal of removal.

Fig. 8.1. Rear suspension (Sec. 1)

1 Shock absorber
2 Support arm
3 Torque rod
4 Track rod
5 Stabilizer

3 Shock absorbers and springs - checking

1 Shock absorbers and springs may be checked as described in Chapter 11. No maintenance or repair is possible.
2 If you renew a spring, be sure to renew its opposite number even if there is nothing apparently wrong with it. Springs should be obtained in matched pairs.

4 Rubber bushes - renewal

1 Generally speaking, renewal of any of the numerous rubber bushes in the rear suspension is a straightforward business. Press out the old one, give the new one a generous coating of washing-up liquid, press it in. Two bushes need further comment
2 Bushes for the torque rods are marked and the marks should be placed at right angles to the rod (see Fig. 8.2).
3 The front bushes for the support arms have flats on them. Fit these so that a flat side is at right angles to the length of the support arm (Fig. 8.3).

5 Rear axle - general description

1 The rear axle is entirely conventional, of the hypoid type with the pinion below the centre-line of the crownwheel. It consists of pinion, crownwheel and differential gear. Gear backlash and differential carrier bearing loading are adjusted by shims inside the differential carrier bearings.
2 The differential gears in the differential carrier consist of two level pinions on a trunnion and two side gears in which the halfshafts are carried by internal splines.
3 The differential gears are journalled so that they can rotate, at different speeds. There is a thrust washer under each of the differential gears.
4 The pinion bearings are taper roller bearings. The axial location of the pinion relative to the crownwheel is adjusted by shims under the outer race of the rear pinion bearing.

6 Halfshaft - removal

1 Jack-up the car and remove the wheel. If you are removing the half-shafts as a preliminary to dismantling the back axle, note the remarks on jacking in Section 11, paragraph 1.
2 Unbolt and remove the brake calipers and brake disc (see Chapter 9).
3 Remove the parking brake shoes and their associated mechanism (Chapter 9).
4 Remove the bolts securing the brake backing plate to the back axle casing. You can get at these through holes in the halfshaft flange.

Fig. 8.2. Correct positioning of torque rod bushes (Sec. 4)

SVO 2732

Fig. 8.3. Correct positioning of front bush in support arm (Sec. 4)

5 The halfshaft is now free to be withdrawn, bringing with it its bearing and the retaining plate which was bolted to the rear axle casing. A little judicious tapping with a hammer on a drift applied behind the flange may be necessary to start it off, but generally it presents no difficulty.

Fig. 8.4. Cut-away view of differential unit (Sec. 5)

1	Tubular shaft	6	Thrust washer
2	Differential carrier bearing	7	Differential side gear
3	Bearing cap	8	Lock pin
4	Shims	9	Differential pinion
5	Differential carrier	10	Crown wheel
		11	Shaft

12	Thrust washer
13	Lock cover
14	Rear axle casing
15	Flange
16	Dust cover plate
17	Oil seal

18	Oil slinger
19	Shims
20	Front pinion bearing
21	Pinion
22	Rear pinion bearing
23	Shims

7 Halfshafts (broken) - removal

1   If the halfshaft is broken, the splined end will of course remain inside the axle when the outer end is withdrawn. Removal of the broken piece can be done without dismantling the rear axle or removing it from the car.

2   Remove the cover to the differential housing, being careful not to get any dirt into the differential as you do so.

3   With a piece of stiff wire or something similar, push the broken end of the halfshaft (which will still be engaged with the side gear) into the axle casing.

4   When you have got it well clear of the side gear, you will be able to fish it out with a hooked wire inserted at the outside end of the casing.

8 Halfshafts - bearings and oil seals - renewal

1   If halfshaft removal is part of a general overhaul of the rear axle, all oil seals should be renewed. This means that the taper bearing must be removed and renewed, even though it may be entirely satisfactory. If you have no facilities for pressing off the bearing and its locking ring, you can remove the locking ring by drilling and splitting (see Fig. 8.5). Use a ¼ inch (6 mm) drill and be careful you do not drill right through to the halfshaft.

2   Extract the inner seal from the axle casing.

3   Remove the bearing using a press or suitable extractor.

4   Remove the outer seal.

Fig. 8.5. Removing halfshaft bearing locking ring by drilling and splitting (Sec. 8)

5   Clean the bearing, giving it a final wash in white spirit to remove every trace of old grease and cleaning fluid. Examine for signs of wear or blueing. Renew if necessary.

6   Reassemble with new oil seals and (if necessary) a new bearing.

7   **Even if the old locking ring is intact, it must be renewed.**

8   Press or drive on the locking ring, making sure that the whole assembly is as close up as possible to the shoulder on the halfshaft.

9 Halfshafts - inspection

Clean and examine the halfshaft. The splines must be clean and sharp with no burrs and there must be no trace of twist or warp.

Fig. 8.6. Sectional view of rear hub and halfshaft (Sec. 8)

1 Halfshaft
2 Axle casing
3 Inner oil seal
4 Locking ring
5 Taper roller bearing
6 Outer oil seal

Fig. 8.8. Pulling off the flange (Sec. 12)

Fig. 8.7. Positioning axle stand correctly (Sec. 11)

Fig. 8.9. Pressing on the flange (Sec. 12)

10 Halfshafts - refitting

1 Pack the bearing with grease and then fit the halfshaft into the axle casing. Hold the halfshaft in a horizontal position and turn it slightly in both directions until the splines at its inner end can be felt to pick up and engage with those of the differential side gears.
2 Refit the bolts securing the backplate and retaining ring, tighten them to the specified torque, and bleed the brakes (see Chapter 9).
3 Refit the brake mechanism, and bleed the brakes (see Chapter 9).

11 Rear axle - removal and refitting

1 Jack-up the rear of the car and support it securely on axle stands placed just in front of the car jacking point. Do not position the axle stands beyond the dotted line shown in Fig. 8.7. Support the rear axle on a jack, preferably a trolley type.
2 Remove the roadwheels.
3 Disconnect the shock absorber upper mounting bolts.
4 Release the brake pipes from the axle casing.
5 Unbolt and tie up the brake calipers with wire taking care not to bend or twist the pipes.
6 Remove the disc/drum assemblies, the handbrake shoes and other components and disconnect the handbrake cables from their operating levers and from their positioning clips either on the suspension arms or axle casing according to layout. These operations are described in Chapter 9.
7 Disconnect the propeller shaft rear flange from the pinion driving flange.
8 Disconnect the Panhard rod from the bracket on the rear axle housing.

9 Disconnect the roadsprings from the suspension arms.
10 Lower the rear axle and remove the springs.
11 Disconnect the suspension arm pivot bolts from the rear axle, also the bolts holding the torque rods to the axle housing.
12 Lower the jack and withdraw the rear axle from underneath and towards the rear of the car.
13 Refitting is a reversal of the removal operations.
14 Bleed the brakes as described in Chapter 9.

12 Pinion shaft oil seal - renewal

1 This can be done without removing the rear axle from the vehicle. Two simple press tools are needed to remove and refit the flange on the pinion shaft. The special Volvo tools are illustrated, and enough information given to enable you to produce adequate substitutes, in Figures 8.8 and 8.9.
2 Disconnect the rear section of the propeller shaft from the flange on the pinion.
3 Take the opportunity of checking the pinion shaft for looseness. If there is any appreciable play, particularly if the differential is noisy, you should be thinking about a complete overhaul.
4 If all is well, prevent the flange from turning while removing the nut from the shaft.
5 Pull the flange off the shaft.
6 Take off the dust cover and oil slinger and extract the oil seal.
7 Coat the new oil seal generously with grease, particularly all round the coil spring. This will prevent any tendency for the coil spring to come off the seal while you are fitting it. (Fig. 8.10).
8 Fit the oil seal, replace the dust cover and oil slinger, press the flange on to the shaft and tighten the nut to the specified torque.

Fig. 8.10. Fitting the pinion shaft oil seal (Sec. 12)

1   *Oil seal*   2   *Coil spring (well greased)*

Fig. 8.11. Driving out the locking pin (Sec. 13)

13 Rear axle - overhaul

1   Unless certain tools are available or suitable substitutes can be made up, it is not recommended that the differential is dismantled as damage to unworn components caused by incorrect removal methods or brute force can be very expensive.

2   Before any work can be carried out the axle housing must be stretched to permit extraction of the crownwheel and differential assembly. The Volvo tools (SVO 2394 and 2601) required for this may possibly be borrowed, alternatively expansion struts can be made up using really heavy duty bolts with fine threads at the strut centres to expand the housing in two directions.

3   A micrometer will also be needed and a new set of crownwheel bolts to offset the stretch which has inevitably occurred in the original ones.

4   Remove the rear axle, as described in Section 11.

5   Take off the cover and look for alignment marks on the bearing caps and case which will tell you exactly where and which way round the bearing caps have to go. If there are no marks to be seen, dot punch the components.

6   At this stage it may be a good idea to check the meshing of the crownwheel and pinion as described in paragraph 28. This might give some fault indication which could be helpful later.

7   Remove the bearing caps.

8   Fit the expansion tool SVO 2394 to the axle housing and the axle casing. Then screw up the bolt three and a half turns. This will stretch the axle housing enough to enable the crownwheel and differential assembly to be lifted out.

9   Wash the interior of the housing with paraffin or cleaning fluid.

10 Undo the nut on the centre of the pinion shaft and pull off the coupling flange.

11 Extract the dust cover, oil slinger and oil seal.

12 Drive out the shaft and pinion. The outer ring of the rear bearing and the whole of the front bearing remain in the housing.

13 Between the rear bearing and housing will be found shims. These determine how far the pinion extends inside the case and hence control the meshing of the pinion with the crownwheel.

14 Between the front bearing and the housing will be found another set of shims. These shims fit against the shoulder on the pinion shaft and take up end play in the shaft.

15 Drive out the front bearing, using a drift just small enough to pass through the rear bearing ring. This need be no more than a disc backed up by a suitable length of rod. Clean the shims and put them on one side, making sure that you will know where they came from when you are reassembling.

16 Drive out the rear bearing ring and treat its shims likewise.

17 Mark the crownwheel and cage, take out the securing bolts and remove the cage from the crownwheel.

18 Drive out the locking pin followed by the shaft for the differential gears (Fig. 8.11).

19 Remove the differential gears and thrust washers.

20 Pull the bearings off the ends of the cage. Store them in such a way that you will know on reassembly which bearing and which shims went on which end of the cage.

21 Thoroughly clean all parts. Check all the bearing races and bearings. The races, rollers or roller containers must not be scratched or damaged, and assembled bearings must have no detectable play.

22 Check the crownwheel and pinion teeth for damage. Slight scuff marks may not mean that renewal is essential. The cause may be incorrect running-in, wrong oil, insufficient clearance or faulty tooth contact.

23 Check the teeth and splines of the side gears for damage.

24 Commence reassembly by refitting the differential cage, side gears and pinions. Whether the parts are new or old, they should be clean and dry so that you can check the thickness and loading tolerances accurately. Assemble the side gears in the cage, using the original positions even if you are putting in new gears. Insert the pinions and their washers and their shaft. Do not install the lock pin at this stage.

25 Check the side play of the side gears with feeler gauges, and if this is greater than 0.006 in (0.15 mm), take it up by increasing the thickness of the thrust washers on both sides by the same amount. The ideal condition is when a slight torque is needed to turn the side gears. Use a torque wrench working on something pushed into the splines (a piece of wood would do) and check that this torque does not exceed 14 lb f ft (2 kg f m). Use marker blue to check that the meshing of each of the side gears with the free pinions is the same. If it is not, transfer side washer thickness from one side to the other by increasing one side washer and decreasing the other by the same amount. When all is well, lock in the shaft with the locking pin. Make sure that the locking pin is firm in the cage.

26 Fit the crownwheel, not forgetting the bolt locking plate. Draw it down with the fixing bolts, and if it has been heated allow it to cool. Finally, tighten the fixing bolts to the specified torque wrench setting.

27 We now turn to the pinion. If you are using the original, assemble it with the original shims between the back bearing and the pinion. Be sure the bearing is pressed well home. If it is a new one, observe the marking code. If it is the same as the old one (very unlikely) use the same shims as before. If not, the shim thickness must be altered in accordance with the markings on the pinions. Mark 33 = 0.33 mm (0.013 in).

28 Having fitted the shims and back bearing on the pinion shaft, assemble it in the case, using only the back bearing for the time being. Now put the bearings on the cage without any shims, put the crown-wheel and cage assembly in the case and temporarily screw down the bearing caps. **Do not** fit the expansion tool SVO 2394 at this stage. Get the crownwheel meshing with the pinion, and using marker blue observe the pattern made on the crownwheel by the pinion. Fig. 8.3 shows what this should look like and how to tell whether your pinion is set too near or too far from the centre of the crownwheel. You can get the areas of the patterns approximately equal by moving the cage assembly slightly from side to side (ultimately the shims fitted behind the bearings will sort this out), but at this stage you are simply concerned with getting them evenly spaced. If they are not, you will have

Fig. 8.12. Location of crownwheel bolt lockplate (A) (Sec. 13)

to drive out the pinion shaft and alter the shims until you get it right. Check the patterns at three points on the crownwheel in case it is warped.

29 When these shims are correct, put back the original front shim thickness altered by the same amount as you have altered the back shim thickness. Fit the front bearing and the flange. Do not bother about the oil seal or slinger and dust cover at this stage as this is only a trial run. Use the original fixing nut, and tighten it carefully. If there is a tendency for the pinion to bind before the nut is fully tightened, remove the nut, remove the flange, and drive out the pinion. Increase the shim thickness and try again. If, on the other hand, you get end play, estimate as best you can (eg. by using feeler gauges between the pinion and case) how much end play there is, take out the pinion, remove the front bearing ring and increase the shim thickness. You should aim to get a very slight stiffness, which can be measured by the bar and spring balance method shown in Fig. 8.14 and should be not less than 0.52 lb and not more than 0.95 lb unless you have fitted new bearings, in which case the reading on the spring balance should be between 0.9 and 2.3 lb. If the stiffness is too great, of course, you will have to reduce the shim thickness. If you are unlucky, you may have to have two or three tries, but there is one consolation - when you have got through this stage you are over the worst of it.

30 When the shims are correct, take off the flange again and fit the oil seal, oil slinger and dust cover. This time fix the flange to the shaft with a new fixing nut and tighten to specified torque.

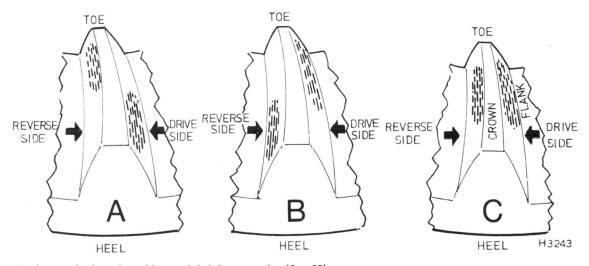

Fig. 8.13. Pinion/crownwheel tooth markings and their interpretation (Sec. 13)

A   Pinion too far from centre of crownwheel - increase shim pack
B   Pinion too near centre of crownwheel - decrease shim pack
C   Pinion to crownwheel mesh correct

Fig. 8.14. Device for measuring pinion bearing pre-load (Sec. 13)

31 It now remains to adjust the play and centring of the crownwheel/cage assembly. Start off by choosing a shim thickness 0.003 in (0.076 mm) less than the original shim thickness on each side, putting the appropriate shims behind the bearings and pushing the bearings well home. If, having done this, the assembly will not go into the car, reduce the shim thickness by another 0.002 in (0.05 mm). We suggest that you try this rather than taking out 0.005 in (0.12 mm) straight away because there is quite a chance that the smaller reduction will give the right answer.

32 Check the end play in each direction, and use marker blue to observe the meshing patterns of the pinion and crownwheel as previously described, but this time you are after equality of area. If necessary, alter shim thickness from one side to the other to get the desired result.

33 Once you have got the shims correct, remove the assembly from the casing and add a further 0.003 in (0.076 mm) to each side. Then reassemble, using the expansion tool to stretch the case and enable the assembly to go in. Three or four turns on the screw of the expansion tool should be sufficient.

34 Fit the bearing caps, but do not at this stage tighten the bolts more than fingertight. Remove the expansion tool, tighten the cap bolts to the specified torque.

35 Fit inspection cover with new gasket, bolt down evenly all round.

36 Reinstall the halfshafts as described in Section 10 and the rear axle is ready to to be refitted to the vehicle.

37 Refill the axle with the correct grade and quantity of oil.

14 Wheels and tyres - general

1 The roadwheels are of pressed steel.

2 Periodically remove the wheels, clean dirt and mud from the inside and outside surfaces and examine for signs of rusting or rim damage. Rectify as necessary.

3 Apply a smear of light grease to the wheel studs before screwing on the nuts and finally tighten them to the specified torque.

4 The tyres are of radial construction. Never mix tyres of different construction and regularly check and maintain the pressures.

5 If the wheels have been balanced on the car then it is important that the wheels are not moved round the vehicle in an effort to equalise tread wear. If a wheel is removed, then the relationship of the wheel studs to the holes in the wheel should be marked to ensure exact replacement, otherwise the balance of wheel, hub and tyre will be upset.

6 Where the wheels have been balanced off the car, then they may be moved round to equalise wear. Include the spare wheel in any rotational pattern. With radial tyres, do not move the wheels from one side to the other but only interchange the front and rear wheels on the same side.

7 Balancing of the wheels is an essential factor in good steering and roadholding. When the tyres have been in use for about half their useful life the wheels should be rebalanced, to compensate for the lost tread rubber due to wear.

8 Inspect the tyre walls and treads regularly for cuts and damage and where evident, have them professionally repaired.

15 Fault diagnosis - rear axle and suspension

Symptom	Reason/s
Rear suspension	
Excessive pitching and rolling on corners and during braking	Defective shock absorbers and/or broken spring.
Suspension 'bottoms' on large bumps (car normally loaded)	Weak or broken springs.
Car sags at one 'corner'	Weak or broken springs.
Rear axle	
Noise on drive overrun	Low oil level. Loose crownwheel bolts. Loose bearing cap bolts. General wear in bearing or gear teeth.
Noise on turn	Seized, broken or damaged pinion side gear or thrust washers.
Knock during gearshift or when taking up drive	Excessive crownwheel to pinion backlash. Worn gears. Worn halfshaft splines. Drive pinion nut loose. Loose crownwheel bolts or bearing cap bolts. Worn side gear splines.

Chapter 9 Braking system

For modifications, and information applicable to later models, see Supplement at end of manual

Contents

Specifications

Front wheel brakes

Type ... ... Discs - Girling or ATE

Brake discs
Outer diameter	10.35 in (263 mm)
Thickness - new	0.563 in (14.3 mm)
- reconditioned	min. 0.517 in (13.14 mm)
Warp	max. 0.004 in (0.10 mm)

Brake linings
Thickness - new	0.394 in (10 mm)
Effective area, Girling	26 sq in (166 sq cm)
ATE	22.5 sq in (145 sq cm)
Designation, Girling	DB 818 FG
ATE	Ferodo 2441 FFG

Wheel cylinders
Area, Girling 1975	1.59 sq in (10.25 sq cm)
1976	1.76 sq in (11.34 sq cm)
ATE	1.58 sq in (10.17 sq cm)

Rear wheel brakes

Type ... ... Discs - Girling or ATE

Brake discs
Outer diameter	11.06 in (281 mm)
Thickness - new	0.378 in (9.6 mm)
- reconditioned	min. 0.331 in (8.4 mm)
Warp	max. 0.004 in (0.10 mm)

Brake linings
Thickness - new, Girling	0.31 in (8 mm)
ATE	0.394 in (10 mm)
Effective area, Girling	15.5 sq in (100 sq cm)
ATE	16.3 sq in (105 sq cm)
Designation, Girling	DB 824 FF
ATE	Ferodo 2442 FFG

Wheel cylinders
Area, Girling	1.77 sq in (11.43 sq cm)
ATE	1.75 sq in (11.33 sq cm)

Master cylinder

Type	Tandem with step piston
Secondary cylinder, nominal diameter	0.621 in (15.75 mm)
Primary cylinder, nominal diameter	0.866 in (22 mm)

Brake valve (pressure regulating) ... ...

	1975	1976
Make, designation	ATE BRM 18	ATE BRM 18
Cut-out points, 242, 244	427 psi (30 kg/sq cm)	483 psi (34 kg/sq cm)
245	640 psi (45 kg/sq cm)	640 psi (45 kg/sq cm)

Servo cylinder

Type										Direct
Make, size, B21E										DBA, tandem 8 in
B20A (auto. transmission)										Girling, 10 in or tandem 8 in
B21A (auto. transmission)										Girling, 10 in or DBA 9 in
B20A (manual gearbox)										DBA 9 in
240 (right-hand steering)										Girling, tandem 8 in

Reduction ratio										
Girling/DBA tandem 8 in										1 : 4
Girling 10 in										1 : 3.5
DBA 9 in										1 : 3.5

Handbrake

Brake drum, diameter									max. 6.32 in (160.45 mm)
radial throw									max. 0.006 in (0.15 mm)
out-of-round									max. 0.008 in (0.2 mm)
Brake linings, effective area									27.28 sq in (176 sq cm)

Torque wrench settings

							lb f ft	kg f m
Retaining bolts, front brake caliper							65 - 72	9 - 10
Retaining bolts, rear brake caliper							38 - 46	5.2 - 6.4
Retaining bolts, armature							33 - 40	4.5 - 5.5
Retaining nuts, rear guard plate							22 - 36	3 - 5
Wheel nuts							72 - 94	10 - 13
Retaining nuts, master cylinder							22 - 36	3 - 5
Bleeder nipples							2.5 - 4	0.35 - 0.55
Brake pipe unions							5.8 - 8.7	0.8 - 1.2
Brake hoses to brake valve							8.7 - 11.5	1.2 - 1.6
Master cylinder stop screw							6	0.8
Pressure warning switch							15	2.1

1 General description

1   The braking system is a four wheel hydraulic operated disc type. The hydraulic system is of dual circuit layout with each circuit operating two of the front four caliper pistons and a rear brake caliper. This arrangement ensures that half the braking system will be effective in the event of a failure of pressure in one circuit. The master cylinder is step-bored which ensures a braking power that is not noticeably diminished should one brake circuit fail. The driver is, however, warned by a warning light which is activated by a warning valve in the brake system.

2   The servo cylinder is directly actuated by the brake pedal. Vacuum assistance, obtained from a vacuum pump and the intake manifold, results in reduced pedal pressure being required for braking.

3   Pressure regulating valves are incorporated in each of the rear wheel brake lines to prevent the rear wheels locking in advance of the front wheels during heavy brake application.

4   The handbrake consists of cable operated brake shoes enclosed in small brake drums on the rear hubs.

2 Bleeding the hydraulic system

1   Whenever the hydraulic system has been overhauled, a part renewed or the level in the reservoir has become too low, air will have entered

Fig. 9.1. Diagram of footbrake system (Sec. 1)

1	Tandem master cylinder	6	Brake switch	11	Brake valve, primary circuit
2	Brake fluid container	7	Warning lamp	12	Brake pedal
3	Vacuum line	8	Rear brake caliper	13	Front brake caliper
4	Check valve	9	Brake disc with drum	14	Brake disc
5	Servo cylinder	10	Brake valve, secondary circuit	15	Warning switch

16	Warning valve
17	6-branch union, (double 3-branch union)
18	Brake pipe
19	Cover plate

1 Lever
2 Yoke
3 Lever
4 Cable
5 Rubber grommet
6 Plastic tube
7 Levers
8 Brake shoes
9 Adjustment device

Fig. 9.2. Handbrake system layout (Sec. 2)

Fig. 9.3. Bleeding sequence (Sec. 2)

1 Left rear wheel
2 Left front wheel, upper, inner
3 Right front wheel, upper, inner
4 Right rear wheel
5 Right front wheel, outer
6 Right front wheel, lower inner
7 Left front wheel, outer
8 Left front wheel, lower inner

Fig. 9.4. Bleeding a front wheel brake unit (Sec. 2)

the system. This will cause some or all of the pedal travel to be used up in compressing air rather than pushing fluid against brake pistons. If only a little air is present the pedal will have a 'spongy' feel, but if an appreciable amount has entered, the pedal will not offer any appreciable resistance to the foot and the brakes will hardly work at all.

2 To overcome this, brake fluid must be pumped through the hydraulic system until all the air has been passed out in the form of bubbles in the fluid. If only one rear brake caliper has been removed and little brake fluid run out, you may get away with bleeding this brake circuit only, but otherwise you should bleed the whole system whenever you have worked on it.

3 The system should be bled in the order shown in Fig. 9.3.

4 One or two points should be watched when bleeding the brakes:

a) Before you start, depress the brake pedal several times in order to

destroy vacuum in the servo cylinder.

b) Make sure that the bleed nipples and their immediate surroundings are thoroughly clean. Dirt is the deadly enemy of hydraulic systems.

c) Remove the switch from the warning valve.

d) Clean round the cap on the brake fluid container and clean the cap itself, making sure that the vent hole of the cap is clean. You are going to have to take the cap on and off to top the reservoir up when you are bleeding the brakes. If you leave the cap off all the time dirt may enter the system. You can see the fluid level perfectly well through the translucent container even when the cap is on.

5 Have a look at Fig. 9.4. This shows a transparent tube fitted over one of the bleed nipples and fed into a bottle containing brake fluid, the end of the tube dipping below the brake fluid. This is essential to avoid air being sucked back into the system as the bleeding procedure

is carried out. The nipple is unscrewed half a turn anticlockwise which enables brake fluid to pass through it from the brake cylinder. Use a 5/16 AF spanner to slacken the nipple.

6   When all is set up, fill the master cylinder reservoir with brake fluid up to the 'Max' mark and have an assistant pump the brake pedal up and down; this will pump fluid through the system and into the bottle. Once you have an inch or so of brake fluid in the bleeding jar, it is essential that the end of the bleed tube remains immersed until the bleed nipple is retightened. Keep the reservoir topped up as the level falls - never let it get as low as the 'Min' mark or air will re-enter the system. The correct method of pumping is to press the brake pedal slowly as far down as it will go, pause a little and then quickly release it.

7   At first, air bubbles will be present in the liquid passing through the tube, but after a while it will be completely free of them. When this is so, press the pedal to the bottom and screw up the bleed nipple. Do not forget to refit the rubber cap on the nipple when you take off the tube and spanner. Recommended tightening torque for the nipple is 12 - 15 lb f ft (1.6 - 2.0 kg f m). Generally it is only necessary to go round the whole car once, but if at the end of this, the brake pedal still feels 'spongy', the process should be repeated until all is well.

8   Finally, fill the brake fluid reservoir up to the 'Max' mark and refit the warning switch, tightening it to a torque of 10-15 lb f ft (1.4-2.0 kg f m).

9   Two final points about the brake fluid itself:
a) Do not let the fluid come in contact with friction surfaces or linings or with paintwork.
b) Do not return any of the fluid pumped out during bleeding to the system.

3 Disc brake caliper - description

1   Fig. 9.5 shows a diagram of the front wheel brake caliper. This caliper consists of a housing in two halves - referred to as the inner and outer half, Nos 6 and 14 in Fig. 9.5 - bolted together and located on either side of the brake disc. Each half contains two cylinders and pistons. In the diagram the outer half is cut away to show the cylinder and piston assembly.

2   The cut away portion carries a bleed nipple which is additional to those illustrated in the diagram.

3   The two upper cylinders are connected together and fed from one of the hydraulic circuits, while the two lower cylinders are fed from the other one.

4   The sealing rings (1) Fig. 9.5 as well as preventing brake fluid from oozing out act as return springs for the pistons. When hydraulic pressure is released these rings, which distort as the piston moves past them, return to their natural shape and in so doing pull back the piston slightly. The amount of withdrawal of the piston is always the same, so that the system automatically compensates for wear in the brake pads and needs no adjustment.

5   Fig. 9.6 shows a diagram of the rear brake calipers, which operate in just the same manner as the front ones except that they only have one cylinder each. Each rear cylinder is fed by a different hydraulic circuit, so that if one circuit fails half the rear braking effort is still present.

4 Brake pads - removal and replacement

1   At intervals, specified in Routine Maintenance, jack-up and remove each road wheel in turn and examine the thickness of the friction material on the disc pads. This can be judged by the nearness of the pad backing plate to the tension spring but for a really accurate assessment it is necessary to remove the damping spring.

2   If the pads have worn down to between 1/8 and 1/16 in (1.6 and 3.2 mm) they must be renewed.

3   *Girling:* Remove the hairpin-shaped locking clips for the guide pins. Pull out one of the retaining pins while holding the damper spring in place. Remove the springs and the other retaining pin (photos).
    ATE: Tap out the upper retaining pin with a drift. Take out the damper spring and tap out the lower retaining pin.

4   Withdraw the disc pads, gripping them with pliers if they prove hard to remove. If the pads are to be used again, mark them to ensure they are restored to their original position (photo).

6   Clean the inside faces of the housings and examine the dust covers

Fig. 9.5. Front brake caliper assembly - Girling (Sec. 3)

1	Seal	8	Bolt
2	Piston	9	Retaining clip
3	Rubber dust cover	10	Brake pad
4	Retaining ring	11	Lower bleeder nipple
5	Channel	12	Damping spring
6	Outer half	13	Retaining pin
7	Upper bleeder nipple	14	Inner half

Fig. 9.6. Rear brake caliper assembly - Girling (Sec. 3)

1	Seal	8	Bolt
2	Piston	9	Retaining clip
3	Rubber dust cover	10	Brake pad
4	Retaining ring	11	Inner half
5	Channel	12	Damping spring
6	Outer half	13	Retaining pin
7	Bleeder nipple	14	Washer

4.3a The hairpin-shaped lock clip (Girling)

4.3b Removing the retaining pin and the springs (Girling)

4.3c Remove the other retaining pin and the springs (Girling)

4.4 Withdraw the brake pad (Girling)

protecting the cylinders. Replace any dust covers that are damaged. They are held on to the housing by clip rings and are easily removed.

7   To make room for the new pads, push the pistons down into the cylinders with a screwdriver or the like, taking great care not to damage the dust covers while you do so.

8   Fitting new pads or refitting the old ones is simply a reversal of the removal procedure.

9   Depress the footbrake pedal several times to position the pads against the disc and then check and top-up the master cylinder fluid reservoir.

10 Disc pads should be renewed in axle sets, not just one wheel only, so repeat the foregoing operations on the opposite wheel.

11 Any nuisance caused by disc pad squeal on the rear brakes may be due to incorrect positioning of the piston cut-out.

5   Front calipers - removal and refitting

1   Jack-up the front end of the car and support it on axle stands placed under the front jack attachments. It is important to do this so that when the hoses are refitted they are free from torsion under normal conditions.

2   Temporarily block the vent hole in the brake fluid container cover to reduce leakage when the brake hoses are disconnected.

Fig. 9.7. Front wheel brake caliper (Sec. 5)

3   Disconnect the brake hoses at the caliper (photo).

4   Remove the two caliper retaining bolts and lift away the caliper (photo).

5   Replacement is in the main simply a reversal of the removal procedure, but it should be done with care. Check that the contact surfaces of the caliper and frame are clean and undamaged.

6   The brake disc should be central in the caliper and parallel to it. This can be checked by measuring the distances between the bosses at the top and bottom of the caliper and the disc, with spacers and feeler gauges. The difference between these distances should not exceed 0.022 in (0.55 mm). The location of the caliper can be adjusted with shims which are available in thicknesses of 0.008 in and 0.016 in (0.2 - 0.4 mm). Coat the fixing bolts with a couple of drops of Loctite, Type AV.

7   When all is finished, do not forget to open the hole in the brake fluid container cover which you blocked up to reduce leakage.

8   Check that the brake discs can rotate easily in the brake pads.

9   Bleed the brake system as described in Section 2.

6   Rear brake calipers - removal and refitting

1   The procedure for rear calipers is basically the same as for the front. The car should be jacked up and supported on its rear axle to ensure that when the hoses are fitted they are not in torsion under

normal load conditions. Fig. 9.8 shows the caliper fitted in position.

7   Brake calipers - overhaul

1   Absolute cleanliness is essential when dismantling and reassembling these units. Clean the outside thoroughly before you start. Before dismantling ATE type brake calipers mark the pistons so that you can refit them in the same position with regard to the rim step.

2   Remove the dust cover retaining rings (if fitted) and the dust covers themselves. Place a piece of wood about ½ in (12.5 mm) thick between the pistons and apply compressed air to one of the hoses connected to the caliper to push the pistons out. A good source of compressed air for this job is a flexible bottle (for example the sort used for washing-up liquid - but be sure that the bottle has been thoroughly cleaned out). If by any chance the piston is jammed in the housing and will not yield to this treatment, a local garage may be able to apply a high pressure air line for you.

3   Remove the inner sealing rings with a small screwdriver, being very careful not to scratch the bore or damage the groove. It is a good idea to round off the corners of screwdrivers used for this sort of thing.

4   Unscrew the bleed nipples, hose connections etc., from the unit but do not attempt to separate the two halves as reassembling them is a factory job needing specialised equipment.

5   Give the various parts and connecting paths a thorough clean

5.3 Front brake caliper (Girling)

5.4 Removing the rear caliper (Girling)

Fig. 9.8. Rear wheel brake caliper - Girling
Arrows show attachment bolts (Sec. 6)

Fig. 9.9. Using special tool SVO 2919 to align ATE caliper piston
(Sec. 7)
A (clearance to cut-out step) = 0.04 in (1 mm)

with methylated spirit - about the only fluid which you can guarantee will not affect the rubber seals. Dry the various bits and pieces with a lint-free rag. A hair drier is very useful for the fluid pathways, to make sure - as you must - that all methylated spirit is removed.

6   Thoroughly inspect the various parts. If any of the cylinders is scored or scratched the entire cylinder housing must be replaced complete. Replace any other damaged or worn parts.

7   Reassembly is straightforward. Coat the various parts with brake fluid before assembling them. Fit the inner sealing rings into their grooves, making sure they are the right way round (see Fig. 9.5). Fit the pistons with the large ends inside the housings. In the case of ATE type brakes the outer end of the piston (stepped part) should incline 20° as shown in Fig. 9.9. You will not need a special template if you marked the piston before dismantling as recommended in paragraph 1. If you are replacing the piston with a new one, compare new with old and mark the new one in the same place.

8   Disc - inspection, removal and refitting

1   Each time that the disc pads require renewal, take the opportunity to examine the surfaces of the discs.

2   Light scoring is normal but deep grooves will mean that the disc must be renewed or machined provided that the thickness is not reduced below 0.51 in (13.4 mm), for the front discs and 0.331 in (8.4 mm) for the rear.

3   Disc run-out (out of true) must not exceed 0.004 in (0.1 mm) and should be measured by turning the disc against the plunger of a dial gauge. If this instrument is not available, feeler blades can give an approximate indication if they are used to measure the gap between the disc and a fixed point.

4   *To remove a front disc,* unbolt the caliper and tie it securely to one side to prevent strain on the flexible hoses.

5   Remove the disc/hub securing screws and withdraw the assembly.

6   *To remove a rear disc,* unbolt the caliper, remove the clip which secures the rigid brake line to the rear axle casing and pull the caliper far enough away from the disc to tie it up without bending the brake pipe. Insert a screwdriver in the adjuster hole in the handbrake drum and release the shoe adjustment.

7   Unscrew and remove the two retaining screws and withdraw the disc/drum assembly.

8   Refitting is a reversal of removal but adjust the handbrake shoes on the rear brake so that the drum is stiff to turn and then back off the adjuster by between 4 and 5 teeth, see Section 18.

9   Master cylinder - removal, overhaul and replacement

1   Fig. 9.10 shows the master cylinder fitted on the front face of the vacuum servo booster unit with the fluid reservoir on top.

2   The basic principle on which the cylinder works is perfectly simple. There are two pistons in tandem, the primary piston and the secondary piston. There is no difference in function - and there is certainly no difference in importance - between primary and secondary pistons and the circuits connected to them; the primary piston is so called because it is the one that gets pushed first. If all is working properly, pressure building up in front of the primary piston pushes forward the secondary piston and the same hydraulic pressure is exerted in both primary and secondary circuits. If the primary circuit develops a leak the primary piston is simply carried on until it meets the secondary piston and pushes it forward physically. If there is a leak in the secondary circuit, the secondary piston will carry on until it hits the end of the master cylinder, but pressure will be maintained in front of the primary cylinder and in the primary circuit.

3   To remove the master cylinder, first lift off the brake fluid reservoir. Nothing has to be unscrewed first - it simply sits on top of two rubber seals. If you put your fingers over the bottom holes quickly you will lose very little fluid. A rag placed underneath the cylinder will help to prevent what you do lose from dripping on to places where it is not wanted.

4   Remove the brake lines from the master cylinder and plug them with plastic plugs. Undo the fixing nuts and remove the cylinder.

5   Clean the outside of the cylinder thoroughly.

6   Lever out the rubber seals from the master cylinder.

7   Unscrew and remove the stop screw.

Fig. 9.10. Master cylinder and reservoir (Sec. 9)

1   Connection for secondary circuit
2   Connection for primary circuit
3   Retaining bolts

Fig. 9.11. Sectional view of master cylinder (Sec. 9)

1	Spring	7	Spring
2	Spring seat	8	Connector sleeve
3	Seal	9	Seal
4	Secondary piston	10	Primary piston
5	Seal	11	Seal
6	Seal	12	Snap ring

Fig. 9.12. Assembling the master cylinder (Sec. 9)

1   Piston assembly   2   Spring seat   3   Spring

8   Extract the circlip from the end of the master cylinder and withdraw the primary and secondary piston assemblies.

9   At this stage, examine the surfaces of the pistons and cylinder. If they are scored or show any evidence of 'bright' wear areas, the master cylinder should be renewed complete.

10 If these components are in good condition, discard all rubber seals and wash the parts in clean hydraulic fluid or methylated spirit - nothing else.

11 Obtain a repair kit which will contain all the necessary renewable items including new seals.

12 Commence reassembly by installing the seals to the secondary piston. Make sure that the seal lips face the correct way.

13 Install the back-up ring, the thrust washer and the spring to the secondary piston and then dip the assembly in clean hydraulic fluid and insert it into the master cylinder. Take care not to turn over or trap the seal lips.

14 To the primary piston, fit the washer, the piston seal, the plastic washer, the second seal and the second washer. Make sure that the seal

lips face the correct direction.

15 Dip the primary piston assembly in clean hydraulic fluid and insert it into the master cylinder. Take care not to trap or bend back the lips of the seals.

16 Depress the piston far enough to be able to fit the circlip.

17 Fit the stop screw using a new sealing washer. Tighten the screw to a torque of 6 lb f ft (0.8 kg f m).

18 Fit new reservoir to master cylinder sealing collars and push the fluid reservoir firmly into position.

19 Fill the reservoir with clean hydraulic fluid which has remained unshaken for 24 hours and has been stored in an airtight container.

20 Depress the master cylinder piston several times to expel any trapped air and then plug the fluid outlet holes to prevent loss of fluid while the cylinder is being installed.

21 Fit the 'O' ring seal to the master cylinder mounting flange, install the cylinder to the front face of the servo unit, fit the washers and nuts and tighten them to the specified torque.

22 Remove the temporary plugs and connect the fluid lines to the master cylinder.

23 Bleed the complete hydraulic system, as described in Section 2.

10 Pressure warning valve - resetting

1 The switch is basically a piston assembly which is kept in balance by the equal pressure in the two hydraulic circuits.

2 When a fault causes a drop in pressure in one of the circuits, the piston is displaced and a plunger type switch actuates a warning lamp on the instrument panel.

3 The following operations are necessary before the piston can return to its 'in balance' position.

4 Disconnect the lead from the switch terminal and unscrew the switch from the valve body.

5 Repair the fault or leak and bleed the faulty circuit.

6 The piston assembly will now have returned to its normal setting and the switch should be screwed in and tightened to a torque of 15 lb f ft (2.1 kg f m).

11 Rear brake valves - removal and refitting

1 Any fault in either of the two brake valves which are incorporated in the rear brake lines can only be rectified by renewing the valve complete.

2 To remove a valve, disconnect the rigid brake pipe from the valve and plug the pipe to prevent loss of fluid.

3 Using a close fitting spanner just release the flexible brake hose from the valve. Do not unscrew it more than a quarter of a turn.

4 Unbolt the brake valve and then unscrew the valve body from the flexible hose. Do not twist the hose during this operation.

5 Refitting of the new valve is a reversal of the removal procedure.

6 On completion bleed the hydraulic circuit as described in Section 2.

12 Brake pedal - dismantling and reassembly

1 Remove the panel under the dashboard.

2 Remove the brake stoplamp switch and bracket.

3 Disconnect the pushrod link from the brake pedal.

4 Unscrew and remove the pedal pivot bolt and nut and lift the pedal away.

5 Bushes and sleeves can be fitted to the pedal and linkage by pressing out the old ones and fitting new ones. Apply grease to the bearing surfaces on reassembly.

6 When fitting the stoplamp switch, adjust it as described in Section 13.

13 Brake stoplamp switch - adjustment

1 Make sure that the footbrake pedal is fully released and then measure the distance between the switch and the pedal arm, A in Fig. 9.16.

2 The distance should be 0.16 in (4 mm). Adjust by slackening the retaining screws and moving the switch bracket. Retighten the retaining screws.

Fig. 9.13. Fitting the piston assembly (Sec. 9)

Fig. 9.14. Pressure warning valve (Sec. 10)

1 Pressure warning valve   2 Retaining screw

Fig. 9.15. Removing a brake valve (Sec. 11)

14 Servo brake booster system - general description

1 A vacuum servo unit is fitted in the brake system between the brake pedal and the master cylinder to provide assistance to the driver when the brake pedal is depressed. This reduces the effort required by the driver to operate the brakes under all braking conditions.

2 The unit operates by vacuum from a separate vacuum pump driven from the engine camshaft, B20 engines, or intermediate shaft, B21 engines. It is connected to the engine intake manifold which means that there is still some vacuum available in the event of pump failure.

3 The brake servo booster unit and hydraulic master cylinder are connected together so that the servo unit piston rod acts as the master

Fig. 9.16. Adjusting the brake stoplamp switch (Sec. 13)

cylinder pushrod. The driver's braking effort is transmitted through another pushrod to the servo unit piston and its built in control system. The servo unit piston does not fit tightly into the cylinder, but has a strong diaphragm to keep its edges in constant contact with the cylinder wall, so assuring an airtight seal between the two parts. The forward chamber is held under vacuum conditions created in the inlet manifold of the engine and, during periods when the brake pedal is not in use, the controls open a passage to the rear chamber so placing it under vacuum conditions as well. When the brake pedal is depressed, the vacuum passage to the rear chamber is cut off and the chamber opened to atmospheric pressure. The consequent rush of air pushes the servo piston forward in the vacuum chamber and operates the main pushrod to the master cylinder.

4   The controls are designed so that assistance is given under all conditions and, when the brakes are not required, vacuum in the rear chamber is established when the brake pedal is released. All air from the atmosphere entering the rear chamber is passed through a small air filter.

5   It is emphasised that the servo unit assists in reducing the braking effort required at the foot pedal and in the event of its failure, the hydraulic braking system is in no way endangered, except that the need for higher pedal pressures will be noticed.

6   The servo unit should not be serviced, overhauled or dismantled and in the event of a fault occurring it should be replaced.

15 Servo booster unit - removal and refitting

1   Remove the master cylinder as described in Section 9.
2   Disconnect the vacuum hose from the booster unit.
3   Disconnect the link arm from the brake pedal.
4   Remove the bracket which supports the clutch pedal stop.
5   Remove the four nuts securing the unit to the bulkhead.

6   Pull the unit forward and then disconnect the pushrod clevis fork from the brake pedal link arm.
7   Refitting is the reverse of the removal procedure.
8   Bleed the hydraulic system as described in Section 2.

16 Servo unit vacuum pump - removal, overhaul and refitting

1   Disconnect both hoses from the vacuum pump.
2   Unscrew and remove the mounting bolts and withdraw the pump.
3   Clean away all external dirt and the secure the pump in a vice. Remove the valve housing cover (Fig. 9.18).
4   Scribe a line across the edges of the upper and lower body flanges to facilitate reassembly.
5   Unscrew the flange screws and separate the upper and lower bodies.
6   Unscrew the centre bolt and remove the diaphragm, washers and spring from the lower housing (Fig. 9.19).
7   Invert the pump and remove the lower cover.
8   Extract the lever shaft, lever and pump rod.
9   Renew worn components by obtaining the appropriate repair kits.
10 Reassembly is a reversal of dismantling but make sure that the diaphragm centre bolt is fitted with its washer and O-ring. Clean the centre bolt threads and coat them with Loctite.
11 Make sure that the raised sides of the diaphragm is upwards and the dished sides of the washers are against the diaphragm.
12 Tighten the centre bolt making sure that the hole in the diaphragm is opposite the one in the housing.
13 Refit the pump to the engine and reconnect the hoses to their respective connections.

17 Non-return valves - removal and refitting

1   Three non-return valves are incorporated in the vacuum system. One is located directly on the servo booster unit, one in the hose to the intake manifold and one in the hose to the vacuum reservoir, see Fig. 9.20.
2   To renew the hoses or non-return valves, release the hose clips and separate the hoses.
3   When fitting the non-return valves, make sure that the arrows on the valve point the right way.

18 Handbrake - description and adjustment

1   The handbrake operates mechanically through cables to shoes and drums at the rear wheels. The layout is shown in Fig. 9.2.
2   The parking brake lever acts on two levers via a yoke. The cables are routed parallel with the propeller shaft tunnel. The cables cross

Fig. 9.17. Sectional view of brake servo unit (Sec. 14)

1   Non-return valve
2   Front thrust rod
3   Return spring
4   Diaphragm, front
5   Diaphragm, rear
6   Guide housing
7   Valve piston seat
8   Seal assembly
9   Spring
10 Rear thrust rod
11 Filter
12 Filter
13 Spring
14 Reaction disc

Fig. 9.18. Cut-away view of vacuum pump (Sec. 16)

1 This lever transfers the cam-   5 Nylon bushing
   shaft movements to the   6 Pump diaphragm
   pump rod   7 Valve housing
2 Roller with needle bearing   8 Suction valve
3 Pump spring   9 Discharge valve (into the air)
4 Pump rod

each other on top of the rear axle before being connected to scissor
type levers between the shoe lower ends. An adjuster is provided
between the shoe upper ends.

3 When correctly adjusted the handbrake should give its full effect
on the third or fourth notch of the lever ratchet.

4 Jack-up the rear of the car and remove the road wheels. Remove
the rear ashtray.

5 Screw out the adjustment screw at the rear end of the parking brake
lever so that the cables are slackened, see Fig. 9.21.

6 Align the brake drum so that its hole is opposite the adjuster screw
and adjust with a screwdriver, you will feel the serrations of the
adjuster clicking. Turn the screw until the shoes can be felt to drag
when the drum is rotated then back-off the adjuster 4-5 serrations.

7 Replace the road wheels and the ashtray.

19 Handbrake shoes - inspection and renewal

1 Remove the rear disc/drum assemblies as described in Section 8
paragraphs 6 and 7.

2 Brush away any accumulated dust and inspect the thickness of the
friction linings. If they are worn down, or nearly down, to the securing
rivets (or in the case of bonded linings they are less than 1/16 in (1.6
mm) in thickness) then they must be renewed.

3 If the linings are satisfactory, refit the disc/drum and caliper,
adjust the handbrake, refit the roadwheel and lower the car.

4 If the linings are worn, detach both shoe return springs and remove
the adjuster.

5 Pull the shoes forward, disconnecting them from the links as they
come.

6 Before installing the new shoes, slacken the handbrake cable at the
handbrake lever.

7 Apply a smear of high melting point grease to the shoe slides on the
brake backplate, also to the adjuster threads.

8 Check that the lever and anchor bolt are correctly fitted.

9 Fit the washer and spring to the leading shoe and then fit the shoes,
adjuster and return springs. Note that the shorter section of the adjuster
faces the front of the car on the right-hand brake and towards the rear
on the left-hand brake. Also set the adjuster to its fully retracted
position.

Fig. 9.19. Removing the diaphragm (Sec. 16)

Fig. 9.20. Location of non-return valves (Sec. 17)

1 Vacuum valve   4 Non-return valve
2 Non-return valve (hose   (on servo unit)
   to intake manifold)   5 Servo unit
3 Non-return valve (hose   6 Hose to vacuum pump
   to vacuum reservoir)   7 Vacuum pump

10 Refit the disc/drum and the caliper.

11 Adjust the shoes and the cable, as described in Section 18.

20 Handbrake cable - renewal

1 The handbrake cables can be renewed individually.

2 Remove the handbrake lever cover and disconnect the lead from
the ashtray lamp.

3 Unscrew the adjustment bolt (1) (Fig. 9.24) and remove the nut
(2) at the same time holding the cable in position with a small screwdriver. It should be realised that the cables cross over each other under
the floor and the left-hand cable at the handbrake lever connects with
the right-hand rear brake and the right-hand cable with the left-hand
brake.

4 Lift the front of the rear seat cushion, peel away the carpet and
loosen the clips which hold the cable to the floor.

5 Disconnect the cable end sleeve and grommet from the rear seat
support.

6 Jack-up the rear of the car and support it on stands and then remove
the rear roadwheel.

7 Remove the clamp which attaches the rigid brake line to the rear
axle casing. Unbolt the caliper and without bending the brake line pull
the caliper from the disc and hang it up with a piece of wire.

8 Remove the brake drum and the brake shoes, as described in
Section 8.

9 Press out the lock pin which retains the cable to the shoe actuating
lever.

10 Remove the bolt from the retainer above the rear suspension arm
and pull out the cable, plastic tube and rubber seal.

11 Withdraw the cable from the centre support and channel in the
floor of the car.

12 Refit the new cable by reversing the removal procedure and then
adjust the cable, see Section 18.

Fig. 9.21. Slackening the adjusting screw at handbrake lever (Sec. 18)

Fig. 9.22. Adjusting the brake shoes (Sec. 18)

Fig. 9.23. Handbrake shoe arrangement (Sec. 19)

1	Shoe	6	Anchor bolt
2	Return spring	7	Lever
3	Adjuster	8	Washer
4	Shoe	9	Spring
5	Shoe steady clip		

Fig. 9.24. Handbrake cable attachment to control lever (Sec. 20)

1   Adjuster bolt
2   Lockscrew

Fig. 9.25. Disconnecting cable from shoe lever (Sec.20)

Fig. 9.26. Handbrake cable support (Sec.20)

1   Attaching screw
2   Cable
3   Plastic tube

21 Fault diagnosis - braking system

Symptom	Reason/s
Brake grab	Excessive run-out of discs. Rust on disc. Oil stained pads.
Brake drag	Faulty master cylinder. Foot pedal return impeded. Reservoir breather blocked. Seized caliper. Incorrect adjustment of handbrake. Crushed, blocked or swollen pipe lines.
Excessive pedal effort required	Pads not yet bedded-in. Pads or discs contaminated with oil or grease. Scored discs. Faulty vacuum servo unit.
Brake pedal feels hard	Glazed surfaces of friction material. Rust on disc surfaces. Seized caliper piston.
Excessive pedal travel	Low reservoir fluid level. Disc run-out excessive. Worn front wheel bearings. Air in system. Worn pads.
Pedal creep during sustained application	Fluid leak. Internal fault in master cylinder. Faulty servo unit non-return valve.
Pedal 'spongy'	Air in system. Perished flexible hose. Loose master cylinder mounting nuts. Faulty breather blocked.
Fall in reservoir fluid level	Normal due to pad wear. Leak in hydraulic system.

Chapter 10 Electrical system

For modifications, and information applicable to later models, see Supplement at end of manual

Contents

Specifications

System voltage   ...   .   12 volts

Battery

Type ... ... ,,, ,,, ...	Tudor 6 EX 3 (or equivalent)
Earth connection	Negative terminal
Battery capacity (standard)	60 Ah
Specific gravity of electrolyte:	
Fully charged battery	1.28
When recharging is required	1.21
Recommended charging current	5.5 A

Alternator (SEV Marchal)

Type	SEV Marchal A 14/30 712 712 12
Output	490 W
Maximum amperage	35 A
Maximum speed	15,000 rpm
Direction of rotation	Optional
Ratio: engine speed - alternator speed	1 : 2
Minimum length of brushes	0.2 in (5 mm)
Tightening torque:	
Attaching screws	2.9 lb f ft (0.4 kg f m)
Nut for pulley	29 lb f ft (4 kg f m)
Test values:	
Field winding resistance	4.9 ohm
Output test	30 A at 3,000 rpm and approx. 13 V

Alternator (Bosch K1 - 14V 35A 20)

Type	Bosch K1 - 14V 35A 20
Output	490 W
Maximum amperage	35 A
Maximum speed	13,500 rpm
Direction of rotation	Clockwise
Ratio, engine speed - alternator speed	1 : 2
Minimum diameter of slip rings	1.24 in (31.5 mm)
Maximum radial throw on:	
Slip rings	0.0012 in (0.03 mm)
Rotor body	0.0020 in (0.05 mm)
Minimum length of brushes	0.31 in (8 mm)
Brush pressure	0.7 - 0.9 lb (0 - 0.4 kg)
Tightening torque, pulley nut	25 - 29 lb f ft (3.5 - 4 kg f m)

Test values:

Resistance in stator	0.26 - 0.29 ohm/phase	
Resistance in rotor	4 - 4.4 ohm	
Output test	30 A at 3,000 rpm and approx. 13 V	

Alternator (Bosch K1 - 14V 55A 20)

Type	Bosch K1 - 14V 55A 20
Output	770 W
Maximum amperage	55 A
Maximum speed	13,500 rpm
Direction of rotation	Clockwise
Ratio: engine speed - alternator speed	1 : 2
Minimum diameter of slip ring	1.24 in (31.5 mm)
Maximum radial throw on:	
Slip rings	0.0012 in (0.03 mm)
Rotor body	0.0020 in (0.05 mm)
Minimum length of brushes	0.31 in (8 mm)
Spring pressure	0.7 - 0.9 lb (0.3 - 0.4 kg)
Tightening torque, pulley nut	25 - 32 lb f ft (3.5 - 4.5 kg f m)
Test values:	
Resistance in stator	0.26 - 0.29 ohm/phase
Resistance in rotor	4 - 4.4 ohm
Output test	48 A at 3,000 rpm and approx. 13 V

Voltage regulator

SEV Marchal 727 105 02:	
Control voltage, after driving 10 minutes	13.5 - 14.1 V
Bosch AD - 14V:	
Control voltage, after driving 10 minutes	13.5 - 14.1 V
Load current, two lower contacts	44 - 46 A
Control range (between two upper and lower contacts)	0 - 0.4 V
Load current, two upper contacts	3 - 8 A

Starter motor

Type	Bosch GF 12V 1.1 PS
Voltage	12 V
Earth connection	Negative terminal
Direction of rotation	Clockwise
Output	810 W (1.1 hp)
Number of teeth on pinion	9
Number of brushes	4
Test values:	
Mechanical:	
Armature endfloat	0.0004 - 0.0118 in (0.01 - 0.30 mm)
Brush spring tension	3 - 3.5 lb (1.4 - 1.6 kg)
Distance from pinion to ring gear	0.047 - 0.173 in (1.2 - 4.4 mm)
Frictional torque of rotor brake	2.18 - 3.48 lb in (2.5 - 4 kg cm)
Pinion idling torque	1.22 - 1.91 lb in (1.4 - 2.2 kg cm)
Backlash	0.012 - 0.020 in (0.3 - 0.5 mm)
Minimum diameter of commutator	1.32 in (33.5 mm)
Minimum length of brushes	0.51 in (13 mm)
Electrical:	
Unloaded starter motor (11.5 volts and 30 - 50A)	5,800 - 7,800 rpm
Loaded starter motor (9 volts and 185 - 220A)	1,050 - 1,350 rpm
Locked starter motor (7 volts and 400 - 490A)	0 rpm
Control solenoid, cut-in voltage	Min. 7.5 V

Light bulbs

	Power	Socket
Headlights	60/55 W	H4
Day running lights	5 W/21 W	Ba 15d
Direction indicators:		
Front	21 W or 32 cp	Ba 15s
Rear	21 W or 32 cp	Ba 15s
Tail lights	5 W or 4 cp	Ba 15s
Brake lights	21 W or 32 cp	Ba 15s
Reversing lights	21 W or 32 cp	Ba 15s
Number plate light	5 W	S 8.5
Interior light	10 W	S 8.5
Glovebox light	2 W	Ba 9s
Instrument lighting	2 W	W 2.2d
Engine compartment light	15 W	S 8.5
Lighting:		
Control panel	1.2 W	W 1.8d
Automatic transmission	1.2 W	W 1.8d
Rear ashtray	1.2 W	W 1.8d
Safety belt lock	1.2 W	W 1.8d

Warning lights:

Charging	...	...	...	...	...	...	...	...	...	...	1.2 W	W 1.8d
Oil pressure	...	...	...	...	...	...	...	...	...	...	1.2 W	W 1.8d
Handbrake	...	...	...	...	...	...	...	...	...	...	1.2 W	W 1.8d
Brake failure	...	...	...	...	...	...	...	...	...	...	1.2 W	W 1.8d
Bulbs	...	...	...	...	...	...	...	...	...	...	1.2 W	W 1.8d

Indicator lights:

Choke	...	...	...	...	...	...	...	...	...	...	1.2 W	W 1.8d
Direction indicators	...	...	...	...	...	...	...	...	...	...	1.2 W	W 1.8d
Full beam	...	...	...	...	...	...	...	...	...	...	1.2 W	W 1.8d
Overdrive	...	...	...	...	...	...	...	...	...	...	1.2 W	W 1.8d
Hazard warning lights	...	...	...	...	...	...	...	...	...	...	1.2 W	W 2 x 4.6d
Heated rear window	...	...	...	...	...	...	...	...	...	...	1.2 W	W 2 x 4.6d
Safety belts	...	...	...	...	...	...	...	...	...	...	2 W	BA 9S

Heated rear window

Output	...	...	...	...	...	...	...	...	...	...	150 ± 30 W

* Fuses

Number	Circuit protected	Fuse rating (amps)
1	Cigar lighter	8A
	Tailgate window wiper/washer (245)	
2	Windscreen wipers	16A
	Heater fan	
	Horn	
3	Electrically heated rear window	16A
	Overdrive	
4	Glove compartment light	8A
	Reversing light	
	Electrically heated driver's seat	
5	Instruments	8A
	Indicators	
	Warning light	
	Fasten seatbelt warning light	
6	Hazard warning lights	8A
	Engine compartment light	
7	Clock	16A
	Fuel pump (injection engines)	
8	Brakelight	8A
	Interior light	
9	Daytime running lights (UK only)	8A
	Ignition interlock buzzer, seatbelt (USA only)	
10	Spare	16A
11	Left-hand parking light	8A
	Rear foglight	
12	Right-hand parking light	8A
	Instrument and panel light	

Typical fuse ratings shown. See the handbook for details

1 General description

The electrical system is of the 12 volt type and the major components comprise a 12 volt battery (of which the negative terminal is earthed), voltage regulator, alternator, which is fitted at the front of the engine and is driven from the pulley on the front of the crankshaft, and a starter motor which is mounted on the rear left-hand side of the engine.

The battery supplies a steady amount of current for the ignition, lighting and other electrical circuits, and provides a reserve of electricity when the current consumed by the electrical equipment exceeds that being produced by the alternator.

When fitting electrical accessories to cars with a negative earth system it is important, if they contain silicone diodes or transistors, that they are connected correctly, otherwise serious damage may result to the components concerned. Items such as radios, tape recorders and electronic tachometers should all be checked for correct polarity.

It is important that the battery is always disconnected if it is to be boost charged when an alternator is fitted. This is also applicable when electric welding equipment is to be used.

2 Battery - removal, maintenance, inspection and refitting

1 The battery is fitted on a shelf in the engine compartment (to the left of the radiator) and is held in position by a bar and clamp. When removing it, first disconnect the negative (earth) lead and then the positive lead. This way you avoid any possibility of damage through shorted circuits. The leads are fastened to the battery either by clamps (the normal Volvo practice) or by caps which are screwed to tapped holes in the battery terminals; this type of fitting may be found as a replacement for the original clamps. Removal of the battery is simply a matter of undoing the nuts holding the retaining bar, removing this and lifting the battery out.

2 Every three months the battery should be removed and cleaned - brush it down and give it a rinse with clean luke warm water. At the same time clean the battery shelf and the terminals, wire brushing these if necessary to remove corrosion.

3 Weekly maintenance consists of checking the electrolyte level in the cells to ensure that the separators are covered by ¼ in (6 mm) of electrolyte. If the level has fallen, top up with distilled water only. Do not overfill. If you find it difficult to judge the correct level of electrolyte, you can buy battery fillers which automatically get it right for you, employing a simple valve or cut away in the spout. If the battery is overfilled or any electrolyte spilled, wipe away the electrolyte immediately as it attacks and corrodes any metal it comes into contact with very quickly.

4 Inspect the retaining bar, securing nuts, tray and battery leads for corrosion (white fluffy deposits on the metal which are brittle to touch). If any corrosion is found, clean off the deposit with ammonia and paint over the clean metal with an anti-rust/anti-acid paint.

5 Keep an eye on the battery case for cracks. It is possible to clean and plug these with proprietary compounds made for this purpose. If an appreciable amount of electrolyte has leaked away through a crack or if electrolyte has been spilt out of the battery it should be

replaced with fresh electrolyte; otherwise all topping-up should be done with distilled water.

6 If topping-up becomes excessive and there is no leakage from the case, the battery is being overcharged and the voltage regulator will have to be checked and reset.

7 As part of the three-monthly check, measure the specific gravity of the electrolyte with a hydrometer. A table of specific gravity is given later in this Section. There should be very little variation between different cells. If a variation greater than 0.025 is present, the cause must either be spillage or leakage - which has been topped-up with distilled water, or an internal short circuit in the cell - an indication that the battery will soon need renewal.

8 To check a suspect cell, discharge the battery completely (for example, by leaving the headlights on). Recheck the specific gravities and if the dubious cell is still lower than the others remove some of the electrolyte if necessary and top it up with a mixture of one part sulphuric acid to 2.5 parts of water, repeating this process until the specific gravity comes up to standard. If it is too high to start with, of course, you will top it up with distilled water after removing the electrolyte, but in practice this never seems to happen.

9 Now recharge the battery at about 5 amps until the specific gravity of the electrolyte in the good cells has remained constant for about four hours. It will take you about 18 hours in all. It does not matter if you charge at a lesser rate, but it will take proportionately longer. You can save time by charging at up to 10 amps but do not be tempted to use a rapid charger which claims to restore the power of the battery in one or two hours. They can be dangerous devices to use with batteries that are past their best.

10 In all probability the suspect cell will now have the same specific gravity as the others. Replace the battery in the car and keep a particular eye on this cell. If in a week or two the specific gravity has again dropped below the level of the others, you can resign yourself to the thought that very soon you will have to renew the battery.

11 When mixing sulphuric acid and water **never add water to sulphuric acid** - always pour the acid slowly on to the water in a glass container. **If water is added to sulphuric acid it will explode.**

12 Refitting is a direct reversal of the removal procedure. Connect the positive lead before the negative lead and smear the terminals with petroleum jelly (Vaseline) to prevent corrosion. Never use an ordinary grease as applied to other parts of the car.

13 In wintertime when a heavy demand is placed on the battery it is a good idea to give the battery an occasional charge at about 5 amps. Ideally you should charge at this rate until the specific gravity has remained constant for four hours. We are usually content to observe the vigorous bubbling from the electrolyte which indicates that the battery is fully charged and let this go on for three or four hours.

14 A final hint - in very cold weather, top your battery up just before you start a run. Distilled water is lighter than electrolyte and may float on top of it instead of mixing with it if the car is cold and stationary. In this case it can easily freeze and may ruin your battery by cracking the case.

SPECIFIC GRAVITY TABLE

Specific gravity - fully discharged

1.098 at 100°F or 38°C electrolyte temperature
1.102 at 90°F or 32°C electrolyte temperature
1.106 at 80°F or 27°C electrolyte temperature
1.110 at 70°F or 21°C electrolyte temperature
1.114 at 60°F or 16°C electrolyte temperature
1.118 at 50°F or 10°C electrolyte temperature
1.122 at 40°F or 4°C electrolyte temperature
1.126 at 30°F or-1.5°C electrolyte temperature

Specific gravity - battery fully charged

1.268 at 100°F or 38°C electrolyte temperature
1.272 at 90°F or 32°C electrolyte temperature
1.276 at 80°F or 27°C electrolyte temperature
1.280 at 70°F or 21°C electrolyte temperature
1.284 at 60°F or 16°C electrolyte temperature
1.288 at 50°F or 10°C electrolyte temperature
1.292 at 40°F or 4°C electrolyte temperature
1.296 at 30°F or-1.5°C electrolyte temperature

3 Alternator - general description

1 In an ordinary generator the armature rotates between what are, in effect, the poles of a magnet or may be several sets of these poles. The magnetism is maintained by the field coils. As the position of the armature relative to the magnetic poles varies, the magnetic field passing through the armature changes and it is this change of magnetism which produces current in the armature coils. It is only when the magnetic field is changing that current is produced, (when the armature is not rotating no current appears) and this current, like the changing field that produces it, is changing all the time. In fact, if it were not for the commutator which acts as a reversing switch operated in time with the changing current, the output of the ordinary generator would be alternating current and not direct current.

2 The alternator differs from the ordinary DC generator in that the armature is stationary and the field coils with their magnetic pole pieces rotate. The output from the armature is alternating current because there is now no rotating commutator to keep changing it over, but the current passes through a system of diodes so arranged that whichever way the current is flowing when it leaves the armature it is always flowing in the same direction at the output terminals. It is easy to get an idea of how these diodes operate by looking at the circuit diagrams (Figs. 10.2 and 10.3) and remembering that the electric current only passes through the diodes in the direction indicated by the arrows, so that it is only possible for current to enter and leave the output terminals in the direction shown, whatever is happening in the alternator coils.

3 There is nothing particularly novel about this idea, but it has only become practicable in the last few years because of a technological break through in rectifier design - the development of materials known as semi-conductors. It brings with it some very considerable design advantages. The first of these is that the brushes now only pass the field current - a matter of two or three amps - instead of the total output current of 30-50 amps, and this current needs no commutation but is simply passed into the field coil via slip rings. Because of this the size of the brushes can be greatly reduced and sparking becomes negligible.

4 In a normal generator, excessive current produces overheating of the brushes and commutator leading to complete breakdown of the armature. Because of this the current output has to be limited by an external regulator. With the alternator, provided that the armature is wound with thick enough wire, and in practice this is quite easy, the output current is limited to a safe value by reason of the magnetic effect it produces which cancels out the magnetism produced by the field coil. Because of this, only voltage regulation is needed with an alternator; the current can be allowed to look after itself.

5 Three different alternators are found on the 240 series models. Two of these, the Bosch K1-14 35A 20 and K1-14V 55A 20, are almost identical, the latter providing a larger current output. The third type, SEV Marchal 712 712 12 has slightly different electrical and mechanical arrangements but works on exactly the same principle.

6 The voltage regulator for the alternator is located on the right-hand wheel housing. Fig. 10.9 shows the Bosch regulator: the SEV regulator look very similar.

Fig. 10.1. Location of alternator - B20 engine (Sec. 3)

Fig. 10.2. SEV alternator and regulator circuit diagram (Sec. 3 and 7)

Fig. 10.3. Bosch alternator and regulator circuit diagram (Sec. 3)

5.3 Disconnecting the leads from the alternator

4   Alternator - special precautions

1   The diodes used in alternator equipment are very sensitive to voltages and currents greater than they are designed to withstand, and in particular they are easily damaged by excessive reverse voltages. To avoid any risk of diode failure or shortened life, take the precautions outlined in the next few paragraphs.
2   When replacing or reconnecting the battery, make sure that it is connected with correct polarity, ie. negative earth.
3   Never run the alternator unless the regulator is connected. If the battery is disconnected, be sure that there is some external load - headlamps, for example - connected across the output terminal.
4   No attempt should be made to polarise the alternator. This is not necessary.
5   When charging the battery while installed in the car, the negative battery lead should be disconnected.
6   A rapid charger should not be used as an aid in starting.
7   When using an extra battery as a starting aid, always connect it in parallel.
8   When carrying out electric welding on the vehicle, disconnect the negative battery lead as well as all the alternator leads. The welder should always be connected as near as possible to where the welding is carried out.

5   Alternator - removal and refitting

1   For safety reasons, disconnect the battery.
2   Slacken the belt tensioner and remove the fanbelt.
3   Make a note of, and then disconnect, the leads to the alternator (photo).
4   Undo and remove the alternator securing bolts and remove the alternator from the engine.
5   Refitting the alternator is the reverse sequence to removal. Adjust the fanbelt tension, as described in Chapter 2.

6   Alternator - dismantling, overhaul and reassembly

1   Give the alternator a good clean before starting to take it apart, using paraffin or a proprietary solvent.
2   Figs. 10.4 and 10.5 give exploded views of Bosch and SEV alternators respectively.
3   Remove the screws attaching the brush holder and take off the holder.
4   Using the fanbelt as protection, hold the pulley in a vice with soft jaws. Undo the fixing nut, lift off the pulley key (watch this - its powers of concealment would do credit to a chameleon!) spacing washer or washers (note the order of assembly) and fan.
5   Remove the two bolts holding together the alternator and take off the drive end shield holding the alternator in a vice by the driveshaft. Be careful when using screwdrivers to part the alternator - do not insert them further than 1/16 in (2 mm) or you may damage the stator winding.
6   Remove the retaining plate which holds the rotor bearing in the drive end shield and knock out the bearing by gently tapping on the rotor shaft with a hide mallet or a piece of wood.
7   In the SEV alternator detach the isolation diode holder by removing the nuts and washers on terminal '61' and the corresponding ones on the other side of the isolation diode. This being done, it is a simple matter to detach the rectifier assembly from the slip ring end shield and withdraw the stator winding with the rectifier assembly still connected to it. The end shield may then be detached.
8   For the Bosch alternator, unsolder the stator winding leads from the terminals on the slip ring end shield, marking the leads and terminals so that you know which goes to which. The stator winding can then be withdrawn from the shield. Remove the positive diode assembly, the magnetizing rectifier assembly and the negative diode assembly from the slip ring end shield, which can then be separated from the stator.

Bearings
1   Generally speaking the bearings for the rotor will stay on the rotor shaft when the alternator is dismantled, though sometimes they may remain in the end shields. Where these bearings are of the open type, they should be removed from the end shield or shaft, thoroughly cleaned in White Spirit and examined carefully for signs of scoring, scuffing, wear or blueing. If such signs are present or there is appreciable play in the bearing it should be replaced. Otherwise, pack the bearing with a suitable grease for further use.
2   If the bearings are of the sealed type, check them for play and smoothness of operation and replace them if you are in any doubt about their condition.

Fig. 10.4. Exploded view of Bosch alternator (Sec. 6)

1 Rectifier (plus diode plate)	3 Brush holder	6 Stator	9 Fan
2 Magnetizing rectifier	4 Slip ring end shield	7 Rotor	10 Pulley
	5 Rectifier (negative diodes)	8 Drive end shield	

Fig. 10.5. Exploded view of SEV alternator (Sec. 6)

1 Brush holder	3 Slip ring end shield	5 Stator	7 Drive end shield
2 Isolation diodes with holder	4 Rectifier (silicon diodes)	6 Rotor	8 Fan

Brushes and slip rings

1　Using a 12v 2.5w bulb connected to a suitable source (three 4½ volt flat flash lamp batteries are very handy) check that the brushes are isolated from each other (ie. the lamp must not light when connected between the brushes). Check that the connection between the brushes and their respective terminals on the holder are good - ie. the test lamp should light when connected between a brush and its terminal.

2　The minimum length of the brush protruding from the holder should be 0.2 in (5 mm) for SEV alternators and 0.31 in (8 mm) for Bosch.

3　The surface of the slip rings should be smooth. You may give them a polish with very fine sand paper (not emery paper), being careful to remove all traces of the sand paper when you have finished. If the slip rings are burnt or damaged in any other way, there is no reason why they should not be skimmed in a lathe, but a glance at the Specifications for run-out given for the Bosch alternator will show that this is a specialist operation. You should resist the temptation to hold the rotor in an electric drill and take a file to the slip rings.

Checking the rotor

1　Check the slip rings, as described in the previous sub-Section.

2　Examine the winding for breakage or damaged insulation.

3　Check the insulation between the winding and the frame by connecting a test lamp and battery between the frame and one of the slip rings. The lamp should not light.

4　Measure the resistance between the slip rings with an ohmmeter or multi-meter. It should be 4.9 ohms for SEV and 4.0 ohms ± 10% for Bosch.

Checking the stator

1　Examine the winding carefully for signs of burning. If this is found, it means that there is a short circuit in the winding and the stator should be replaced or rewound.

2　Connect a test lamp between one of the winding terminals and the frame, the lamp should not light. If there is the smallest glow, the

Fig. 10.6. Test circuit for Bosch alternator (Sec. 6)

A Alternator	D Ammeter 0 - 50 amps
B Test lamp 12V, 2w	E Battery 60 Ah
C Voltmeter 0 - 20V	F Load resistance

stator should be replaced.

3　Using an ohmmeter or multi-meter, measure the resistance between each pair of winding terminations (in the case of the Bosch alternator, these are the leads that are connected to the diodes - not the star point which has three wires going to it). The presence of the diodes on the SEV stator windings will not affect these measurements unless the diodes are defective. The three different measurements should give the same value of resistance - certainly within 2%. For the Bosch alternator the resistance value should lie within 0.26 ± 0.03 ohms.

Checking the diodes

1　The diode is simply a device which will allow electric current to pass through it one way and not the other way. In diagrams such as Figs. 10.2 and 10.3 the direction in which current is able to flow through the diode is indicated by the black arrowhead. Electric current flows from positive to negative, so if you connect a positive voltage (for example, the positive lead of your battery/test bulb combination) to the broad end of the arrow and the negative lead to the other end, current will flow and the lamp will light. If you reverse the connections, the lamp will not light. Normally, you do not have to worry about which way round you connect your lamp, because if the lamp lights when connected one way round and does not light when connected the other way round, the diode must be all right. A faulty diode either lights the lamp both ways or not at all. Note that the positive voltage on a rectifier diode appears at the pointed end of the arrow. The diodes are made up to produce positive voltage at the casing or at the centre lead as required; both types are used in the alternator.

2   Unless specialised apparatus is available, it is necessary to unsolder the leads from the SEV alternator to the diodes mounted on it in order to check them. To someone not experienced in working with electronic equipment, this soldering is a tricky business and best left to a specialist. There is no reason why the local radio shop should not do this for you. Check the diodes as just described with the test lamp and voltage source. In no circumstances should the test voltage exceed 14v. If any defective diodes are found, replace the relevant assembly or have a diode fitted to the existing plate by a specialist. In the Bosch alternator, the diode plate is disconnected from the stator winding when the alternator is dismantled and there is no need to unsolder the diodes themselves. The battery and lamp can be connected across each diode in turn.

Reassembly

1   Reassembly in the main is a reversal of the dismantling process, and presents no special problems. In the Bosch alternator, fit the bearing and retaining plate to the drive end bearing shield before assembling this to the rotor. Coat the slip ring end shield bearing seat with a light layer of 'Molycote' paste or similar and assemble the alternator. Do not forget the spring ring, on the slip ring end shield bearing seat. Fixing screws and nuts should be tightened to a torque of 3.6-4.3 lb f ft (0.50-0.60 kg f m).

2   For the SEV alternator, the fixing screws should be tightened to a torque of 2.0 - 2.2 lb f ft (0.28 - 0.30 kg f m).

3   Be sure that the isolation diode holder on the SEV alternator is fitted with the full complement of plastic tube and isolation washers on its fixing screws.

4   Fit the spacer washer, key, fan, pulley, washer and finally the pulley nut in the order in which you took them off. Tightening torque for the pulley nut is 29 lb f ft (4 kg f m) for both SEV and Bosch alternators.

7   Alternator regulator - checking

1   The SEV regulator does not depend on spring tension, contact clearance etc for its correct operation, being controlled by a voltage sensitive resistor element (R3, Fig. 10.2). No means of adjustment is available and if it does not meet the checking procedure which follows, it should be replaced.

2   To check the SEV regulator, start up the engine and run the alternator at about 5,000 rpm (engine speed 2,500 rpm) for 15 seconds. Switch everything off except the ignition and read the voltage between 'B+' and 'D-' on the alternator. This should lie within the shaded area of Fig. 10.7. Note that the temperature referred to is the air temperature, not the temperature of the regulator itself. The reading should change very little when the alternator is loaded with, for example, full beam headlights. Now drive the vehicle for 45 minutes and repeat the procedure. The readings should now be within the shaded area of Fig. 10.8. If they are not, you will either have to live with it or replace the regulator.

3   To check the Bosch regulator, you will need to load the alternator with 28-30 amps (ie. full beam headlights plus as much again - another pair of bulbs, for example). The check must be carried out quickly, before the regulator has a chance to get really warm. Run the alternator to a speed of 4,000 rpm (engine speed 2,000 rpm) rapidly lower it to about 1,000 rpm (ie. idling speed), raise the speed again to 4,000 rpm and read the voltage between 'B+' and 'D-' on the alternator. This should be 14-15v. Reduce the load on the alternator to 3-8 amps (ie. one dipped headlight equivalent) and read the voltage again. It should now be between 0 and 0.3v less than the first reading. If the voltage is outside specification - particularly if it is too high - the regulator should be adjusted by a specialist or replaced.

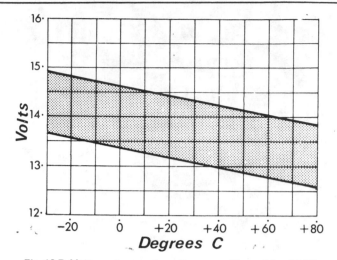

Fig. 10.7. Voltage - temperature diagram, cold regulator (SEV) (Sec. 7)

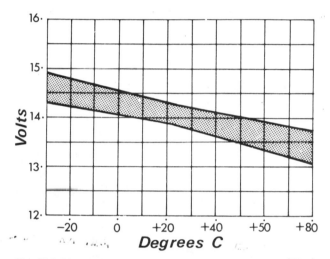

Fig. 10.8. Voltage - temperature diagram, warm regulator (SEV) (Sec. 7)

Fig. 10.9. Bosch voltage regulator (Secs. 3 and 7)

1   *Contact for lower control range*
2   *Contact for upper control range*
3   *Stop arm*
4   *Spring. Steel upper section*
      Bi-metal lower section

10.3a Bolts securing the starter to the flywheel housing (B21 engine)

10.3b Starter motor support bracket (B21 engine)

Fig. 10.10. Cut-away view of starter motor (Sec. 11)

1	Shift lever	9	Connection lead to field	17	Brush holder	25	Drive end frame
2	Pivot pin (bearing screw)	10	Screw	18	Brush	26	One-way clutch
3	Plunger	11	Rubber gasket	19	Brush spring	27	Pinion
4	Steel washer	12	Shims	20	Commutator	28	Stop ring
5	Rubber washer	13	Snap ring	21	Armature	29	Snap ring
6	Winding	14	Bush	22	Pole shoe	30	Bush
7	Contact plate	15	Commutator end frame	23	Stator		
8	Terminal for battery lead	16	Adjusting washers	24	Field winding		

8 Starter motor - general description

1   The starter motor is of the pre-engaged type, in which the pinion is mechanically engaged with the flywheel ring gear before the motor is switched on, a roller clutch drive in the pinion assembly allowing the pinion to free-wheel when the engine starts. The mechanical engagement is driven by a solenoid which operates the starter motor switch after it has pushed the pinion into position.

2   If properly lubricated before assembly, the self-lubricating bearings of the starter motor will last as long as the engine.

9 Starter motor - testing on engine

1   If the starter motor fails to operate, first check the condition of the battery by turning on the headlamps. If they shine brightly for several seconds and then gradually dim, the battery needs charging.

2   If the headlights remain bright and it is obvious that the battery is in good condition, check the connections between the battery and the starter - this includes the earth lead from the battery terminal to the bodyframe and the lead from the starter switch to the solenoid.

3   If all the connections are sound, listen for a click from the solenoid when the starter switch is operated. If there is no click, a fault in the solenoid is suggested. If there is a click but the starter motor does not turn, there is probably a fault in the motor itself. In either event the starter motor will have to be removed for inspection.

10 Starter motor - removal and refitting

1   Disconnect the battery, for safety reasons.

2   Make a note of, and then disconnect, the leads from the starter motor solenoid.

3   Undo and remove the bolts and spring washer that secure the starter motor to the flywheel housing. On B21 engines remove the bracket attaching the starter motor to the engine block (photos).

4   Lift away the starter motor.

5   Refitting the starter motor is the reverse of the removal sequence.

11 Starter motor - dismantling, overhaul and reassembly

1   Refer to Fig. 10.10 and remove the small cover located at the front end of the shaft.

2   Lift away the locking washer and the adjustment washer.

3   Suitably mark the drive bearing and commutator bearing brackets.

4   Undo and remove the two through-bolts.

5   Lift off the commutator bearing shield. The brushes and retainers will remain in position on the armature.

6   Remove the brush retaining plate from the armature.

7   Note the position of the washers.

8   The brushes may now be pulled from their holders.

9   Remove the brush gear from the armature taking care not to lose the shims.

10 When the brush gear is removed the negative brushes will also be detached but the positive brushes will remain attached to the field winding.

11 Unscrew the nut that holds the field terminal connection to the solenoid.

12 Undo and remove the screws which hold the solenoid to the drive-shaft end. Lift away the solenoid.

13 Remove the drive end shield and armature from the starter body.

14 Remove the pivot pin from the engagement lever, lift away the rubber washer and also the metal washer.

15 Lift the armature together with the pinion and lever from the drive end shield.

16 Knock back the stop washer and remove the circlip from the armature.

17 Finally pull off the stop ring and drive pinion assembly.

18 Clean off the various components using a compressed air jet.

19 Carefully examine the rotor for signs of mechanical damage such as a worn or bent shaft, scored or burnt commutator or damaged windings. If the rotor shaft is bent or worn, it must be renewed.

20 If the commutator is scored or worn unevenly it may be skimmed on a lathe. Take small cuts each time so that the minimum amount of material is removed. The insulation between the laminations should now be undercut to a depth of 0.016 in (0.4 mm) using a hacksaw blade with the tooth sides ground off.

21 Examine the housing and the field winding for signs of damage caused by the rotor.

22 If possible test the field winding to ensure that it is not earthed by connecting the contact points of a test light and battery to the housing and field winding. If the light comes on, the winding or lead

Fig. 10.11. Starter motor - general arrangement (Sec. 11)

Fig. 10.12. Starter motor - lubrication points (Sec. 11)

*1   Lightly grease insulation washers, shaft end, adjusting washers
     and lock washer*
2   Soak bush in oil for 30 minutes
3   Well grease rotor thread and engaging lever groove
4   Lightly grease rotor shaft
5   Soak bush in oil for 30 minutes
6   Lightly grease engaging lever joints and iron core of solenoid

Fig. 10.13. Exploded view of headlamp (Sec. 12)

through the body is damaged. Remove the through lead and re-test.
If the light still remains on the field coils are earthed and must be
renewed.
23 Carefully examine the brush holders. If any parts are worn or
damaged they must be renewed.
24 Generally inspect all other parts and renew any parts that are worn
or damaged. During reassembly new circlips should always be used.
25 To remove the brushes they must be unsoldered from their attachments in the brush holder and field winding respectively. Solder the
new brushes into position taking care not to allow solder to run down
onto the brush leads as this can prevent the necessary movement of the
brushes in the brush holders and may also reduce brush spring. Ideally
the brushes should be renewed when they have worn down to a length
of 0.51 in (13 mm).
26 Reassembly of this starter motor is a direct reversal to the dismantling procedure. Lubricate the starter motor as shown in Fig. 10.12.

12 Headlights - general

1   To remove a headlight pull out the socket connection at the rear
and remove the rubber cover. Turn the chromed ring slightly anticlockwise, remove the chromed ring and lift out the headlight (photos).
2   The bulb is removed by releasing the retaining clip and withdrawing
the bulb (photo).
3   The beam alignment of the headlights should be adjusted by a
service station using modern optical setting equipment.
4   The two adjusting screws are located at the rear of each headlight
in the engine compartment.

13 Rear lights - general

1   To change the bulbs remove the lens assembly by undoing the four
retaining screws (photos).
2   Disconnect the leads from inside the boot and remove the defective
bulb (photo).
3   When refitting the lens ensure the seal is in position .

14 Number plate light - general

1   The rear number plate light is removed by releasing the spring clips,
which retain it in position, with a screwdriver (photo).
2   Unclip the cover and remove the bulb (photo).

15 Parking light and direction indicators (front) - general

1   Remove the screws retaining the lens (photo).

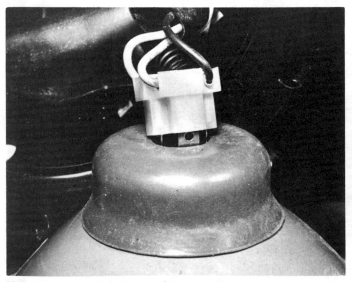

12.1a Removing the headlamp socket connection

12.1b Removing the chromed ring

12.2a Bulb retaining clip

12.2b Removing the bulb

13.1a Lens assembly securing screws

13.1b Rear lights cluster with lens removed

13.2 Rear lights connections in the boot

14.1 Removing the number plate light

14.2 Remove the cover to get at the bulb

15.1 The two screws securing the lens on the front parking light and direction indicator light

15.2 The lens removed exposing the bulbs

2   Lift out the lens and renew the bulb (photo).
3   When refitting the lens ensure the seal is in position.

16 Interior light - general

1   Remove the lens by inserting a screwdriver into the small cut-out and prising out the assembly (photo).
2   The bulb can now be renewed.

17 Flasher unit - general

1   The flasher unit controls the operation of the direction indicators and the hazard warning lights.
2   The unit is located behind the control panel.
3   If a fault occurs in either system, check the wiring and bulbs. If these are in order, pull out the flasher unit from the terminal block and install a new one.

18 Horns and horn switch - general

1   Twin horns are mounted behind the radiator grille (photo).
2   The horns normally require no attention. If they fail to operate, check the circuit fuse and the connecting wiring.
3   To check the horn switch, lever off the crash-pad from the centre of the steering wheel, unscrew the retaining screws and remove the contact bar (photo).
4   If the fuse, wiring and switch is in order but the fault persists, renew the horn.

19 Windscreen wiper blades and arms - removal and refitting

1   Whenever the wiper blades fail to clean the windscreen effectively, they must be renewed.
2   Pull the wiper arm away from the screen until it locks in position. Depress the small locking tab and pull the wiper blade from the wiper

16.1 Changing the interior roof light bulb

18.1 The horns are fitted behind the radiator grille

18.3 Checking the horn switch

19.2 Pulling the wiper blade from the upper arm

19.4 Wiper arm removed from its spindle

20.4 Windscreen wiper motor - location

arm (photo).

3   It may be possible to obtain new rubber inserts otherwise the wiper blade and holder will have to be renewed complete.

4   A wiper arm can be removed by lifting the small locking tab and pulling it from the splines of its driving spindle (photo).

5   Refitting is a reversal of removal but make sure that the wiper arms are fitted to their splines in such a way that the blades are parallel with the bottom edge of the windscreen.

20 Windscreen wiper motor - removal and refitting

1   Disconnect the battery earth terminal. Remove the wiper arms.

2   Remove the panel under the dashboard.

3   Remove the demister hoses.

4   Disconnect the wiper motor leads. Undo and remove the securing screws and linkage. Lift away the motor (photo).

5   Refitting is the reversal of the removal procedure.

21 Windscreen wiper motor - servicing

1   The windscreen wipers are operated by an electric motor which is fitted under the dashboard and drives the wiper arms by linked arms.

2   The electric motor is of the two pole, compound motor type with a parking switch built into the gear housing. The motor has two speeds.

3   Two motors have been fitted, SWF or Electrolux, but their principle of operation is the same.

4   If the motor operation is faulty it is far better to obtain a replacement unit rather than try to repair it as spares can be very difficult to

Fig. 10.14. Windscreen wiper motor and linkage (Sec. 21)

Fig. 10.15. Windscreen wiper motor - exploded view (Sec. 21)

1	Terminal contact	8	End
2	Screw	9	Brush holder
3	Cover	10	Brush
4	Contacts	11	Rotor
5	Housing	12	Nut
6	Gear	13	Stator
7	Screw		

obtain. For the more ambitious, the following notes are given.

5   On the early type of motor the bushes are of the self-lubricating type. When overhauling the motor a few drops of engine oil should be applied to the armature shaft and the gear housing three quarters filled with lithium based grease. If the motor is noisy in operation this is usually caused by excessive endfloat of the armature shaft and this is adjustable by means of a screw. The correct clearance is 0.004-0.012 in (0.1-0.3 mm).

6   On the later type of motor a lubricating wick is used for the bearings. This should be dipped in engine oil. At the same time the gear housing should be filled with lithium based grease. The clearance between the worm screw and the gear wheel should be 0.002-0.006 in (0.05-0.15 mm). Lubricate the linkage joints with a little lithium based grease for refitting.

Self parking position - changing

1   On all models, the windscreen wiper blades are parked on the right when viewed from the driver's seat.

2   The parking position can be changed over, so that the blades park on the left, by turning the contact plate through 180° for Electrolux

Fig. 10.16. Tailgate window wiper motor (Sec. 22)

1	Rotor	6	Permanent magnet
2	Brush spring	7	Parking switch
3	Brush	8	Diode
4	Brush holder	9	Pole shoe
5	Stop tab for rotor		

Fig. 10.17. Tailgate window wiper drive housing (Sec. 22)

1	Drive on output shaft	3	Rotor shaft drive
2	Intermediate drive, fibre		

wiper motors.

3   The nut, steel washer and fibre washer are first removed after which the contact plate can be lifted up and turned.

4   On cars fitted with the SWF wiper motor the parking position can be changed by removing the shaft and turning it through 180°.

22 Tailgate window wiper (245 models) - general

1   The tailgate window wiper is operated by a single speed permanent magnet electric motor. It is connected to the wiper blade by a link arm.

2   The wiper is removed by taking off the panel on the inside of the tailgate and unscrewing the screws securing the reinforcing plate under the wiper motor which are found under this panel. The battery positive lead should be disconnected before you start as you will have to unscrew leads from terminals on the motor. These leads should, of course, be marked before removal. When the link arm has been disconnected and the reinforcing plate pushed to one side, the motor can be removed.

3   Dismantling and inspecting the motor and gear housing is a simple matter with the guidance of Figs. 10.16, 10.17 and 10.18. Clean all the parts and check them for wear and mechanical damage. Check the armature for short circuiting between commutator and frame and also for short circuiting, and breakage in, the winding coils.

This is usually indicated by signs of overheating in the armature. Signs of burning on the commutator, on the other hand, indicate open circuit armature windings. If you are dubious about the armature, have it tested by a specialist.

Fig. 10.18. Tailgate window wiper - parking switch (Sec. 22)

1	Connection 31b	6	Contact (2) 53
2	Diode	7	Contact 31b
3	Connection 53	8	Connection 53a
4	Lift tab	9	Connection 31
5	Contact 53a		

Fig. 10.19. Tailgate window wiper wiring diagram (Sec. 22)

a - connection to window washer

4   On reassembly the drive housing should be well greased. The armature shaft and its bush should be very lightly oiled. Renew the brushes if they are worn.

5   The wiring diagram (Fig. 10.19) illustrates the switching and parking arrangements which are quite different from those for the windscreen wiper. The tailgate wiper switch has three positions - park, wiper operating, wiper and washer operating. The connection 'a' in the diagram takes battery positive to the window washer. When the switch is in the parking position (as shown in the diagram) the wiper motor continues to run until the changeover contact connected to the brush which is not permanently earthed switches over from 12v positive to earth (reached via the switch) and this exerts a braking action on the motor which immediately comes to rest. The normal position of the contact, of course, connects battery positive to the motor brush.

6   When the switch is in one of the running positions, battery positive is connected to terminals '31B' and '53A'. In this case, when the contact is actually changing over the current from the battery flows via '31B' through the diode to the motor so that there is no interruption in the supply while the contacts are actually changing over - a comparatively slow process. When the switch is in the parking position but before the contacts change over, the diode is connected between the motor and earth but does not present a short circuit to the battery because it does not permit current flow in the direction opposite to that indicated by the black arrow head.

7   Failure of this diode would be indicated by some hesitancy in leaving the parking position when the wiper is operating, but in all probability more noticeably by clicks in the car radio each time the wiper passes through this position. This assumes that the diode goes

Fig. 10.20. Screen washer (Sec. 23)

1	Brush holder	9	Pump housing
2	Commutator	10	Shaft
3	Brush	11	Hose
4	Thermal fusing	12	Container
5	Spring	13	Flange
6	Terminal pin	14	Stator
7	Water outlet	15	Rotor
8	Pump impeller	16	Field winding

open circuit when it fails; if it goes short circuit it will either burn itself out very quickly (thus going open circuit) or blow the supply fuse.

23 Windscreen and tailgate window washers - general

1   Both these washers are of the same type. They consist of a centrifugal pump driven by a small permanent magnet motor. They need little maintenance apart from an occasional clean out of the system. Repair of the motor is not a practical proposition.

2   The windscreen washer is located on the right-hand wheel housing, where its position is obvious. The tailgate window washer is placed in a cavity to the right under the floor of the cargo space.

24 Instrument panel - removal and refitting

1   Disconnect the battery earth terminal.

2   Remove the covers round the steering column. Remove the bracket retaining screws and allow the bracket to slip down on the steering column.

3   Remove the instrument panel retaining screws and pull the panel forward out of the dashboard. The electrical connections can now be disconnected and warning light bulbs changed. This is a simple operation: the holders may be twisted and removed from the panel and the bulbs pushed into the holders.

4   Dismantling the panel to remove the various instruments is a straightforward process.

25 Speedometer and speedometer cable - general

1   It is most important that the speedometer cable is correctly fitted if the speedometer is to function without trouble. It is vitally important that the cable is not bent too sharply. At no point must the radius of a bend be less than 4 in (100 mm). If the bending radius is less than this, vibration and noises can occur in the instrument. The drive couplings must run true in the outer casing of the cable.

2   This being said, fitting is not difficult. We suggest that you start at the speedometer end, because this is the cleanest. Withdraw the old cable as you go and fit the new one.

3   If a speedometer starts giving trouble, it should be renewed. Faulty operation is almost always the result of wear which cannot really be

Fig. 10.21. Instrument panel (Sec. 24)

A Odometer	F Brake circuits failure warning light
B Speedometer	G Turn right signal light
C Turn left signal light	H Oil pressure failure light
D Parking brake light	I Battery charging failure light
E Headlamp main beams	

J Trip, odometer	N Temperature gauge
K Trip meter reset knob	O Overdrive light
L Tachometer (certain models)	P Choke light
M Bulb failure warning light	Q Fuel gauge

compensated by adjustment.

26 Fuel gauge - testing

1 Before removing an apparently faulty fuel gauge always check to see that it is the gauge that is at fault.
2 First check that all terminal connections at the rear of the gauge and on the top of the tank unit are clean and secure.
3 Switch on the ignition and using a test light check that there is current on the feed side of the gauge.
4 Gauge reads empty:

    a) Disconnect the lead on the sender unit and insulate the end so that it cannot earth against the body or tank.
    b) Switch on the ignition and the gauge should read 'full'.
    c) If the gauge shows 'empty' disconnect the lead on the gauge (the one which connects the gauge to the tank sender unit).
    d) Switch on the ignition and if the gauge reads 'full' there is no fault in the gauge and the wiring or sender unit must be suspect.

5 Gauge reads 'full':

    a) Disconnect the lead on the tank sender unit.
    b) Switch on the ignition and earth the lead to the tank sender unit using a piece of spare wire.
    c) If the gauge shows 'empty' the lead and gauge are satisfactory. The fault must therefore be in the tank sender unit.
    d) Should the gauge not show 'empty' also disconnect the lead at the terminal on the gauge.
    e) Earth the contact screw using a piece of spare wire. If the gauge is satisfactory it should show 'empty'.
    f) Should the gauge show anything other than 'empty' the fault is due either to dirty contact on the terminals between the gauge and lead to the sender unit or a breakage in the lead. It is very rare for the gauge to fail.

6 Removal and refitting of the fuel tank sender unit is described in Chapter 3.

27 Voltage stabilizer - general

1 Electric current is supplied to the combined water and oil temperature gauges and the fuel gauge via a voltage stabilizer in order to ensure that the readings given do not fluctuate with the state of charge of the battery.
2 The stabilizer supplies the instruments with a constant voltage of approximately 10 volts.
3 The stabilizer is mounted on the reverse side of the combined instrument. To remove it, pull straight out so that the three pins come loose from their retainers.

Fig. 10.22. Voltage stabilizer (Sec. 27)

28 Seatbelt interlock system - general

1 This system is fitted to cars produced for the North American market. If the front seats are occupied but either seatbelt has not been fastened, the car cannot be started and a warning buzzer (USA only) and lamp are actuated if any attempt is made to do so.
2 Apart from checking the interconnecting wiring and connections, special test equipment is needed to check out a major fault.

29 Bulb failure warning light - general

1 This light comes on if any of the following lights are defective:

    One of the lower beams.
    One of the tail lights.
    One of the number plate lights.
    One of the brakelights (when the brake pedal is depressed).

2 The system consists of a Reed relay and a warning light. It indicates a failure of one of the above lights if the light comes on.
3 The relay is located to the left, under the dashboard, and the warning light is located in the instrument panel (Fig. 10.23).

Fig. 10.23. Bulb failure warning light relay - location (Sec. 29)

Fig. 10.24. Fuse box with cover removed (Sec. 30)

30 Fuses - general

1 The fusebox is located at the front of the left-hand door. The cover is removed by turning the small knob a quarter-turn.

2 If a fuse blows, temporarily connect a headlamp bulb (main beam) across the fuse holder. If this bulb glows at full strength, you have a complete short circuit. This is certain to be caused by a nipped wire, a broken connection with one end of the wire touching metal, or a connector being bent over to touch metal. If the bulb glows faintly, it may be replaced by an ammeter which will indicate how much the overload current is. Do not leave the ammeter connected for any length of time in case the cause of the overload suffers damage from which it has been protected by the blowing of the fuse.

3 Tracing the cause of a blown fuse is a matter of logic and perseverance. Disconnect each of the switches, lamps etc fed by the fuse in turn until the overload disappears, thus revealing the culprit. If all the items fed by the fuse are dismantled and you are still getting trouble, the fault must lie in the wiring.

4 Intermittent short-circuits are almost invariably due to wiring and connector faults. These are often difficult to trace as they always seem to disappear when you are looking for them, but patience and thoroughness will lead you to them in the end.

5 Always use fuses having the values depicted on the appropriate circuit diagram. This way you can be sure of adequate protection without unnecessary replacement.

31 Faults - tracing (general)

1 Electrical faults fall into three classes:

a) *Failure to generate.*
b) *Failure to start.*
c) *Failure of instrument, accessories or lighting to function properly in an otherwise satisfactory electrical system.*

2 Faults in the first two classes are dealt with in the table that follows. This table concludes with an example of a fault in the third class; this part of the table may be adapted to deal with almost any accessory, and certainly the first two or three possible reasons or remedies are of almost universal application, especially if we take the words 'faulty control switch' to include faulty control relays where applicable.

32 Fault diagnosis - electrical system

Symptom	Reason/s	Remedy
Starter motor turns engine very slowly	Battery in discharged condition	Charge battery.
	Starter brushes badly worn, sticking, or brush wires loose	Examine brushes, renew as necessary, tighten down brush wires.
	Loose wires in starter motor circuit	Check wiring and tighten as necessary.
	Worn bearing bushes in starter motor	Renew starter motor.
Starter motor operates without turning engine	One-way clutch slipping	Clean clutch thoroughly - if this does not prove successful, renew motor.
	Pinion or ring gear teeth broken or worn	Fit new gear ring, and new pinion to starter motor drive.
Starter motor noisy or excessively rough engagement	Pinion or ring gear teeth broken or worn	Fit new ring gear, or new pinion to starter motor drive.
	Starter drive main spring broken	Dismantle and fit new main spring.
	Starter motor retaining bolts loose	Tighten starter motor securing bolts. Fit new spring washer if necessary.
	Worn bearing bushes	Renew starter motor.

Symptom	Reason/s	Remedy
Battery will not hold charge for more than a few days	Battery defective internally	Remove and fit new battery.
	Electrolyte level too low or electrolyte too weak due to leakage	Top-up electrolyte level to just above plates
	Plate separators no longer fully effective	Remove and fit new battery.
	Battery plates severely sulphated	Remove and fit new battery.
	Drivebelt slipping	Check belt for wear, renew if necessary, and tighten.
	Battery terminal connections loose or corroded	Check terminals for tightness, and remove all corrosion.
	Short in lighting circuit causing continual battery drain	Trace and rectify.
	Regulator unit not working correctly	Check setting, adjust where possible, renew, if defective.
	Faults listed under next heading may also apply	
Ignition light fails to go out, battery runs flat in a few days	Drivebelt loose and slipping, or broken	Check, renew and tighten as necessary.
	Brushes worn, sticking, broken or dirty	Examine, clean, or renew brushes as necessary.
	Brush springs weak or broken	Examine and test. Renew as necessary.
	Commutator or slip rings dirty, greasy, worn or burnt	Clean commutator and undercut segment separators; in alternator, clean slip rings.
	Armature/rotor badly worn or shaft bent	Fit new or reconditioned armature/rotor.
	Faulty regulator unit or isolation diode	Check, renew.
Wipers do not function correctly Wiper motor fails to work	Blown fuse	Check and renew fuse if necessary.
	Faulty control switch	Renew.
	Wire connections loose, disconnected or broken	Check wiper wiring. Tighten loose connections.
	Brushes badly worn	Remove and fit new brushes.
	Armature worn or faulty	If electricity at wiper motor remove and overhaul and fit replacement armature.
	Field coils faulty	Purchase reconditioned wiper motor.
Wiper motor works very slowly and takes excessive current	Commutator dirty, greasy or burnt	Clean commutator thoroughly.
	Drive to spindles unlubricated	Examine drive. Lubricate.
	Wheelbox spindle binding or damaged	Remove, overhaul, or fit replacement.
	Armature bearings dry or unaligned	Replace with new bearings correctly aligned.
	Armature badly worn or faulty	Remove, overhaul, or fit replacement armature.
Wiper motor works slowly and takes little current	Brushes badly worn	Remove and fit new brushes.
	Commutator dirty, greasy or burnt	Clean commutator thoroughly.
	Armature badly worn or faulty	Remove and overhaul armature or fit replacement.
Wiper motor works but wiper blades remain static	Driving linkage disengaged	Examine and if faulty, renew.
	Wheelbox gear and spindle damaged or worn	Examine and if faulty, renew.
	Wiper motor gearbox parts badly worn	Overhaul or fit new gearbox.

Fig. 10.15. Wiring diagram (to 1975)

Key to wiring diagram

1 Battery
2 Connection plate
3 Ignition switch
4 Ignition coil
5 Distributor, firing sequence 1-3-4-2
6 Spark plug
7 Starter motor
8 Alternator
9 Charging regulator
10 Fusebox
11 Lighting switch
12 Bulb failure warning unit
13 Step relay for fullbeams, dipped beams and headlight flasher
14 Fullbeams
15 Dipped beams
16 Parking light
17 Day notice light
18 Tail light
19 Side marking light
20 Sign light
21 Stop light contact
22 Stop light
23 Contact on M 40, M 41 gearbox
24 Contact on BW 35 automatic transmission
25 Back-up spotlight
26 Direction indicator lever
27 Hazard warning lights switch
28 Flasher unit
29 Front flasher light
30 Rear flasher light
31 Conn. to instrument
32 Conn. to instrument
33 Conn. to instrument
34 Conn. to instrument
35 Oil pressure warning light
36 Choke light
37 Parking brake warning light
38 Brake warning light
39 EGR - indicator light
40 Battery charging warning light
41 Bulb failure warning light
42 Full beams indicator light
43 Flasher indicator light
44 Overdrive indicator light
45 Fasten seat belt tight
46 Engine compartment
47 Buckle lighting
48 Rear ashtray lighting
49 Gear position lighting
50 Rheostat for instrument panel light
51 Instrument panel light
52 Control panel light
53 Glove locker light
54 Courtesy light
55 Door contact, driver's side
56 Door contact, passenger's side
57 Fuel level sender
58 Temperature sender
59 Oil pressure sensor
60 Choke control contact
61 Parking brake contact
62 Brake warning contact
63 EGR - warning contact
64 Contact, seat belt, pass. seat
65 Contact, seat belt, driver's seat
66 Contact, passenger seat
67 Contact, driver's seat
68 Light buzzer
72 Rev counter
73 Fuel gauge
74 Thermometer
75 Voltage stabilizer
76 Horns
77 Horn ring
78 Cigar lighter
79 Fan
80 Fan switch
81 Windscreen wiper/washer switch
82 Windscreen wipers
83 Windscreen washers
84 Relay for headlight wipers
85 Headlight wipers
86 Switch for tailgate window wiper/washer
87 Tailgate window wiper
88 Tailgate window washer
89 Rear door contact
90 Rear cargo space light
91 Electrically heated rear window switch
92 Electrically heated rear window
93 Switch for overdrive M 41
94 Contact for overdrive on M 41 gearbox
95 Control magnet for overdrive on M 41 gearbox
96 Heater element with thermostat, driver's seat
97 Heater element, driver's seat
98 Clock
99 Diode
100 Joint
101 Relay, start inhibitor
102 Start inhibitor unit
103 Start valve
104 Thermal timer contact
105 Air pressure gauge
106 Main relay, fuel injection
107 Fuel pump relay
108 Fuel pump
109 Pressure regulating valve
110 Auxiliary air valve
111 Resistor
112 Ignition control unit
113 Solenoid on compressor
114 Solenoid valve
115 Switch, AC compressor
116 Thermostat
118 Relay for back-up light

Chapter 11 Front suspension and steering

For modifications, and information applicable to later models, see Supplement at end of manual

Contents

Specifications

Front suspension

Type	Coil spring	
Wire thickness	0.545 in (13.85 mm)	0.553 in (14.05 mm)
Outer diameter	6.531 in (165.9 mm)	6.540 in (166.1 mm)
Number of turns	6.5	6.5
Shock absorbers	Double-acting hydraulic telescopic	

Steering gear (mechanical)

Type ... ...   Rack and pinion
Make ... ...   Cam gear or ZF
Cam gear:
    Number of turns, lock-to-lock 4.34
    Reduction ratio ... ...   21.4 : 1
    Rack preload ... ...   0.0039 in (0.1 mm)
    Preload, rack-pinion ... ...   0.4 - 1.2 lb f ft (0.06 - 0.17 kg f m)
    Lubricant ... ...   Engine oil, SAE 20W-50 or 20W-40
    Oil capacity ... ...   0.35 Imp. pint (0.2 litre/0.4 US pint)
ZF:
    Number of turns, lock-to-lock 4.34
    Reduction ratio ... ...   21.4 : 1
    Preload, rack-pinion ... ...   0.4 - 1.2 lb f ft (0.06 - 0.17 kg f m)
    Lubricant ... ...   Grease, Calypsol D4024-OK
    Grease quantity ... ...   1 oz (25 gram)

Power steering

Type ... ...   Rack and pinion
Make ... ...   Cam gear
Number of turns, lock-to-lock 3.5
Reduction ratio ... ...   17.2 : 1
Preload, rack-pinion ... ...   0.6 - 1.2 lb f ft (0.09 - 0.17 kg f m)
Checking the servo balance:
    Pump pressure when torque on steering column is checked ... ...   170 lb f ft (12 kg f m)
    Torque on steering column ... ...   2.5 - 3.3 lb f ft (0.35 - 0.45 kg f m)
    Maximum difference between right and left front wheel turn ... ...   0.7 lb f ft (0.1 kg f m)
Lubricant ... ...   Engine oil SAE 20W-50 or 20W-40
Oil capacity ... ...   0.35 Imp. pint (0.2 litre/0.4 US pint)
Hydraulic oil ... ...   Automatic Transmission Fluid, Type A or Dexron
Oil capacity ... ...   1.9 Imp. pint (1.1 litre/2.3 US pint)
Power pump:
    Type ... ...   Vane type pump
    Make ... ...   ZF
    Maximum pressure ... ...   995 - 1,138 psi (70 - 80 kg / sq cm)
    Drive ... ...   Belt-driven
    Ratio, engine speed - pump speed ... ...   1 : 1

Wheel alignment (vehicle unloaded)

Castor ... ...   +2° - +3°
Camber ... ...   +1° - +1.5°
Toe-in:

A - measured from centre of tyre treads
B - measured from tyre walls
C - measured from inner rims of wheels

	Angle (2 α)	A — a, mm (in.)	B — b, mm (in.)	C — c, mm (in.)
Mechanical steering	24'±8'	4.5±1.5 (0.18±0.06)	3.5±1 (0.14±0.04)	2.5±1 (0.1±0.04)
Power steering	16'±8'	3.0±1.5 (0.12±0.06)	2.0±1 0.08±0.04	1.5±1 (0.06±0.04)

Steering axis inclination at a camber of 0° ... ... 12°
Turning angles ... ... 20° outer wheel, 20.8° inner wheel

Torque wrench settings

	lb f ft	kg f m
Nut, ball joint (on strut) - early type strut	36 - 50	5 - 7
Bolts, ball joint attachment - later type	15 - 20	2.0 2.7
Steering wheel nut	29 - 43	4 - 6
Steering coupling pinch-bolts	18	2.5
Strut upper mounting nuts	18	2.5
Track control arm (front bolt)	60	8.2
Track control arm (rear nut)	40	5.4
Track control arm (bracket bolts)	35	4.8
Roadwheel nuts	70 to 100	10 to 14

1 General description

1 The front suspension is of the MacPherson type with a shock absorber inside the coil spring. It consists of a strut and coil spring assembly, attached at the top to the wheel housing and at the bottom to a control arm. A stabiliser bar, supported in rubber bushings, connects the control arms.

2 The strut assembly contains the shock absorber. The coil spring bottom support and the hub are welded to the strut casing. The shock absorber spindle functions as the strut upper guide and is pivoted in the strut upper attachment.

3 The steering gear is of the rack and pinion type. There are two versions: manual and power-assisted. There are two makes of manual steering gear, one grease-lubricated and the other oil-lubricated.

4 The power pump is a vane-type pump driven by a belt from the crankshaft pulley.

5 The top section of the steering column is provided with a splined sliding joint which, in case of accident, prevents the shaft from being driven into the car. As a further safety measure the steering wheel is connected to the steering column by a steel sleeve which collapses under excessive pressure.

2 Steering mechanism - maintenance and inspection

1 At the intervals specified in 'Routine Maintenance' check and top-up the fluid level in the steering pump. Check the level when the engine is not running. The level should be about ¼ in (6.35 mm) above the mark on the pump reservoir. When the engine is started, the level will fall to the mark (Power steering) (Fig. 11.3).

2 Use only specified (automatic transmission) fluid for topping-up.

3 Wear in the steering gear and linkage is indicated when there is considerable movement in the steering wheel without corresponding movement at the roadwheels. Wear is also indicated when the car tends to 'wander' off the line one is trying to steer. There are three main steering 'groups' to examine in such circumstances, these are the wheel bearings, the linkage joints and bushes and the steering gear itself.

4 First jack-up the front of the car and support it on stands under the side frame members so that both front wheels are clear of the ground.

5 Grip the top and bottom of the wheel and try to rock it. It will not take any great effort to be able to feel any play in the wheel bearing. If this play is very noticeable it would be as well to adjust it straight away as it could confuse further examinations. It is also possible that during this check play may be discovered also in the lower suspension ball joint. If this happens the ball joint will need renewal.

6 Next grip each side of the wheel and try rocking it laterally. Steady pressure will, of course, turn the steering but an alternated back and forth pressure will reveal any loose joint. If some play is felt it would be easier to get assistance from someone so that while one person rocks the wheel from side to side, the other can look at the joints and bushes on the track rods and connections.

7 The most likely places for wear or play to occur are at the track rod end ball joints.

Fig. 11.1. Front suspension (Sec. 1)

1	Stabilizer bar	4	Strut upper pivot point	7	Ball joint
2	Bracket	5	Spring	8	Control arm
3	Link	6	Strut assembly	9	Rear bracket for control arm

10 Front bracket for control arm
11 Front axle member

Fig. 11.2. Manual steering gear (Sec. 1)

1 Steering shaft
2 Steering gear
3 Steering rod
4 Steering arm

8 Check the security of the steering box mountings.

3 Front hubs - adjustment

1 Jack-up the front of the car and support the control arm by placing a jack under it.
2 Remove the roadwheel.
3 Tap off the grease cap. This can usually be removed quite easily using a brass drift to drive it off outwards.
4 Extract the split pin.
5 Extract the disc pads (see Chapter 9).

6 Turn the hub in its normal forward direction of rotation and at the same time tighten the nut to a torque of 50 lb f ft (7 kg f m). Unscrew the nut 1/3rd of a turn and insert a new split pin.
7 Half fill the cap with wheel bearing grease and tap it into position.

Fig. 11.3. The fluid reservoir (power steering) (Sec. 2)

1 Suction line   3 Cover
2 Filter   4 Return line

Fig. 11.2A. Power steering system (Sec. 1)

1 Steering gear   4 Oil input
2 Power pump   5 Return oil
3 Oil output   6 Oil reservoir

A. Normal position

B. Compressed

Fig. 11.4. Steering column (Sec. 1)

1 Lower U-joint
2 Flange
3 Steering shaft, bottom section
4 Upper U-joint
5 Lower bearing
6 Steering shaft, top section
7 Lower attachment
8 Column jacket (below)
9 Serrated sleeve
10 Upper attachment steering lock
11 Upper bearing
12 Steering wheel hub
13 Collapsible steel sleeve
14 Nut, retaining the wheel

8 Refit the disc pads.
9 Refit the roadwheel and lower the car to the ground.

4 Front hubs - overhaul

1 If the front wheel bearings become worn, this will usually be indicated by roadwheel rock which cannot be removed even though the wheel bearings have been correctly adjusted.
2 Jack-up the front of the car, support it securely and also support the control arm with a second jack. Remove the roadwheel.
3 Remove the disc caliper assembly, as described in Chapter 9.
4 Remove the grease cap, extract the split pin and unscrew and remove the castellated nut.
5 Pull off the hub/disc assembly and catch the outer bearing.
6 Pull the inner bearing from the stub axle.
7 Extract the oil seal.
8 Drive out the bearing tracks from the hub/disc assembly and wipe out all internal grease.
9 Install the new bearing tracks to the hub/disc assembly.
10 Pack the interior of the hub with grease, leaving an opening in the centre which is equal to the diameter of the stub axle.
11 Fit the oil seal and the inner bearing to the stub axle. Press grease into the bearing.
12 Install the hub/disc to the stub axle, fit the outer bearing having first packed grease into it.
13 Fit the thrust washer and castellated nut and adjust the hub, as described in the preceding Section. Fit the cap.
14 Refit the caliper and bleed the brake hydraulic system.
15 Fit the roadwheel and lower the car to the ground.

5 Control arms and bushings - removal and refitting

1 Jack-up the front end and place stands at the front jack-up points. Remove the wheels.
2 Disconnect the stabiliser bar from the link rod.
3 Remove the three retaining nuts and disconnect the ball joint from the control arm.
4 Remove the control arm front retaining bolt.
5 Remove the bolts securing the rear attachment bracket and lower the control arm. Remove the bracket from the control arm.
6 Press out the bushings from the control arm and bracket.
7 When fitting the new bushing in the control arm the flanged end of the bush is towards the front.
8 When fitting the new bushing in the control arm bracket it should be positioned so that the small slots, Fig. 11.7, point horizontally when fitted on the car.
9 After replacing the bushings fit the bracket to the control arm but do not tighten the nut.
10 Fit the rear end of the control arm in position, fit the three securing bolts but do not tighten them.
11 Fit the front retaining bolt but do not tighten the nut.
12 Attach the ball joint to the control arm and tighten the bolts to a torque of 7 - 9 lb f ft (1 - 1.3 kg f m).
13 Position a jack under the outer end of the control arm, jack-up and compress the spring.
14 Connect the stabiliser bar and link rod.
15 Tighten the front retaining bolt to the specified torque.
16 Tighten the nut for the rear bushing to the specified torque.
17 Tighten the bracket bolts to the specified torque.
18 Fit the roadwheel and lower the car.

Fig. 11.5. Ball joint to control arm retaining nuts (Sec. 5)

Fig. 11.6. Front control arm (Sec. 5)

1 Hole for ball joint	5 Rear rubber bushing
2 Front axle member	6 Nut
3 Front rubber bushing	7 Rear bracket
4 Bolt	

Fig. 11.7. Replacing control arm bracket bushing (Sec. 5)

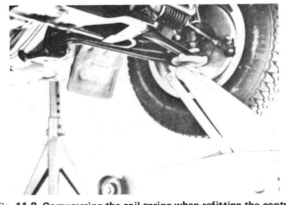

Fig. 11.8. Compressing the coil spring when refitting the control arm (Sec. 5)

6 Ball joints (later type) - renewal

1   Renewal of early type ball joints is dealt with in Section 7.
2   Jack-up and support the car at the front jacking points.
3   Slacken the strut shock absorber cap nut a few turns. For this you will need a peg spanner. The Volvo tool is shown in Fig. 11.9.
4   Remove the four bolts retaining the ball joint attachment.
5   Remove the three retaining nuts and remove the ball joint from the control arm.
6   Remove the ball joint nut and press out the ball joint.
7   Fit a new ball joint in the attachment, making sure the ball stud is free from grease, otherwise it might seat too deeply, causing the rubber bellows to jam on the strut. Tighten the nut to the specified torque.
8   Refitting to the strut is the reversal of removal procedure.

7 Spring, shock absorber, ball joint (early type) and strut top mounting - removal and refitting

1   Fit a spring compressor on the spring to catch up on five coils. Fig. 11.11 shows the Volvo tool for this job. If you decide to make one yourself ensure that it is of solid construction as a spring coming free at the wrong time could be dangerous.
2   Support the car on stands at the front jacking points and remove the wheel.
3   Disconnect the trackrod from the steering arm, for this you will require a ball joint separator of which there are several types. One type is shown in Fig. 11.12.
4   Disconnect the stabiliser bar from the link rod and remove the bolt securing the brake line bracket.

5   Remove the cover for the spring and strut assembly upper attachment. Remove the centre nut. Use a pipe wrench or pliers to restrain the shock absorber from turning (Fig. 11.13).
6   Tie up the strut assembly when lowering the jack so that brake lines and hoses do not get damaged.
7   Remove the spring seat, rubber bumper and shock absorber protection sleeve. Lift out the coil spring (Fig. 11.14).
8   Remove the shock absorber retaining nut and pull the shock absorber out of its housing.
9   Slacken the ball joint retaining nut a few turns until the ball joint bracket comes loose. Use a 19 mm socket with extension and hold the strut with a pipe wrench (Fig. 11.15).
10 Using a drift and a hammer loosen the ball joint stud from the strut assembly. When it comes free use the socket and extension to remove the nut. Coat the inside of the socket with grease so that the nut will come out with the socket. Remove the three retaining bolts and disconnect the ball joint from the control arm.

Fig. 11.9. Slackening the shock absorber cap nut (Sec. 6)

Fig. 11.10. Front strut and spring assembly (Sec. 7)

1 Strut	6 Coil spring
2 Spring seat plate	7 Shock absorber protection
3 Shock absorber	8 Stabilizer
4 Rubber buffer	9 Stabilizer attachment
(rebound stopper)	10 Stabilizer link
5 Upper mounting	

Fig. 11.11. Tools for compressing the coil spring (Sec. 7)

5040 Tool for compressing the spring for removal from the car
5041 Tool for removing the spring from 5040

Fig. 11.12. Using a ball joint separator (Sec. 7)

11 Mark the position of the strut top mounting and then remove the three retaining nuts. Remove the mounting (Fig. 11.16).

12 To release the spring from the compressor tool you will require another type of spring compressor tool or clamp. The Volvo tool for this is shown in Fig. 11.11.

13 Check the shock absorber for leaks and test it by extending and contracting it a few times. Any lack of resistance indicates it requires renewing.

14 Refitting is the reverse of the removal procedure. When fitting the strut top mounting ensure the marks made at removal are in alignment. Tighten the ball joint nut to 36 - 50 lb f ft (5 - 7 kg f m). Take care not to put any strain on brake pipes and hoses when tightening bolts.

8 Stabiliser bar (front) - removal and refitting

1 Disconnect the stabiliser bar from the link rods.

2 Remove the bolts which secure the stabiliser bar supports to the bodyframe and lift out the bar.

3 Any rubber bushes or mountings which are worn or have deteriorated must be renewed.

4 Refitting is the reverse of the removal procedure.

9 Steering wheel - removal and refitting

1 Remove the impact pad from the centre of the steering wheel by compressing it sideways and easing off the upper edge.

2 Remove the horn ring (see Chapter 10).

3 Remove the centre nut and pull off the steering wheel with a puller.

4 When replacing the wheel check that the roadwheels are in the straight-ahead position. Position the steering wheel spoke horizontally and fit the centre nut. Tighten to the specified torque.

5 Fit the horn ring and the impact pad.

Fig. 11.13. Removing the cover for the upper attachment (Sec. 7)

Fig. 11.14. Removing the rubber bumper and shock absorber sleeve (Sec. 7)

Fig. 11.15. Slackening the ball joint retaining nut (Sec. 7)

Fig. 11.16. Top mounting retaining nuts and alignment mark (Sec. 7)

10 Steering column - removal and refitting

1 Disconnect the battery earth terminal.
2 Remove the clamping screw for the upper steering shaft joint in the engine compartment.
3 Remove the steering wheel as described in Section 9.
4 Remove the upper steering column covers. Remove the turn indicator switch and wiper switch and disconnect the leads.
5 Remove the housing for the switches.
6 Remove the spring and column upper bearing.
7 Remove the screws for the steering lock by drilling a hole in the centre of the screws and then removing them with a screw extractor.
8 Remove the rubber grommet from the bulkhead, and the lower attachment for the steering column.
9 Push the steering column in through the bulkhead and pull the steering column into the car.
10 Remove the steering lock.
11 The upper and lower bearings can be renewed but any other wear or damage will necessitate a new steering column.
12 Refitting is the reverse of the removal sequence. Turn the steering wheel and check that it can rotate freely. Connect the battery earth cable and check the operation of the horn, indicators and windscreen wipers.

11 Trackrod end ball joints - removal and refitting

1 The trackrod ball joints require no routine lubrication. When wear occurs the ball joints on the trackrods are renewed.
2 Place stands under the front jacking points.
3 Remove the nut and disconnect the ball stud from the steering arm using a suitable ball joint separator.
4 Remove the splash guard from under the car.
5 Slacken the clips at the outboard end of the bellows.
6 Using an open-ended spanner on the flats provided to prevent the trackrod rotating, release the locknut at the trackrod end ball joint.
7 Unscrew the ball joint assembly from the trackrod, counting the number of turns.
8 Screw the new ball joint onto the trackrod by the same number of turns and connect it to the steering arm. Check the wheel alignment as described in Section 23.
9 Tighten the bellows clamp on completion.

12 Steering gear (manual) - removal and refitting

1 Remove the clamp bolt from the universal shaft joint flange. Open the flange slightly with a screwdriver.
2 Raise the front end of the car and put stands under the jacking points. Remove the wheels.
3 Remove the nuts from the trackrod-end ball joints and, using a suitable tool, disconnect the ball joints from the steering arms.
4 Remove the splash guard from under the car.
5 Remove the four bolts securing the steering gear to the front axle member.
6 Disconnect the steering gear from the steering shaft flange and remove the steering gear complete with trackrods.
7 Refitting is the reversal of the removal procedure. Check the wheel alignment, as described in Section 23.

13 Manual steering gear (Cam gear type) - dismantling and inspection

1 Clean off all external dirt. Before dismantling check the inner ball joints for wear.
2 Undo the left side bellows clip, ease off the bellows and drain the oil.
3 Bend up the peening lock on the inner ball joint, and remove the

left side trackrod. Remove the right side trackrod.
4 Remove the cover for the pre-loading device and lift out the spring, 'O' ring and piston.
5 Remove the pinion cover and lift out the pinion, top bearing and spacer sleeve. Collect the shims.
6 Pull out the rack towards the pinion side of the steering gear.
7 Clean all the parts in white spirit. Check the rack bush for wear and renew if necessary. Check the pinion lower bearing, if it requires renewing a puller will be required to remove it, see Fig. 11.17. Examine the rack and pinion for wear and damage. Renew all seals and gaskets.

14 Manual steering gear (Cam gear type) - reassembly

1 Oil all the parts before assembly with engine oil (SAE 20W-50 or SAE 20W-40).
2 If new rack bushing is being fitted, position it so that the locks on the bush align with the slots in the housing and drive it in with a drift.
3 Fit the pinion with upper bearing in the housing (no shims) and fit the spacer sleeve. Fit the pinion cover, with a gasket but without the seal.
4 Using a dial gauge check the end play of the pinion. Remove the pinion cover and determine a shim thickness equal to the measured endplay plus 0.0039 in (0.1 mm) for preloading. Shims are available in thicknesses of 0.005-0.0075-0.01 in (0.127-0.191-0.254 mm).
5 Fit a new seal on the pinion cover. Apply a non-hardening gasket compound on the seal and fit the seal on the pinion cover using a suitably sized tube to drive it on.
6 Fit the rack from the pinion side taking care not to damage the bushing.
7 Fit the pinion, with upper bearing, shims and spacer sleeve. Fit the pinion cover gasket and the cover.
8 Fit the preloading piston in the housing without the 'O' ring and spring. Use a steel ruler and feeler gauge to measure the end clearance, see Fig. 11.20. Determine the thickness of shims required. Shims and gasket together should equal the measured end clearance plus 0.0008-0.0059 in (0.02-0.15 mm) for the piston endplay. Shims are available in thicknesses of 0.005-0.01-0.015-0.02 in (0.127-0.254-0.381-0.508 mm).
9 Place the spring and 'O' ring in the piston and fit the gasket and cover.
10 Connect a torque gauge to the pinion shaft and crank the rack back and forward to each end of its travel. The torque should be 5-15 lb f in (0.06 - 0.17 kg f m) if the preloading is correct.
11 Fit the left side trackrod. If fitting the same rod, place a thin shim

Fig. 11.17. Removing the pinion lower bearing (Sec. 13)

Fig. 11.18. Exploded view of manual steering gear (Cam gear) Sec. 13)

1	Housing	8	Bolt	14	Shim	20	Bellows
2	Rack	9	Spacer	15	Cover	21	Bellows
3	Bearing bushing	10	Ball bearing	16	Bolt	22	Clamp
4	Pinion	11	Shim	17	Steering rod	23	Clamp
5	Cover	12a	Pre-load piston	18	Ball joint	24	Clamp
6	Seal	12b	O-ring	19	Nut	25	Cap
7	Gasket	13	Spring				

Fig. 11.19. Fitting the rack bushing (Sec. 14)

Fig. 11.20. Measuring the pre-loading piston end clearance (Sec. 14)

Fig. 11.21. Fitting shim to provide a new locking position (Sec. 14)

between the ball joint and rack shoulder so that an unused part of the ball joint can be used for locking by peening the edge of the ball joint into the rack groove. Fit the bellows and tighten the inner clamp. Fit the right side rod in the same way. Both rods should be the same length within 0.06 in (1.6 mm).
12 Fill the steering gear with specified oil by inserting an oil gun under the lip of the bellows.

15 Manual steering gear (ZF type) - dismantling and inspection

1   Carry out the operations described in Section 13, paragraphs 1-3.
2   Remove the dust seal for the preloading device and remove the split pin (Fig. 11.24).
3   Remove the cover and spring for the preloading device and remove the piston, tapping the rack with the palm of your hand will help to remove it.
4   Remove the pinion dust seal and the circlip. Remove the pinion

Fig. 11.22. Removing the pinion (Sec. 15)

Fig. 11.23. Fitting a new O-ring in the pinion nut (Sec. 16)

nut.
5   To remove the pinion from the housing, clamp the pinion shaft in a vice with soft grips and tap lightly on the housing with a soft-nosed hammer.
6   Pull out the rack towards the pinion side of the housing.
7   Press in the locking tabs for the rack bushing and lever out the bushing.
8   Remove the thrust washer and circlip from the pinion shaft and press off the bearing.
9   Clean all the parts and examine them for wear or damage. Renew 'O' rings and rack bushing.

16 Manual steering gear (ZF type) - reassembly

1   Press the ball bearing on to the pinion shaft and fit the circlip and thrust washer.
2   Fit new 'O' rings on the rack bushing and press it into the housing. Check that the locking tabs for the bearing fit correctly into the recesses in the housing.
3   Grease the rack with Calypsol D4024-OK grease and insert it in the pinion side of the housing. Be careful not to damage the bushing with the rack teeth.
4   Grease and insert the pinion. Pack the bearing with grease. Fit a new 'O' ring on the pinion nut, fit the nut and the locking circlip. Fill the cavity on top of the nut with grease and fit the pinion dust seal.
5   Fit a new 'O' ring on the preloading piston, grease the pinion and fit the piston and spring. Fit the cover but do not finally tighten the cover yet.
6   Connect a torque gauge to the pinion and check the torque. Crank back and forward to each end of travel. The torque should be 5-15 lb f in (0.06 - 0.17 kg f m). To increase the torque, screw in the preload piston cover. When the correct torque is obtained, fit the split pin to lock the cover and fit the dust cover (Fig. 11.25).
7   Crank the rack fully out and fill the tooth spaces with grease. Crank in the rack then out again and apply more grease. The grease charge will be approximately 1 oz (25 gram).
8   Fit the steering rods, as described in Section 14.

Fig. 11.24. Exploded view of manual steering gear (ZF) (Sec. 15)

2   Housing
3   Rack
4   Bearing
5   O-ring
6   Lockwasher
7   Pinion
8   Bearing
9   Ball bearing
10 Washer
11 Lockring
12 O-ring
13 Pinion nut
14 Lockwasher
15 Seal
16 Piston
17 O-ring
18 Spring
19 Pre-load piston cover
20 Split pin
21 Cover
22 Steering rod
23 Ball joint
24 Nut
25 Bellows

Fig. 11.25. Checking the pinion torque (Sec. 16)

17 Power steering gear - removal and refitting

Removal and refitting of the steering gear is as described for the manual steering gear described in Section 12, with the addition of disconnecting the hoses and plugging them to prevent loss of fluid. Checking and adjusting after refitting is described in Section 20.

18 Power steering gear - dismantling and inspection

1   Carry out the operations described in Section 13, paragraphs 1-3.
2   Remove the oil pipes.
3   Remove the preloading device cover, the piston, 'O' ring and sleeve. Do not turn the pinion shaft or you are likely to get an oil spray.
4   Remove the lower cover and spacer sleeve for the pinion. Release the locking tab and remove the nut. Unscrew the inner bearing race with ball retainer and outer race.
5   Remove the valve housing cover and the spring. Lift off the valve housing taking care not to damage the valve housing or valve. Lift out the pinion.

Fig. 11.26. Exploded view of power steering gear (Sec. 18)

2	Rack	16	O-ring	30	Cover	44	O-ring
3	O-ring	17	Dowel	31	Gasket	45	Spring
4	Piston ring	18	Washer	32	Bolt	46	O-ring
5	Bearing housing	19	Circlip	33	Ball bearing	47	Bolt
6	Lead	20	O-ring	34	Lockwasher	48	Pipe
7	Plastic ring	21	Piston	35	Locknut	49	Pipe
8	O-ring	22	Shim	36	Spacer	50	Steering rod
9	Spacer ring	23	Spring	37	Seal ring	51	Ball joint
10	O-ring	24	Cover	38	Bearing	52	Locknut
11	Plastic ring	25	Bolt	39	Valve housing	53	Bellows
12	Inner tabs	26	O-ring	40	Circlip	54	Clamp
13	Spacer ring	27	By-pass	41	O-ring	55	Clamp
14	Circlip	28	Seal	42	Cover	56	Cap
15	Washer	29	Pinion	43	Seal		

6 Remove the lock bolt for the right side housing, pull off the housing and the connecting tube.

7 Pull out the rack and bearing sleeve. Pull the sleeve off the rack.

8 Remove the bolt for the left side housing and pull out the outer tube from the housing, then pull out the inner tube.

9 Remove the upper bushing. For this you will need a puller like the one shown in Fig. 11.17. Use the tool in the middle of the sleeve.

10 Using two thin screwdrivers lever out the upper outer race of the pinion lower bearing.

11 Remove both 'O' rings and spacer from the right side housing. Remove the bearing, 'O' ring and seal from the valve housing cover.

12 Remove the seal, 'O' ring and plastic rings from the rack bearing sleeve.

13 Remove the plastic ring and the 'O' ring under it from the rack.

14 Remove the oil seal, washer and circlip from the inner tube.

15 Clean all parts with white spirit. Examine all the parts for wear or damage. If a pinion, control valve or valve housing is faulty all the assembly parts should be renewed. Also, if the bearing is renewed the bearing sleeve for the rack should be renewed. Renew all seals and 'O' rings.

19 Power steering gear - reassembly

1 Oil all the parts before assembly with engine oil.

2 Fit the oil seal, bearing and 'O' ring on the valve housing cover. Fit the plastic ring and 'O' ring on the rack bearing sleeve.

3 Fit the circlip on the inner tube. Fit the 'O' ring and plastic ring on the rack piston with the 'O' ring under the plastic ring.

4 Fit the spacer sleeve, oil seal and plastic ring on the rack. Fit them from the teeth side of the rack but cover the teeth with a wide tape to protect the oil seal from damage as it is fitted, then remove the tape and fit the spacer sleeve on the rack.

5 In the left side housing fit the oil seal with the lip facing outwards, the bushing (use a suitable drift to drive it in) and the two 'O' rings.

6 Fit the spacer washer and two 'O' rings in the right side housing.

7 On the left side housing fit the inner tube and its spacer washer. Fit the rack, equipped with seal and spacer rings, into the inner tube and press in the seal and spacer rings. Fit the retaining circlip.

8 Fit the outer tube on the left side housing, with the hole for the lock bolt aligned with the hole in the housing, and fit the lock bolt.

9 Fit the bearing sleeve in the outer tube with the holes for the lock bolt in alignment.

10 Fit the seal and plastic ring in the bearing sleeve, use a tape round the sharp edge of the rack to protect the seal.

11 Fit the connecting pipe with rubber seal in the right side housing and then fit the right side housing, so that the holes for the lock bolts and the connecting pipe are in alignment. Fit the lock bolt and connect up the pipe.

12 Fit the outer race for the pinion lower bearing. Fit the pinion taking care not to damage the valve and fit the inner race and ball retainer on the pinion. Fit the lock ring and nut, but do not lock the nut.

13 Fit the outer race and the spacer sleeve.

14 Press down the spacer sleeve so that it bottoms on the bearing and using a feeler gauge and steel ruler measure the distance between the spacer ring and housing (see Fig. 11.20) to determine thickness of gasket required.

15 Fit the selected gasket(s) and the Volvo tool 5054, this represents the cover with the centre removed so that the nut is accessible for adjusting the steering gear when it is fitted in the car, see the following Section.

16 Fit the 'O' ring in the valve housing, fit the housing and then place the coil spring in the valve housing with the big end in first. Fit the valve housing cover making sure that the spring does not get caught between the valve housing and the cover. The pinion shaft shoulder should be 0.06 in (1.5 mm) above the cover face. Adjust the position, if necessary, by moving the lower bearing inner race.

17 Fit the preloading piston, without 'O' ring, in the housing. Using feeler gauge and steel ruler, measure the distance between housing and piston face. Select shims equal to the measured distance plus 0.002-0.006 in (0.05-0.15 mm) for correct end clearance.

18 Fit the 'O' ring and spring for preloading piston, fit selected shims and cover.

19 Connect a torque gauge to the pinion shaft and move the rack back and forward over its full travel. Torque should be 5-15 lb f in (0.09-

0.17 kg f m). If the torque is excessive stop the rack in that position and re-adjust the preloading piston. If the rack jams with the piston removed, the rack is distorted and must be renewed.

20 Fit the oil pipes.

21 Fit the steering rods, as described in Section 14.

22 Valve adjustment, filling power steering oil and lubricating oil is carried out after the steering gear is refitted in the car - see the following Section.

20 Power steering gear - checking and adjusting balance

1 To carry out the following checks and adjustments, special tools are required, the illustrations show the Volvo tools, but suitable equivalents could be used (ie. tool 5054 could be made by cutting the centre out of a pinion cover).

2 Connect the test gauge as shown in Fig. 11.32. Position the gauge in front of the windscreen so that it can be read from the driver's seat.

3 Fill oil almost up to the edge of the reservoir. Start the engine and let it idle. Top-up with oil when the level drops, until the level is stabilised at the correct level. Use ATF Type A or Dexron oil.

4 Turn the steering wheel slowly, from side-to-side several times, topping-up with oil when necessary. Keep turning the steering wheel until the reservoir is almost free of air bubbles. Top-up, if necessary, and fit reservoir cap.

5 Remove the steering wheel impact pad. Turn the steering wheel nearly to the right end position and connect a torque gauge to the steering wheel centre nut with a 27 mm socket and extension. Use the torque gauge to turn slowly to the right and read the torque at the moment the pressure gauge approaches 170 psi (12 kg/sq cm). It is most important that the torque is read exactly when this pressure is reached, as the pressure will remain, even if the torque is lowered in this position.

6 Now check the balance when turning the steering wheel to the left in the same way. The torque should be 2.5-3.3 lb f ft (0.35-0.45 kg f m). The difference between right and left sides must not be more than 0.7 lb f ft (0.1 kg f m).

7 If the torque difference between sides is excessive, switch off the engine and remove the lock nut and lockwasher from the pinion lower bearing. If the torque has to be increased for left side - decreased for right side proceed as follows: Straighten the lockwasher tab which was bent for locking the bearing race (adjustment nut), bend over the next tab to the left. Turn the adjustment nut to the left until its groove fits the lockwasher tab. Fit the lockwasher and locknut. If the torque has to be altered in the opposite direction move one tab to the right. Changing to the next tab alters the torque by 4 lb f in (0.05 kg f m).

8 To check the pump pressure at the left side end position turn the steering wheel fully to the left and hold it there for a maximum of 10 seconds while reading the gauge. The pressure should be 995-1,150 psi (70-80 kg/sq cm). Check the right side end position in the same way.

9 If the pump pressure is incorrect, check the pump by closing the pressure gauge valve for 10 seconds maximum. If the pressure does not reach the figure specified above the pump is faulty.

10 Re-check the balance when turning the steering to the right and then to the left. The torque difference must be within the limit specified in paragraph 6.

11 Switch off the engine and lock the pinion nut with the lockwasher. Remove the adjusting flange taking care not to damage the gasket and fit the pinion cover.

12 Fill the steering gear with lubricating oil, by inserting an oil gun under the lip of the bellows, then carefully compress the bellows so that some oil flows to the other side.

13 Disconnect the test gauge and connect the pressure hose to the steering gear. Fit the steering wheel impact pad.

14 Start the engine. Turn the steering wheel to left and right end positions, check the reservoir oil level and top-up, if necessary.

15 Fit the roadwheels and lower the car.

21 Power steering pump - removal and refitting

1 Place a container to collect the oil below the pump and disconnect the pump hydraulic connections.

2 Remove the nuts on the two long bracket bolts. Remove the

Fig. 11.27. Levering out the upper outer race of the pinion lower bearing (Sec. 18)

Fig. 11.31. Check the position of the pinion shaft shoulder (Sec. 19)

Fig. 11.28. Rack teeth covered with tape when fitting seal (Sec. 19)

1 Spacer   3 Plastic ring
2 Seal   4 Tape

Fig. 11.29. Fitting the rack into the inner tube (Sec. 19)

Fig. 11.32. Test equipment connections (Sec. 20)

Fig. 11.30. Fitting the inner race and ball retainer on the pinion (Sec. 19)

Fig. 11.33. Turning the adjusting nut to the left (Sec. 20)

tensioner locking screws on both sides of the pump and lift off the drivebelt.

3 Swing the pump up and remove the three screws securing the bracket to the engine block, then remove the pump and bracket.

4 Separate the bracket from the pump.

5 Refitting is the reverse of the removal procedure. Tension the drivebelt to give a deflection of 0.12 in (5 mm) at the centre of its longest run.

6 Fill and bleed the system, as described in Section 20, paragraphs 3 and 4.

Fig. 11.34. Exploded view of power steering pump (Sec. 22)

1 Nut for pulley	9 Housing	16 O-ring
2 Lock washer	10 Thrust plate	17 End plate
3 Shaft key	11 Rotor with vanes	18 Retaining ring
4 Shaft	12 Cam ring	19 Control valve
5 Seal	13 O-ring	20 Spring
6 Retaining ring	14 Pressure plate	21 Copper seal
7 Retaining ring	15 Spring	22 Plug
8 Ball bearing		

22 Power steering pump - overhaul

1   Remove the pulley nut and the pulley. Remove the mounting bracket from the pump. Remove the front seal, Fig. 11.34.
2   Remove the circlip.
3   Using multi-grip pliers remove the spring and pressure plate. Turn the pump over and tap lightly on the end until the rotor and cam ring falls free. If the cam ring does not come loose leave it for now.
4   Remove the ball bearing retaining circlip and push the shaft out of the housing. Push out the thrust plate and, if it did not come out before, the cam ring.
5   Remove the plug, control valve and spring.
6   Renew all 'O' rings. Examine parts for wear and damage. If the pump housing bushing is worn or damaged renew the housing assembly. The rotor, vanes and cam ring are a matched set, if any one is defective they must be renewed as an assembly.
7   Fit the bearing on the shaft and fit the retaining circlips on each side. Press the shaft into the housing.
8   Fit the thrust plate with the dowel located in one of the holes. Fit the cam ring on the dowel with the arrow side upwards, Fig. 11.35. Fit the inner 'O' ring.
9   Fit the rotor with the recess round the shaft hole down towards the drive side. Fit the vanes with the rounded ends towards the cam ring. Fit the pressure plate so that one of the holes locates on the dowel.
10 Fit the outer 'O' ring and spring. Fit the endplate and retaining circlip. It will be necessary to push on the endplate to fit the circlip in its groove.
11 Fit the control valve, spring and plug. Use a new copper washer on the plug.
12 Fit the shaft seal, tap it in lightly until it is properly seated.
13 Fit the pulley and mounting bracket.
14 When overhauling the pump it is a good idea to renew the filter in the reservoir. Remove the cover, spring retaining nut and spring. Lift out the filter and fit a new one. Refit the spring, nut and cover.

Fig. 11.35 Fitting the cam ring and O-ring (Sec. 22)

23 Steering geometry - general

1   Accurate front wheel alignment is essential for good steering and tyre wear. Before considering the steering angle, check that the tyres are correctly inflated, that the front wheels are not buckled, the hub bearings are not worn or incorrectly adjusted and that the steering linkage is in good order, without slackness or wear at the joints.
2   Wheel alignment consists of four factors:
Camber, which is the angle at which the front wheels are set from the vertical when viewed from the front of the car. Positive camber is the amount (in degrees) that the wheels are tilted outwards at the top from the vertical.
Castor, is the angle between the steering axis and a vertical line when viewed from each side of the car. Positive castor is when the steering

Fig. 11.36. Diagram showing 'A' vertical line and 'B' camber (Sec. 23)

axis is inclined rearward.
Steering axis inclination is the angle, when viewed from the front of the car, between the vertical and an imaginary line drawn between the upper and lower suspension ball joints.

Toe-in is the amount by which the distance between the front inside edges of the front roadwheels (measured at hub height) is less than the diametrically opposite distance measured between the rear inside edges of the front roadwheels.

3   It is recommended that all the steering angles are set by a service station on modern equipment. Castor cannot be adjusted on the 240 series, if it is outside the specification the front suspension must be checked for damage.

4   Camber is adjusted by moving the upper strut attachment in or out. Incorrect camber causes uneven tyre wear.

5   Front wheel alignment can be carried out by the home mechanic if the following operations are followed.

6   Place the car on level ground with the wheels in the straight-ahead position.

7   Obtain or make a toe-in gauge. One may be easily made from tubing, cranked to clear the sump and bellhousing, having an adjustable nut and setscrew at one end.

8   With the gauge, measure the distance between the two inner rims of the front roadwheels, at hub height and at the rear of the wheels.

9   Push the vehicle so that the roadwheel turns through half a turn (180⁰) and measure the distance between the two inner rims at hub height at the front of the wheel. This last measurement should be less than the first by the specified toe-in which is:

> 0.1 ± 0.04 in (2.5 ± 1 mm) for manual steering and
> 0.06 ± 0.04 in (1.5 ± 1 mm) for power steering.

10 If the toe-in is incorrect, slacken the trackrod locknuts and the bellows outboard clips and turn the rods into the trackrod-ends to increase the toe-in, or out, to decrease the toe-in. Make sure you turn both rods the same amount so that they are the same length within 0.06 in (1.6 mm).

11 Re-check the toe-in and then tighten the trackrod locknuts and clips.

24 Fault diagnosis - front suspension and steering

Symptom	Reason/s
Excessive movement of steering wheel before roadwheel movement is apparent	Wear in the steering gear and ball joints.
Car difficult to steer in a straight line - wandering	Wear in steering gear and ball joints. Wheel alignment incorrect (indicated by excessive and uneven tyre wear). Front wheel hub bearings loose. Worn strut ball joints.
Steering stiff and heavy	Incorrect wheel alignment. Excessive wear or binding in the steering gear.
Wheel wobble and vibration	Roadwheels out of balance. Wheel alignment incorrect. Wear in steering gear or ball joints.
Excessive pitching or suspension bottoming	Defective shock absorbers and/or coil springs.
Faults usually attributed to the power steering system Car wanders	Low fluid level. Air in the system.
Steering stiff	Low fluid level. Air in system. Pump control valve seized. Reservoir filter blocked. Defective seals in steering gear.
Steering stiff on one lock only	Lack of pressure on one side of the rack piston due to wear.
Front wheel wobble	Air in the system.
Steering heavy if steering wheel is turned rapidly	Pump control valve blocked. Air in system.

Chapter 12 Bodywork

For modifications, and information applicable to later models, see Supplement at end of manual

Contents

1 General description

1 The Volvo 240 series is of integral monocoque construction. The all steel body and frame are welded into one unit. Heat transfer from the exhaust system to the body is reduced by three heat shields and insulation is provided against noise.

2 A heater and ventilating system is fitted as standard but a full air-conditioning system is available as an optional fitting.

3 To assist in the prevention of corrosion the underside is comprehensively rustproofed and undersealed. Hot dipped galvanised (zinc coated) steel is used for many metal components normally subjected to high weather exposures.

4 The grille is made of ABS plastic and retained by spring locks. The front end and front wings are attached by bolts and can be replaced.

2 Maintenance - bodywork

1 The condition of the bodywork is of considerable importance as it is on this, in the main, that the second-hand value of the car depends. Maintenance is easy but needs to be regular and careful. Neglect, particularly after minor damage, can lead quickly to further deterioration and costly repair bills. It is important also to keep watch on those parts of the car not immediately visible, for instance the underside, and inside all the wheel arches.

2 The basic maintenance routine for the bodywork is washing, preferably with a lot of water, from a hose. This will remove all the solids which may have stuck to the car. It is important to flush these off in such a way as to prevent grit from scratching the finish. The wheel arches and underbody need washing in the same way to remove any accumulated mud which will retain moisture and tend to encourage rust. Paradoxically enough, the best time to clean the underbody and wheel arches is in wet weather when the mud is soft.

3 Once a year, or every 12,000 miles, it is advisable to visit a garage equipped to steam clean the body. This facility is available at many commercial vehicle garages. All traces of dirt and oil will be removed and the underside can then be inspected carefully for rust, damaged pipes, frayed electrical wiring and so forth. The car should be greased on completion of this job. The engine compartment should be cleaned in the same way.

4 If steam cleaning is not available, brush 'Gunk' or a similar cleaner over the whole of the engine and engine compartment with a stiff brush, working it well in where there is an accumulation of oil and dirt. Do not forget to cover the ignition system and protect it with oily rags when the 'Gunk' is washed off. As it is washed away, it will take with it all traces of oil and dirt, leaving the engine looking clean and bright.

5 The wheel arches should be given particular attention, as under-sealing can easily come away here, and stones and dirt thrown up from the roadwheels can soon cause the paint to chip and flake and so allow rust to set in. If rust is found, clean down to the bare metal with wet and dry paper, paint on an anti-corrosive coating such as 'Kurust' or red lead and renew the undercoating and top coat.

6 The body should be washed once a week or more often if necessary. After washing paintwork, wipe it with a chamois leather to give an unspotted clear finish. If a car is frequently washed, it only needs a very occasional waxing as a protection against chemical pollutants in the air. Wax the chromium plated parts as well as the paintwork. To keep windscreens and windows clear of film wash them with water to which a little ammonia has been added.

Keep wax polish away from glass - the smallest trace will cause smeariness in wet weather.

7 Spots of tar and grease thrown up from the road can be removed by a rag dampened in petrol. Tar should not be allowed to linger on the paintwork, nor should bird droppings, which sometimes discolour paint.

3 Maintenance - upholstery and floor coverings

1 Mats and carpets should be brushed or vacuum cleaned regularly to keep them free of grit. If they are badly stained remove them for sponging and make sure they are quite dry before replacement. Seats and interior trim panels can be kept clean by a wipe over with a damp cloth. If they do become stained, use a little liquid detergent and a soft nail brush to scour the grime out of the grain of the material.

2 Do not forget to keep the head lining clean in the same way as the upholstery.

3 When using liquid cleaners inside the car do not over-wet the surfaces being cleaned. Excessive damp could get into the seams and padded interior causing stains, offensive odours or even rot. If the inside of the car gets wet accidentally it is worthwhile taking some trouble to dry it out properly, particularly where carpets are involved.

4 Minor body damage - repair

The photographic sequence on pages 190 and 191 illustrates the operations detailed in the following sub-Sections.

Repair of minor scratches in the car's bodywork

If the scratch is very superficial, and does not penetrate to the metal of the bodywork, repair is very simple. Lightly rub the area of the scratch with a paintwork renovator (eg. T-cut), or a very fine cutting paste, to remove loose paint from the scratch and to clear the surrounding bodywork of wax polish. Rinse the area with clean water.

Apply touch-up paint to the scratch using a thin paint brush, continue to apply thin layers of paint until the surface of the paint in the scratch is level with the surrounding paintwork. Allow the new paint at least two weeks to harden, then, blend it into the surrounding paintwork by rubbing the paintwork, in the scratch area with a paintwork renovator (eg. T-cut or a very fine cutting paste). Finally apply wax polish.

Where the scratch has penetrated right through to the metal of the bodywork, causing the metal to rust, a different repair technique is required. Remove any loose rust from the bottom of the scratch with a penknife, then apply rust inhibiting paint (eg Kurust) to prevent the formation of rust in the future. Using a rubber or nylon applicator fill the scratch with bodystopper paste. If required, this paste can be mixed with cellulose thinners to provide a very thin paste which is ideal for filling narrow scratches. Before the stopper paste in the scratch hardens, wrap a piece of smooth cotton rag around the top of a finger. Dip the finger in cellulose thinners and then quickly sweep it across the surface of the stopper paste in the scratch; this will ensure that the surface of the stopper paste is slightly hollowed. The scratch can now be painted over as described earlier in this Section.

Repair of dents in the car's bodywork

When deep denting of the car's bodywork has taken place, the first task is to pull the dent out, until the affected bodywork almost attains its original shape. There is little point in trying to restore the original shape completely, as the metal in the damaged area will have stretched on impact and cannot be reshaped fully to its original contour. It is better to bring the level of the dent up to a point which is about 1/8 inch (3 mm) below the level of the surrounding bodywork. In cases where the dent is very shallow anyway, it is not worth trying to pull it out at all.

If the underside of the dent is accessible, it can be hammered out gently from behind, using a mallet with a wooden or plastic head. Whilst doing this, hold a suitable block of wood firmly against the impact from the hammer blows and thus prevent a large area of bodywork from being 'belled-out'.

Should the dent be in a section of the bodywork which has a double skin or some other factor making it inaccessible from behind, a different technique is called for. Drill several small holes through the metal inside the dent area - particularly in the deeper sections. Then screw long self-tapping screws into the holes just sufficiently for them to gain a good purchase in the metal. Now the dent can be pulled out by pulling on the protruding heads of the screws with a pair of pliers.

The next stage of the repair is the removal of the paint from the damaged area, and from an inch or so of the surrounding 'sound' bodywork. This is accomplished most easily by using a wire brush or abrasive pad on a power drill, although it can be done just as effectively by hand using sheets of abrasive paper. To complete the preparations for filling, score the surface of the bare metal with a screwdriver or the tang of a file, or alternatively, drill small holes in the affected area. This will provide a really good 'key' to the filler paste.

To complete the repair see the sub-Section on filling and respraying.

Repair of rust holes or gashes in the car's bodywork

Remove all paint from the affected area and from an inch or so of the surrounding 'sound' bodywork, using an abrasive pad or a wire brush on a power drill. If these are not available a few sheets of abrasive paper will do the job just as effectively. With the paint removed you will be able to gauge the severity of the corrosion and therefore decide whether to replace the whole panel (if this is possible) or to repair the affected area. Replacement body panels are not as expensive as most people think and it is often quicker and more satisfactory to fit a new panel than to attempt to repair large areas of corrosion.

Remove all fittings from the affected area except those which will act as a guide to the original shape of damage bodywork (eg. headlamp shells etc.). Then, using tin snips or a hacksaw blade, remove all loose metal and any other metal badly affected by corrosion. Hammer the edges of the hole inwards in order to create a slight depression for the filler paste.

Wire brush the affected area to remove the powdery rust from the surface of the remaining metal. Paint the affected area with rust inhibiting paint (eg. Kurust); if the back of the rusted area is accessible treat this also.

Before filling can take place it will be necessary to block the hole in some way. This can be achieved by the use of zinc gauze or aluminium tape.

Zinc gauze is probably the best material to use for a large hole. Cut a piece to the approximate size and shape of the hole to be filled, then position it in the hole so that its edges are below the level of the surrounding bodywork. It can be retained in position by several blobs of filler paste around its periphery.

Aluminium tape should be used for small or very narrow holes. Pull a piece off the roll and trim it to the approximate size and shape required, then pull off the backing paper (if used) and stick the tape over the hole; it can be overlapped if the thickness of one piece is insufficient. Burnish down the edges of the tape with the handle of a screwdriver or similar, to ensure that the tape is securely attached to the metal underneath.

Bodywork repairs - filling and re-spraying

Before using this Section, see the Sections on dent, deep scratch, rust hole and gash repairs.

Many types of bodyfiller are available, but generally speaking those proprietary kits which contain a tin of filler paste and a tube of resin hardener (eg. Holts Cataloy) are best for this type of repair. A wide, flexible plastic or nylon applicator will be found invaluable for imparting a smooth and well contoured finish to the surface of the filler.

Mix up a little filler on a clean piece of card or board - use the hardener sparingly (follow the maker's instructions on the packet) otherwise the filler will set very rapidly.

Using the applicator, apply the filler paste to the prepared area; draw the applicator across the surface of the filler to achieve the correct contour and to level the filler surface. As soon as a contour that approximates the correct one is achieved, stop working the paste - if you carry on too long the paste will become sticky and begin to 'pick-up' on the applicator. Continue to add thin layers of filler paste at twenty-minute intervals until the level of the filler is just 'proud' of the surrounding bodywork.

Once the filler has hardened, excess can be removed using a Surform plane or Dreadnought file. From then on, progressively finer grades of abrasive paper should be used, starting with a 40 grade production paper and finishing with 400 grade 'wet-and-dry' paper, Always wrap the abrasive paper around a flat rubber, cork, or wooden block - otherwise the surface of the filler will not be completely flat. During the smoothing of the filler surface the 'wet-and-dry' paper should be periodically rinsed in water. This will ensure that a very smooth finish is imparted to the filler at the final stage.

At this stage the dent should be surrounded by a ring of bare metal, which in turn should be encircled by the finely 'feathered' edge of the good paintwork. Rinse the repair area with clean water, until all of the dust produced by the rubbing-down operation is gone.

Spray the whole repair area with a light coat of grey primer - this will show up any imperfections in the surface of the filler; repair these imperfections with fresh filler paste or bodystopper, and once more smooth the surface with abrasive paper. If bodystopper is used, it can be mixed with cellulose thinners to form a really thin paste which is ideal for filling small holes. Repeat this spray and repair procedure until you are satisfied that the surface of the filler, and the feathered edge of the paintwork are perfect. Clean the repair area with clean water and allow to dry fully.

The repair area is now ready for spraying. Paint spraying must be carried out in a warm, dry, windless and dust free atmosphere. This condition can be created artificially if you have access to a large indoor working area, but if you are forced to work in the open, you will have to pick your day very carefully. If you are working indoors, dousing the floor in the work area with water will 'lay' the dust which

would otherwise be in the atmosphere. If the repair area is confined to
one body panel, mask off the surrounding panels; this will help to
minimise the effects of a slight mis-match in paint colours. Bodywork
fittings (eg. chrome strips, door handles etc) will also need to be
masked off. Use genuine masking tape and several thicknesses of
newspaper for the masking operation.

Before commencing to spray agitate the aerosol can thoroughly,
then spray a test area (an old tin, or similar) until the technique is
mastered. Cover the repair area with a thick coat of primer; the thickness should be built up using several thin layers of paint rather than
one thick one. Using 400 grade 'wet-and-dry' paper, rub down the
surface of the primer until it is really smooth. While doing this,
the work area should be thoroughly doused with water, and the
'wet-and-dry' paper periodically rinsed in water. Allow to dry before
spraying on more paint.

Spray on the top coat, again building up the thickness by using
several thin layers of paint. Start spraying in the centre of the repair
area and then, using a circular motion, work outwards until the whole
repair area and about 2 inches of the surrounding original paintwork
is covered. Remove all masking material 10 to 15 minutes after spraying
on the final coat of paint.

Allow the new paint at least 2 weeks to harden fully; then, using a
paintwork renovator (eg. T-cut) or a very fine cutting plaste, blend the
edges of the new paint into the existing paintwork. Finally, apply wax
polish.

7.1 Front grille lock

5 Major body damage - repair

Where serious damage has occurred or large areas need renewal due
to neglect, it means certainly that completely new sections or panels
will need welding in and this is best left to professionals. If the damage
is due to impact it will also be necessary to completely check the
alignment of the body shell structure. Due to the principle of
construction the strength and shape of the whole can be affected by
damage to a part. In such instances the services of a Volvo agent with
specialist checking jigs are essential. If a body is left misaligned it is
first of all dangerous as the car will not handle properly and secondly
uneven stresses will be imposed on the steering, engine and transmission,
causing abnormal wear or complete failure. Tyre wear may also be
excessive.

Fig. 12.1. Adjusting bonnet hinges (Sec. 9)

1   Lock bolt

6 Door rattles - tracing and rectification

The most common cause of door rattles is a misaligned, loose or
worn latch plate but other causes may be:

a) loose door handles, window winder handles or door hinges;
b) loose, worn or misaligned door lock components;
c) loose or worn door locking linkages;
d) any combination of the above three.

Worn parts should be renewed as described in later parts of this
Chapter.

7 Replacing the grille

1   Depress and turn the spring locks 90° then lift up the spring locks.
(photo).
2   Pull the grille forward to free it from the upper member and lift it
out.
3   Transfer the springs to the new grille.
4   Position the grille and the spring locks, depress the locks and turn
so that they lock. Check that the grille is held securely.

8 Front wing - removal and replacement

1   Remove the side and indicator lamp cluster (see Chapter 10).
2   Remove the four bolts to the stay.
3   Remove the four bolts at the rear end. These bolts are accessible
when the front door is opened.
4   Remove the three bolts attaching the wing to the front section and
the eight bolts from inside the wheel housing.
5   Remove the wing.
6   Replacement is the reverse of removal.

9 Bonnet - removal, refitting and adjustment

1   Open the bonnet to its fullest extent.
2   Mark the location of the hinge plates on the underside of the
bonnet to facilitate refitting.
3   Obtain the help of an assistant to support the bonnet and then
unscrew and remove the bolts which secure the hinges to the bonnet.
Lift the bonnet from the car.
4   Any adjustment can be made when refitting the bonnet by moving
it within the limits of the hinge plate elongated bolt holes.
5   Positive closure of the bonnet can be provided by moving
the positions of the bonnet lock and spring-loaded lock bolt within

the limits of their mounting plate bolts. The lock bolt is also adjustable in length so that the bonnet when closed will be flush with the tops of the front wings. If the lock bolt is adjusted then the two rubber buffers at the corners of the bonnet will also probably need screwing in or out (photo).

Fig. 12.2. Bonnet lock (Sec. 9)

10 Front door lock - removal and refitting

1 Take out the two plastic plugs from the arm rest and remove the attaching screws located on the inside (photos).
2 Turn the plastic ring at the front edge of the armrest several turns to the left, push the arm rest forwards and the hook at the front edge disengages, allowing the arm rest to be removed (photo).
3 Remove the window winding handle by removing the cover, then the retaining screw and the handle (photos).
4 Unscrew the door lock button and the screws at the top edge of the door interior trim panel.
5 Remove the interior trim panel by inserting a screwdriver, or similar flat tool, between the panel and door and then carefully prise off the trim panel.
6 Remove the lock cylinder attaching screw from the rear edge of the door, Fig. 12.4.
7 Release the securing clip and remove the pushrod from the door lock knob.
8 Disconnect the pullrod from the door interior handle.
9 Disconnect the pullrod from the door exterior handle.
10 Unscrew and remove the three screws which secure the door lock assembly to the edge of the door. Withdraw the lock from the door cavity.
11 The exterior handle may be removed, if required, after removing the two securing screws, accessible with the window lowered.
12 If the lock is worn or damaged, renew it as an assembly.
13 Refitting the lock assembly is the reverse of the removal procedure. Make any necessary adjustment by altering the length of the exterior handle pullrod, Fig. 12.3.

11 Rear door lock - removal and refitting

1 Carry out the operations described in Section 10, paragraphs 1 to 5 and 7 to 9.

9.5 Bonnet lock

10.1a Removing a plastic plug from arm rest

10.1b Removing the arm rest attaching screws

10.2 Disengaging the arm rest

10.3a Taking off the window winding handle cover

10.3b Removing the winding handle retaining screw

Fig. 12.3. Front door lock components (Sec. 10)

1   Lever
2   Lever
3   Lever
4   Pull rod for lock button
5   Outer handle
6   Cover for outer handle
7   Screws for outer handle
8   Return spring for outer handle
9   Pull rod for outer handle
10   Lock cylinder
11   Lock device
12   Inner door opener
13   Return spring for inner door opener

Fig. 12.4. Front door lock attaching screws (Sec. 10)

1   Door lock screws
2   Hole for the lock cylinder attaching screw
3   Hole for rear view mirror installation

Fig. 12.5. Rear door lock components (Sec. 11)

1   Lever for remote control
2   Lever for child safety door lock
3   Lever
4   Pull rod for outer handle
5   Outer handle
6   Cover for outer handle
7   Screws for outer handle cover
8   Return spring for outer handle
9   Pull rod for lock button
10   Inner door opener
11   Return spring for inner door opener

2   Disconnect the interior lock plunger rod by removing the locking clip.

3   Remove the screw from the rear window guide channel and the lock securing screws, all of which are located on the rear edge of the door.

4   The exterior handle can now be removed, if necessary, after removing the securing screws.

5   Refitting is the reverse of the removal procedure but adjust the rod for the exterior handle to provide a clearance, 'A' in Fig. 12.5, of 0.04 in (1 mm) between the pullrod eyelet and the pin in the lock lever.

12 Door stop - removal and refitting

The door stop is shown in detail in Fig. 12.6. It is fastened to the door by two bolts and to the pillar by a single bolt. When these are removed the complete assembly comes away. When replacing it, do not forget the rubber seal.

13 Other locks and latch plates

1   Figs. 12.7, 12.8 and 12.9 give sufficient detail of these to enable the owner to carry out whatever adjustment or replacement is necessary.
2   An interesting example of Volvo thoroughness is their specification for the tilt of the latch plate, which is actually the same plate whether fitted to front or rear doors.

14 Front door window - removal and replacement

1   Lower the window to its bottom position.
2   Remove the interior trim as described in Section 10.
3   Remove the lock springs and washers on the inside of the winding arms. Bend the arms outwards and separate them from the window channel.
4   Remove the window by lifting and turning it towards the car as shown in Fig. 12.10.

Fig. 12.6. Door stop (Sec. 12)

Fig. 12.7. Luggage compartment lock (Sec. 13)

1   Lock catch, fitted in lid
2   Lock mechanism, fitted in rear section
3   Lock knob, fitted in rear section

Fig. 12.8. Tailgate lock, 245 (Sec. 13)

1   Outer handle
2   Inside opener
3   Latching device for inner opener
4   Control for latching device
5   Eccentric
6   Lock cylinder

Fig. 12.9. Latch plate (Sec. 13)

$A = 1.5^o$ - Front door
$A = 2.5^o$ - Rear door

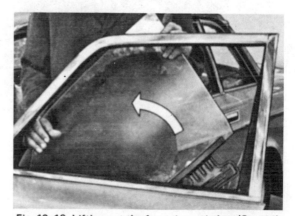

Fig. 12.10. Lifting out the front door window (Sec. 14)

This sequence of photographs deals with the repair of the dent and paintwork damage shown in this photo. The procedure will be similar for the repair of a hole. It should be noted that the procedures given here are simplified — more explicit instructions will be found in the text

In the case of a dent the first job — after removing surrounding trim — is to hammer out the dent where access is possible. This will minimise filling. Here, the large dent having been hammered out, the damaged area is being made slightly concave

Now all paint must be removed from the damaged area, by rubbing with coarse abrasive paper. Alternatively, a wire brush or abrasive pad can be used in a power drill. Where the repair area meets good paintwork, the edge of the paintwork should be 'feathered', using a finer grade of abrasive paper

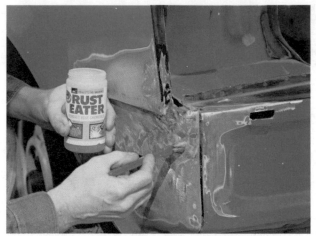

In the case of a hole caused by rusting, all damaged sheet-metal should be cut away before proceeding to this stage. Here, the damaged area is being treated with rust remover and inhibitor before being filled

Mix the body filler according to its manufacturer's instructions. In the case of corrosion damage, it will be necessary to block off any large holes before filling — this can be done with zinc gauze or aluminium tape. Make sure the area is absolutely clean before...

...applying the filler. Filler should be applied with a flexible applicator, as shown, for best results; the wooden spatula being used for confined areas. Apply thin layers of filler at 20-minute intervals, until the surface of the filler is slightly proud of the surrounding bodywork

Initial shaping can be done with a Surform plane or Dreadnought file. Then, using progressively finer grades of wet-and-dry paper, wrapped around a sanding block, and copious amounts of clean water, rub down the filler until really smooth and flat. Again, feather the edges of adjoining paintwork

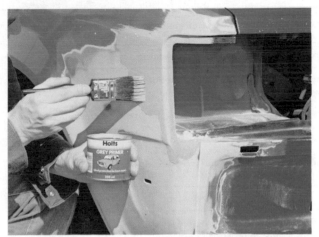

The whole repair area can now be sprayed or brush-painted with primer. If spraying, ensure adjoining areas are protected from over-spray. Note that at least one inch of the surrounding sound paintwork should be coated with primer. Primer has a 'thick' consistency, so will fill small imperfections

Again, using plenty of water, rub down the primer with a fine grade of wet-and-dry paper (400 grade is probably best) until it is really smooth and well blended into the surrounding paintwork. Any remaining imperfections can now be filled by carefully applied knifing stopper paste

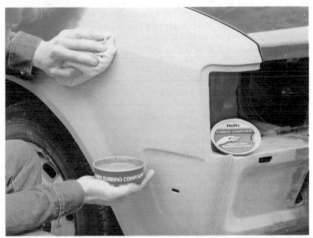

When the stopper has hardened, rub down the repair area again before applying the final coat of primer. Before rubbing down this last coat of primer, ensure the repair area is blemish-free – use more stopper if necessary. To ensure that the surface of the primer is really smooth use some finishing compound

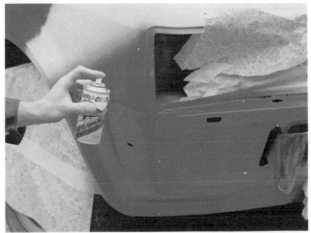

The top coat can now be applied. When working out of doors, pick a dry, warm and wind-free day. Ensure surrounding areas are protected from over-spray. Agitate the aerosol thoroughly, then spray the centre of the repair area, working outwards with a circular motion. Apply the paint as several thin coats

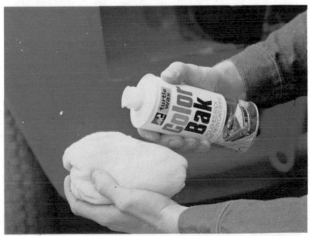

After a period of about two weeks, which the paint needs to harden fully, the surface of the repaired area can be 'cut' with a mild cutting compound prior to wax polishing. When carrying out bodywork repairs, remember that the quality of the finished job is proportional to the time and effort expended

5   Replacement is the reverse of the removal procedure.

15 Front door window winding mechanism - removal and replacement

1   Carry out operations 1 to 3 in Section 14.
2   Remove the clip at one of the winding arm's securing points in the door, see Fig. 12.11.
3   Remove the winding mechanism four retaining screws and withdraw the mechanism from the cavity in the door.
4   Replacement is the reverse of the removal sequence, but after refitting the retaining screws, wind the window up to the fully closed position before tightening the screws.

16 Rear door window and winding mechanism - replacement

The procedure for replacing the window and door winding mechanism is the same as described in Sections 14 and 15.

17 Doors and tailgate - removal, refitting and adjustment

1   To remove the doors, take out the upholstery panels (Section 10) you have to do this to get at the nuts on the hinge bolts - remove the door stops (Section 12), disconnect the heated rear window and unscrew the bolts between the hinges and the door. Elongated holes in the hinges where they fit to the door and oversized holes in the pillar where the hinges are attached provide for adjustment of the door position.

18 Tailgate - removal and replacement

1   To remove the tailgate, you will have to take off the upholstery panel on the inside. Then remove the left-hand number plate lamp and its cable, disconnect the other out-going cables from the tailgate, remove the gas spring, undo the bolts connecting the hinges to the tailgate and lift it off. The tailgate hinges can be removed from the body by easing the hinge out of its groove at the rear, pushing the electric cables out of the way and thus enabling yourself to get at the nuts holding the hinge bolts. Replacement is straightforward, the only problem being to compress the gas spring. To keep it compressed a simple bracket, like that shown in Fig. 12.12, is very little trouble to make.

19 Luggage compartment lid

1   The luggage compartment lid is mounted on two hinges both of

which are attached by two bolts to the inner plate of the lid and by three bolts to the pillar under the rear window.
2   The lid is counterbalanced by a spring support. When fitting a new spring support use a clamp as shown in Fig. 12.12. The holes in the hinges are elongated to provide adjustment when refitting the lid.

20 Windscreen glass - removal and refitting

1   This is a job for specialists. Due to the method of sealing the glass, the old windscreen must be released using a hot soldering iron of special shape.
2   Fitting the new screen requires special adhesive and butyl tape and when one considers the cost involved if the windscreen should get broken during fitting it is recommended that you leave this job to your Volvo agent.

21 Rear window glass - removal and refitting

1   Disconnect the leads from the heated rear window. Move the bright trim clips aside and prise off the time (Fig. 12.13).
2   Release the rubber surround from the glass and the body flange by sliding a thin plastic blade round the joint.
3   Working inside the car but with an assistant outside to catch the glass, prise the lip of the rubber surround from the body starting at the top left-hand corner and pushing the glass outwards at the same time.
4   Clean all old sealant from the glass, body flange and the rubber surround. If the latter is damaged, hardened or sealant is stuck to it, renew the surround.
5   Cut a piece of strong cord greater in length than the periphery of the glass and insert it into the body flange locating channel of the rubber surround (Fig. 12.14).
6   Apply a thin bead of sealant to the face of the rubber channel which will eventually mate with the body.
7   Offer the glass to the body aperture and pass the end of the cord, previously fitted and located at bottom centre into the vehicle interior.
8   Press the glass into place, at the same time have an assistant pulling the cords to engage the lip of the rubber channel over the body flange (Fig. 12.15).
9   Remove any excess sealant with a paraffin soaked rag.
10 Refit the bright trim. This is best done by inserting a 5/32 in (4 mm) diameter cord (or leather thong) in the groove in the rubber surround. Soak the cord in paraffin or soapy solution beforehand. Press the trim into position at the same time pulling the cord out and upwards. Fit the trim joint clips (Fig. 12.16).

Fig. 12.11. Removing the window winding mechanism (Sec. 15)

1   Lock   2   Winding mechanism retaining
                                        screws

Fig. 12.12. Compressing the gas spring for luggage compartment lid or tailgate (Sec. 18)

Fig. 12.13. Removing the trim from rear window surround (Sec. 21)

Fig. 12.15. Pulling the edge of the rubber strip over the surround (Sec. 21)

Fig. 12.14. Fitting the cord in rubber strip (Sec. 21)

Fig. 12.16. Fitting the metal trim (Sec. 21)

22 Rear quarter glass - removal and refitting

1   The method of replacing these windows is very similar to the procedure described in Section 21.

23 Sun roof

1   Enough details are given in Fig. 12.17 to enable anyone looking at it, in conjunction with an actual sun roof, to see how the whole thing works. It can be removed as follows.
2   Open the sun roof and release the clips securing the roof upholstery at the front end. Move the upholstery back to leave an opening.
3   Crank the sun roof forwards and slacken the screws at its four attachments (9 and 11, Fig. 12.17). Bend the blade springs (10) to one side and remove the reinforcing plates (13) at the rear attachments. The sun roof can now be lifted off.

24 Sun roof - replacing cables

1   Remove the sun roof as described in Section 23.
2   Remove the wind deflector (2, Fig. 12.17).
3   Remove the intermediate pieces (8) covering strip (3) and holders above the drive. Release the front guide rails (6) and pull out the cables (5).
4   Fit replacement cables so that the attachments for the sun roof come opposite each other at the rear end of the roof opening. Screw the front guide rails on securely.
5   Refit the intermediate pieces, holders, covering plate and the wind deflector.
6   Screw on the roof securely and put back the leaf springs.
7   Crank the sun roof forwards until it is completely closed and check that it is level with the main roof. If necessary adjust at the front and rear attachments (7 and 12, Fig. 12.17). Check that the lifts on the rear attachments are pushed up when the roof is closed. (B, Fig. 12.17).

8   When the roof is closed the crank should point straight forwards in the vehicle. If it does not, unscrew the crank and gear housing, turn the crank to the stop position and replace.

25 Bumpers - removal and refitting

1   Various types of bumper section may be encountered, also different methods of mounting them.
2   On some cars the bumpers are mounted on rigid brackets while on others, including those destined for North America, the mountings may be of coil spring, hydraulic or gas-filled type. These impact absorbing type bumpers are removed as with the other designs, simply by releasing the mounting nuts or bolts.
3   Where the gas-filled shock absorbing type mountings are installed, do not attempt to open them or weld or heat them as the gas can explode.
4   Before discarding a defective impact absorber it should be emptied by drilling holes to release the gas. Use safety glasses while drilling the holes.

26 Driver's seat heater pads - renewal

1   On some cars, an electrically heated driver's seat is fitted.
2   Disconnect the leads to the seat heating pads at the junction box (Fig. 12.18).
3   Unbolt and remove the seat, complete with runners, from the car floor.
4   Disconnect the leads between the seat back panel and the seat cushion pad.
5   Remove the screws which secure the seat cushion and remove the cushion (Fig. 12.19).
6   Place the seat upside down on the bench and cut and remove the upholstery front retaining clamps.
7   Release the plastic hooks and pull out the heater pad from the seat back (Fig. 12.20).
8   When installing the new heater pad to the seat back, make sure

Fig. 12.17. Sun roof (Secs. 23 and 24)

A. Rear attachment when roof is open
B. Rear attachment when roof is closed

1 Drain hose
2 Wind deflector
3 Cover strip
4 Crank housing with crank
5 Cables
6 Front guide rail
7 Front adjustment

8 Intermediate piece
9 Front attachment
10 Leaf spring
11 Rear attachment
12 Rear adjustment
13 Reinforcing plate

Fig. 12.18. Leads and connectors for driver's seat heater pads
(Sec. 26)

Fig. 12.19. Seat cushion retaining screws (Sec. 26)

Fig. 12.20. Removing heater pad from driver's seat back (Sec. 26)

Fig. 12.21. Fitting heater pad to driver's seat cushion (Sec. 26)

that the barbed side of the elements faces the seat padding and the electrical leads run on the inner side of the seat back (nearer the transmission terminal).

9   To renew the pad in the seat cushion, place the cushion upside down and remove the cover plate.

10 Cut and remove the clamp at the rear end of the cushion. With-draw the heater pad. Note that a thermostat is fitted in the cushion heater pad.

11 When installing the new pad, make sure that the barbed side of the heater element is towards the padding, and the electrical leads run on the inner side of the cushion (nearer the transmission tunnel).

12 Connect the upholstery using new clamps.

Chapter 13 Supplement

Contents

---

1 Introduction

1 Since its introduction in 1974, the 240 Series has been the subject of continuous development and modification with detailed design changes to many components. It is not the intention of this Supplement to list these changes unless their inclusion affects the specifications or the original overhaul operations given in this manual.

2 In order to use this Supplement to the best advantage, it is suggested that it is referred to before the main Chapters of the manual, where the date of production of the vehicle being worked upon falls within the years 1977 on.

Vehicle designations

3 Commencing with the 1980 models, for operation in North America, the individual model types have been changed as follows:

   242 to DL
   244 to GL
   245 to GT

Routine maintenance

4 Due to the improvement in lubricants and the development of longer wearing materials of construction, the servicing periods for later models have now been extended.

To 1976	1977 on
6000 miles (10 000 km)	*7500 miles (12 000 km)*
12 000 miles (20 000 km)	*15 000 miles (24 000 km)*
24 000 miles (40 000 km)	*30 000 miles (48 000 km)*
36 000 miles (60 000 km)	*45 000 miles (72 000 km)*

5 The following maintenance tasks should be added to those listed in the Routine Maintenance Section at the beginning of this manual for later models equipped with automatic transmission and emission control devices:

   15 000 miles (24 000 km) - Check Air Injection Reactor system.

   30 000 miles (48 000 km) - Renew EGR valve. Adjust rear brake band (BW 35 transmission). Adjust kickdown cable (BW 35 transmission).

   45 000 miles (72 000 km) - Renew charcoal canister (fuel evaporative emission control system).

---

2 Specifications

Note: *The information given below is supplementary to the Specifications in the twelve main Chapters of the manual*

Engine

B19 engine (special territories only)
As B21 engine except for the following:

Cylinder bore	3.499 in (88.9 mm)
Displacement	121.2 cu in (1986 cc)

Compression ratio:
    B19A (carburettor engines) ... ...   8.5 : 1 or 8.8 : 1
    B19E (fuel injection engines) ... ...   8.8 : 1
Max output @ rpm, DIN: **kw**   **hp**
    B19A (8.5 : 1 CR) ... ...   66 @ 5000   90 @ 5000
    B19A (8.8 : 1 CR) ... ...   71 @ 5400   97 @ 5400
    B19E ... ...   86 @ 6000   117 @ 6000
Max torque @ rpm, DIN: **kgf m**   **lbf ft**
    B19A (8.5 : 1 CR) ... ...   15.5 @ 3200   114 @ 3200
    B19A (8.8 : 1 CR) ... ...   16.0 @ 3200   118 @ 3200
    B19E ... ...   16.0 @ 4500   118 @ 4500

B17A engine (special territories only)
As B19 engine except for the following:
Cylinder stroke ... ...   2.84 in (72 mm)
Displacement ... ...   109 cu in (1787 cc)
Compression ratio ... ...   8.4 : 1
Max output @ rpm, DIN ... ...   66 kw (90 hp) @ 5750
Max torque @ rpm, DIN ... ...   13.5 kgf m (98 lbf ft) @ 2500

Fuel system
Zenith-Stromberg 175 CD-2SE carburettor
    B20A engine, 1975/76 ... ...   Needle BICC
    B21A engine:
        1975 ... ...   Needle B2BB
        1976 ... ...   Needle B1ED
        1977 ... ...   Needle B1EE
CO %:
    B20A engine:
        1975 ... ...   2.5
        1976 ... ...   1.5
    B21A engine 2.5

SU HIF-6 carburettor
B21A engine ... ...   Needle BDJ

Ignition system
Ignition timing, 1976 on*
Vacuum pipe disconnected and plugged, engine speed 700 to 800 rpm
Engine:
    B17A ... ...   12° BTDC
    B19A ... ...   12° BTDC (15° pre-1978)
    B19E ... ...   8° BTDC
    B20A ... ...   10° BTDC
    B20E and F† ... ...   5° BTDC
    B21A (1979 on) ... ...   12° BTDC
    B21E† ... ...   10° BTDC
    B21F† ... ...   8° BTDC
Refer also to individual vehicle decal
†*Air conditioner off, air injection system disconnected*

Clutch
Hydraulically-actuated clutch
Application ... ...   RHD cars, 1975 on
Fluid type ... ...   Castrol Girling Universal Brake and Clutch Fluid
Release arm free movement ... ...   0.2 in (5 mm)

Clutch driven plate
Number of splines on hub:
    M45/46 gearbox, 1979 on   22
    All other models   10

Automatic transmission
Approximate shift speeds (AW55 and BW55)

Engine	Throttle	1 – 2	2 – 3	3 – 2	3 – 1
B21 with 3.91 : 1 final drive	Full open	35 to 44 mph (55 to 70 km/h)	62 to 71 mph (100 to 115 km/h)	56 mph min (90 km/h min)	22 to 35 mph (35 to 55 km/h)
B21 with 4.10 : 1 final drive	Full open	31 to 40 mph (50 to 65 km/h)	60 to 68 mph (95 to 110 km/h)	53 mph min (85 km/h min)	22 to 35 mph (35 to 55 km/h)

Normal stall speeds
BW55 ... ...   2400 to 2650 rpm
AW55 ... ...   2500 rpm

Torque wrench settings (BW55, AW55)

	lbf ft	Nm
Torque converter housing-to-engine	35	48
Torque converter housing-to-transmission casing:		
M10 bolts	25	34
M12 bolts	40	54
Driveplate-to-torque converter	35	48
Fluid cooler pipeline connections	20	27
Extension housing-to-transmission casing	25	34
Drive flange	35	48
Oil pan bolts	7	10
Dipstick guide tube union nut	60	82

Limited slip differential
Torque wrench setting

	lbf ft	Nm
Differential case bolts (left-hand thread)	50	68

Braking system
Front discs (1975 on)

Type	Ventilated
Thickness (new)	0.94 in (24.0 mm)
Minimum refinishing thickness:	
1975 models	0.90 in (22.8 mm)
1976 on models	0.82 in (20.8 mm)
Maximum run-out	0.004 in (0.10 mm)

Electrical system
Starter motor

Make and type	Hitachi 5114—232
Direction of rotation	Clockwise
Output	1.4 kW (2 hp)
Minimum brush length	0.43 in (11.0 mm)
Minimum diameter of commutator	1.54 in (39.0 mm)

Alternator
SEV—Marchal A14/55A

Maximum amperage	55A
Maximum wattage	770W
Minimum diameter, slip rings	1.34 in (34.0 mm)
Minimum brush length	0.20 in (5.0 mm)
Tightening torque - pulley nut	30 lbf ft (41 Nm)
Test values:	
Rotor winding resistance	3.5 to 4.3 ohms
Stator resistance	0.17 to 0.23 ohm/phase
Output at 14V	48A at 3000 rpm

SEV—Marchal D14/70A

Maximum amperage	70A
Maximum wattage	980W
Minimum diameter, slip rings	1.34 in (34.0 mm)
Minimum brush length	0.20 in (5.0 mm)
Tightening torque - pulley nut	30 lbf ft (41 Nm)
Test values:	
Rotor winding resistance	3 to 5 ohms
Stator resistance	0.08 to 0.18 ohm/phase
Output at 14V	62A at 3000 rpm

Bosch N1 14V 70A 20

Maximum amperage	70A
Maximum wattage	980W
Minimum diameter, slip rings	1.24 in (31.5 mm)
Minimum brush length	0.20 in (5.0 mm)
Tightening torque - pulley nut	26 lbf ft (35 Nm)
Test values:	
Rotor winding resistance	4 to 4.4 ohms
Stator resistance	0.1 ohm/phase
Output at 14V	58A at 3000 rpm

Transistor type voltage regulator

Make and type	Bosch EF 14V 3B or SEV—Marchal 723 17102
Regulator temperature with fully charged battery	77°F (25°C)
Test voltage between B+ and D— terminals (engine at 3000 rpm, alternator load 5 to 10A):	
Cold	13.7 to 14.5V
Warm (15 minutes running)	13.5 to 14.1V

Front suspension and steering
Power steering pump (1977 on)

Make ...	...	...	...	...	...	...	...	Saginaw
Maximum pressure	...	...	...	...	...	...	...	853 to 996 lbf/in² (60 to 70 kgf/cm²)

Steering angles

Castor (1979 on with power-assisted steering)	...	...	...	3° to 4° positive
Camber (1980 on GT) ...	...	...	...	¼° to ¾° positive

Steering gear lubrication

Type ...	...	...	...	...	...	...	...	Cam gears
Lubricant ...	...	...	...	...	...	...	...	Engine oil SAE 20W/50 or 20W/40
Capacity ...	...	...	...	...	...	...	...	0.35 Imp pts (0.21 US qt, 0.2 litre)
Type ...	...	...	...	...	...	...	...	ZF
Lubricant ...	...	...	...	...	...	...	...	Grease (Volvo Part No 1161001)
Capacity ...	...	...	...	...	...	...	...	75g (manual), 100g (power-assisted)

Power-assisted steering fluid

Fluid type ...	...	...	...	...	...	...	...	ATF type A, F or Dexron R
Capacity:								
1975 to 1976	...	...	...	...	...	...	...	1.94 Imp pt (1.16 US qt, 1.1 litre)
1977 on ...	...	...	...	...	...	...	...	1.23 Imp pt (0.74 US qt, 0.7 litre)

---

3 Engine

B19 type engine - description

1 This engine was introduced in 1977 for use in cars destined for operation in a few special territories only. Three versions are available: one fuel injection model (B19E) and two carburettor versions (B19A).

2 Apart from its displacement, achieved by reducing the cylinder bore, the engine is identical to the B21 Series engine.

North American engine - designation

3 Commencing with 1980 models, the B21E engine is designated the B21F.

B17A type engine - description

4 This engine was introduced in 1979 exclusively for vehicles destined for operation in Israel and Nigeria.

5 The engine is very similar to the B19 engine mentioned in this Supplement apart from its smaller capacity, achieved by reducing the stroke.

Engine sump pan (1980 models) - removal and refitting

6 A deeper type of sump pan was introduced early in 1979 and if it is to be removed from the car with the engine in position, the following operations must be adhered to.

7 Raise the front end and support the car under the jacking points.

8 Drain the engine oil.

9 Remove the splash shield from under the engine.

10 Remove the engine mounting nuts from the underside of the cross-member.

11 Release both pinch-bolts from the universal joint coupling on the steering shaft and slide the coupling up the splines on the shaft.

12 The engine must now be raised slightly. Do this by attaching a hoist to the lifting lugs or by using a crossbar and threaded hook similar to the arrangement shown (Fig. 13.3).

Fig. 13.1. Engine mounting nuts (arrowed) (Sec. 3)

Fig. 13.2. Steering coupling pinch-bolts (arrowed) (Sec. 3)

13 Unscrew and remove the bolts which secure the crossmember and lower it.
14 Unbolt and remove the engine mounting from the left-hand side.
15 Unbolt the bracing brackets from the rear corners of the sump pan.
16 Unbolt the sump pan, lower it and turn it to remove it.
17 Refitting is a reversal of removal. Use a new gasket and tighten the steering coupling pinch-bolts to the specified torque.
18 Fill the engine with oil.

4 Cooling system, heater and air conditioner

Fan coupling

1 The slip coupling type radiator cooling fan has been modified on certain models. As well as being speed sensitive, the fan is also temperature sensitive by the inclusion of a bi-metal spring in its hub.
2 The spring controls a valve which in turn regulates the coupling internal oil flow, so permitting the fan to revolve faster or slower according to the cooling requirements of the engine.

Air conditioner - drier

3 The drier is located next to the radiator on 1978 and later models.

5 Fuel system

Zenith 175 CD-2SE (tamperproof) carburettor - idle (CO) mixture adjustment

1 This type of carburettor can be recognised by the fact that a plug is not fitted to the underside of the float chamber. The idle mixture is normally set during production and unless the carburettor is completely overhauled or has new internal parts fitted, it should not require adjustment.
2 A special tool (No 999 5159) will be required to adjust the jet on this type of carburettor.
3 Have the engine at normal operating temperature and adjust the idle speed to 900 rpm (refer to paragraph 32).
4 Using an exhaust gas analyser or other device such as a 'Colortune', connected in accordance with the maker's instructions, check that the CO level is between 1.5 and 3.5% or that the combustion flame colour is correct.
5 Where adjustment is required, remove the damper and insert the special tool, pushing it down until the lugs on the tool engage with the notches in the air valve spindle. If the engine is inclined to stall during installation of the tool, hold the throttle open until the tool is engaged.

Fig. 13.3. Volvo tools for supporting the engine (Sec. 3)

5006 Crossbar
5033 Side members
5115 Threaded hook

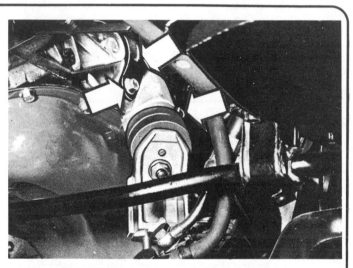

Fig. 13.5. Engine mounting bolts (arrowed) (Sec. 3)

Fig. 13.4. Front crossmember bolts (arrowed) (Sec. 3)

Fig. 13.6. Sump-to-bellhousing bracing bracket bolts (arrowed) (Sec. 3)

Fig. 13.7. Modified radiator cooling fan with bi-metal spring (arrowed) (Sec. 4)

Fig. 13.10. Topping-up the carburettor dashpot (Sec. 5)

Fig. 13.8. Air conditioner drier is located next to radiator on later models (Sec. 4)

Fig. 13.11. Fitting the metering needle with special tool 5159 (175 CD-2SE) (Sec. 5)

Fig. 13.9. Zenith 175 CD-2SE carburettor jet adjusting tool (Sec. 5)

Fig. 13.12. Carburettor flexible diaphragm locating lug (arrowed) (Sec. 5)

Plugged channel (used if solenoid for air conditioning is fitted)

Idle channel

Fuel nozzle

Adjuster screw (CO)

Bimetal washers (temperature compensation)

Fig. 13.13. Sectional view of Zenith DVG 175 CDSU carburettor (Sec. 5)

Fig. 13.15. Mixture screw (arrowed) on Zenith DVG 175 CDSU carburettor is sealed with a plastic plug (Sec. 5)

Fig. 13.16. Adjusting idle speed (later type carburettor with independent idling circuit) (Sec. 5)

Cold fuel (engine)   Warm fuel (engine)

Fig. 13.14. Position of spring-loaded fuel nozzle at different temperatures (Sec. 5)

A-B = 0,7-0,9 mm

Fig. 13.17. Throttle butterfly basic setting (carburettors with independent idling circuit) (Sec. 5)

Fig. 13.18. Exploded view of Zenith DVG 175 CDSU carburettor (Sec. 5)

6 Now turn the inner member of the tool to adjust the jet and the mixture. Clockwise rotation of the tool enriches the mixture, anti-clockwise weakens it.

7 Make sure that the outer member of the tool is not allowed to rotate during the adjustment operation, otherwise the flexible diaphragm within the carburettor will tear.

8 After each movement of the adjusting tool, rev up the engine to about 3000 rpm before checking the mixture evaluating instrument.

9 When the mixture is correct, withdraw the tool, top up the damper cylinder and refit the damper.

10 Remove the analysing device.

Zenith 175 CD-2SE carburettor metering needle - removal and refitting

11 Remove the carburettor from the engine and clean its external surfaces.

12 Remove the suction chamber cover, extract the coil spring and lift out the air valve piston and flexible diaphragm.

13 Insert the special adjusting tool (inner member) and turn the metering needle until it releases from the adjuster screw.

14 Unscrew the spring-loaded guide screw and remove the needle and retainer if required.

15 To fit the needle/retainer, insert the assembly into the base of the air valve piston and then insert the guide screw so that it engages in the groove in the needle retainer.

16 Again using the special tool, screw up the needle until its floating washer is flush with the base of the piston. This is the basic mixture setting position and the mixture must be finally adjusted as described above (paragraphs 3 to 10) once the carburettor is installed on the engine.

17 Refit the air valve and diaphragm, making sure that the alignment projection on the diaphragm engages in the recess in the carburettor body.

18 Fit the coil spring and the suction chamber cover.

19 Fill the damper with oil of the specified type and fit the damper piston.

20 Install the carburettor on the engine using new flange gaskets.

Zenith DVG 175 CDSU carburettor - description

21 This carburettor was introduced on UK models for 1978. It differs from other Zenith carburettors fitted to the range mainly by a special fuel nozzle. The mixture is varied by an adjustable fuel nozzle which incorporates temperature-variable bi-metal washers (temperature compensator).

22 When the fuel is cold, these washers come together, causing the coil spring to force the fuel nozzle downward so creating a greater space between nozzle and metering needle to permit a larger fuel flow and in consequence a richer mixture.

23 As the fuel temperature increases, the bi-metal washers separate, causing a smaller space between nozzle and metering needle to give a weaker mixture.

24 The fuel nozzle/washer/spring assemblies are only supplied as complete units.

25 This carburettor also incorporates a manually-operated cold start device (choke).

Zenith DVG 175 CDSU carburettor - idle mixture (CO) adjustment

26 The mixture (CO) is set during production of this carburettor and should not be tampered with unless the unit has been the subject of major overhaul with the renewal of some internal components.

27 Have the engine at normal operating temperature with the idle speed set to the specified level (refer to paragraph 32).

28 Connect an exhaust gas analyser or combustion flame viewer such as a 'Colortune' in accordance with the manufacturers' instructions. Check that the CO level is between 1.5 and 3.5% or that the combustion flame colour is correct.

29 Where adjustment is required, prise out the plastic plug which seals the mixture adjusting screw and turn the screw — clockwise to enrich the mixture and anti-clockwise to weaken it.

30 On completion, refit the plastic plug.

Carburettors - idle speed adjustment

31 The later type of carburettors described in this Supplement have an independent idling circuit which provides a smoother idle and

eliminates run-on by means of a solenoid-operated valve.

32 Idle speed adjustment should normally be carried out only by means of the screw located in the intake manifold connecting flange. With the engine at normal operating temperature, turn the screw in or out to bring the idle speed to between 850 and 950 rpm.

33 The basic setting of the throttle butterfly is adjusted during production and it should not be altered unless the normal adjusting method proves unsatisfactory or new carburettor components have been fitted.

34 To alter the basic setting, first remove the carburettor from the engine. Close the butterfly valve fully and measure the dimension A shown in Fig. 13.17.

35 Now adjust the butterfly so that when it is fully closed, dimension B will be between 0.028 and 0.036 in (0.7 and 0.9 mm) less than A previously measured. Adjustment on Zenith-Stromberg carburettors is made by bending the spindle, while on SU carburettors a screw and locknut are fitted.

DVG 175 CDSU carburettor - dismantling and reassembly

36 Remove the carburettor from the intake manifold and clean external dirt and grease from it.

37 Remove the damper piston, the suction chamber and the return spring. Carefully lift out the air valve and the diaphragm.

38 Remove the float chamber cover and its gasket.

39 Remove the adjuster screw from the float chamber cover. Extract the O-ring from the screw.

40 Remove the fuel nozzle with temperature compensator and spring.

41 Remove the fuel inlet needle valve and its washer.

42 Remove the cold start device.

43 Clean, examine and renew components as necessary. If the butterfly valve is dismantled, refit it so that the engraved face is downwards and towards the float chamber.

44 Check the float level by inverting the chamber so that the fuel inlet valves are depressed by the weight of the floats only. Measure as shown in Fig. 13.19, adjusting if necessary by bending the tongues which bear on the fuel inlet valves.

45 When fitting the metering needle, make sure that it is not worn, bent or scored (an unevenly running engine is an indication of a worn needle).

Fig. 13.19. Float level adjustment on DVG 175 CDSU carburettor (Sec. 5)

The needle must be marked PN. Locate the flat side of the needle against the end of the retaining screw.

46 When fitting the float chamber adjuster screw, remember the O-ring and screw it into the cover until the nozzle is 0.10 in (2.5 mm) under the carburettor housing bridge.

47 Make sure that the diaphragm is not perforated and engage the pip on the diaphragm in the recess in the carburettor housing.

48 Tighten the suction chamber cover screws evenly. Lift the piston with a finger and allow it to drop unaided. It should fall smoothly without any tendency to stick and strike the bridge with a distinct metallic click.

49 Check that the damper piston has an endfloat on its rod of between 0.020 and 0.060 in (0.5 and 1.5 mm). Lack of clearance can cause delay in acceleration.

50 Fill the damper with automatic transmission fluid.

51 When installing the carburettor, use a new gasket and make sure that its straight edges are located as shown in Fig. 13. 22.

Fig. 13.20. Suction chamber alignment marks (arrowed) on DVG 175 CDSU carburettor (Sec. 5)

Fig. 13.21. Damper piston endfloat (Sec. 5)
A = 0.020 to 0.060 in (0.5 to 1.5 mm)

Fig. 13.22. Correctly fitted carburettor flange gasket (Sec. 5)

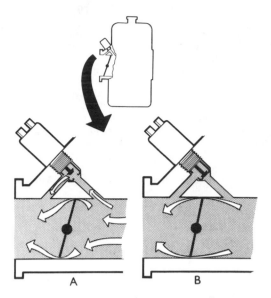

Fig. 13.23. Operation of constant idle speed valve (models with air conditioning) (Sec. 5)

A   Air conditioner on
B   Air conditioner off

Fig. 13.24. Coolant-heated manifold. Arrows show direction of coolant flow (Sec. 5)

Fig. 13.25. Idle speed adjuster (arrowed) on fuel injection models, 1978 on (Sec. 5)

Constant idle speed valve (air conditioned models)
52 On later models equipped with an air conditioner, an additional solenoid valve is incorporated in the carburettor in order to maintain the engine idle speed when the air conditioner compressor is switched on. This is achieved by opening a passage to admit extra fuel/air mixture as soon as the solenoid valve is energised by completion of the air conditioner electrical circuit.

Manifold pre-heating (carburettor models)
53 The intake manifold is coolant-heated on models built after 1978 to ensure more rapid warm-up.
54 All later models are also equipped with an automatic temperature-controlled air cleaner.

Idle and CO adjustment (fuel injection, 1978 on)

55 The idle speed should be adjusted when the engine is at normal operating temperature. Start the engine and turn the screw in or out as necessary to set the engine speed to 900 rpm (manual transmission) or 800 rpm (automatic transmission).

56 To check the CO level, insert an exhaust gas analyser probe into the end of the exhaust pipe on vehicles without a catalytic converter or into the exhaust pipe (plug provided) just forward of the catalytic converter on vehicles provided with this device.

57 Using the special tool (5015) inserted into the hole in the airflow sensor, adjust the screw until the CO reading is within the specified tolerance (see Specifications, Chapter 3, Part B).

Air injection system ('Pulsair' type)

58 This type of emission control system is fitted to engines on some models, depending upon operating territory.

59 The purpose of the system is to inject air into the exhaust manifold to promote the combustion of unburnt gases leaving the cylinders.

60 The main difference between this and other air injection systems is that an air pump is not required. Pressure changes in the exhaust system are used to inject the air.

Fuel tank cap

61 On later models with a fuel evaporative control system, a special fuel tank filler cap is used. The cap has two integral valves to control excess pressure or vacuum within the tank.

62 It is important that the cap seal is kept in good condition.

Roll-over valve (evaporative emission control system)

63 Commencing with 1980 models, a valve is fitted to prevent fuel spillage through the charcoal filter in the event of the vehicle turning over.

64 The valve closes once it is tipped more than 45° from horizontal.

Carbon canister (evaporative emission control system)

65 Commencing with 1980 models, a larger carbon canister is fitted with integral vacuum valve operated by the engine intake manifold vacuum.

66 The new canister is located under the left-hand front wing.

67 Always keep the drain hole at the base of the canister clear by probing periodically.

Fuel filter

68 On later engines, a larger capacity fuel filter is located on the engine compartment rear bulkhead. The filter is a snap-on fit to its bracket.

Cruise control system - description and adjustment

69 The cruise control system is designed to enable the driver to select and maintain a constant roadspeed (over 30 mph - 48 km/h) without the need to continually adjust the position of the accelerator pedal. The system is immediately overridden if the brake or clutch pedals are depressed.

70 Earlier versions incorporated a mechanically controlled system but later models are electronically controlled.

71 The system should not be engaged in heavy traffic or when driving on wet or slippery roads.

72 If the system is in use and the gearchange lever is inadvertently knocked into the neutral position, quickly depress the clutch or brake pedal which will switch the system off to prevent overrevving of the engine.

73 If the system is disengaged by a depression of the clutch or brake pedal, the set speed can be re-introduced if the control switch is momentarily moved to the RESUME position, but anticipate violent acceleration if the speed differential between the actual roadspeed and the set speed is excessive. Momentary rapid acceleration for over-taking will not interrupt the set speed setting which will be resumed on completion of the acceleration without having to touch the RESUME switch.

74 To set the desired roadspeed, move the switch (1) on the steering column stalk to ON. Accelerate to the desired roadspeed and when it is reached, depress the button (2). If a lower set speed is subsequently desired, depress the button (2) and hold it depressed until the speed has dropped to the required level, then release it.

Fig. 13.26. Mixture adjusting tool 5015 - fuel injection models, 1978 on (Sec. 5)

Fig. 13.27. 'Pulsair' air injection system (Sec. 5)

Fig. 13.28. Fuel tank filler cap for evaporative emission control system. Note vent holes (arrowed) (Sec. 5)

Fig. 13.29. Sectional view of fuel tank filler cap (Sec. 5)

Carbon filter and vacuum valve assy.

Rubber cap

Hose from fuel tank

Drain hole. Must not be blocked

Fig. 13.31. Later type carbon canister (Sec. 5)

Roll-over valve

open

closed

To canister

Fig. 13.30. Roll-over fuel valve (Sec. 5)

Fig. 13.32. Later type fuel filter (Sec. 5)

throttle actuator

retard switch

governor

turn signal switch with cruise control

brake light switch

clutch

vacuum valve

speed pickup coil

throttle control

Fig. 13.33. Cruise control system layout (Sec. 5)

Fig. 13.34. Cruise control system wiring diagram (Sec. 5)

Fig. 13.35. Cruise control operating switch (Sec. 5)

1 On/off/resume
2 Set speed

Fig. 13.36. Cruise control retard switch setting (Sec. 5)

Fig. 13.37. Cruise control governor adjustment points (arrowed) (Sec. 5)

75 The main components of the cruise control system are:

(a) Steering column switch (slide and push-button) to select ON-OFF-RESUME-SET SPEED
(b) Speed pick-up coil, located in the speedometer to sense speedo revolutions and relay to governor
(c) Governor, receives signals from the pick-up coil and then controls the throttle actuator
(d) Throttle actuator, receives signals from the governor and in turn controls the throttle setting
(e) Clutch and brake switches, interrupt the system when clutch or brake pedals are depressed
(f) Retard switch, cuts out system when deceleration exceeds a pre-determined value
(g) Vacuum valve, opens when brake pedal depressed to open throttle cable actuator motor to atmospheric pressure so removing tension from throttle operating cable

76 If a fault occurs in the system, the following simple checks can be carried out. More extensive investigation should be left to your dealer:

(a) Check the circuit fuse
(b) Check for secure wiring connections
(c) Check for loose or perforated vacuum hoses
(d) Check that the retard switch is set at an angle of 17° to the horizontal. This is a mercury switch and the correct setting is very important

77 It should be noted that the governor is earthed through the brake stoplamp bulbs and if both these bulbs blow, the governor will be inoperative.

78 Failure of the system to operate at the specified speed levels may indicate that the governor requires adjustment. Adjustment is carried out while the vehicle is being road tested and an assistant should be engaged for this purpose.

79 Remove the governor from its mounting but do not disconnect its electrical leads. If the engaging speed is out of line with the indicated roadspeed, insert a screwdriver in the LOW SPEED hole and turn the screw clockwise to increase, or anti-clockwise to decrease, the engaging speed. If the set speed is not maintained to within ± 3 mph (4.8 km/h), insert a screwdriver into the CENTERING hole and turn the screw clockwise to increase the engaging speed or anti-clockwise to decrease it.

80 The governor is adjusted during production for maximum sensitivity which ensures that the throttle control is continuously adjusted to take care of variations in road and other conditions. The sensitivity can be reduced to improve fuel economy for vehicles driven almost entirely with driver only and no luggage, by inserting a screwdriver into the SENSITIVITY hole and turning the screw anti-clockwise. Turning the screw clockwise increases the sensitivity of the governor.

6 Ignition system

Ignition coil

1 After 1978, cars built for operation in cold climates have a ballast resistor fitted in series with the ignition coil.

2 When the starter motor is operated, full battery voltage is applied to terminal 15 of the coil, the power coming directly from terminal 16 on the starter motor solenoid.

3 As soon as the engine starts, reduced voltage reaches the coil through the ballast resistor.

4 The arrangement provides better cold starting and prevents the flow of excessive current through the coil.

7 Hydraulically actuated clutch

General description

1 From 1975 onwards, right-hand drive models are fitted with a hydraulically actuated clutch. This is basically the same as the cable operated clutch system, except in the method of clutch actuation.

2 The pendant clutch pedal is connected to the clutch master cylinder and hydraulic fluid reservoir by a short pushrod. The master cylinder and hydraulic reservoir are mounted on the engine side of the bulkhead in front of the driver.

3   Depressing the clutch pedal moves the piston in the master cylinder forwards, so forcing hydraulic fluid through the hydraulic pipe to the slave cylinder (photo).

4   The piston in the slave cylinder moves forward on the entry of the fluid and actuates the clutch release arm by means of a short pushrod.

5   From this point on the clutch is disengaged in the same manner as the cable actuated clutch. It must be noted, however, that owing to the fact that a cable pulls the release arm and hydraulic pressure can only push it, the arm used in conjunction with the hydraulically actuated system is of different design to that used in the cable operated system. Instead of the release arm pivot being on the opposite side of the release bearing to the actuated end of the arm as in the cable actuated system, it is situated *between* the release bearing and the actuated end of the arm.

Clutch - adjustment

6   The free movement at the release arm must be maintained at 0.2 in (5 mm).

7   To alter the free play, release the locknut on the slave cylinder pushrod, and turn the adjuster nut until the correct clearance is obtained between this nut and the release arm (see Fig. 13.40).

8   Tighten the locknut.

Clutch hydraulic system - bleeding

9   Whenever the clutch hydraulic system has been overhauled, a part renewed, or the level in the reservoir is allowed to get low, air will enter the system, necessitating bleeding. During this operation the level of hydraulic fluid in the reservoir should not be allowed to fall below half-full, otherwise air will be drawn in again.

10 Obtain a clean dry glass jar, plastic tubing at least 12 inches (305 mm) long and able to fit tightly over the bleed screw of the slave cylinder, and a supply of the specified hydraulic fluid. The services of an assistant will be required.

7.3 Clutch slave cylinder mounted on bellhousing

Fig. 13.38. Hydraulic clutch system components (Sec. 7)

1 Pedal carrier   4 Slave cylinder
2 Master cylinder   5 Release arm
3 Hydraulic line

Fig. 13.39. Cutaway view of clutch master cylinder (Sec. 7)

1 Reservoir   6 Outer piston seal
2 Washer   7 Piston
3 Lockring   8 Inner piston seal
4 Dust cover   9 Spring
5 Pushrod   10 Cylinder

Fig. 13.40. Cutaway view of clutch slave cylinder (Sec. 7)

1	Bleed nipple	4	Piston seal	7	Stop ring
2	Cylinder	5	Piston	8	Dust cover
3	Spring	6	Pushrod	9	Adjuster nuts

11 Check that the master cylinder reservoir is full, and if not, fill it. Cover the bottom 1 inch (22 mm) of the jar with hydraulic fluid.
12 Place one end of the tube securely over the end of the bleed screw after removing the dust cap (if fitted) and insert the other end in the jar so that the tube end is below the level of the fluid.
13 With a suitable spanner, open the bleed screw one turn.
14 An assistant should now depress the clutch pedal and allow it to return slowly.
15 Repeat this sequence, until no more air bubbles appear. Tighten the bleed screw during the next pedal downstroke.
16 Do not forget to check the reservoir frequently to ensure that the hyraulic fluid does not drop too far, so letting air into the system.
17 Refit the rubber dust cap over the bleed screw after removing the bleeding tube. **Note: Never re-use the fluid bled from the hydraulic system.**

Clutch master cylinder - removal, overhaul and refitting
18 Connect up the end of a suitable length of tubing to the bleed screw of the slave cylinder and place the other end in a jam jar. Undo the bleed screw one turn and pump the clutch pedal up-and-down until the clutch fluid reservoir is empty of fluid. Remove the tube and tighten the bleed screw.
19 Disconnect the fluid outlet pipe from the master cylinder.
20 Remove the panel under the dashboard and then disconnect the pushrod from the clutch pedal by removing the clevis pin.
21 Unscrew and remove the bolts from the master cylinder mounting flange and remove the master cylinder.
22 Clean away all external dirt before taking the master cylinder to a totally clean working area.
23 Pull off the dust excluding cover and withdraw the pushrod.
24 Extract the circlip now visible at the end of the master cylinder and remove the washer, piston, seals and return spring.
25 Examine the surfaces of the piston and the cylinder bore for scoring or bright wear areas. If such conditions are evident, renew the master cylinder complete.
26 If these components are unmarked and in good condition, discard the rubber seals and wash each part in clean hydraulic fluid or methylated spirit. **Do not use any other fluid.**
27 Obtain a repair kit which will contain all the necessary seals and other renewable items.
28 Dip the new seals in clean hydraulic fluid and position them on the piston using the fingers only.
29 Insert the spring, piston and seals and washer carefully into the master cylinder and secure with the circlip.
30 Insert the pushrod and refit the dust cover.
31 Refitting the master cylinder is a reversal of the removal procedure.
32 Check that there is a clearance of 0.04 in (1 mm) between the pushrod and the piston. If not, adjust the clearance by turning the adjusting nuts on each side of the pushrod yoke that connects to the pedal.

33 Refit the pedal mounting cover panel under the dashboard.
34 Fill up the master cylinder reservoir with hydraulic fluid and bleed the system as described in paragraphs 9 to 17.
35 Finally, check the release arm free movement as described in paragraphs 6 to 8.

Clutch slave cylinder - removal, overhaul and refitting
36 Disconnect the flexible hose from the rigid hydraulic pipe by unscrewing the union nut from the latter.
37 Disconnect the hose from its securing bracket and plug the open end of the fluid line to avoid loss of fluid.
38 Remove the lockring securing the slave cylinder to the clutch casing.
39 Remove the return spring from the release arm if fitted.
40 Carefully withdraw the cylinder from the clutch casing.
41 Clean away all external dirt from the slave cylinder and remove the rubber dust cover and pushrod.
42 Extract the circlip (which is now visible at the end of the cylinder) and withdraw the piston assembly and spring.
43 Inspect the surfaces of the piston and cylinder bore for scoring or bright wear areas. If these are evident, the complete slave cylinder must be renewed.
44 If the components are in good condition, wash them in clean hydraulic fluid or methylated spirit. **Do not use any other fluid.**
45 Obtain a repair kit which will contain a new seal and other renewable items.
46 Dip the new piston seal in clean hydraulic fluid and manipulate into position on the piston using the fingers.
47 Refit the spring and piston assembly into the cylinder and secure with the circlip. Refit the pushrod and dust cover.
48 Refitting is a reverse of the removal procedure. The system must be topped up with the specified hydraulic fluid and then bled, as described in paragraphs 9 to 17.
49 Finally, check the release arm free movement as described in paragraphs 6 to 8.

Clutch pedal - removal, overhaul and refitting
50 This is basically similar to the method described for the cable-actuated mechanism in Chapter 5. Detail differences will be apparent, notably that the master cylinder pushrod must be disconnected from the pedal by removal of the clevis pin instead of detaching the clutch cable.

8   Manual gearbox and automatic transmission

Manual gearbox - oil changing and oil type
1   Commencing with 1979 models, the transmission is 'filled for life' and routine oil changes are no longer specified by the manufacturer.

2   However, in the light of operating experience, it is still advisable to renew the oil periodically to remove accumulations of metallic swarf and to make good the inevitable deterioration in the oil additives and anti-friction qualities.

3   It is suggested that the oil is renewed whenever the clutch driven plate is changed.

4   The recommended lubricant for Type M45/46 gearboxes is now automatic transmission fluid type F.

Manual gearbox - modifications to Type M45/46 gearboxes

5   On later gearboxes (1979 on); only one selector shaft is used instead of the three previously used. Two shift forks and the gearchange selector dog are attached to the selector shaft.

6   Two selector plates are retained in position by a spring and the transmission cover. Movement of the plates by the selector shaft/dog is controlled by three projecting guides which allows them to move sideways when the gearchange control lever is moved.

7   A leaf spring is incorporated in the gearbox cover to keep the reverse selector in position. Also cast into the underside of the cover are three stop lugs for the selector plates.

8   It is emphasised that many components of this modified gearbox have been redesigned and are not interchangeable with earlier models. These include:

(a) Input shaft with 22 splines (different type of clutch driven plate required in consequence)
(b) 3rd/4th gears and synchroniser
(c) Steel shift forks with renewable brass friction pads

9   The gearchange control lever used with this later type of gearbox has been modified at its lower end as shown. The reverse gear slot is now on the left-hand side instead of at the rear. The gear lever extension support is now of square section steel tubing.

Automatic transmission type BW 55 - downshift cable renewal

10 On BW 55 transmissions, renewal of the downshift cable should

Fig. 13.41. Selector shaft (arrowed) on later type M45/46 gearbox (Sec. 8)

Fig. 13.43. Selector plates and guides, later type M45/46 gearbox (Sec. 8)

Fig. 13.42. Interior view of later type selector mechanism (Sec. 8)

1 Selector dogs   2 Selector shaft   3 Selector forks

Fig. 13.44. Reverse selector leaf spring and selector plate stop lugs (arrowed) on later type M45/46 gearbox cover (Sec. 8)

Fig.13.45. Later type gearchange lever (Sec. 8)

Fig. 13.47. Downshift cable adjustment — BW 55 transmission (Sec. 8)

A = 2.0 in (50.8 mm), accelerator fully depressed

Fig. 13.48. Propeller shaft with rubber damping inserts (arrowed)
(Sec. 9)

Fig. 13.46. Gearchange control lever showing reverse slot (arrowed) on
later models (Sec. 8)

not be attempted as it involves removing the valve blocks and the use
of special tools. However, the cable at the throttle control end should
always be adjusted to provide the following tolerances and movement.
11 With the accelerator pedal released, the clearance between the end
of the threaded adjuster on the outer cable and the crimped ferrule on
the inner cable should be between 0.010 and 0.040 in (0.25 and 1.0
mm). Adjust by means of the nut and locknut.
12 Depress the accelerator fully. The distance between the end of the
threaded adjuster and the crimped ferrule should now be 2.0 in (50.8
mm).
13 If the inner cable is now gripped and pulled, it should be possible
to pull it out a further 0.08 in (2.0 mm). This proves that the
adjustment is correct.

Automatic transmission type AW 55 - general description
14 This type of transmission is manufactured in Japan under Borg-
Warner licence and is fitted to some later models. The transmission
is almost identical to the BW 55 except that the valve bodies and the
front and rear clutches vary slightly in design.
15 The two types of transmission are interchangeable but the fluid
cooler connecting pipes are not.

9 Propeller shaft

Modification (1979 on)
    On vehicles equipped with a type M46 manual gearbox, after
1979 a propeller shaft with rubber damping inserts is used to reduce
transmission noises.

10 Rear axle

Limited slip differential - description
1   Later models can be fitted with a limited slip differential rear
axle as an option. The axle is identical to the standard type axle
except for the differential.
2   The purpose of this type of axle is to limit the differences in
rotational speed between the two halfshafts by means of internal
clutches.
3   With this type of axle, never jack up one rear wheel and turn it
while the opposite wheel is still on the ground. Always jack up both
wheels together, otherwise damage may be caused to the unit.

Limited slip differential - overhaul
4   The overhaul operations are as described for the standard axle
in Chapter 8, except for the following special work which must be
done once the differential carrier is removed.
5   With a suitable tool, remove the differential case bearings.

Fig. 13.49. Limited slip differential (Sec. 10)

1	Differential case (smaller section)	5	Spider
2	Clutch discs	6	Differential case (larger section)
3	Gear retainer	7	Side gear
4	Pinion gear	8	Clutch discs

Fig. 13.50. Differential case alignment marks (arrowed) (Sec. 10)

Fig. 13.51. Reassembling the limited slip differential (Sec. 10)

6 Using quick-drying paint, mark the ends of the differential gear shafts in relation to their holes in the case. Also mark the two halves of the differential case.

7 Unscrew and remove the bolts which hold the differential case together. *These bolts have left-hand threads.*

8 Lift the case from the crownwheel and extract the clutch discs and gears, keeping them all in fitted order.

9 If the crownwheel is to be removed, unscrew the retaining bolts and discard them. Purchase new ones for reassembly.

10 Commence reassembly by fitting the crownwheel, using new bolts with thread locking fluid applied to their threads, and tighten them to the specified torque.

11 With the teeth of the crownwheel towards you, insert the shafts, gears and the discs correctly aligned. Apply specified oil to all the components as they are fitted.

12 Fit the differential case, screw in the bolts *(left-hand thread)* and tighten to the specified torque.

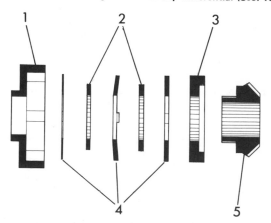

Fig. 13.52. Correct orientation of limited slip differential components (Sec. 10)

1	Differential case (smaller section)	4	Clutch discs
2	Clutch discs	5	Side gear
3	Gear retainer		

Fig. 13.53. Ventilated type brake disc (Sec. 11)

11 Braking system

Front disc brakes

1   On cars built from late 1975 on (except DL models), the front brake discs are of ventilated type. Reference should be made to the Specifications in this Supplement for details of new and refinishing dimensions for these later type discs.

Handbrake ratchet

2   On later models (1979 on), the handbrake control lever ratchet pawl is of double-toothed type to provide an additional safety feature.

Caliper units

3   Up until 1975, the front and rear calipers may be of ATE or Girling manufacture. The make can be determined from the code number on the label which is affixed to the centre door pillar. Code 1 denotes Girling, code 2 denotes ATE.

4   Commencing with 1976 models, the code numbers apply only to the rear wheels as the front brakes are exclusively of Girling manufacture.

Hydraulic system - bleeding

5   If the services of an assistant are not available to bleed the brakes as described in Chapter 9 then one of the two following methods may be used. If the master cylinder or pressure regulating valve have been disconnected and reconnected, then the complete system (both circuits) must be bled. If only one circuit has been disturbed, then only that particular circuit need be bled.

Bleeding using a one-way valve kit

6   There are a number of one-man brake bleeding kits currently available from motor accessory shops. These devices simplify the bleeding process and reduce the risk of expelled air or fluid being drawn back again into the system.

7   To use this type of kit, connect the outlet tube to the bleed nipple and then open the nipple half a turn. If possible, position the unit so that it can be viewed from inside the car. Depress the brake pedal to the floor and slowly release it. The one-way valve in the bleed kit will prevent expelled air or fluid from returning to the system at the end of each pedal return stroke. Repeat this operation until clean hydraulic fluid, free from air bubbles, can be seen coming through the bleed tube. Tighten the bleed nipple and remove the tube.

8   Repeat the operations on the remaining bleed nipples in the sequence given in Chapter 9. Make sure that throughout the process the fluid reservoir level never falls so low that air can be drawn into the master cylinder, otherwise the work up to this point will have been wasted.

Fig. 13.54. Exploded view of ATE front brake caliper (Sec. 11)

1	Disc shield	7	Anti-squeal shim
2	Pad retaining pin	8	Dust-excluding boots
3	Caliper body	9	Pistons
4	Anti-squeal shim	10	Seals
5	Pads	11	Bleed nipple and dust cap
6	Anti-rattle spring	12	Ventilated disc

Fig. 13.55. Exploded view of ATE rear caliper (Sec. 11)

1	Disc shield	4	Piston seal	7	Boot retaining clip	10	Anti-squeal shims (if fitted)
2	Disc/drum	5	Piston	8	Pad	11	Bleed nipple and dust cap
3	Caliper body	6	Dust-excluding boot	9	Anti-rattle spring	12	Pad retaining pin

Fig. 13.56. Exploded view of Girling front brake caliper (Sec. 11)

1	Disc shield	4	Bleed screw and dust cap	7	Piston	10	Anti-squeal shim
2	Disc	5	Caliper body	8	Dust-excluding boot	11	Pad
3	Pad retaining pin and spring clip	6	Piston seal	9	Boot retaining clip	12	Anti-rattle spring

Fig. 13.57. Exploded view of Girling rear brake caliper (Sec. 11)

1	Disc shield	5	Pad retaining pin	8	Piston seal	11	Boot retaining clip
2	Disc/drum	6	Spring clip	9	Piston	12	Pad
3	Dust cap	7	Caliper body	10	Dust-excluding boot	13	Anti-rattle spring
4	Bleed nipple						

Bleeding using a pressure bleeding kit

9   These, too, are available from motor accessory shops and are usually operated by air pressure from the spare tyre.

10 By connecting a pressurised container to the master cylinder fluid reservoir, bleeding is then carried out by simply opening each bleed nipple in turn and allowing the fluid to run out, rather like turning on a tap, until air bubbles are no longer visible in the fluid being expelled.

11 Using this system, the large reserve of hydraulic fluid provides a safeguard against air being drawn into the master cylinder during the bleeding process.

12 This method is particularly effective when bleeding 'difficult' systems and when bleeding the entire system at the time of routine fluid renewal.

13 When the bleeding operations are completed, check and top up the fluid level in the master cylinder. Check the feel of the brake pedal, which should be firm and free from any sponginess which would indicate air still being present in the system.

14 Discard any expelled hydraulic fluid as it is likely to be contaminated with moisture, air and dirt, which makes it unsuitable for further use.

15 Hydraulic fluid should always be stored in an airtight container as it absorbs moisture from the air which tends to lower its boiling point. Never shake a tin of hydraulic fluid before using it.

---

12 Electrical system

Starter motor

1   Additional makes of starter motor may be encountered (see

Specifications at the beginning of this Supplement). Although the design of individual components may vary, the procedures described in Chapter 10 will still apply.

2   After 1978, the front starter motor mounting bracket is no longer fitted to cars having B19 or B21 series engines.

Headlamps

3   On 1978 models, the headlamps project further forward to accommodate a new design of radiator grille. A spacer and mounting plate are used to achieve this.

4   Adjustment of the headlamp beam is carried out by inserting a screwdriver into the cut-outs in the headlamp trim.

Running lights

5   On 1976 models, daytime running lights are fitted in the front parking and tail lamps. The circuit is fused and is operative when the ignition is switched on.

Boot interior lamp

6   A luggage boot lamp is fitted on DL models after 1978. Access to the bulb is obtained after extracting the securing screw and separating the lens.

Heated rear window

7   The element on the inside of the heated rear window (or tailgate) glass should be treated with care. Do not allow luggage to rub against it during journeys. Clean the glass with water and detergent only, wiping the glass in the direction of the elements, and avoid scratching them with rings on the fingers.

8   Do not stick labels across the heater element.

9   It is possible to repair a broken element by using a special conductive paint available from your Volvo dealer.

Relays

10 A relay panel is located on the engine compartment rear bulkhead and may include relays to actuate any of the following components and accessories according to the particular model and date of production (see wiring diagram):

    (a)   *Fuel injectors*
    (b)   *Fuel pump*
    (c)   *Window regulator*
    (d)   *Headlamp relay*
    (e)   *Emission control (Lambda Sond)*
    (f)   *Spotlamp*

An interval relay for the windscreen wipers is fitted to later models and located under the facia panel on the left-hand support.

Fuses

11 The fuses are of 8A or 16A rating. The circuits protected vary according to the year of production of the vehicle and the extent of its equipment.
12 Refer to the fusebox cover or to the appropriate wiring diagram for fuse and circuit details.

Electrically-operated window regulator - description

13 On later models, some versions (GLE - UK) are equipped with an electrically-operated window lift mechanism.
14 Access to the motors is obtained as described for manually-operated regulators in Chapter 12.
15 Failure of the system may be due to a blown fuse, check this first.
16 The control switches are located in the door armrests, those at the driver's door being of master type to control and override all the other switches.

Fig. 13.60. Luggage boot interior lamp (Sec. 12)

Fig. 13.58. Later type headlamp mounting with spacer (A) (Sec. 12)

Fig. 13.61. Typical relay panel and junction box (Sec. 12)

Fig. 13.59. Adjusting later type headlamp alignment (Sec. 12)

Fig. 13.62. Windscreen wiper interval relay (arrowed) (Sec. 12)

Front door

Rear door

Fig. 13.63. Later type window lift switches (Sec. 12)

Electrically-operated window regulator - removal, refitting and adjustment

17 With the door interior panel removed as described in Chapter 12, peel away the waterproof sheet.

18 Fully lower the window to its stop.

19 Release the regulator arms from the glass rail. Do this by pushing the safety brackets to loosen them, extracting the washers and levering the arms towards you.

20 Raise the glass fully by hand and prop or wedge it.

21 Disconnect the battery negative lead.

22 Remove the panel from under the end of the facia, also the side panel from just forward of the front pillar.

23 Disconnect the electrical leads from the regulator motor. On some models this will mean dismounting the fusebox to disconnect the leads. In this case it is recommended that the leads are cut and a suitable connecting plug fitted to facilitate the operation on any future occasion.

24 Release the lifting arm from the side rail in the door, extract the regulator mounting screws and withdraw the mechanism through the access hole in the door.

25 To dismantle the mechanism, secure it in a vice as shown and remove the electric motor.

26 Release the vice only very slowly and keep the fingers away from the mechanism as it is under spring tension.

27 When reassembling, grip the toothed ratchet quadrant in the vice and tension the regulator spring again as shown, before fitting the electric motor.

28 Refitting to the door is a reversal of removal. Adjust in the following way.

29 Raise the window to its stop and then release the stop lug.

30 Try to raise the window further by operating the lift button. Adjust the stop lug against the toothed quadrant, then tighten the lug locknut.

31 Lower the window fully to its stop and then check that the lifting arm does not bottom in the slide fork. Adjust the stop lug if necessary to provide a clearance in the fork of approximately 1/32 in (1.0 mm).

Radio - general

32 A typical factory-option radio installation would include a facia mounted receiver, loudspeakers fitted into the front doors and an electrically-operated aerial located in the rear wing.

33 The radio is normally fused through the No 1 circuit in the fusebox.

34 Alternative types of radio and tape players can be fitted, but it is recommended that the position in the facia is used, also the rear wing mounting position for the aerial, in order to give the best reception.

35 To remove the standard type of radio, pull off the control knobs and release the spindle locknuts. Remove the escutcheon panel and withdraw the receiver until the connecting leads can be detached.

36 When fitting a radio, make sure that the casing is well earthed. The aerial body must contact bare metal on the wing. If a new receiver is being fitted, trim the set to the aerial as instructed by the radio manufacturer.

37 Suppression of interference can sometimes present a problem with a newly fitted radio. The ignition leads and plugs will already

Fig. 13.64. Electric window winding mechanism removed (Sec. 12)

Fig. 13.65. Tensioning the window lift regulator spring (Sec. 12)

Fig. 13.66. Stop lug adjustment (arrowed) - window in raised position (Sec. 12)

Fig. 13.67. Stop lug adjustment (arrowed) - window in lowered position (Sec. 12)

have been suppressed during manufacture but if a persistent 'clicking' noise is heard when the radio is on and the engine running, try fitting a 1.5 mF capacitor between the coil (+) terminal and earth.

38 If a whining is heard, varying in intensity with the speed of the engine, a 1.0 to 1.3 mF capacitor should be fitted between the alternator large (B+) terminal and earth.

Central door locking system

39 On later models, a central door locking system is fitted either as standard or as an option depending upon the version.

40 Either by turning the cylinder lock on the driver's door or by depressing the interior lock plunger knob, all other doors are automatically locked. All doors are unlocked simultaneously when the driver's door is unlocked.

41 On 5-door Estate models, the tailgate is included in the central locking circuit.

42 Actuation is accomplished by relays and solenoids (in the doors). The opening and closure of the driver's door is mechanical, simultaneous with the electrical switching of the other door locks.

43 The relays are mounted behind the clock on the facia panel. Access to the door lock solenoids is obtained after removing the door interior trim panel as described in Chapter 12.

Fig. 13.68. Typical radio installation diagram (Sec. 12)

A   Speakers   D   Aerial control switch
B   Ignition switch   E   Electrically-operated aerial
C   Fuse block

Fig. 13.69. Typical central door locking circuit (Sec. 12)

10/8	Fuse block (8A)	191	Exterior switch (cylinder lock)
91	Clock	192	Solenoid (front passenger door)
93	Connector	193	Solenoid (left-hand rear)
188	Relay	194	Solenoid (right-hand rear)
189	Relay	195	Tailgate solenoid (245 Estate)
190	Interior switch		

Fig. 13.71. Central door locking relays located behind clock in facia panel (Sec. 12)

Fig. 13.72. Typical headlamp wash/wipe mechanism (Sec. 12)

Fig. 13.70. Electric door locking mechanism on a front door (Sec. 12)

Fig. 13.73. Headlamp wiper adjustment diagram (Sec. 12)

Headlamp wipers/washers

44 These were introduced in 1979. Each headlamp has an independent motor. The washer jet is located in the wiper arm and fed by a flexible pipe.

45 Removal and refitting is quite straightforward once the radiator grille and the headlamp trim panel have been withdrawn but on completion, the following adjustment must be carried out.

46 Pull back the cover to expose the wiper arm-to-motor spindle locknut. Release the locknut so that the arm is free and then set the wiper blade immediately below the lower stop lugs. Reconnect the wiper arm to the spindle and tighten the locknut. Finally lift the wiper blade and locate it above the stop lugs.

Key to Fig. 13.74. Not all items listed are fitted to all vehicles

1 Battery
2 Connection plate
3 Ignition switch
4 Coil
5 Distributor
6 Spark plugs
7 Starter motor
8 Alternator
9 Charging regulator
10 Fuse box
11 Light switch
12 Bulb failure warning unit
13 Relay (headlights)
14 High beam
15 Low beam
16 Parking light
17 Day running light
18 Tail light
19 Side marker light
20 Number plate light
21 Stoplamp switch
22 Stoplamp
23 Gearbox contact (manual)
24 Transmission contact (automatic)
25 Reversing lamp
26 Direction indicator switch
27 Hazard warning switch
28 Flasher unit
29 Front direction indicator
30 Rear direction indicator
31 Instrument connector
32 Instrument connector

33 Instrument connector
34 Instrument connector
35 Oil pressure warning lamp
36 Choke warning lamp
37 Handbrake warning lamp
38 Brake failure warning lamp
39 EGR warning lamp
40 No-charge warning lamp
41 Bulb failure warning lamp
42 Main beam warning lamp
43 Direction indicator warning lamp
44 Overdrive warning lamp
45 Seat belt warning lamp
46 Under-bonnet lamp
47 Buckle lamp
48 Rear ashtray lamp
49 Gear selector lamp
50 Panel lighting rheostat
51 Instrument lamp
52 Control panel lamp
53 Glovebox lamp
54 Interior lamp
55 Door switch (driver's side)
56 Door switch (passenger's side)
57 Fuel gauge
58 Temperature gauge
59 Oil pressure gauge
60 Choke switch
61 Handbrake switch
62 Brake failure switch
63 EGR warning switch

64 Passenger's seat belt switch
65 Driver's seat belt switch
66 Passenger seat contact
67 Buzzer
68 Tachometer
69 Fuel gauge sender
70 Temperature sender
71 Voltage stabiliser
72 Horn
73 Horn push
74 Cigarette lighter
75 Fan
76 Fan switch
77 Windscreen wipe/wash switch
78 Windscreen wiper
79 Windscreen washer
80 Relay for headlamp wipers
81 Headlamp wipers
82 Rear window wipe/wash switch
83 Rear window wiper
84 Rear window washer
85 Rear door switch
86 Rear interior light
87 Heated rear window switch
88 Heated rear window element
89 Heated driving seat cushion
90 Heated driving seat backrest
91 Clock
92 Diode
93 Junction
94 Seat belt reminder

95 Starting valve
96 Temperature/time contact
97 Airflow meter
98 Main relay, fuel injection
99 Fuel pump relay
100 Fuel pump
101 Pressure regulating valve
102 Extra air valve
103 Resistor
104 Ignition control unit
105 Compressor solenoid
106 Solenoid valve
107 Compressor switch
108 Carburettor solenoid valve
109 Overdrive switch
110 Gearbox overdrive contact
111 Overdrive solenoid
112 Bridge connector
113 Under-bonnet start terminal
114 RANCO solenoid (California)
115 Microswitch
116 Suppressor
117 Loudspeakers
118 Aerial
119 TDC sensor
120 Capacitor
121 Floor thermostat
122 Exhaust temperature warning lamp
123 Diode box
124 Temperature warning unit
125 Catalytic converter thermo-element
126 Air conditioning thermostat

Fig. 13.74. Wiring diagram, 1976/77 models (Sec. 12)

Fig. 13.75. Wiring diagram, 1978/79 models (Sec. 12)

Fig. 13.75. Wiring diagram, 1978/79 models (Sec. 12) - continued

Key to Fig. 13.75. Not all items listed are fitted to all models

1	Battery	54	Courtesy light bulb	106	Solenoid valve
2	Connection plate	55	Door switch, driver's side	107	Switch for air conditioning
3	Ignition switch	56	Door switch, passenger's side	108	Solenoid valve, carburettor
4	Ignition coil	57	Fuel gauge sender	109	Switch for overdrive
5	Distributor	58	Temperature gauge sender	110	Switch for overdrive on gearbox
6	Spark plugs	59	Oil pressure sensor	111	Control magnet for overdrive
7	Starter motor	60	Choke contact	112	Coupling
8	Alternator	61	Parking brake switch	113	Power output
9	Charging regulator	62	Brake warning switch	114	Thermostat
10	Fuse box	63	EGR/EXH warning switch	116	Suppression, resistor
11	Light switch	64	Switch, seat belt, passenger's seat	117	Loudspeaker, front doors
12	Bulb failure warning light	65	Switch, seat belt, driver's seat	118	Antenna, windscreen
13	Headlamp relay	66	Switch, passenger's seat	119	TDC sender
14	Main beams	67	Headlights on reminder buzzer	120	Capacitor
15	Dipped beams	68	Rev counter	121	Thermostat, floor
16	Parking lights	69	Fuel gauge	122	Exhaust temperature indicator light
17	Day running lights	70	Thermometer	123	Diode box
18	Tail lights	71	Voltage stabilizer	124	Temperature sender
19	Side marker lights	72	Horn	125	Thermo-element, catalyst
20	Number plate light	73	Horn switch	126	Relay for window winders
21	Stoplight switch	74	Cigar lighter	127	Rear fog lights
22	Stoplight	75	Fan	128	Switch for rear fog lights
23	Switch (gearbox)	76	Fan switch	129	Relay for air conditioning
24	Switch (automatic transmission)	77	Switch for windscreen wipers/washers	130	Rear cargo space light
25	Reversing lights	78	Windscreen wipers	131	Switch for window winder, LH side, front
26	Direction indicator stalk	79	Windscreen washer	132	Motor for window winder, LH side, front
27	Switch for hazard warning flashers	80	Relay for headlight wipers	133	Switch for window winder, RH side, front
28	Flasher device	81	Headlight wipers	134	Motor for window winder, RH side, front
29	Front direction indicator light	82	Switch for tailgate wiper/washer	135	Fasten seat belt warning light
30	Rear direction indicator light	83	Tailgate wiper	136	Main switch for window winders, rear
31	Connection at instrument	84	Tailgate washer	137	Switch for window winder, LH side, rear
32	Connection at instrument	85	Rear door switch	138	Motor for window winder, LH side, rear
33	Tank pump	86	Rear cargo space light	139	Switch for window winder, RH side, rear
34	Connection at instrument	87	Switch for electrically heated rear window	140	Motor for window winder, RH side, rear
35	Oil pressure warning light	88	Electrically heated rear window	145	Cable fusing
36	Choke light	89	Heater element with thermostat, driver's seat cushion	146	Connector, 8-pole
37	Handbrake indicator light	90	Heater element, driver's seat backrest	147	Fuse box, headlights, Italy
38	Brake warning light	91	Clock	148	Interval relay for windscreen wipers
39	EGR indicator light	92	Diode	149	Test point, Lambda-sond
40	Battery charging warning light	93	Joint	150	Side flashers
41	Bulb failure warning light	94	Fasten seat belt reminder	151	Cable fusing
42	Main beam indicator light	95	Cold start valve	152	Spotlight
43	Hazard warning lights light	96	Thermal timer switch	153	Relay for spotlight
44	Overdrive indicator light	97	Air flow sensor	154	Switch for spotlight
45	Fasten seat belt warning light	98	Main relay, fuel injection	155	Curve and fog light
46	Engine compartment light	99	Relay for fuel pump	156	Relay for curve and fog light
47	Fasten seat belt light	100	Fuel pump	157	Switch for curve and fog light
48	Ashtray light	101	Control pressure regulator	158	Temperature gauge sender
49	Selector lever light	102	Auxiliary air valve	159	Relay for lambda system
50	Rheostat for instrument panel light	103	Resistance	160	Frequency valve
51	Instrument panel light	104	Control unit, ignition system	161	Control unit, lambda system
52	Control panel light	105	Control magnet, compressor	162	Lambda-sond sensor
53	Glove locker light				

Key to Fig. 13.76. Not all items listed are fitted to all models

Component or system	Location	Component or system	Location
Alternator	B1	Parking lights, front	C1, E1
Ashtray light	B8	Parking lights, rear	B9, E9
Auxiliary air valve	A3	Relay, high/low beam	E3
Ballast resistor	A3	Remote starter pick-up	B4
Battery	A1	Reversing lights	B9, E9
Blower	D2	Rheostat, panel lights	E5
Boot (trunk) light	D8	Seat belt reminder lights	B6
Brake failure switch	A6	Seat belt buckle light	B8
Brake lights	B9, E9	Seat heater	C7
Bulb failure sensor	E4	Senders for gauges	A5/A6
Buzzer	D4	Sensor, bulb failure	E4
Carburettor solenoid	D3	Spark plugs	A4
Cigarette lighter	B4	Starter motor	A1
Clock	E6	Switches:	
Cold start injector	A2	Brake light	E5
Control panel lights	E6, E7	Brake failure	A6
Control pressure regulator	A2	Door	D2
Distributor	A3	Hazard warning	D7
Door switches	D3	Ignition	C4
Electrically heated rear window	C7	Interior lights	D2
Engine compartment light	C2	Overdrive	C7
Flasher unit	D6	Rear door	D9
Fuel gauge	B5	Rear window heater	C7
Fuel pump relay	B1	Reversing lights	D7
Fuse box	C4	Seat belt	A6, B7
Gearshift light	E6	Seat heater	C7
Glovebox light	E7	Tailgate wiper/washer	B10
Horns	C2	Turn signal	D7
Ignition coil	B3	Windscreen wiper/washer	A8
Ignition module	A4	Tail lights, Estate	B9, E10
Indicator lights	A5, A6	Tail lights, Saloon	B9, E9
Instrument lights	E6, E7	Thermal time switch	A2
Interior light	D3	Turn signal, front	C1, E1
Interior light, Estate	D9	Turn signal, rear	B9, E9
Interval relay, tailgate window wiper	C10	Voltage regulator	B1
Interval relay, windscreen wiper	A7	Voltage stabiliser	B6
Light switch	E2	Washer, tailgate window	C10
Number plate light	C9	Washer, windscreen	A9
Overdrive solenoid	C7	Wiper motor, tailgate window	B9
Overdrive switch	C7	Wiper motor, windscreen	A8

Fig. 13.76. Wiring diagram, 1980 models (Sec. 12)

Fig. 13.76. Wiring diagram, 1980 models (Sec. 12) - continued

Fig. 13.77. Electric window winding circuit diagram, 4-door, 1980 models (Sec. 12)

Fig. 13.78. Auxiliary lights wiring diagram, 1980 models (Sec. 12)

Fig. 13.80. Automatic transmission wiring diagram, 1980 models (Sec. 12)

Fig. 13.81. Lambda-sond system wiring diagram, 1980 models (Sec. 12)

Fig. 13.79. Electric window winding circuit diagram, 2-door, 1980 models (Sec. 12)

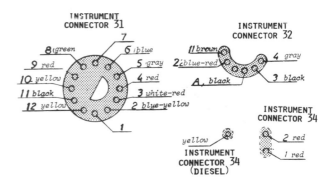

Fig. 13.82. Instrument connectors, 1980 models (Sec. 12)

Fig. 13.83. Air conditioning/heater wiring diagram, 1980 models (Sec. 12)

Fig. 13.84. Seat belt reminder system, 1980 models (Sec. 12)

Fig. 13.85. Interior light delay wiring diagram, 1980 models (Sec. 12)

Fig. 13.86. Steering shaft taper (arrowed) is modified on later models (Sec. 13)

Fig. 13.87. Using special tool 5173 to release a gas-pressurised front suspension strut (Sec. 13)

Fig. 13.88. Gas-pressurised front shock absorber in extended position (Sec. 13)

Fig. 13.89. Gas-pressurised rear shock absorber in compressed position (Sec. 13)

Fig. 13.90. Method of securing roadwheel hub cap (Sec. 13)

1 Spring clips
2 Hub cap
3 Emblem disc

13 Steering and front suspension

Steering wheel - removal and refitting
1   On later models (1979 on) a puller is no longer required to remove the steering wheel. This has been achieved by altering the taper angle at the upper end of the steering shaft.
2   The advantage of this modification is somewhat offset by the need for a special tool (No 1158146) in order to reach the steering wheel nut on these models.

Front suspension struts
3   Commencing with 1979 models, the fluid in the suspension struts is gas-pressurised to provide better damping action.
4   When removing a strut from one of these vehicles, a special tool (5173) must be used.

Rear shock absorbers
5   Also on 1979 vehicles, the rear shock absorbers are of gas-pressurised type. In the event of wear or a fault developing, renew the shock absorber complete.

Roadwheel hub caps
6   On certain 1980 models equipped with pressed steel roadwheels, a new type of hub cap is fitted. The cap is secured on three wide spring clips.
7   Before removing the main hub cap, prise out the small emblem disc from its centre as this acts as a wedging device to keep the spring clips apart. Refit in the reverse order.

14 Bodywork

Front wing liners
1   Commencing with 1978 models, protective plastic liners are fitted under the front wings. They are retained by small set bolts.

Door locks
2   On later models (1978 on), modified door locks are fitted and are the only type supplied as spares for earlier versions.
3   To renew the earlier type of lock, it will only be necessary to carry out a direct substitution, but note that the newer type of lock cylinder is retained by a spring clip.
4   To renew a later type of lock, carry out the following operations. If a front door lock is being removed, withdraw the stowage compartment first from the inner surface of the door.
5   Remove the window regulator handle, the lock interior handle, the armrest and the lock plunger knob.
6   Remove the door interior trim panel and the waterproof sheet.
7   Extract the spring retainers from the interior and exterior handle linkage and the plunger rod (Fig. 13.94).
8   Using an Allen key, unscrew the two socket-headed screws from the lock at the door edge. Withdraw the lock outer section and then remove the inner section from the door interior.
9   If a front door is being worked on, the lock cylinder can be removed if the retaining clip is first prised out with a screwdriver.
10 Refitting is a reversal of removal, but make sure that there is a gap of 0.040 in (1.0 mm) at the exterior handle link rod to lever (Fig. 13.97) before fitting the securing spring clip.

Luggage boot lid lock (not with central locking system)
11 A key opening lock is fitted to 1979 and later models which cannot be opened by turning with the fingers as was the case on earlier models.
12 The lock is retained by a forked clip as is used on later type door lock cylinders.
13 To dismantle the lock, prise out the E-clip and remove the latch and the return spring.
14 When reassembling, engage the end of the return spring in the recess in the latch, connect the latch/return spring to the lock cylinder and then pre-tension the spring by one notch by turning the latch clockwise. Refit the E-clip.

Fig. 13.91. Front wing plastic liners (Sec. 14)

Fig. 13.92. Later type door lock components (Sec. 14)

Fig. 13.93. Door stowage compartment securing screws (Sec. 14)

Fig. 13.97. Exterior handle link rod adjustment diagram (Sec. 14)

1mm

Fig. 13.94. Spring retainers on door lock linkage (Sec. 14)

Fig. 13.98. Later type luggage boot lock (Sec. 14)

Fig. 13.95. Extracting a door lock screw (Sec. 14)

Fig. 13.99. Extracting lock cylinder E-clip (Sec. 14)

Fig. 13.96. Removing a door lock cylinder retaining clip (Sec. 14)

Fig. 13.100. Latch return spring (Sec. 14)

Fig. 13.101. Pre-tension latch return spring in direction arrowed (Sec. 14)

Fig. 13.102. Internally controlled exterior rear view mirror (Sec. 14)

Exterior rear view mirrors
15 The externally-mounted rear view mirrors are remotely controlled from inside the vehicle on 1980 models.
16 The mirror can be removed once the interior control handle screw has been extracted and the handle removed.

Conversion factors

Length (distance)

Inches (in)	X	25.4	= Millimetres (mm)	X 0.039	= Inches (in)
Feet (ft)	X	0.305	= Metres (m)	X 3.281	= Feet (ft)
Miles	X	1.609	= Kilometres (km)	X 0.621	= Miles

Volume (capacity)

Cubic inches (cu in; in^3)	X	16.387	= Cubic centimetres (cc; cm^3)	X 0.061	= Cubic inches (cu in; in^3)
Imperial pints (Imp pt)	X	0.568	= Litres (l)	X 1.76	= Imperial pints (Imp pt)
Imperial quarts (Imp qt)	X	1.137	= Litres (l)	X 0.88	= Imperial quarts (Imp qt)
Imperial quarts (Imp qt)	X	1.201	= US quarts (US qt)	X 0.833	= Imperial quarts (Imp qt)
US quarts (US qt)	X	0.946	= Litres (l)	X 1.057	= US quarts (US qt)
Imperial gallons (Imp gal)	X	4.546	= Litres (l)	X 0.22	= Imperial gallons (Imp gal)
Imperial gallons (Imp gal)	X	1.201	= US gallons (US gal)	X 0.833	= Imperial gallons (Imp gal)
US gallons (US gal)	X	3.785	= Litres (l)	X 0.264	= US gallons (US gal)

Mass (weight)

Ounces (oz)	X	28.35	= Grams (g)	X 0.035	= Ounces (oz)
Pounds (lb)	X	0.454	= Kilograms (kg)	X 2.205	= Pounds (lb)

Force

Ounces-force (ozf; oz)	X	0.278	= Newtons (N)	X 3.6	= Ounces-force (ozf; oz)
Pounds-force (lbf; lb)	X	4.448	= Newtons (N)	X 0.225	= Pounds-force (lbf; lb)
Newtons (N)	X	0.1	= Kilograms-force (kgf; kg)	X 9.81	= Newtons (N)

Pressure

Pounds-force per square inch (psi; lbf/in^2; lb/in^2)	X	0.070	= Kilograms-force per square centimetre (kgf/cm^2; kg/cm^2)	X 14.223	= Pounds-force per square inch (psi; lbf/in^2; lb/in^2)
Pounds-force per square inch (psi; lbf/in^2; lb/in^2)	X	0.068	= Atmospheres (atm)	X 14.696	= Pounds-force per square inch (psi; lbf/in^2; lb/in^2)
Pounds-force per square inch (psi; lbf/in^2; lb/in^2)	X	0.069	= Bars	X 14.5	= Pounds-force per square inch (psi; lbf/in^2; lb/in^2)
Pounds-force per square inch (psi; lbf/in^2; lb/in^2)	X	6.895	= Kilopascals (kPa)	X 0.145	= Pounds-force per square inch (psi; lbf/in^2; lb/in^2)
Kilopascals (kPa)	X	0.01	= Kilograms-force per square centimetre (kgf/cm^2; kg/cm^2)	X 98.1	= Kilopascals (kPa)

Torque (moment of force)

Pounds-force inches (lbf in; lb in)	X	1.152	= Kilograms-force centimetre (kgf cm; kg cm)	X 0.868	= Pounds-force inches (lbf in; lb in)
Pounds-force inches (lbf in; lb in)	X	0.113	= Newton metres (Nm)	X 8.85	= Pounds-force inches (lbf in; lb in)
Pounds-force inches (lbf in; lb in)	X	0.083	= Pounds-force feet (lbf ft; lb ft)	X 12	= Pounds-force inches (lbf in; lb in)
Pounds-force feet (lbf ft; lb ft)	X	0.138	= Kilograms-force metres (kgf m; kg m)	X 7.233	= Pounds-force feet (lbf ft; lb ft)
Pounds-force feet (lbf ft; lb ft)	X	1.356	= Newton metres (Nm)	X 0.738	= Pounds-force feet (lbf ft; lb ft)
Newton metres (Nm)	X	0.102	= Kilograms-force metres (kgf m; kg m)	X 9.804	= Newton metres (Nm)

Power

Horsepower (hp)	X	745.7	= Watts (W)	X 0.0013	= Horsepower (hp)

Velocity (speed)

Miles per hour (miles/hr; mph)	X	1.609	= Kilometres per hour (km/hr; kph)	X 0.621	= Miles per hour (miles/hr; mph)

Fuel consumption*

Miles per gallon, Imperial (mpg)	X	0.354	= Kilometres per litre (km/l)	X 2.825	= Miles per gallon, Imperial (mpg)
Miles per gallon, US (mpg)	X	0.425	= Kilometres per litre (km/l)	X 2.352	= Miles per gallon, US (mpg)

Temperature

Degrees Fahrenheit (°F) $= (°C \times \frac{9}{5}) + 32$

Degrees Celsius (Degrees Centigrade; °C) $= (°F - 32) \times \frac{5}{9}$

*It is common practice to convert from miles per gallon (mpg) to litres/100 kilometres (l/100km), where mpg (Imperial) x l/100 km = 282 and mpg (US) x l/100 km = 235

Index

**Printed by
Haynes Publishing Group
Sparkford Yeovil Somerset
England**